Sunbeam Rapier / Alpine Owners Workshop Manual

by J H Haynes

Associate Member of the Guild of Motoring Writers

and J R S Hall

Models covered:

Sunbeam Rapier 1725 cc
Sunbeam Rapier H120 1725 cc
Sunbeam Alpine 1725 cc

ISBN 978 0 85733 737 5

(051-8A1)

Haynes Group Limited
Haynes North America, Inc

www.haynes.com

The manufacturer's authorised representative in the EU for product safety is:

HaynesPro BV
Stationsstraat 79 F, 3811MH Amersfoort, The Netherlands
gpsr@haynes.co.uk

Acknowledgements

Our thanks are due to Chrysler/Rootes for their assistance with technical material and illustrations; to Castrol for lubrication details; to 'Motor' for the cutaway illustration on the cover.

There was invaluable assistance from Rod Grainger in preparing the engine photographs and from Len Tooze for those for the gearbox. The author is also grateful to David Stead for additional technical information.

About This Manual

Its aims

This is a manual by a practical owner/maintainer for practical owner/maintainers. The author, and those assisting him, learned about this range of models the only thorough way, by studying all available information and then going ahead and doing the work, under typical domestic conditions and with a typical range of tools, backed only by their experience as keen car men over a number of years.

Unlike other books of this nature, therefore, the hands in most of the photographs are those of the author, and the instructions cover every step in full detail, assuming no special knowledge on the part of the reader except how to use tools and equipment in a proper manner, firmly and positively but with due respect for precise control where this is required.

Its arrangement

The manual is divided into twelve chapters, each covering a logical sub-division of the vehicle. The chapters are each divided into sections, numbered with single figures, e.g. 5; and the sections into paragraphs (or sub-sections), with decimal numbers following on from the section they are in, e.g. 5.1, 5.2, 5.3, etc.

It is freely illustrated, especially in those parts where there is a detailed sequence of operations to be carried out. There are two forms of illustration: figures and photographs. The figures are numbered in sequence with decimal numbers, according to their position in the chapter: e.g. Fig.6.4 is the 4th drawing/illustration in Chapter 6. Photographs are numbered (either individually or in related groups) the same as the section or sub-section of the text where the operation they show is described.

There is an alphabetical index at the back of the manual as well as a contents list at the front.

References to the 'left' or 'right' of the vehicle are in the sense of a person in a seat facing forwards towards the engine.

Points for the reader

The accumulation of good tools normally must take place over a period of time and this is the one expense which the do-it-yourself owner must face. Cheap tools are never worth having, as they are not cheap in the long run. They rarely last, often make the work more difficult, and may even cause accidental damage which could cost more to put right than the cost of a good tool in the first place.

Certain jobs require special tools and where these are essential the manual points this out. Otherwise, alternative methods are given.

Be discreet about borrowing tools; even with great care, accidents still happen, and the replacement of a lost or damaged tool can be costly. Do not be offended, if refused; he may have had an unhappy experience already!

Where appropriate, fault finding instructions are given at the end of chapters. Accurate diagnosis of troubles depends on a careful, and, above all, systematic approach, so avoid the attitude "if all else fails, read the handbook". It is better, and almost always quicker, to say: "This could be one of several things, so let's have a look at the Haynes manual before trying anything".

Modifications

The policy of the manufacturer of these vehicles is one of continuous development, and designs and specifications are frequently being changed as a result. It follows naturally that spares may sometimes be purchased which differ both from the original part removed and from the part referred to in this manual. However, suppliers of genuine Chrysler/Rootes spare parts can usually settle queries about interchangeability by reference to the latest information issued by the manufacturer. **(Read the section Ordering Spare Parts).**

Contents

Introduction to the Sunbeam Rapier and Alpine

The Sunbeam Rapier belonged originally to the Chrysler/Rootes range known as the Arrow, which embraced a number of models marketed internationally under various names. It was conceived as a sports saloon and all versions have 'fast-back' styling.

The Rapier was first introduced in October 1967, and one year later the Rapier H120 became available. Both use the well-proved 1725 cc engine and gearbox from the Hunter/Vogue/Sceptre, but that in the H120 is fitted with twin Weber 40 DCOE carburettors instead of the twin Stromberg 150 CDS of the standard model, and other changes by Holbay Engineering result in its producing considerably more power.

The Alpine is the economy version, with a single Stromberg carburettor and lower standards of performance, but offering most of the other facilities and selling at an appreciably lower price.

The Rapiers and Alpines have caused no great sensation in the motoring world, but their appearance is well-balanced and their construction gives an impression of rugged strength and an ability to cover long distances without fuss. Their reputation generally lives up to their appearance, and although owners may not find them exciting, many will speak with respect of the robust good service they have had from them.

Dates of introduction

Rapier Saloon October 1967
Rapier H120 October 1968

Alpine October 1969

Dimensions (overall)

Length	14 ft 6½ in (443.2 cm)
Width	5 ft 4¾ in (164.5 cm)
Height	
Rapier, Alpine	4 ft 7½ in (141.0 cm)
H120	4 ft 5½ in (135.9 cm)
Ground clearance	
Rapier, Alpine	6¾ in (16.8 cm)
H120	5 in (12.7 cm)
Weights	
Rapier	2277 lb (1032.8 kg)
Rapier (automatic)	2288 lb (1037.8 kg)
Alpine	2221 lb (1008.0 kg)
Alpine (overdrive)	2241 lb (1017.0 kg)
Alpine (automatic)	2232 lb (1013.0 kg)
H120	2298 lb (1043.0 kg)

Routine maintenance

Maintenance is essential for ensuring safety and desirable for the purpose of getting the best in terms of performance and economy from the car. Over the years the need for periodic lubrication - oiling, greasing and so on - has been drastically reduced if not totally eliminated. This has unfortunately tended to lead some owners to think that because no such action is required the items either no longer exist or will last for ever. This is a serious delusion. If anything, there are now more places, particularly in the steering, and suspension where joints and pivots are fitted. Although you do not grease them any more you still have to look at them - and look at them just as often as you may previously have had to grease them. It follows therefore that the largest initial element of maintenance is visual examination. This may lead to repairs or renewals.

At the beginning of each chapter in the manual the routine maintenance details covering that chapter are given.

In the summary given here the 'essential for safety' items are shown in **bold type. These must** be attended to at the regular frequencies shown in order to avoid the possibility of accidents and loss of life. Attention to the other items will help to avoid problems of unreliability, increased running costs and increasing wear and depreciation. Neglect only leads to poor service and unnecessarily high costs and losses all round.

250 miles

EVERY 250 miles travelled or weekly - whichever comes first.

STEERING

Check tyre pressures
Examine tyres for wear or damage
Check steering remains smooth and precise

BRAKES

Is there any fall off in braking efficiency?
Try an emergency stop. Is adjustment necessary?

LIGHTS, WIPERS & HORNS

Do all bulbs work at the front and rear?
Are the headlamp beams aligned properly?
Do wipers and horns work?

ENGINE

Check the sump oil level and top up if required
Check the radiator coolant level and top up if required
Check the battery electrolyte level and top up just above the level of the plates with distilled water if needed

1,000 miles

EVERY 1,000 miles or monthly, whichever comes first - or earlier if indications suggest that safety items in particular are not performing correctly

STEERING

Is there any free play between the steering wheel and the road wheels?

BRAKES

Check the fluid reservoir (hydraulic) level. If significantly lower examine the system immediately for signs of leaks

5,000 miles

EVERY 5,000 miles or six monthly, whichever comes first, or earlier if indications suggest that safety items in particular are not performing correctly

STEERING

Examine all steering linkage rods, joints and bushes for signs of wear or damage
Check front wheel hub bearings and adjust if necessary
Check tightness of steering box mounting bolts
Check the steering box oil level
Inspect rubber dust seals and boots for damage or deterioration

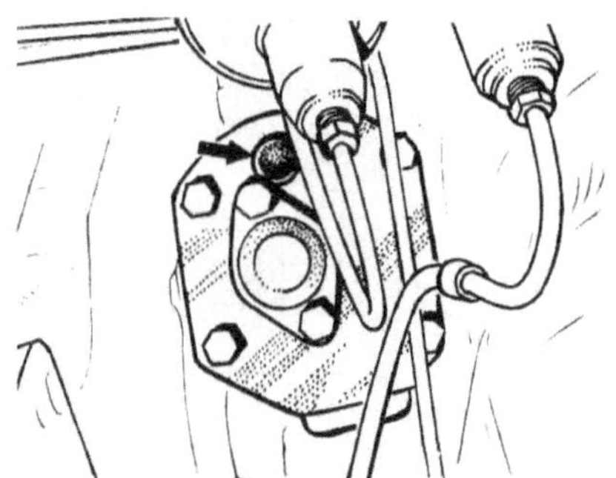

Steering box filler/level plug

Sump drain plug.

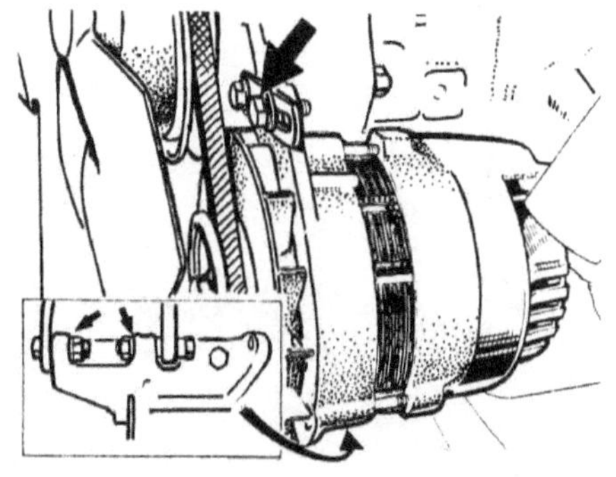

Fan belt adjustment - alternator retaining bolts

SUNBEAM RAPIER

SUNBEAM RAPIER H120

BRAKES

Examine disc pads and drum shoes to determine the amount of friction material left. Renew if necessary
Examine all hydraulic pipes, cylinders and unions for signs of chafing, corrosion, dents or any other form of deterioration or leaks
Lubricate the handbrake pull off springs

SUSPENSION

Examine all nuts, bolts and shackles securing the suspension units, front and rear. Tighten if necessary
Examine the rubber bushes for signs of wear and play

ENGINE

Change oil and filter element
Check valve clearances and adjust if necessary
Check distributor contacts gap and lubricate the spindle and cam
Check fan belt tension
Clean and reset spark plug gaps
Lubricate the generator rear bearing (not on alternators)
Top up the carburettor damper oil
Clean the air cleaner element and casing
Clean the crankcase breather valve and flame trap
Check specific gravity of antifreeze, if used
Top up gearbox/automatic transmission, rear axle and steering gear

CLUTCH

Check and top up if necessary the hydraulic fluid reservoir
Examine for any signs of leaks if the level has dropped significantly

BODY

See that the water drain holes at the bottom of all doors are clear and that the drain tube from the heater air intake box is clear

10,000 miles

EVERY 10,000 miles or annually

BODYWORK

Examine the underbody for signs of rust, particularly where the rear suspension is anchored
Check the condition of the body frame mounting for the upper end of the front suspension units

ENGINE

Fit new distributor contact points
Fit new spark plugs
Fit new carburettor air cleaner element
Flush out the cooling system
Clean fuel pump sediment bowl and filter gauze

GEARBOX

Check and top up oil level

REAR AXLE

Check the oil level and top up as necessary

STEERING

Remove front wheel hubs, flush out bearings, inspect and repack with grease

BRAKES

Renew servo air filter element (if fitted)

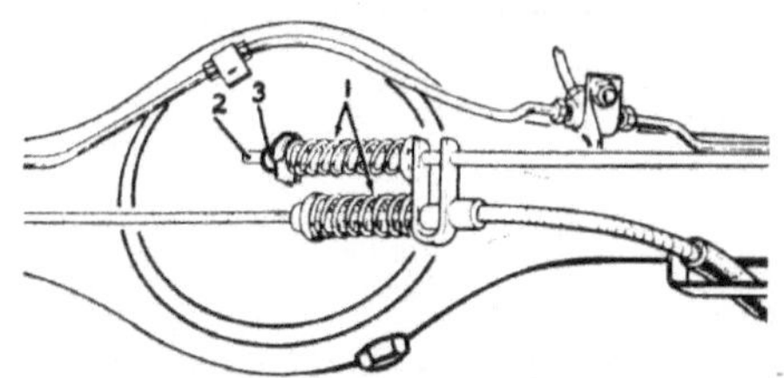

Handbrake pull-off springs, rod and bush greasing points.

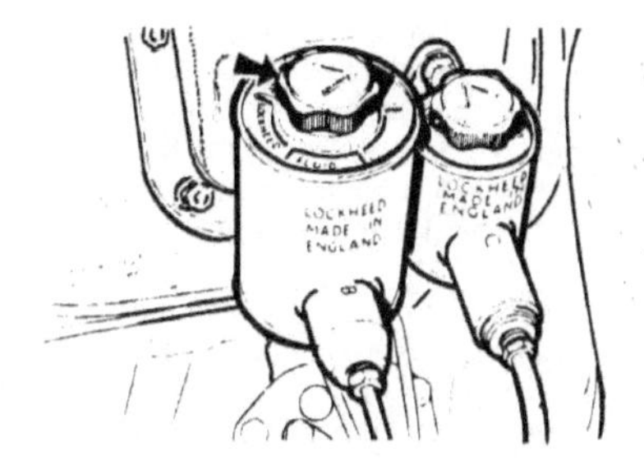
Hydraulic fluid reservoirs - larger reservoir for braking system.

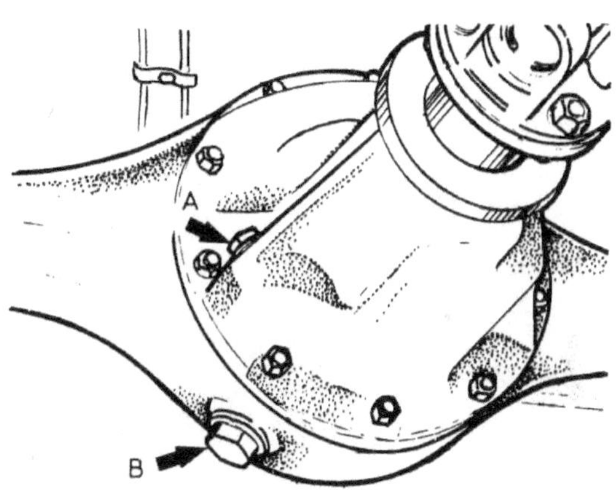

Rear axle filler/level plug (A) and drain plug (B).

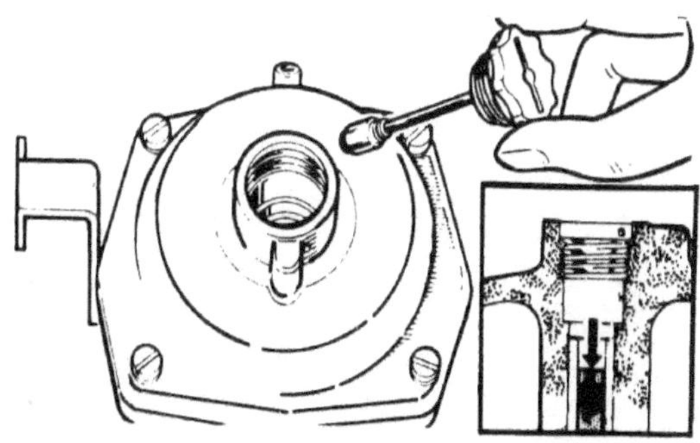
Carburettor dashpot damper removed and (inset) oil level height.

30,000 miles

GEARBOX
Drain and refill with fresh oil

REAR AXLE
Drain and refill with fresh oil

TRANSMISSION
Check tightness of propeller shaft coupling bolts and condition of universal joints

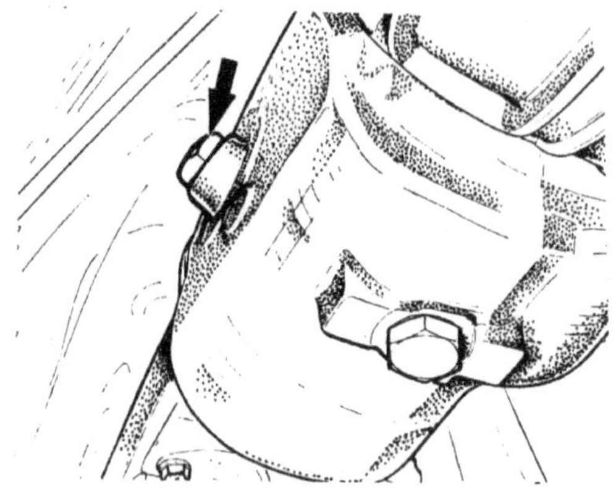

Gearbox filler/level plug.

In addition, time should be spent on the following:—

CLEANING
The best way to examine a car and know what sort of a state it is in, is to thoroughly clean it, inside and out. One of the principal results of this, which is not covered by other maintenance operations, is the finding of any traces of rust in the body panels. If rust is allowed to go unchecked it could affect certain structural panels which may make the car unsafe and keep it off the road.

EXHAUST SYSTEM
An exhaust system must be leakproof and keep engine noise below a level of 86 decibels. Leaks may cause dangerous fumes to enter the interior and affect the driver and passengers - thus having an adverse effect on the driver's capabilities. Excessive noise constitutes a public nuisance. Both these faults can result in the vehicle being declared unfit for use.

Ordering spare parts

Buy genuine Chrysler/Rootes spare parts from a Rootes dealer direct, or through a local garage. If you go direct to an authorised dealer the correctly fitting genuine parts can usually be supplied from stock which, of course, is a greatly added convenience.

The full details of the car's serial number should be available when the parts are ordered or obtained. If the actual part being renewed can also be produced it is often useful. Modifications are a continuing and unpublicised process in car manufacture, apart from all the model variations. If a parts storeman says that he cannot guarantee that a part he supplies is correct because the car number is unknown, he is perfectly justified. Variations can occur from month to month.

The vehicle serial number and suffix letters are stamped on a plate which is fixed to the bonnet lock platform. A drawing of the plate is given below although it shows only load and axle load figures (and these refer to the Avenger series!).

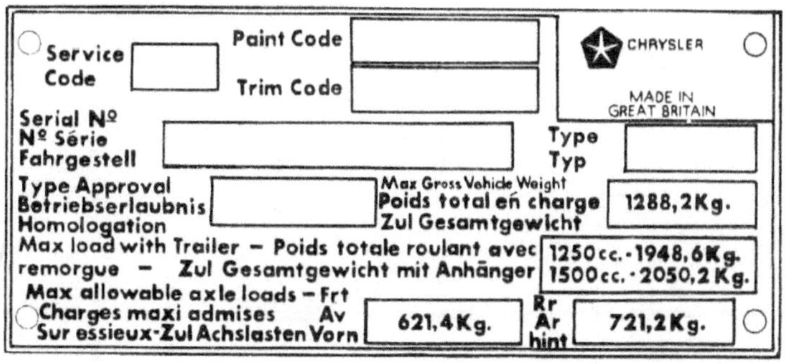

Service Code
Paint Code
Trim Code
CHRYSLER
MADE IN GREAT BRITAIN
Serial Nº
Nº Série
Fahrgestell
Type
Typ
Type Approval
Betriebserlaubnis
Homologation
Max Gross Vehicle Weight
Poids total en charge
Zul Gesamtgewicht
1288,2Kg.
Max load with Trailer – Poids totale roulant avec remorgue – Zul Gesamtgewicht mit Anhänger
1250cc.-1948,6Kg.
1500cc.-2050,2Kg.
Max allowable axle loads – Frt
Charges maxi admises Av
Sur essieux-Zul Achslasten Vorn
621,4Kg.
Rr
Ar
hint
721,2Kg.

RECOMMENDED LUBRICANTS

COMPONENT	TYPE OF LUBRICANT OR FLUID	CASTROL PRODUCT
ENGINE SUMP	Multigrade engine oil	G.T.X.
GEARBOX	Multigrade engine oil	G.T.X.
REAR AXLE	S.A.E. 90 E.P.	Castrol Hypoy
STEERING BOX	S.A.E. 90 E.P.	Castrol Hypoy
FRONT WHEEL HUB BEARINGS	Lithium based grease	Castrol L.M.
DISTRIBUTOR, STARTER & DYNAMO BUSHES	Light engine oil	G.T.X.
DISTRIBUTOR CONTACT BREAKER CAM & BATTERY TERMINALS	Petroleum jelly	
HYDRAULIC PISTONS	Rubber grease	
BRAKE MECHANISMS (ADJUSTER CAM & SHOES TO BACKPLATES)	High melting point white grease	Castrol P.H.
HYDRAULIC SYSTEM	Hydraulic fluid	Castrol Girling Brake Fluid
CARBURETTOR DAMPER	Light engine oil	G.T.X. or Everyman

Additionally Castrol Everyman oil can be used to lubricate door, boot and bonnet hinges, and locks, pivots, etc.

LUBRICATION CHART

CASTROL GTX.
An ultra-high performance motor oil incorporating for the first time every necessary high performance quality. Recommended for the engine in summer and winter. Castrolite should be used in the gearbox.

CASTROL HYPOY GEAR OIL.
A powerful extreme pressure lubricant recommended for the steering unit and rear axle.

CASTROL LM GREASE.
A lithium based high melting point grease recommended for the front hub bearings.

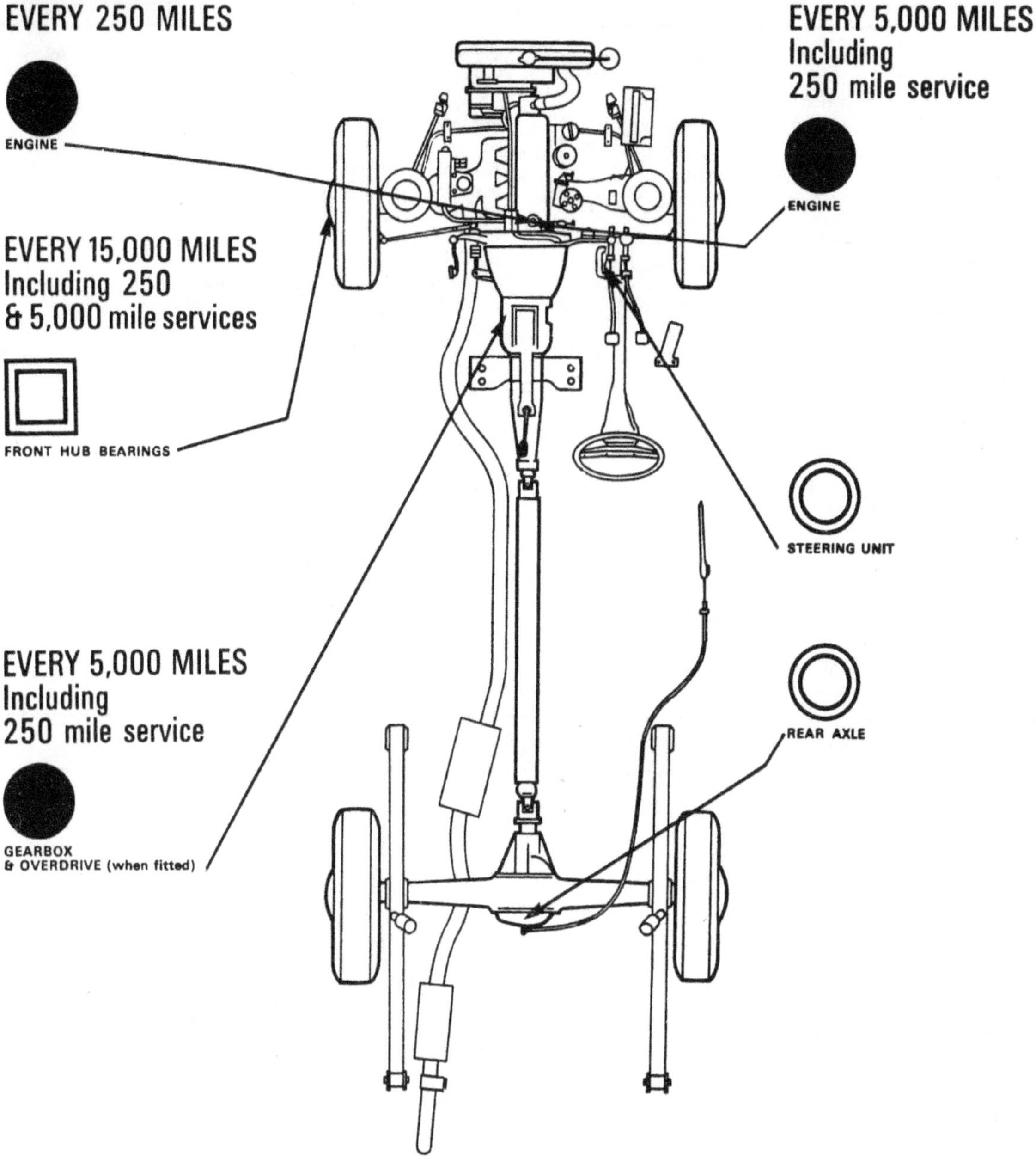

EVERY 250 MILES

ENGINE

EVERY 15,000 MILES
Including 250 & 5,000 mile services

FRONT HUB BEARINGS

EVERY 5,000 MILES
Including 250 mile service

GEARBOX
& OVERDRIVE (when fitted)

EVERY 5,000 MILES
Including 250 mile service

ENGINE

STEERING UNIT

REAR AXLE

Chapter 1 Engine

Contents

Specifications – Engine Specifications and Data – 1725 cc Standard and H120

Engine - General

Type	4 cylinder in line ohv pushrod operated

Cylinder Block

Material	Cast iron
Bore - Grade A	3.2102–3.2106 in (81.539–81.549 mm)
- Grade B	3.2106–3.2110 in (81.549–81.559 mm)
- Grade C	3.2110–3.2114 in (81.559–81.569 mm)
- Grade D	3.2114–3.2118 in (81.569–81.579 mm)
Stroke	3.25 in (82.55 mm)
Capacity	1724 cc (105.1 cu in)
Firing order	1, 3, 4, 2
No 1 cylinder position	Front of engine, next to radiator
Compression ratio	
- Standard	9.2 to 1
- H120	9.6 to 1
Compression pressure	
- Standard	160–180 lb sq in (11.3–12.7 kg/cm^2)
- H120	200–210 lb sq in (14.0–14.8 kg/cm^2)
Fuel octane - Standard	96/98
- H120	101
Max bhp (net)	
- Standard	88 at 5,200 rpm
- H120	105 at 5,200 rpm

Max torque (net)	
- Standard	100 lb/ft (13.8 kg.m) at 4,000 rpm
- H120	120 lb/ft (16.59 kg.m) at 4,000 rpm

Camshaft

Bearings	3 steel shell lined with white metal
Journal diameter	1.7477–1.7470 in (44.39–44.37 mm)
Bearing running clearance	0.003–0.0013 in (0.07–0.03 mm)
End float	0.002–0.003 in (0.05–0.07 mm)

Crankshaft

Throw	1.625 in (41.28 mm)
Bearings	5 steel backed, lined with white metal
Journal diameter (A)	2.375 in (60.325 mm)
Journal diameter (B)	2.365 in (60.071 mm)
Max regrind undersize	0.040 in (1.01 mm)
Crankpin diameter (A)	2.125 in (53.975 mm)
Crankpin diameter (B)	2.115 in (53.721 mm)
Thrust washers	Two semi-circular - copper lead face
End float	0.002–0.008 in (0.05–0.20 mm)
Main bearing running clearance	0.0025–0.0010 in (0.063–0.025 mm)

Connecting Rods

Type	H section steel forging
Distance between centres	5.625 in (14.28 cm)
Big end bore (no bearings)	2.2715–2.2710 in (57.69–57.68 mm)
Big end running clearance	0.002–0.0015 in (0.05–0.03 mm)
Big end endfloat	0.0125–0.0075 in (0.32–0.19 mm)
Big end bearings	Steel backed alum/tin or copper/lead indium coated
Small end bore (with bush)	
White - High grade	0.9378–0.9377 in (23.820–23.817 mm)
Green - Med grade	0.9377–0.9376 in (23.817–23.815 mm)
Yellow - Low grade	0.9376–0.9375 in (23.815–23.812 mm)

Gudgeon Pins

Type	Fully floating with circlip location
Fit in piston	Push fit at 68°F (20°C)
Diameter - Service grade (blue)	0.9378–0.9377 in (23.820–23.817 mm)
- High grade (white)	0.9377–0.9376 in (23.817–23.815 mm)
- Med grade (green)	0.9376–0.9375 in (23.815–23.812 mm)
- Low grade (yellow)	0.9375–0.9374 in (23.812–23.809 mm)

Pistons

Type	
- Standard	Aluminium alloy, tin plated with slotted skirt
- H120	Aluminium alloy, tin plated, solid skirt
Length	
- Standard	3.25 in (82.57 mm)
- H120	2.848 in (72.33 mm)
Rings fitted	2 compression, 1 scraper
Diameter	
- Standard - Grade A	3.2096–3.2092 in (81.524–81.514 mm)
- Grade B	3.2100–3.2096 in (81.534–81.524 mm)
- Grade C	3.2104–3.2100 in (81.544–81.534 mm)
- Grade D	3.2108–3.2104 in (81.555–81.544 mm)
- Grade E	3.2112–3.2108 in (81.565–81.555 mm)
- H120 - Grade A	3.2080–3.2076 in (81.48–81.47 mm)
- Grade B	3.2084–3.2080 in (81.49–81.48 mm)
- Grade C	3.2088–3.2084 in (81.50–81.49 mm)
- Grade D	3.2092–3.2088 in (81.51–81.50 mm)
(service only) - Grade E	3.2096–3.2092 in (81.52–81.51 mm)
Oversize available (Grade B only)	0.030 in (0.76 mm)
Clearance at skirt in cylinder measured at right angles to gudgeon pin axis	
- Standard	0.0006–0.0014 in (0.015–0.035 mm)
- H120	0.0022–0.0030 in (0.05–0.07 mm)
Ring gap	
Top ring (Grade A bore)	0.032–0.024 in (0.81–0.60 mm)
Second and scraper	0.014–0.009 in (0.35–0.22 mm)

Cylinder Head

Material	Aluminium
Gasket type	Steel, copper asbestos
Valve position	Overhead with rockers and pushrods
Valve clearances (hot)	
- Standard - Inlet	0.012 in (0.30 mm)
- Exhaust	0.014 in (0.35 mm)
- H120 - Inlet	0.013 in (0.33 mm)
- Exhaust	0.013 in (0.33 mm)
Valve seat and face angle	45°
Valve stem diameter - Inlet	0.3110–0.3105 in (7.90–7.89mm)
- Exhaust	0.3100–0.3095 in (7.87–7.86 mm)
Valve stem to guide clearance	
- Inlet	0.0015–0.0030 in (.038–.076 mm)
- Exhaust	0.0025–0.004 in (.063–.102 mm)
Valve length	4.66 in (118.3 mm)
Valve guides - O.D	0.5640–0.5635 in (14.30–14.27 mm)
- interference fit	0.0025–0.0045 in (0.063–0.114 mm)
- length - inlet	2.0 in (50.8 mm)
- length - exhaust	2.15 in (54.6 mm)
- fitted height above head	0.50 in (12.7 mm)

Valve Timing

Standard	
Inlet opens	29° BTDC
Inlet closes	63° ABDC
Exhaust opens	69° BBDC
Exhaust closes	23° ATDC
H120	
Inlet opens	58° BTDC
Inlet closes	66° ABDC
Exhaust opens	84° BBDC
Exhaust closes	40° ATDC
Valve head diameter - Inlet	1.503 in (38.17 mm)
- Exhaust	1.204 in (30.58 mm)
Valve springs type	Dual
Length fitted - Inner	1.38 (32.5 mm)
- Outer	1.40 in (35.6 mm)
Load fitted	
Standard - Inner	21.2 lb (9.6 kg)
- Outer	50.2 lb (22.9 kg)
H120 - Inner	28.3 lb (12.8 kg)
- Outer	52.0 lb (23.6 kg)

Lubrication

Sump capacity (incl filter)	7½ pints (9 US pints, 4.2 litres)
Filter capacity	½ pint (0.6 US pint, 0.28 litre)
Oil pump type	Eccentric lobe
Pump drive	Skew gear from camshaft
Normal pressure - hot	48–52 lb sq in (3.4 to 3.5 kg cm^2)
Oil filter type	Full flow disposable

Torque Wrench Settings

Cylinder head nuts	48 lb/ft (6.6 kg.m)
Main bearing caps	55 lb/ft (7.6 kg.m)
Big end caps	29 lb/ft (4.0 kg.m)
Rocker shaft standards	11 lb/ft (1.5 kg.m)
Manifolds	33 lb/ft (4.6 kg.m)
Flywheel bolts	41 lb/ft (5.7 kg.m)

Approx Weights

Engine	295 lb (134 kg)
Engine with gearbox	365 lb (166 kg)

Castrol GRADES

Castrol Engine Oils

Castrol GTX

An ultra high performance SAE 20W/50 motor oil which exceeds the latest API MS requirements and manufacturers' specifications. Castrol GTX with liquid tungsten† generously protects engines at the extreme limits of performance, and combines both good cold starting with oil consumption control. Approved by leading car makers.

Castrol XL 20/50

Contains liquid tungsten†; well suited to the majority of conditions giving good oil consumption control in both new and old cars.

Castrolite (Multi-grade)

This is the lightest multi-grade oil of the Castrol motor oil family containing liquid tungsten†. It is best suited to ensure easy winter starting and for those car models whose manufacturers specify lighter weight oils.

Castrol Grand Prix

An SAE 50 engine oil for use where a heavy, full-bodied lubricant is required.

Castrol Two-Stroke-Four

A premium SAE 30 motor oil possessing good detergency characteristics and corrosion inhibitors, coupled with low ash forming tendency and excellent anti-scuff properties. It is suitable for all two-stroke motor-cycles, and for two-stroke and small four-stroke horticultural machines.

Castrol CR (Multi-grade)

A high quality engine oil of the SAE-20W/30 multi-grade type, suited to mixed fleet operations.

Castrol CRI 10, 20, 30

Primarily for diesel engines, a range of heavily fortified, fully detergent oils, covering the requirements of DEF 2101-D and Supplement 1 specifications.

Castrol CRB 20, 30

Primarily for diesel engines, heavily fortified, fully detergent oils, covering the requirements of MIL-L-2104B.

Castrol R 40

Primarily designed and developed for highly stressed racing engines. Castrol 'R' should not be mixed with any other oil nor with any grade of Castrol.

†Liquid Tungsten is an oil soluble long chain tertiary alkyl primary amine tungstate covered by British Patent No. 882,295.

Castrol Gear Oils

Castrol Hypoy (90 EP)

A light-bodied powerful extreme pressure gear oil for use in hypoid rear axles and in some gearboxes.

Castrol Gear Oils (continued)

Castrol Hypoy Light (80 EP)

A very light-bodied powerful extreme pressure gear oil for use in hypoid rear axles in cold climates and in some gearboxes.

Castrol Hypoy B (90 EP)

A light-bodied powerful extreme pressure gear oil that complies with the requirements of the MIL-L-2105B specification, for use in certain gearboxes and rear axles.

Castrol Hi-Press (140 EP)

A heavy-bodied extreme pressure gear oil for use in spiral bevel rear axles and some gearboxes.

Castrol ST (90)

A light-bodied gear oil with fortifying additives

Castrol D (140)

A heavy full-bodied gear oil with fortifying additives.

Castrol Thio-Hypoy FD (90 EP)

A light-bodied powerful extreme pressure gear oil. This is a special oil for running-in certain hypoid gears.

Automatic Transmission Fluids

Castrol TQF (Automatic Transmission Fluid)

Approved for use in all Borg-Warner Automatic Transmission Units. Castrol TQF also meets Ford specification M2C 33F.

Castrol TQ Dexron® (Automatic Transmission Fluid)

Complies with the requirements of Dexron® Automatic Transmission Fluids as laid down by General Motors Corporation.

Castrol Greases

Castrol LM

A multi-purpose high melting point lithium based grease approved for most automotive applications including chassis and wheel bearing lubrication.

Castrol MS3

A high melting point lithium based grease containing molybdenum disulphide.

Castrol BNS

A high melting point grease for use where recommended by certain manufacturers in front wheel bearings when disc brakes are fitted.

Castrol Greases (continued)

Castrol CL

A semi-fluid calcium based grease, which is both waterproof and adhesive, intended for chassis lubrication.

Castrol Medium

A medium consistency calcium based grease.

Castrol Heavy

A heavy consistency calcium based grease.

Castrol PH

A white grease for plunger housings and other moving parts on brake mechanisms. *It must NOT be allowed to come into contact with brake fluid when applied to the moving parts of hydraulic brakes.*

Castrol Graphited Grease

A graphited grease for the lubrication of transmission chains.

Castrol Under-Water Grease

A grease for the under-water gears of outboard motors.

Anti-Freeze

Castrol Anti-Freeze

Contains anti-corrosion additives with ethylene glycol. Recommended for the cooling systems of all petrol and diesel engines.

Speciality Products

Castrol Girling Damper Oil Thin

The oil for Girling piston type hydraulic dampers.

Castrol Shockol

A light viscosity oil for use in some piston type shock absorbers and in some hydraulic systems employing synthetic rubber seals. It must not be used in braking systems.

Castrol Penetrating Oil

A leaf spring lubricant possessing a high degree of penetration and providing protection against rust.

Castrol Solvent Flushing Oil

A light-bodied solvent oil, designed for flushing engines, rear axles, gearboxes and gearcasings.

Castrollo

An upper cylinder lubricant for use in the proportion of 1 fluid ounce to two gallons of fuel.

Everyman Oil

A light-bodied machine oil containing anti-corrosion additives for both general use and cycle lubrication.

1. General Description

The 1725 cc engine fitted to models covered by this manual is virtually 'square' in that the bore and the stroke are almost exactly the same. The engine has four cylinders in line, an aluminium cylinder head, fitted with two valves per cylinder which are operated by overhead rockers and pushrods from a single camshaft mounted in the right hand side of the engine block.

The crankshaft runs in five main bearings and the endfloat is controlled by a pair of semi-circular thrust washers located in the upper half of the centre main bearing journal. The camshaft is driven by a duplex chain from a sprocket on the forward end of the crankshaft and this chain is tensioned by a hard rubber slipper supported on a steel leaf pivoting inside the cover. The camshaft, in turn, drives the oil pump through a skew gear and the oil pump drive shaft also drives the distributor.

The pistons are a fully floating fit to the connecting rods and the gudgeon pins are retained in the piston with circlips. The connecting rod small end bush is renewable and gudgeon pins are available in different sizes as required for the fit of the piston to the small end of the connecting rod. The lubrication system is of the forced feed type through a full flow oil filter to the crankshaft main bearings, connecting rod big end bearings, camshaft bearings and valve rocker gear. The oil pump is fully submersed and is of the eccentric lobe twin rotor type.

The engine is flexibly mounted into the body frame at three points. There is one mounting bracket fitted to each side of the engine block, centrally, and the third suspension point is on to a crossmember which runs underneath the gearbox. It will be appreciated, therefore, that neither the engine nor the gearbox is fully supported when either one is removed.

2. Routine Maintenance

1. Once a week, or more often if high mileages are being driven, remove the oil level dipstick and check the level of the oil in the sump which should be at the full mark. Top up the level with the recommended grade of oil (see page II for details). The difference between the two marks is two pints. If an engine appears to be using oil at a rate of more than 1 pint per 500 miles it should be considered as excessive and steps should be taken to discover whether there is a leak in the system or whether the oil is being consumed due to excessive wear in the engine.
2. Every 5,000 miles, or every 6 months if 5,000 miles are not completed, run the engine until it is hot. Then place a container with a minimum capacity of one gallon under the drain plug in the sump, undo the drain plug and allow the old oil to drain out for at least ten minutes. The oil filter cartridge should also be unscrewed and a new one fitted as described in Section 20 of this Chapter.
3. Carefully clean the drain plug and make sure that the washer is clean and intact and replace the plug in the sump tightening it firmly. Then refill the sump with 7½ pints of Castrol GTX oil and run the engine and recheck the level on the dipstick. Examine the point where the new filter cartridge has been screwed in to make sure that there are no oil leaks of any sort.
4. If the car is regularly used in extreme conditions of heat, cold or excessively dusty atmospheres, it is advantageous to change the engine oil more often. In such circumstances a frequency of 3,000 miles between changes is recommended.
5. Clean flame trap every 5,000 miles. Slacken the clip retaining screw and detach the rubber pipe from the oil filler neck. Detach the rubber hose from the other side and the flame trap may now be completely removed. Soak in paraffin bath, swilling trap to loosen dirt; drain; dry through with low pressure air line. (Do not use petrol). Refit trap securely.
6. Part of preventive maintenance is keeping a check on various aspects of performance. See comments under Section 21 'Engine Examination - General'.

3. Major Operations which may be carried out with engine in place

1. The following work may be conveniently carried out with the engine in place:—

1) Removal and replacement of the cylinder head assembly.
2) Removal and replacement of the clutch assembly.
3) Removal and replacement of the engine front mountings.
4) Removal and replacement of the timing chain cover, timing chain and timing chain sprockets.

2. The following work can be carried out with the engine still mounted in the car but it is preferable, if possible, to remove the engine from the car.

If the engine is left in position it is very easy for extraneous dirt to find its way in where it should not be. Great care must always be taken to ensure that all parts removed and replaced are kept scrupulously clean.

1) Removal and replacement of the sump.
2) Removal and replacement of the oil pump.
3) Removal and replacement of the connecting rod big end bearings.
4) Removal and replacement of pistons and connecting rods (after the removal of the cylinder head and sump).
5) Removal and replacement of the camshaft.
6) Removal and replacement of the flywheel (after removing the gearbox and clutch).
7) Removal and replacement of the crankshaft main bearing shells.

4. Major Operations for which the engine must be removed from the car

1. Removal and replacement of the crankshaft.
2. Renewal of the camshaft bearings.

5. Engine - Removal

1. The description which follows will assume that the engine is being removed from the car by itself, that is, with the gearbox left in the car. For occasions when it is required to remove the engine and gearbox together as one unit from the car the necessary information is given towards the end of this Section. It is necessary to disconnect and remove several items from the engine before it can be lifted from the car, and this Chapter only indicates what has to be removed. Instructions for removal of individual items will be found under their appropriate Chapter headings. For example, where an instruction to 'remove carburettor' is given details are given in Chapter 3. Before starting work on the actual removal of the engine, it is well worthwhile to spend some time in getting the engine thoroughly cleaned off away from the area where the actual removal and subsequent dismantling may be taking place. If this cleaning can be done at a service station which may be equipped with pressure cleaning equipment, so much the better. Otherwise one should use paraffin and stiff brushes and scrapers to remove the bulk of the caked on dirt before removing the engine. The final thorough cleaning of the exterior of the engine may be left until it is removed from the car. Decide whether you are going to jack up the car and support it on actual stands or raise the front end of the car on to wheel ramps. If the latter method, run the car up (and chock the rear wheels) whilst you still have engine power available. Remember that with the front wheels supported on ramps the working height and engine lifting height are going to be increased. If stands are to be used the front of the car can be jacked up later when ready.
2. Once you are sure that the car is in the correct position, which should be on level ground or level floor, the work of removing the engine may begin.
3. Open the bonnet and disconnect the battery leads of the battery

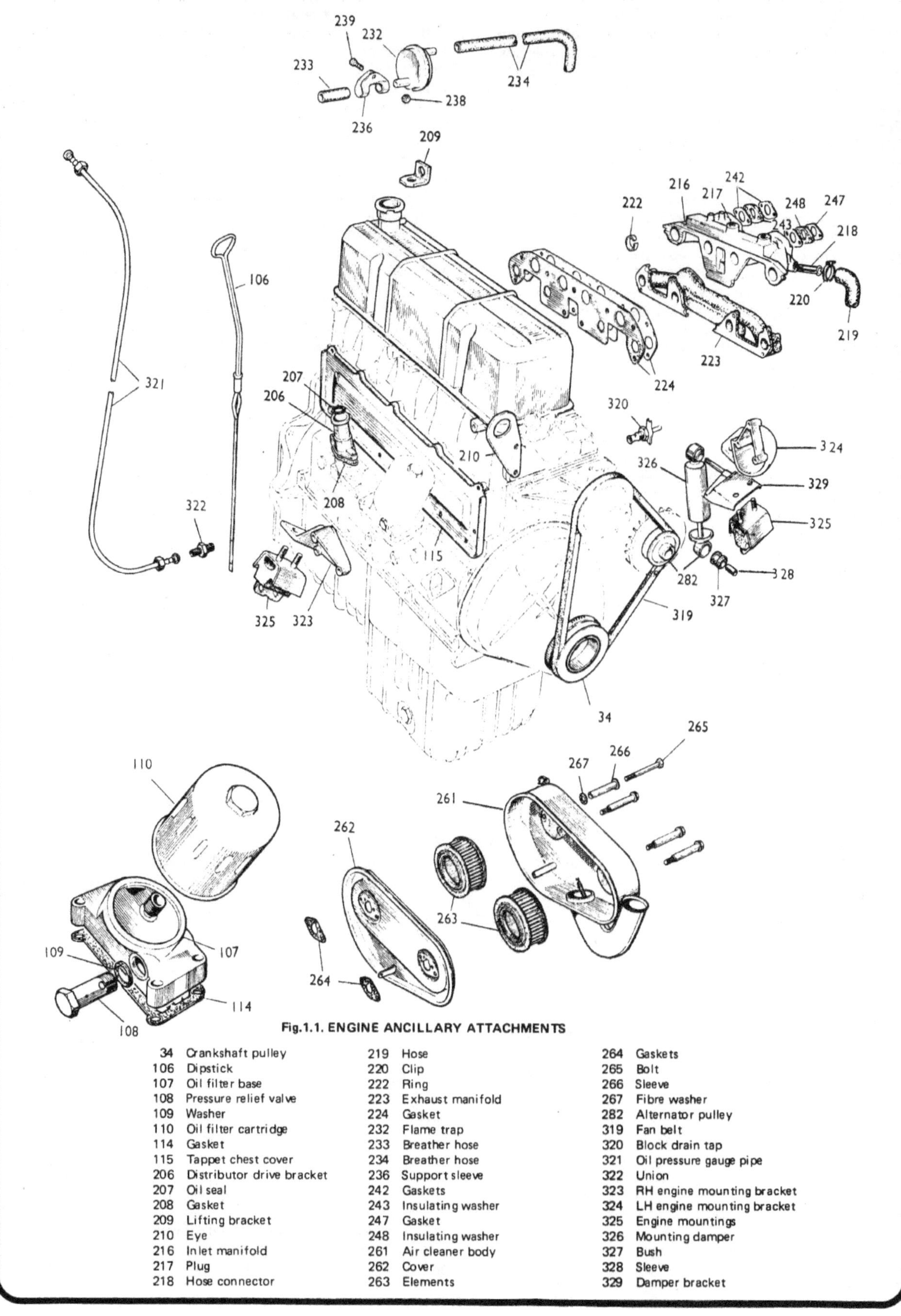

Fig.1.1. ENGINE ANCILLARY ATTACHMENTS

34	Crankshaft pulley	219	Hose	264	Gaskets
106	Dipstick	220	Clip	265	Bolt
107	Oil filter base	222	Ring	266	Sleeve
108	Pressure relief valve	223	Exhaust manifold	267	Fibre washer
109	Washer	224	Gasket	282	Alternator pulley
110	Oil filter cartridge	232	Flame trap	319	Fan belt
114	Gasket	233	Breather hose	320	Block drain tap
115	Tappet chest cover	234	Breather hose	321	Oil pressure gauge pipe
206	Distributor drive bracket	236	Support sleeve	322	Union
207	Oil seal	242	Gaskets	323	RH engine mounting bracket
208	Gasket	243	Insulating washer	324	LH engine mounting bracket
209	Lifting bracket	247	Gasket	325	Engine mountings
210	Eye	248	Insulating washer	326	Mounting damper
216	Inlet manifold	261	Air cleaner body	327	Bush
217	Plug	262	Cover	328	Sleeve
218	Hose connector	263	Elements	329	Damper bracket

clamp and remove the battery from the car. (Photos).

4. With the bonnet propped open, mark the position of the bonnet hinges, preparatory to removing the hinge clamping bolts. It is easier if you have someone to help you at the next stage, to lift the bonnet off. Care is required if damage is to be avoided to the surrounding paintwork as the bonnet is quite heavy and it could easily slip and scratch the paint nearby. It can be done single handed, however, by supporting the rear of the bonnet corners by blocks of wood. Full details can be found in Chapter 12. When the bonnet is finally removed place it somewhere where it cannot be damaged and where the edges will not be scratched nor chipped by hard surfaces.

5. Drain the oil from the sump of the engine.

6. Drain the liquid from the cooling system.

7. Detach both hose pipes from the top and bottom of the radiator by slackening the hose clips and carefully pulling the pipes from the radiator shell (Photos). Detach the heater water hoses from their connections on the bulkhead. Also unclip the two hoses from the top of the cylinder head. When this has been done both of these hoses may be put to one side clear of the engine.

8. Undo the four bolts which secure the radiator to the front body panel of the car and holding the radiator vertical to prevent it being damaged on the fan blades lift it out carefully (Photo).

9. Detach the high tension lead from the centre of the coil by simply pulling it out and then pull off all the high tension leads from the spark plugs. After unclipping the distributor cap, the cap and leads may be lifted away. Disconnect the leads from the terminals at the end of the alternator.

10 Disconnect the low tension lead from one of the coil terminals to the distributor.

11 Disconnect the lead wire from the terminal on the thermostat sender unit which is mounted in the water pump housing (Photo).

12 Disconnect the wire lead attached to the oil pressure gauge sender unit underneath the distributor in the side of the block.

13 Remove the carburettors. Although not essential, this is done for safety's sake. Disconnect the earthing cable strip which is attached to one of the bolts securing the timing cover case to the front of the engine (Photo). The other end of the cable is attached to the body frame nearby. Undo the union connecting the fuel pipe to the inlet side of the fuel pump on the right hand side of the engine (Photo).

14 Remove the nut on the terminal of the starter motor securing the lead from the solenoid (Photo).

15 Detach the exhaust pipe from the exhaust manifold by unscrewing the two nuts which hold the flange of the pipe to the manifold.

16 Remove the two bolts and the nuts holding the starter motor to the clutch flywheel bellhousing and remove the starter motor.

17 It is now time to go underneath the car so if it has not already been put up on wheel ramps and it is necessary to support it and raise it at the front on stands, do so now. It is best if the stands are placed underneath the side frame members in a position just behind the anti-roll bar clamps. It is most important that the car is properly and firmly supported because there are some bolts to be undone which may be quite stiff and the force required to turn them could well move the car off a shaky form of support.

18 Undo the nuts and bolts securing the clutch hydraulic slave cylinder to the bellhousing and lift it to one side. It is not necessary to disconnect any of the hydraulic lines for this, but ensure that nobody inadvertently puts his foot on the clutch pedal otherwise the piston will blow out of the cylinder and deposit hydraulic oil either over your floor or someone underneath the car. Some people block up the clutch pedal with a piece of wood to prevent this happening.

19 Remove the two clamps which hold the centre of the anti-roll bar to the side frame members. Each clamp is held by two bolts which locate into captive nuts in the side frame members. It is necessary to do this in order to enable the torsion bar to drop down a few inches. This will permit the sump of the engine to clear the torsion bar when the engine is drawn forward eventually to detach it from the gearbox input shaft.

20 Remove the bolts attaching the aluminium sump to the clutch bellhousing and remove the servo pipe from the inlet manifold (Photo) and the oil pressure gauge pipe from the block (Photo).

21 If everything has been done correctly the engine is now attached to the car at only three points, namely, the left and right hand side engine mountings and by the top bolts on to the gearbox bell-housing. Before proceeding further it will be necessary to provide support underneath the gearbox so that it will not tip right forward when the engine is taken away from it. This should now be done either using a jack or supporting the gearbox under the drain plug with a suitable stand or wooden blocks. This must be done before any attempt is made to detach the engine from its mountings.

22 The engine should now be supported by the hoist of whichever type is being used, so that the weight of it may be taken before disconnecting the mounting brackets. On the left hand side of the cylinder head, at the front and rear, are two holding down studs each with two nuts. In addition to the hose clips which are attached to them the rear stud also has a strong lifting bracket fitted to it. It is advisable to obtain another bracket exactly the same as this which should then be fitted underneath the top nut of the forward stud. A sling between these two brackets is the best means of lifting the engine out. It is possible to use the eye of the large plate bracket attached to the front right hand side of the engine block, but this would impart a slight twist when the engine is lifted and this makes it difficult to draw the engine forward off the gearbox input shaft. This twist causes even greater problems when the engine is being fitted back.

23 Once the sling has been satisfactorily attached the strain should be taken on it sufficiently to permit the engine mounting bracket bolts to be removed without undue strain or without allowing the engine to drop.

24 The engine mountings should be undone by using the two bolts which attach the lower part of the flexible mounting to the chassis frame. Do not detach the bracket on the engine from the top of the mounting by undoing the two uppermost nuts. If the latter method is used it means that it is very difficult, if not impossible, to lift the engine vertically upwards as the mounting studs will be inclined at an angle of 45°.

25 The remainder of the bolts holding the gearbox bellhousing to the engine should now be removed. It should be noted that one of the long bolts on the lower left hand side of the bellhousing is, in fact, a dowel pin and once the nut has been removed it is not necessary to attempt to remove it as it will remain where it is when the engine is drawn away.

26 With all attachments now removed, other than the connection between the engine and gearbox input shaft, the whole engine should be drawn forward in order to disengage it from the gearbox. This normally presents no difficulties but in case the two are reluctant to part it will be necessary, perhaps, to do a bit of rocking in order to get it to come forward. It is very important to remember that the engine should not be raised or lowered at this stage in an attempt to separate it from the gearbox. Until it is clear of the gearbox input shaft any upwards or downwards strain could cause severe damage to the clutch or the gearbox.

27 Once the engine has been drawn forward from the gearbox, it may be lifted straight up and clear of the car without any tilting whatsoever.

28 If the engine is being removed together with the gearbox the procedures are exactly the same except that the bolts which join the engine and gearbox together at the bellhousing do not have to be removed. The starter motor may also remain in place.

29 In addition, however, it is necessary to remove the gearbox supporting crossmember in order that the rear end of the gearbox may be allowed to drop down sufficiently far for the engine to be tilted up to clear it through the engine compartment on the way out. Details of removal of the crossmember may be found in Chapter 6 under the Section concerned with gearbox removal. It will also be necessary to remove the gearchange lever from inside the car as also described in Chapter 6.

30 The gearbox crossmember should only be removed after the full weight of the engine has been supported at the front and the engine mountings have been unbolted. As soon as this situation is reached, a support in the form of a jack or suitable blocks should be placed

Section 5.3 Disconnecting and unclamping the battery

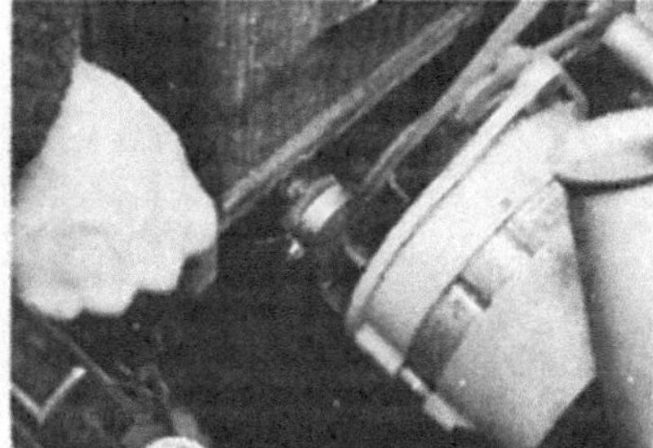

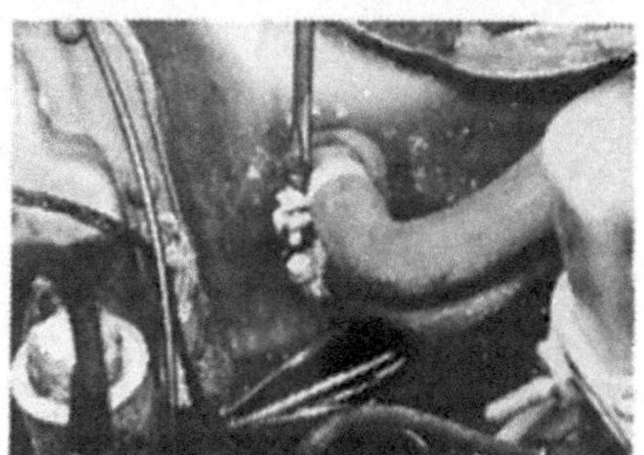

Section 5.7 and 5.8 Disconnecting coolant and heater hoses and removing radiator

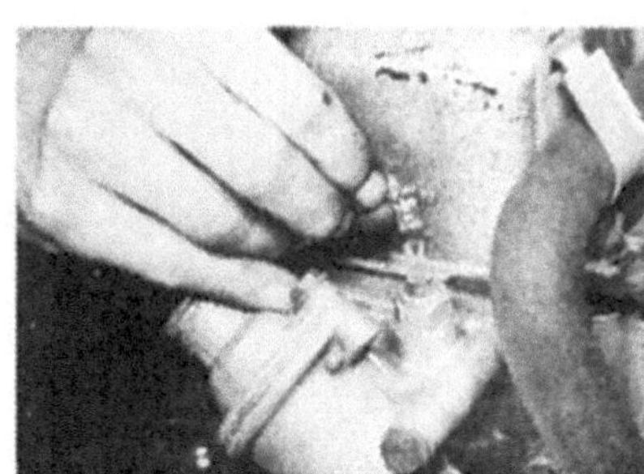

Section 5.11 Disconnecting thermostat sender

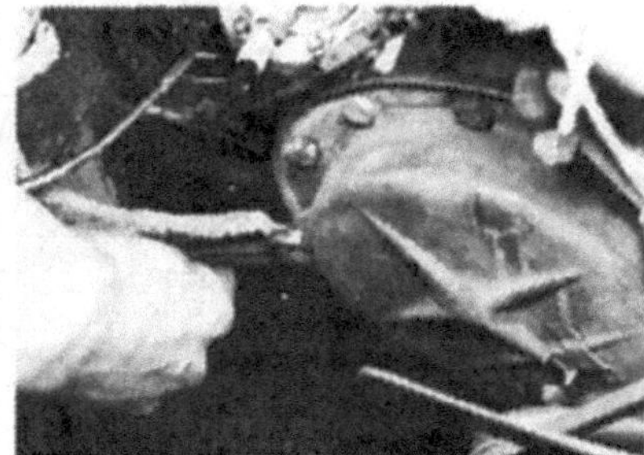

Section 5.13 Disconnecting earthing cable strip (timing cover) and fuel pump pipe on fuel pump

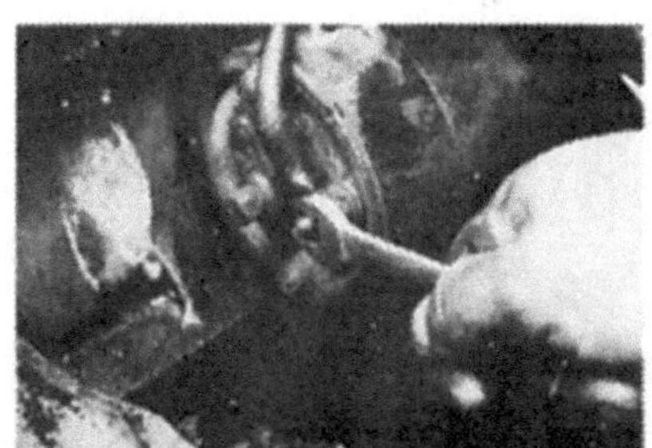

Section 5.4 Disconnecting starter motor

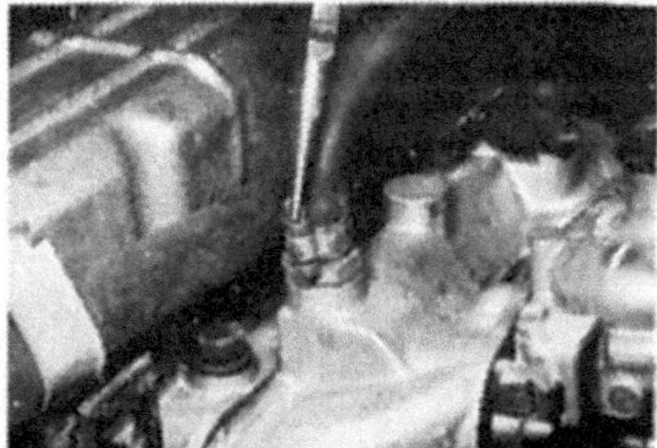

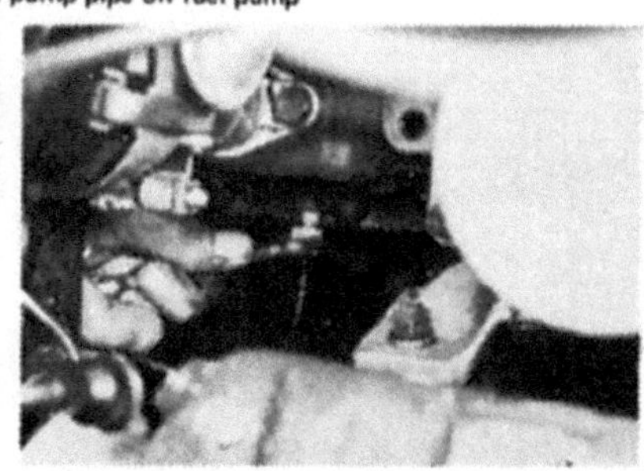

Section 5.20 Removing servo pipe and oil pressure gauge pipe.

PREPARING TO REMOVE THE ENGINE

under the gearbox and the gearbox crossmember support detached from the bodywork of the car and then from the bottom of the gearbox itself.

31 Detach the speedometer cable from the side of the gearbox by unscrewing the milled retaining screw.

32 Without moving the support immediately from under the gearbox start to lift the engine forward and up. It will immediately be noted that the propeller shaft will have to be carefully lowered before it drops out of the tail end of the gearbox and also the gearbox itself will have to be lowered which will mean gradual or total removal of the support which has been placed underneath it. Prepare to collect any oil which may drop from the gearbox rear extension cover. It is in order to let the gearbox come to rest on the floor, but do not let it drop or scrape along the floor. By a gradual process of lifting and moving forward on the hoist the whole assembly can be drawn up through the engine compartment, but it will be considerably more difficult than lifting out the engine by itself and additional help will certainly be necessary if damage or accidents are to be avoided for sure (Photo).

33 Once the engine is clear of the car, either with or without the gearbox attached, lower it as soon as possible to the ground or area where it is to be externally cleaned. It is better if this place is not right close to where the engine is going to be dismantled. Further cleaning at this stage is well worth the time spent on it as the risk of filth and grit getting into the engine later on is greatly reduced. Be careful not to let paraffin or cleaning fluids of any kind contaminate the clutch friction disc during this process. Once the engine is cleaned put it in the position where it is to be dismantled and prop it securely to prevent any damage either to itself or to people.

Slow, easy stages

Section 5.32

Nearly ready for final withdrawal

Fig.1.2. Part of crossmember lowered to facilitate removal of aluminium sump (when engine is left in car)

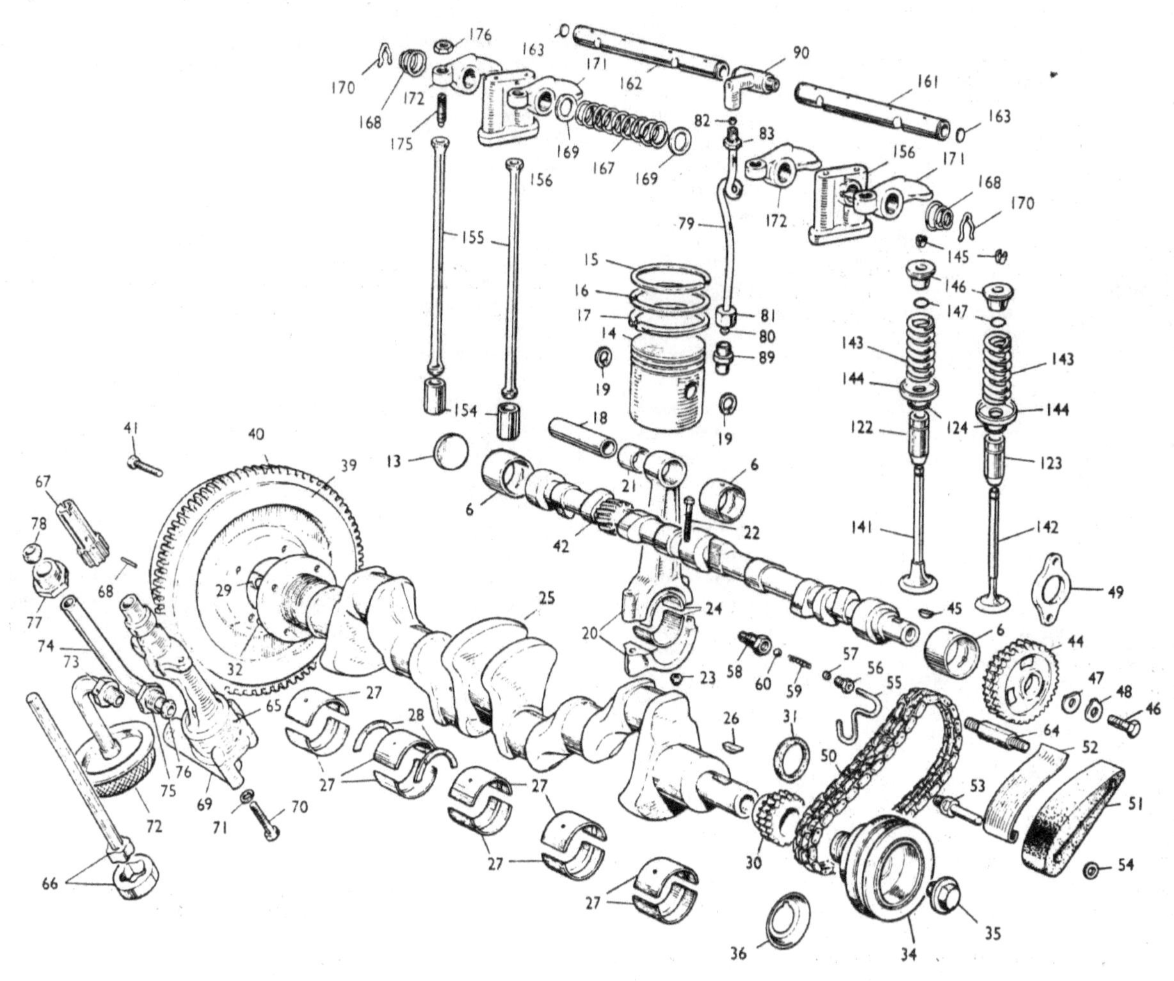

Fig,1.3. THE MOVING COMPONENTS OF THE ENGINE

6 Camshaft bearing
13 Sealing disc
14 Piston
15 Top compression ring
16 Second compression ring
17 Oil control ring
18 Gudgeon pin
19 Circlip
20 Connecting rod and cap
21 Small end bush
22 Big end bolt
23 Nut
24 Big end bearing shells
25 Crankshaft
26 Pulley key
27 Main bearing shells
28 Thrust washers
29 Bush
30 Crankshaft sprocket
31 Damper ring
32 Flywheel dowel
34 Crankshaft pulley
35 Pulley bolt
36 Oil thrower
39 Flywheel
40 Starter ring
41 Bolt
42 Camshaft
44 Camshaft sprocket
45 Camshaft key
46 Bolt
47 Washer
48 Lockwasher
49 Camshaft thrust plate
50 Timing chain
51 Chain tensioner
52 Tensioner blade
53 Pivot pin
54 Washer
55 Oil pipe
56 Nut
57 Olive
58 Adaptor
59 Spring
60 Ball
64 Stud
65 Oil pump body
66 Outer rotor shaft
67 Pump gear
68 Pin
69 Pump cover
70 Bolt
71 Washer
72 Filter screen
73 Nut
74 Oil pipe
75 Nut
76 Olive
77 Nut
78 Olive
79 Rocker oil feed pipe
80 Olive
81 Nut
82 Olive
83 Nut
89 Union
90 'T' piece adaptor
122 Valve guide (inlet)
123 Valve guide exhaust
124 Retaining ring
141 Inlet valve
142 Exhaust valve
143 Valve springs
144 Valve spring cup
145 Valve collets
146 Valve collars
147 Sealing rings
154 Tappets
155 Pushrods
161 Front rocker shaft
162 Rear rocker shaft
163 Plug
167 Rocker shaft inner spring
168 Rocker shaft outer spring
169 Spring spacers
170 Clip
171 Rockers (1, 3, 5, 7)
172 Rockers (2, 4, 6, 8)
175 Rocker adjusting screw
176 Locknut

6. Engine Dismantling - General

1. Owners who have dismantled engines will know the need for a strong work bench and many tools and pieces of equipment, which make their life much easier. For those doing a dismantling job for the first time, there are a few 'musts' in the way of preparation which, if ignored, will only cause frustration and long delays in the job in the long run. It is essential to have sufficient space in which to work. Dismantling and reassembly is not going to be completed all in one go and it is therefore absolutely essential that you have sufficient area to leave things as they are when necessary. A strong work bench is also necessary together with a good engineer's vice. If you have no alternative other than to work at ground level, make sure that the floor is at least level and covered with a suitable wooden or wood composition material on which to work. If dirt and grit are allowed to get into any of the component parts all work which you carry out may be completely wasted. Before actually placing the engine wherever it is that you may be carrying out the dismantling, make sure that the exterior is now completely and thoroughly cleaned.
2. Once dismantling begins it is advisable to clean the parts as they are removed. A small bath of paraffin is about the best thing to use for this, but do not let parts which have oilways in them become immersed in paraffin otherwise there may be a residue which could cause harmful effects later on. If paraffin does get into oilways every effort should be made to blow it out. For this it may be necessary to carry the particular part to a garage fitted with a high pressure air hose. Short oilways such as there are in the crankshaft can be cleared easily with pipe cleaners.
3. Always obtain a complete set of gaskets when the engine is being dismantled - no gaskets on an engine are normally re-usable and any attempt to do so is quite unjustified in view of the relatively small cost involved. Before throwing any gaskets away, however, make sure that you have the replacements to hand. If, for example, a particular gasket cannot be obtained it may be necessary to make one, and the pattern of the old one is useful in such cases.
4. Generally speaking, it is best to start dismantling the engine from the top downwards. In any case, make sure it is firmly supported at all times so that it does not topple over whilst you are undoing the very tight nuts and bolts which will be encountered. Always replace nuts and bolts into their locations once the particular part has been removed, if possible. Otherwise keep them in convenient tins or pots in their groups, so that when the time comes to reassemble there is the minimum of confusion.

7. Engine Dismantling - Ancillaries

1. If you are intending to obtain an exchange engine complete, or what is called a half engine, which is basically the cylinder block, crankshaft and pistons, it will be necessary first of all to remove all those parts of the engine which are not included in the exchange. If you are stripping the engine completely yourself with the likelihood of some outside work to be done by specialists, all these items will be taken off anyway.
2. It is as well to check with whoever may be supplying the replacement exchange unit what is necessary to remove, but as a general guide the following items will have to be taken off. Reference is given to the appropriate Chapter for details of removal of each of these items:—

Alternator - Chapter 10
Distributor - Chapter 4
Thermostat and housing - Chapter 2
Oil filter (expendable) - Chapter 1
Carburettor - Chapter 3
Inlet manifold - Chapter 1
Exhaust manifold - Chapter 1
Water pump - Chapter 2
Fuel pump - Chapter 3
Engine mounting brackets - Chapter 1

3. If a half engine only is being obtained on a replacement exchange basis, the following items in addition to those already removed will have to be taken off:—

Cylinder head complete with valve rocker gear
Flywheel
Sump
Oil pump

8. Valve Rocker Gear - Removal

1. The valve rocker gear will need to be removed if it is desired to remove the cylinder head, either with the engine out of the car or in the car.
2. Remove the four screws which secure the rocker box cover to the cylinder head. It will be necessary to disconnect the breather pipe which goes into the cover and also to unclip the high tension plug leads from the rear end of the engine in order to remove it.
3. The rocker gear may be removed as an assembly complete. The shaft and rocker arms are mounted on four standards, each of which is held to the head by two long bolts. All eight bolts should be undone evenly so as to permit any springs which may be in compression to ease themselves into their free state without unduly distorting the rocker shaft during the process of removing it. Undo the small brass union which connects the oil feed pipe to the T-piece

Fig.1.4. EXPLODED VIEW OF THE STATIC ENGINE COMPONENTS

1 Cylinder block
2 Plug
3 Copper washer
4 Plugs
5 Plug
7 Oilway plug
8 Plug
9 Main bearing cap bolts (front)
10 Main bearing cap bolt (centre & rear)
11 Main bearing cap bolt (intermediate)
12 Washer
37 Engine front plate
38 Gasket
61 Timing cover
62 Gasket
63 Collar
92 Sump
93 Sump baffle
94 Drain plug
95 Copper washer
96 Sump gasket RH)
97 and LH)
98 Oil seal
115 Tappet chest cover
116 Gasket
117 Cylinder head
118 Plug
119 Washer
120 Plug
121 Water jet
134 Gasket
136 Cylinder head stud
137 Bolt
138 Washer
140 Nut
157 Rocker gear stud
158 Washer
177 Rocker cover
178 Oil filler cap
179 Gasket
320 Block drain tap

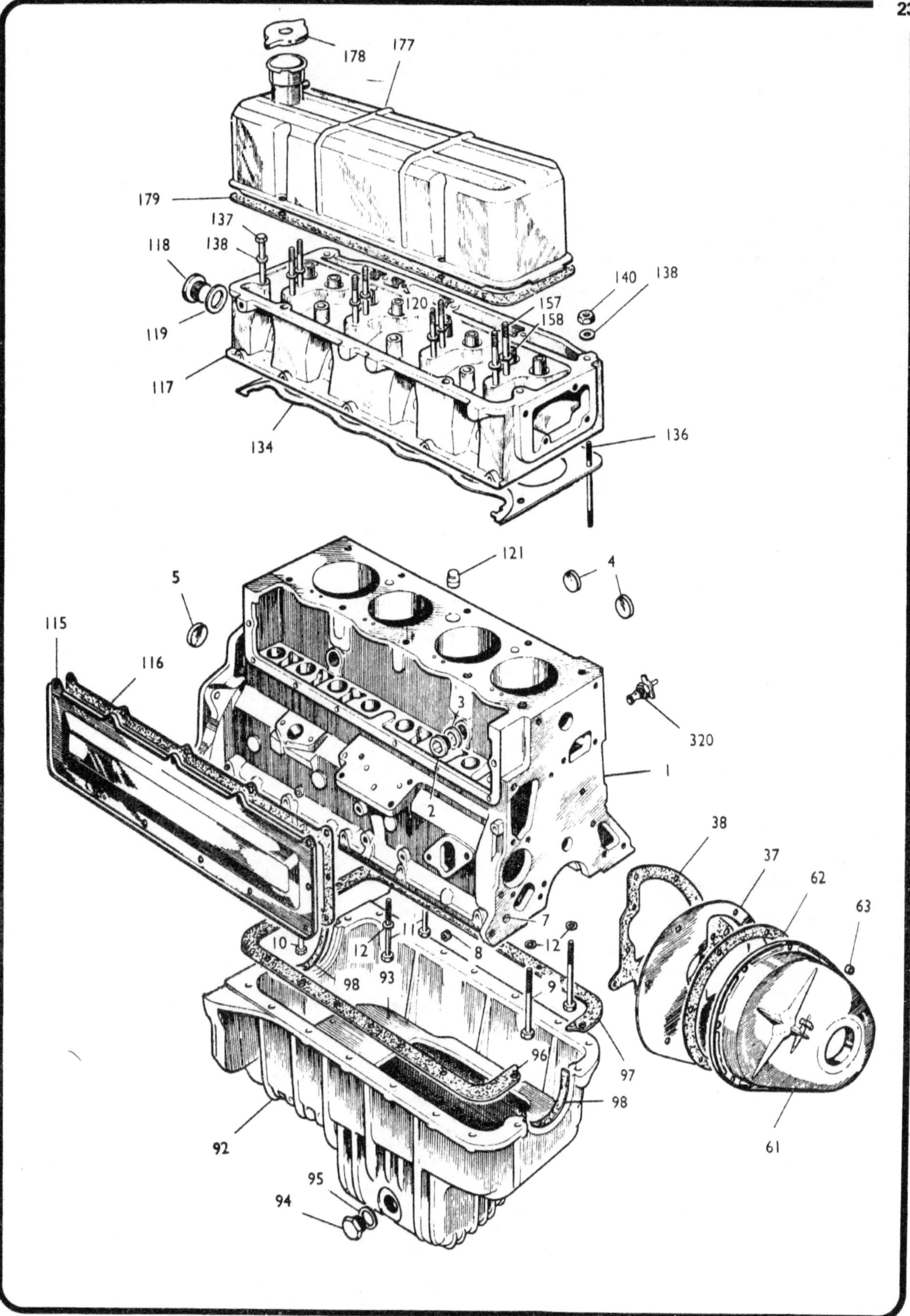
178
177
179
137
118
138
140
138
120
157
158
119
117
134
136
121
4
5
115
116
3
320
2
1
38
37
62
63
7
11
12
10
12
8
98
93
9
96
97
98
92
61
95
94

in the centre of the rocker shaft assembly. By gripping the assembly with a hand at each end, it may now be lifted straight up off the head. Be careful not to let it separate in the centre as it will come apart quite easily, and the T-piece may drop somewhere difficult to reach.

9. Inlet & Exhaust Manifold

1. If the standard engine is being completely dismantled or if the cylinder head is being removed, it is not necessary to detach the manifolds prior to carrying out this work. On H120 models both manifolds should be removed before the cylinder head is taken off.
2. Normally the only occasions one would expect to have to remove either of the manifolds would be to renew a suspected leaking gasket or, of course, a cracked or damaged manifold.
3. The inlet manfold must always be removed before it is possible to remove the exhaust manifold.
4. First of all disconnect all the carburettor controls and fuel pipe connections to the carburettors and remove the carburettors from the manifold. Should it be the exhaust manifold that is to be worked on it is wise at this stage to leave the carburettors attached to the inlet manifold so as to lessen the risk of upsetting their synchronisation.
5. Disconnect the brake servo vacuum pipe at the inlet manifold and also remove the accelerator cable bracket from the manifold by undoing its two retaining nuts.
6. On Rapier and Alpine models undo and remove the four bolts and one nut retaining the inlet manifold in place and lift it off. On the H120 model a 5/16 inch Allen key is required to remove the inlet manifold end screws, the centre being held by two nuts.
7. Disconnect the exhaust pipe from the manifold by undoing the two brass nuts, or in the case of the H120 the clip below the 'Y' junction, then undo the exhaust manifold nuts and bolts and remove the manifold and gasket.

10. Cylinder Head - Removal

1. The cylinder head may be removed with the engine either in or out of the car.
2. If the engine is to remain in the car, the following must be done first:–

a) Drain the cooling system
b) Remove the air cleaner from the carburettors and preferably remove the carburettors also as a safety precaution
c) Disconnect the top radiator hose from either the radiator or the cylinder head
d) Remove the electrical lead from the water temperature gauge sender unit at the front of the cylinder head
e) Disconnect all the leads from the sparking plugs
f) Disconnect the heater water pipes from the water pump housing at the front of the cylinder head and also unclip them from the two clips mounted on to the cylinder head studs
g) Disconnect the fuel feed pipe union from the outlet side of the fuel pump and also detach it from its clip bolted to the front of the cylinder head
h) Disconnect the exhaust pipe from the exhaust manifold by unscrewing the nuts underneath the flange
i) In the case of the H120 model remove both the inlet and exhaust manifolds as described in the previous Section.

3. With the foregoing completed, removal of the cylinder head is now the same whether the engine is in or out of the car. Remove the screws which hold the top edge of the rocker cover to the cylinder head and slacken the other screws which hold the bottom edge of the rocker cover to the cylinder block. Remove the rocker cover and valve rocker gear assembly.
4. Next carefully remove all the pushrods. When lifting them out, make sure that they are not still attached to the tappets. If the tappets are inadvertently lifted up they could become dislodged inside the tappet chest involving a lot of extra work when the head is replaced. This, of course, applies only when the engine is in the car. Keep the pushrods in the same order and the same way up as they were removed from the engine. This can be done by putting them through a piece of pierced cardboard to arrange them in order. The head is held in position by eight bolts and two nuts on studs, one at the front and one at the rear on the left hand side of the head. These bolts and nuts should be slackened off in the reverse order of the tightening sequence which is indicated in Fig.1.11 in Section 47 'Cylinder Head - Replacement'.
5. It should now be possible to lift the head straight off the top of the cylinder block complete with the manifolds which provide a useful hand-hold when lifting the head (not H120).
6. Should there be any difficulty in removing the head, under no circumstances should any attempt be made to force any form of lever into the space between the head and cylinder block. This could cause damage to the finely machined surfaces of the two parts. With the engine still in the car, it is possible to use the piston compression in order to help lift the head and break the tight joint. The engine can be turned by either putting the car in gear and moving it forwards or backwards, or reconnecting the battery, and giving the engine a quick turn on the starter motor. With the engine out of the car, it may be necessary to strike against the side of the head with a wooden block or soft faced mallet. When the head has been satisfactorily lifted off remove also the old cylinder head gasket.

11. Sump Removal

1. Removal of the sump with the engine in the car is possible, but not easy. The engine will need to be removed from its forward mountings and it will be necessary to drop the front axle crossmember away from the body side frame (Fig.1.2).
2. First of all disconnect the battery, and drain the sump of oil.
3. Next, raise the car sufficiently high so that it is possible to work underneath it comfortably. If working with the car over a pit or on a ramp, it should also be raised sufficiently to allow the wheels to clear the ground. The car must then be supported on proper body stands.
4. The weight of the engine must be supported during the sump removal operation, and this can be done by using a conventional hoist and supporting the engine as would be done for removing it.
5. Completely remove the anti-roll bar, which runs across the front of the sump, to allow the sump to be moved forward when it is lowered away.
6. There are four 5/8 inch AF bolts which hold the front crossmember to the underframe. Once these have been removed the whole of the crossmember and front suspension can be pulled down against the springs and held down by putting suitable blocks of wood between the ends of the crossmember and the side frames. Once this has been done the sump can be unbolted from both the cylinder block and the bellhousing, lowered and removed.
7. With the engine on the bench, sump removal is perfectly straightforward, although it is much better if the cylinder head is also removed so that the engine can be stood inverted. Before the engine is inverted see precautions under the Section headed 'Tappets'.

12. Crankshaft Pulley, Timing Gear Cover & Timing Gear - Removal

1. Removal of the crankshaft pulley, timing gear cover and timing gear will be necessary if the timing chain should be slack and noisy, or the tensioner needs attention. It is possible to carry out this work with the engine in the car. If the engine is in the car, first of all remove the radiator completely as described in Chapter 2.

2. Slacken the alternator mounting bolts so as to slacken the fan belt and then remove the fan belt. For details see Chapter 2. The crankshaft pulley is held in position by a large bolt through the centre boss, and this must be undone using a suitable socket wrench. With the engine in the car a gear should be engaged to prevent the engine from turning when the bolt is being undone. If the engine is out of the car it will be necessary to hold the flywheel ring with a suitable lever engaged in the ring gear teeth.
3. The crankshaft pulley is keyed on to the end of the crankshaft and under normal circumstances it should be possible to pull it straight off. If some resistance is met, it is in order to lever it from behind equally on each side simultaneously but if reasonable pressure still fails to dislodge it, it may be necessary to obtain a hub puller in order to draw it off properly without damaging anything.
4. Once the crankshaft pulley wheel has been removed the bolts which hold the timing case cover to the front of the engine block should next be taken out. The cover can then be removed and when this is done the timing chain tensioner, which is held in position by the cover, will fall down and hang on its pivot.
5. To remove the timing chain and sprockets, first take out the split pin from the tensioner pivot and remove the tensioner from the pivot.
6. The timing chain and the two sprockets on which it runs have all to be removed together. First remove the screw, tab washer and plain washer from the front of the camshaft tab. Take off the oil thrower which is mounted on the crankshaft in front of the crankshaft sprocket.
7. The crankshaft sprocket is a tight fit on to the keyed end of the crankshaft and will most probably require a puller in order to draw it off. Once the puller is in position and ready to move the sprocket, the camshaft sprocket should also be moved forward with the aid of suitable levers at the same time as the other sprocket is being moved forward. Both sprockets and the chain can then be drawn off together.

13. Pistons, Connecting Rods & Big End Bearings - Removal

1. It is possible to remove the pistons, connecting rods and big end bearings from the engine with the engine still in the car provided that the cylinder head and sump are also removed first. With the engine removed from the car, the task is much easier and generally cleaner, but, of course, it is understood that if a quick emergency repair job is to be done and speed is of the essence, then it would be in order to do any work with the engine still in the car. With the sump removed and the crankshaft exposed, each of the big end bearing caps can be detached after removing the two self-locking nuts which hold each cap to the connecting rod stud. Rotate the crankshaft to bring each connecting rod cap suitably into position for unscrewing the nuts.
2. With the nuts removed, each big end bearing cap can be pulled off. It must be noted that the connecting rods and big end caps are not marked in any way, other than with a small forging flash on the side of the connecting rod and cap, which matches up on each one. It is, nevertheless, wise to make a mark of your own if the same connecting rods and caps are to be re-used, as they must be replaced exactly as they came out. The same applies to the big end bearing shells which will be released as soon as the connecting rods are detached from the crankshaft. It is inadvisable to re-use these shells anyway, but if they are not renewed they must be put back in exactly the same location from which they came.
3. If any difficulty is experienced in removing the big end bearing caps from the studs of the connecting rods, it will help if the crankshaft is revolved in order to dislodge them. If this is done, however, care must be taken to ensure that nothing gets jammed when the connecting rod comes away from the crankshaft at the top of its stroke. Once released, the connecting rods and pistons can be pushed up through the cylinder bores and out of the top of the block. Make sure that the pistons are kept in such a way that they can be easily identified and replaced in the same bore, if necessary.

14. Gudgeon Pins - Removal

The gudgeon pins will be removed if it is desired to fit new pistons to the existing connecting rods or vice versa. The gudgeon pins are held in position by a circlip in each side of the piston and after this is removed any carbon should be cleaned away. Warm the piston and connecting rod assemblies, preferably in warm oil, when the gudgeon pin can be pushed out with the finger. If the piston is cold and the gudgeon pin is tight, it should not be forced out.

15. Flywheel - Removal

1. The flywheel may be removed with the engine in the car provided that the gearbox and clutch assemblies are both removed first. The flywheel would normally be removed in these circumstances for purposes of renewing the starter ring, which may have damaged teeth, or because of a badly scored face due to a badly worn clutch friction disc.
2. With the gearbox and clutch removed as described in Chapters 6 and 5 respectively, the five bolt heads which secure the flywheel to the crankshaft flange will come into view. These bolts are locked into position by tab washers. Knock back the tabs and then undo and remove the five securing bolts. The flywheel is located to the crankshaft flange on a register and is positioned by a dowel pin. It will be necessary to use a little leverage in order to draw the flywheel off and great care should be taken that it does not come off with a sudden jerk and fall down. One way of preventing this is by putting a stud, or another longer bolt with the head sawn off, into one of the bolt holes so that when the flywheel comes free, the end of the stud will support it. If the dowel comes out together with the flywheel it should be remembered that the dowel should be removed from the flywheel and replaced in the crankshaft flange before the flywheel is replaced.

16. Oil Pump - Removal

1. The oil pump may be removed from the engine whilst the engine is still in the car. It is necessary first of all to remove the sump. As the oil pump drive spindle also drives the distributor, care must be taken to ensure that the ignition timing is not lost when the oil pump is removed and eventually replaced. It is, therefore, necessary also to remove the distributor cap and turn the engine until the rotor is in line with the number one plug high tension lead contact. The timing marker on the crankshaft pulley wheel must then also be set against the top dead centre position. For full details of engine timing refer to Chapter 4.
2. Once the crankshaft has been set to the correct position the distributor should be removed. By looking down into the distributor mounting opening it will be possible to see the top of the oil pump spindle and the position of the offset slot. Take a careful note of this position.
3. Disconnect the oil delivery pipe union from the pump and also at the other end from inside the crankcase. The two bolts holding the pump to the crankcase can then be removed and the pump drawn out.

17. Camshaft - Removal

Although it is possible to remove the camshaft from the engine whilst the engine is still in the car, it is not recommended. The occasions when it is necessary to remove the camshaft other than during the course of a complete engine overhaul must be so few that it is considered unnecessary to go into the details of how to set about removing it in this fashion. A point to note is that the Rapier/Alpine and H120 camshafts are different, and therefore not interchangeable.

With the engine inverted on the bench (before inverting the engine, take the precaution noted under the Section 'Tappets') and the timing sprockets and timing chain removed, all that is required is to undo the two bolts holding the camshaft thrust plate to the front of the block. When these are taken out the thrust plate may be taken off and the camshaft is then ready to be drawn out. Make sure that the tappets are all clear of the cam lobes. When withdrawing the camshaft from the block, care should be taken to avoid chipping the camshaft shell bearings with the sharp hardened edges of the cam lobes. It is quite easy to gouge a deep line out of a shell bearing with one of the cam lobes, and if this is done, the bearing will possibly be damaged seriously enough to warrant replacement, and this is a specialist task. When taken out, put the camshaft where it cannot fall or be damaged as it is of a hard and brittle nature and could easily be cracked or chipped.

18. Tappets - Removal

1. It should always be remembered, when the engine is removed from the car and the valve rocker gear detached, that if the engine is inverted, the tappets are liable to fall out of their bores. If it is not intended to remove the tappets, then this can be a nuisance as they should normally only be refitted into the bores from which they have come. It is, therefore, desirable to remove the tappet chest cover plate at an early stage in engine dismantling, lift the tappets from their bores, and mark them with a pencil accordingly so that they may be returned to the same bore.
2. Normally it is not necessary to renew tappets unless they are severely scored or badly worn, and this is a feature which is normally associated with a damaged camshaft. Certainly if one or the other is badly damaged it is advisable to renew both. If it is wished to invert the engine, yet retain the tappets in position (for example, when removing the camshaft for examination), then it is simple enough to remove the tappet chest cover, and stuff rags inside sufficient to prevent the tappets from dropping down. However, it must be remembered that they should drop down far enough to clear the lobes of the camshaft when it is withdrawn from the engine block.

19. Crankshaft & Main Bearings - Removal

1. It is possible to examine the crankshaft and the crankshaft shell bearings without removing the engine from the car. It is also possible to replace the shell bearings with new ones if required, also without removing the engine from the car. However, as crankshaft shell bearings are not items which are replaced as a matter of routine except where doing a complete engine overhaul, we do not recommend this practice as it may very well be as a result of a wrong diagnosis of some engine fault. If the main bearing shells appear to be in need of renewal, it is more than likely that all the other bearings are in a similar state and that the crankshaft itself needs regrinding.
2. With the engine removed from the car it is necessary for the sump, oil pump, timing chain and sprockets tc be removed, together with the flywheel. It is also desirable that the cylinder head should have been removed so that the engine may be stood inverted. The front plate will also have to come off. This is held by the two bolts near the camshaft thrust plate, and the timing cover mounting stud.
3. The connecting rod bearing caps should all have been removed and, of course, this will have been done if the pistons are being removed from the engine as well.
4. Using a good quality socket spanner remove the two bolts from each of the three main bearing caps, then lift off each of the caps.
5. Note that the front cap has the timing chain tensioner pivot pin screwed into it. With the three main bearing caps removed the crankshaft may be carefully lifted out of the block and it should then be placed somewhere safe where it cannot fall or be damaged. The upper half main bearing shells may then be removed from the crankcase.

20. Oil Filter Element - Removal & Replacement

1. The oil filter element is a throw-away disposable cartridge which is screwed into an adaptor casting bolted to the right hand side of the engine block. This casting comprises the inlet and outlet passages from the filter and also the oil pressure release valve and it can be detached for further investigation if necessary. The rubber jointing ring on the base of the filter cartridge has a tendency to stick and the cartridge therefore can be very difficult to turn. In such cases it will be necessary to fit some form of strap around the cartridge with a suitable lever to apply sufficient pressure to turn it.
2. Some versions have a hexagon on the top face and with these, of course, a spanner can be used. When refitting a new element make sure first of all that the jointing faces of the element and the casting are perfectly clean and lightly smeared with engine oil. Then screw in the cartridge by hand, making sure that the screw threads are running true, until the mating faces just touch. Then screw the cartridge by hand another two-thirds of a revolution only. Do not overtighten otherwise it will be difficult to unscrew later. After fitting a new element the engine should always be run and a check made for signs of any leakage. Filters with a hexagon on their top face must not be tightened with a spanner (Photo).

21. Engine - Examination - General

1. Examination of an engine runs in two phases. The first is a visual and aural examination when it is running and in the car, and the second is when it is out of the car, having decided that something is wrong and needs repairing. It is not difficult for any owner to find garages, friends and relatives all willing to tell him precisely what is wrong with his engine as they listen to it turning in his car! It is a different matter altogether to decide when to take the car off the road, and do something about putting right whatever faults there may be. In general, if the oil and fuel consumption are typical, the performance is satisfactory, and it is not suffering from overheating, underheating, or any other fault which causes aggravation and irritation on the road to a large degree, it is best left alone. Provided the regular maintenance requirements are carried out there is no need to take it to pieces.
2. The first indications of an engine becoming worn (if one has not been able to get the exact mileage that the engine has travelled) are an increase in oil consumption and possibly a corresponding increase in fuel consumption. This may also be accompanied by a falling off in performance. On an average family saloon car it is not always easy to detect a falling off in performance and it is quite a good idea to drive another car of the same type, which is known to be in very good condition, to make a comparison. If the signs are that the engine is performing poorly, using too much petrol and beginning to burn oil, then one of the first things to do is to test the compression in each cylinder with a proper compression testing gauge. This will indicate whether the pistons are leaking in the cylinders or the valves are leaking in the head. Depending on the results, the cylinder head may be removed and further examinations carried out to the bores and head as described in subsequent sections. Early action at this stage could well restore the engine to a satisfactory condition. Furthermore, such action would not call for a great deal of expense of either money or time. If the condition is left, however, it will get progressively worse until major operations are necessary. This will be proportionately much more expensive and time consuming than the simple repairs which would have been adequate earlier.

22. Crankshaft & Crankshaft Main Bearings – Examination & Renovation

1. Remove the crankshaft and examine all the crankpins and main bearing journals for signs of scoring or scratches. If all the surfaces of the bearing journals are obviously undamaged, check next that

all the journals are round. Thsi can be done with a micrometer or caliper gauge, taking readings across the diameter of each journal at six or seven points. If you do not own a micrometer and do not know how to use one, you should have little difficulty at any garage that has good mechanics to get someone to measure it for you.

2. If the crankshaft has ridges or severe score marks in it, it must be reground. The manufacturers of the Rapier/Alpine series go further and say that a crankshaft in this condition should be renewed but as this can be a very expensive procedure, it is felt that regrinding should suffice in all but the most extraordinary situations. If there are no signs of ridging or severe scoring of the journals, it may be that the measurements indicate that the journals are not round. If the amount of ovality exceeds 0.002 inch it is possible that regrinding may be necessary. Certainly if it is more than this figure it is necessary. Here again it is best to get the advice of someone who is experienced and familiar with crankshafts and regrinding crankshafts to give an opinion.

3. The main bearing shells themselves are normally a matt grey in colour all over and should have no signs of pitting or ridging or discolouration which usually indicates that the surface bearing metal has worn away and the backing material is showing through. It is worthwhile renewing the main bearing shells anyway if you have gone to the trouble of removing the crankshaft, but they must, of course, be renewed if there is any sign of damage to them or if the crankshaft has been reground. When the crankshaft is reground the diameter is reduced and consequently one must obtain the proper sized bearing shells to fit. These will normally be supplied by the firm which has reground the crankshaft. Regrinding is usually done in multiples of 0.010 inch as necessary and bearing shells are obtainable

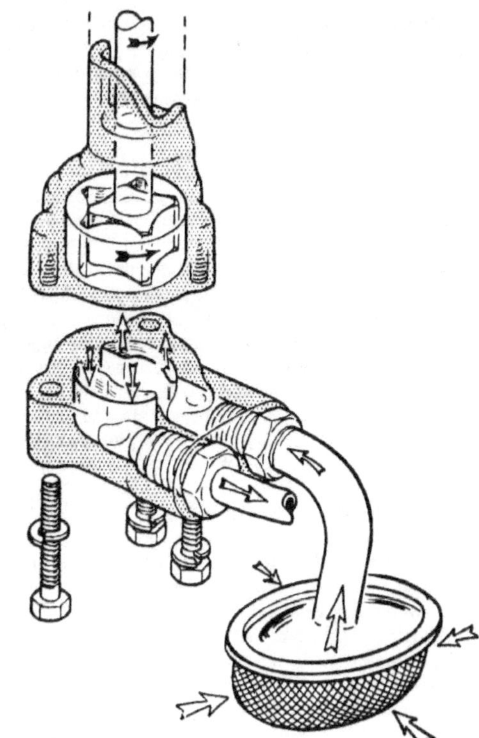

Fig.1.5. Internal flow of oil pump

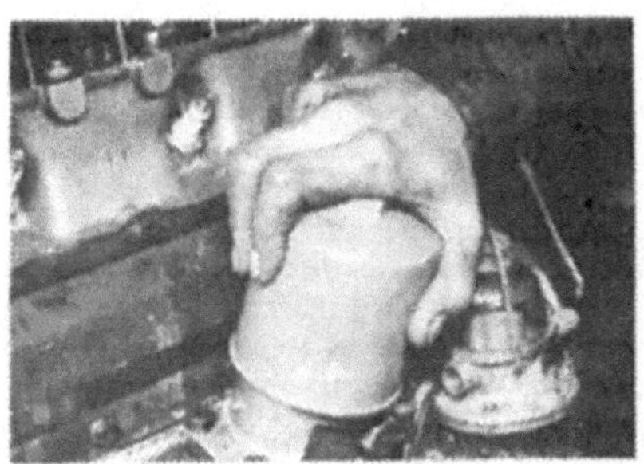

Section 20.
Removing and renewing oil filter cartridge

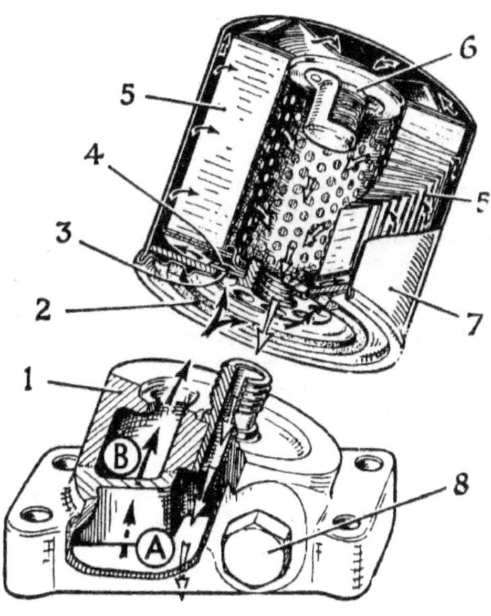

Fig.1.6. CUT–AWAY DRAWING OF OIL FILTER SHOWING OIL FLOW

1	Adaptor plate	5	Filter media
2	Cartridge sealing ring	6	By-pass valve
3	Anti-drain valve	7	Cartridge case
4	Anti-drain valve	8	Pressure relief valve

to suit these standard regrinding sizes. If the crankshaft is not being reground, yet bearing shells are being renewed, make sure that you check whether or not the crankshaft has been reground once before. Look at the back of the bearing shell and this will indicate whether or not it is minus 0.010 inch or more. The same version of shell bearing must be used when they are renewed.

23. Big End (Connecting Rod) Bearings - Examination & Renovation

1. The connecting rod, or big end, bearings as they are more commonly known are subject to wear at a greater rate than those for the crankshaft. Signs that one or more big end bearings is getting badly worn are a pronounced knocking noise from the engine, accompanied by a significant drop in oil pressure caused by oil flowing more freely through the enlarged gap between the journal and the bearing. If this should happen quite suddenly and action is taken immediately, and by immediately is meant within a few miles, then it is possible that the only work needed will be the replacing of the bearing shell.
2. If this happens in an engine which has been neglected and oil changes and oil filter changes have not been carried out as they should have been, it is most likely that the rest of the engine is in poor condition anyway and will need attention. If it occurs in an engine which has been recently overhauled, then it is almost certainly due to a piece of grit or swarf which has got into the oil circulation system and finally come to rest in the bearing shell and scored it. It is in this instance where a replacement of the shell alone accompanied by a thorough flush out of the lubrication system may be all that is required.

24. Cylinder Bores - Examination & Renovation

1. The cylinder bores may be examined for wear with the engine in the car once the cylinder head has been removed. Each bore may be examined in turn with the piston at the bottom of its stroke. A perfect cylinder is, as its name implies, perfectly cylindrical in shape. That is, the sides are parallel and a cross section is perfectly circular.
2. First of all, examine the top of the cylinder about a quarter of an inch below the surface of the block and with the finger feel if there is any ridge running round the circumference of the bore. In a worn cylinder bore a ridge will develop at the point where the top ring on the piston comes to the uppermost limit of its stroke. An excessive ridge indicates that the bore below the ridge is worn. If there is no ridge it is reasonable to assume that the cylinder is not badly worn.
3: Measurement of the diameter of the cylinder bore both in line with the piston gudgeon pin and at right angles to it, and at the top and bottom of the cylinder, is also another check to be made. A cylinder is expected to wear at the sides where the thrust of the piston presses against it. In time this causes the cylinder to assume an oval shape. Furthermore, the top of the cylinder is likely to wear more than the bottom. It will be necessary to use a proper bore measuring instrument in order to measure the differences in bore diameter across the cylinder and variations between the top and bottom ends of the cylinder. As a general guide it may be assumed that any variations more than 0.010 inch indicate that the cylinders need re-boring. Provided all variations are less than 0.010 inch it is probable that the fitting of new piston rings will cure the problems of piston to cylinder bore clearances.
4. Once again it is difficult to give a firm ruling on this as so much depends on the amount of time and effort which the individual owner is prepared or wishes to spend on the task. Certainly, if the cylinder bores are obviously deeply grooved or scored, they must be re-bored regardless of any measurement differences in the cylinder diameter. If the engine has already been removed from the car for overhaul, any cylinder bore wear in excess of 0.005 inch certainly qualifies it for a re-bore; to do otherwise would be a waste of time and effort. However, a re-bore will require the fitment of new pistons, and the expense of this could affect the owner's decision.

25. Connecting Rods, Pistons & Piston Rings - Examination & Renovation

1. Pistons and rings are usually examined in relation to the cylinder bores. With the cylinder head removed it is possible to check the amount of movement between the piston and the wall, both visually and with the aid of a feeler gauge. If the condition of the bore seems to be satisfactory, any excessive clearance between piston and bore (0.010 inch and upwards) could be due to wear on the piston itself. Piston ring wear is almost certain to have taken place also if this is the case, and will necessitate removal of the pistons for further examination. First of all, look for signs of damage to the piston ring grooves, and to the sides of the piston where scoring may be apparent. Any deep scoring or any obvious breakage between the piston ring grooves and the top of the piston wall, of course, call for a new piston. If the pistons do not appear worn or damaged, next check the clearance between the piston rings and the piston ring grooves. This can be done with a feeler gauge and if it is in excess of the specified clearance the pistons should be renewed. Excessive clearance between the rings and the grooves allows the rings to chatter and they will break very easily. Unfortunately, the wear usually occurs on the piston rather than on the piston rings, although new rings should be used as a check before condemning the pistons.

2. To check the condition of the rings it will be necessary to remove them from the piston. Only the top ring on each piston need be checked and, in fact, if one of the four piston rings is bad it is reasonable to assume that the others will be similar and the whole set should be replaced. Remove the top piston ring by spreading the ends apart sufficiently to enable it to be pulled out of the groove and over the top of the piston. Care must be taken not to twist the ring or draw it off unevenly, otherwise it could easily break. The ring should then be placed inside the cylinder bore from which it came and pressed down approximately two inches. It should lie perfectly horizontal across the bore and this can be achieved by using a piston from which all the rings have been removed to press it down square. Then the gap between the ends of the piston rings should be measured with a feeler gauge; if the piston ring gap exceeds that specified then the piston ring is worn out and should be replaced. If the top ring is worn it is reasonable to assume that the other two are worn on the same piston as well. Rings are normally only obtainable in sets anyway so any thoughts of economy by renewing one or two rings on a set of four pistons are really not worthwhile.

3. Provided the engine has not seized up or had some other calamitous damage caused to it, it is most unlikely that the connecting rods are in need or renewal at any time. In cases of seizure one or more could have become bent and to check this they will need setting up on a special jig. This is normally only within the competence of a specialist engineering organisation.

4. The small end bush of the connecting rod is a floating fit on the gudgeon pin. This means, therefore, that if new pistons are to be fitted, and new pistons come supplied with new gudgeon pins as a matter of course, the new gudgeon pin will need to be fitted correctly to the existing bush. The correct fit of a connecting rod small end to the gudgeon pin is when the connecting rod will fall under its own weight if the piston is held horizontal. At the same time there must be no play or rocking movement possible between the rod and the gudgeon pin. If the small end bush does not fit correctly onto the gudgeon pin it will need renewal and reaming out to fit. This, once again, is a tricky specialist task which must be left to people who have got the proper jigs. If it is decided to re-use the same pistons and the gudgeon pin is a slack fit in both the piston boss and the connecting rod small end bush, it is possible for oversize gudgeon pins to be fitted to the existing pistons and connecting rods. Here again, specialist facilities will be necessary in order that this work can be carried out.

26. Valve Rocker Gear - Examination & Renovation

1. Each rocker should move freely on the rocker shaft without any signs of looseness or slackness. If any slackness is apparent it will be necessary to dismantle the assembly as follows.
2. Remove the spring clip from one end of each half of the complete assembly and remove the rockers, spacers, standards and springs, one at a time, laying them out carefully and noting the order in which they were removed. If either the rocker bushes or the rocker shaft are obviously scored and worn at those points where the rockers are pivoting then they should be renewed. The rockers themselves should also be examined on the faces where they bear on to the top of the valve stems and if signs of wear are excessive they should also be renewed.

27. Cylinder Head & Valves & Valve Springs - Examination & Renovation

1. Once the cylinder head has been removed, it should be placed upon a work bench so that a thorough examination can be carried out.
2. First of all the valves should be removed. The valves are located by a collar on two compressed springs which grips two collets (or a split collar) into a groove in the stem of the valve. The springs must be compressed with a special G clamp in order to release the collets and then the valve. Place the specially shaped end of the clamp over the spring collar with the end of the screw squarely on the face of the valve. Screw up the clamp to compress the springs and expose the collet from the valve stem. Sometimes the spring collar sticks and the clamp screw cannot be turned. In such circumstances, with the clamp pressure still on, give the head of the clamp (over the spring) a tap with a hammer, at the same time gripping the clamp frame firmly to prevent it slipping off the valve.
3. Take off the two collets, release the clamp, and the collar and springs can be lifted off. The valve can then be pushed out through its guide and removed. Make sure that each valve is kept in such a way that its position is known for eventual replacement. Unless new valves are being fitted, each valve must go back where it came from. The springs, collars and the collets should also be kept with their respective valves. A piece of card with eight holes punched in it is a good way to keep the valves in order.
4. The valves should be examined for signs of pitting or burning, particularly around their edges and where they seat into the cylinder head. If the valves are very much contaminated with carbon, this should first of all be removed with a wire brush. Very hard spots of carbon may need chipping off with the edge of a very hard blade or tool. Exhaust valves are the ones most likely to suffer from burning and if this is apparently quite severe, then the valves should be discarded.
5. Next replace each valve into its own guide, after thoroughly cleaning the guide and valve stem, and check to see that there is no sideways movement of the valve in the guide. A very small amount of play is permissible but if it is considerable, then it means that oil and exhaust gases can all make their way past the stem of the valve and this is not conducive to good performance. If the guides are obviously badly worn, then it will be necessary to have new ones fitted, together with new valves. The fitting of valve guides on this engine is a specialist task as they have to be reamed out to give a very close tolerance after fitting. If it is thought that the wear is on the valve stem rather than in the guide, the best way to check is to obtain a new valve and try it in position.
6. If the valves are apparently in good general condition the next thing to do is to examine the valve seats themselves in the cylinder head. Here again, there should be no signs of pitting or burning. The valve seats should also be checked to make sure there are no cracks. If there are signs of damage to the seat in any way, then the head itself may need fitting with new valve seat inserts. Possibly, the existing valve seats may be recut; if you have the special tools for recutting valve seats, then these can be done by the owner but if not, it is recommended that the job is given to a specialist. Provided the valves and seats are in good condition, then it is possible to re-seat them by grinding in position using a carborundum paste. This grinding-in process should also be carried out when a new valve is being fitted.
7. The carborundum paste for this job is usually supplied in a double ended tin with coarse paste at one end and fine paste at the other. In addition, a suction tool is required for holding the valve head so that it may be rotated. To grind in a valve, first smear a trace of the coarse paste on to the seat face and fit the suction tool to the valve head. Then with a semi-rotary motion grind the valve head on to its seat, lifting the valve occasionally to re-distribute the grinding paste. If a light spring is placed over the valve stem behind the head this can often be of assistance in raising the valve. When a dull matt continuous line has been produced on both the valve seat and the valve then the coarse paste can be wiped off. Apply a little fine paste and finish off the grinding process.
8. The width of the line which is produced after grinding should not be more than 0.07 inch (1.8 mm). If after a moderate amount of grinding it is apparent that the seating line is much wider than this then it either means that the seat has already been cut back once or more times previously, or else the valve has been ground in several times. Specialist advice is best sought on occasions such as this.
9. After each valve has been ground in, the traces of carborundum paste which will remain in the area of the seat and port must be thoroughly flushed away with paraffin. If possible, a high pressure air line should be used to blow away the final traces. Obviously, particles of carborundum grit are not wanted anywhere inside the engine.
10 Before the valves are finally replaced, all traces of carbon should be cleaned from them and also from the cylinder head itself. A wire cup brush and an electric drill are very useful in doing this work in the head. The face of the cylinder head should also be scraped perfectly clean and free from accumulations of gasket cement or carbon which may be upon it. Do not use any abrasive paper for cleaning but rather a flat bladed scraper. Make sure that no odd particles of gasket or carbon fall into the orifices in the casting. If they do, get them blown out.
11 Examine all the valve springs to make sure that they are of the correct length according to the specifications. It will have been noticed when they were being removed whether any were broken, and if they are then they should be replaced. It is a good idea to replace all the valve springs if one is broken as this may be a sign that all of them are weakening.
12 Inside each valve spring collar there is a small rubber ring which acts as an oil seal on the valve stem. New rings are usually supplied with a cylinder head gasket set and it is wise to renew them also.
13 Before reassembling the valves and springs to the cylinder head, make a final check that everything is thoroughly clean and free from grit and then lightly smear all the valve stems with engine oil.

28. Timing Chain & Sprockets - Examination & Renovation

Examine the teeth of both sprockets for wear. Each tooth on the sprocket is in the shape of an inverted V and if the side of the tooth is concave in shape it is an indication that the tooth is worn badly and the sprocket should, therefore, be replaced. If the sprockets are renewed then the chains should also be renewed. If the sprockets are satisfactory, examine the chain to make sure there is no play between the links and if the chain is held out it should not bend when held horizontal. In view of the relative cheapness of these items it is worthwhile putting on a new chain anyway. Examine the tensioner pivot for signs of excessive wear which could cause rattling and also the tensioner itself. If the chain has gouged a deep groove into the tensioner renew it.

29. Camshaft, Camshaft Bearings & Tappets – Examination & Renovation

1. The camshaft lobes should be examined for signs of flats or scoring or any other form of wear and damage. At the same time the tappets should also be examined for signs of wear, particularly on the faces where they bear against the camshaft. If the case hardened surfaces of the cam lobes or tappet faces have been penetrated it will be quite obvious as there will be a darker, rougher pitted appearance to the surface in question. In such cases, the tappet or the camshaft will need renewal. Where the camshaft or tappet surface is still bright and clean and showing slight signs of wear it is best left alone. Any attempt to re-face either will only result in the case hardened surface being reduced in thickness with the possibility of extreme and rapid wear later on. Having ascertained that the faces of the tappets are satisfactory, check also that the tappets are not a loose fit in their respective bores. It is not likely that they are loosely fitting, but if so they should be renewed.
2. The skew gear in the camshaft which drives the oil pump shaft and indirectly the distributor should be examined for signs of extreme wear on the teeth. Here again, if the skew gear teeth are very badly worn and ridged, it will mean renewal of the complete camshaft. Examine also in conjunction with this the teeth on the driven gear.
3. The camshaft bearing journals should be perfectly smooth and show no signs of pitting or scoring, as should the camshaft bearing shells. Replacement of the camshaft bearing shells is a specialist task as each of the three bearings has to be positioned correctly and must be perfectly lined up with its counterpart. Fortunately, it is rare for the camshaft journals and bearings to wear out at anything like the same rate as the rest of the engine.
4. The camshaft thrust plate which retains the camshaft in the cylinder block should also be examined for any ridging or scoring on its thrust face, and should be renewed if any signs of these are present.

30. Flywheel - Examination & Renovation

1. There are two areas in which the flywheel may have been worn or damaged. Firstly, on the driving face where the clutch friction plate bears against it. Should the clutch plate have been permitted to wear down beyond the level of the rivets, it is possible that the flywheel has been scored. If this scoring is severe it may be necessary to have it re-faced or even renewed.
2. The other part to examine is the teeth of the starter ring gear around the periphery of the flywheel. The edges of the teeth towards the clutch side of the flywheel are designed with a bevel on them to start with so do not confuse this bevel with wear. If, however, several of the teeth are broken or missing, or the front edges of all teeth are obviously very badly chewed up, then it would be advisable to fit a new ring gear.
3. The old ring gear can be removed by cutting a slot with a hacksaw down between two of the teeth as far as possible, without cutting into the flywheel itself. Once the cut is made a chisel will split the ring gear which can then be drawn off. To fit a new ring gear requires it to be heated first to a temperature of 220°C, no more. This is best done in a bath of oil or an oven, but not, preferably, with a naked flame. It is much more difficult to spread the heat evenly and control it to the required temperature with a naked flame.
4. Once the ring gear has attained the correct temperature it can be placed on to the flywheel making sure that it beds down properly on to the register. Make sure the bevel edges of the teeth are facing towards the clutch face side of the flywheel. It should then be allowed to cool down naturally. If by mischance, the ring gear is overheated, it should not be used. The tempering will have been lost, therefore softening it, and it will wear out in a very short space of time.
5. Although it is not actually fitted into the flywheel itself, there is a bush in the centre of the crankshaft flange on to which the flywheel fits. Although this bush is more correctly associated with the gearbox or clutch it is mentioned here as well as it would be a pity to ignore it whilst carrying out work on the flywheel. If it shows signs of wear it should be renewed. If suitable extractors are not available to get it out another method is to fill the recess with grease and then drive in a piece of close fitting steel bar. This should force the bush out. A new bush may be pressed in.

31. Oil Pump - Examination & Renovation

1. With the oil pump removed from the engine, it should be inverted and the hexagon headed screws securing the base plate to the pump body removed. The outer rotor ring may then be lifted out and this should be done carefully as if dropped it could easily crack and therefore become unserviceable.
2. The interior of the pump body may then be thoroughly cleaned with petrol or paraffin to remove all traces of oil.
3. The efficiency of any oil pump depends on the clearances between the inner rotor tips and outer rotor and the outer rotor fit in the pump body. These are set to very fine tolerances on manufacture; if any excessive wear occurs, then some of the oil which is normally forced round by the increasing and decreasing size of the apertures between the inner and outer rotors will escape through the increased clearances between them, and thus pumping efficiency will suffer and pressure will be reduced at the output side of the pump.
4. The main feature of checking the pump, therefore, is measuring the clearances (Fig.1.7). The first clearance to measure is that between the ends of the rotors and the face of the body of the pump. This can be done by putting a steel straight edge across the pump body and measuring with a feeler blade the gap between it and the faces of both rotors. The gap should be between 0.001 and 0.003 inch (0.025 mm and 0.075 mm).
5. The next clearance to be measured is that between the tip of the inner rotor and the high point of the convex section of the outer rotor, also with a feeler blade. The gap here should be between 0.001 and 0.006 inch (0.025 mm and 0.15 mm).
6. The third clearance to be measured is that between the outside of the outer rotor and the pump body. This measurement should be between 0.005 inch and 0.008 inch (0.125 to 0.20 mm).
7. If any of the clearances exceed the limits specified or if the centre rotor spindle should be slack in its bush then a replacement oil pump should be fitted.
8. It is possible to rectify an excessive gap between the end faces of both rotors and the pump body (the first check made) by filing down the face of the body. This calls for a degree of fitting skill in the use of a file and should only be attempted by someone who has the ability to file dead square and dead flat and to measurements of a thousandth of an inch. If not done properly this could make the pump far worse than it was originally, and if replaced in this state could cause irreparable damage to the engine in due course.
9. Whilst the pump is dismantled the opportunity should be taken to examine and clean the inlet filter gauze screen. If the engine has been properly looked after this screen should be perfectly clean. If it is not, however, clean it thoroughly in petrol or paraffin and blow it dry. Do not dry it off on any material or cloth which could leave particles remaining hooked up in the gauze.

32. Exhaust & Inlet Manifolds - Inspection

Exhaust and inlet manifolds should be examined for signs of cracks or other breakages, particularly on the mounting lugs. The mating faces of both manifolds where they join the cylinder head should be examined to make sure that they are completely flat and free from pitting or burrs of any sort. Use a straight edge to check the faces of the manifold for distortion. If there is any distortion or signs of severe pitting or burning the manifold should be renewed.

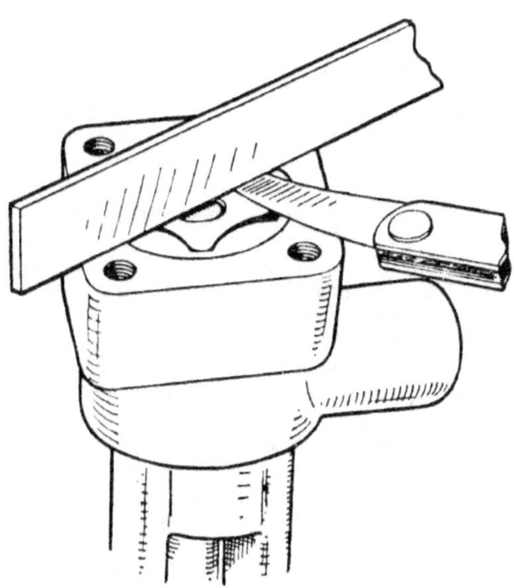

Using straight edge and feeler blade to check end clearance

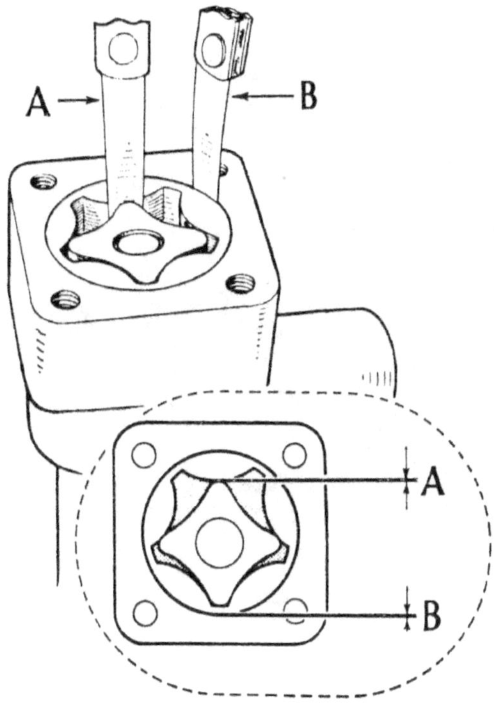

Fig.1.7. Checking oil pump wear
A Rotor top clearance
B Outer rotor clearance

Examine also the exhaust manifold to exhaust pipe flange mounting studs. In time these tend to corrode away and are consequently weakened and it is a simple task to extract them and fit new ones. This is well worth doing. Provided the manifolds are sound, accumulations of carbon within the ports may be removed with a wire brush or scraper.

33. Decarbonisation

1. Modern engines, together with modern fuels and lubricants, have virtually nullified the need for the engine to have a 'de-coke' which was common enough only a few years ago. Carbon deposits are formed mostly on the modern engine only when it has to do a great deal of slow speed, stop/start running; for example, in busy traffic and city traffic conditions. If carbon deposit symptoms are apparent, such as pinking or pre-ignition and running on after the engine has been switched off, then a good high speed run on a motorway or straight stretch of road is usually sufficient to clear these deposits out. It is beneficial to any motor car to give it a good high speed run from time to time.
2. There will always be some carbon deposits, of course, so if the cylinder head is removed for some reason or another, it is a good idea to remove the carbon deposits at the same time. Carbon deposits in the combustion chambers of the cylinder head can be dealt with as described under the Section 'Cylinder Head - Inspection & Renovation'. The other carbon deposits which have to be dealt with are those on the crowns of the pistons. This work can easily be carried out with the engine in the car, but great care must be taken to ensure that no particles of dislodged carbon fall either into the cylinder bores and down past the piston rings or into the water jacket orifices in the cylinder block.
3. Bring the first piston to be attended to, to the top of its stroke, and then using a sheet or strong paper and some self adhesive tape, mask off the other three cylinders and surrounding block to prevent any particles falling into the open orifices in the block. To prevent small particles of dislodged carbon from finding their way down the side of the piston which is actually being decarbonised, press grease into the gap between the piston and the cylinder wall. Carbon deposits should then be scraped away carefully with a flat blade from the top of the crown of the piston and the surrounding top edge of the cylinder. Great care must be taken to ensure that the scraper does not gouge into the soft aluminium surface of the piston crown.
4. A wire brush, either operated by hand or a power drill, should not be used if decarbonising is being done with the engine still in the car. It is virtually impossible to prevent carbon particles being distributed over a large area and the time saved by this method is very little.
5. In addition to the removal of carbon deposits on the pistons, it is a good time also to make sure that traces of gasket or any sealing compound are removed from the mating face of the cylinder block top face.
6. After each piston has been attended to, clean out the grease and carbon particles from the gap where it has been pressed in. As the engine is revolved to bring the next piston to the top of its stroke for attention, check the bore of the cylinder which has just been decarbonised and make sure that no traces of carbon or grease are adhering to the inside of the bore.

34. Engine Reassembly - General

It is during the process of engine reassembly that the job is either made a success or a failure. From the very word go there are three basic rules which it is folly to ignore, namely:

1. Absolute cleanliness. The working area, the components of the engine and the hands of those working on the engine must be

completely free of grime and grit. One small piece of carborundum dust or swarf can ruin a big end in no time, and nullify all the time and effort you have spent.

2. 'Don't spoil the ship for a ha'porth of tar'. Yes, an old fashioned proverb, but if you have spent many hours and several pounds on new parts it is ridiculous to jeopardise the job for the sake of a seal or a gasket which costs a few pence. One is tempted to say 'Oh it'll be all right'. If you can really convince yourself, well and good, but it will be far better for your peace of mind to get the appropriate new piece even though it may mean a little delay.

3. Don't rush it. The most skilled and experienced mechanic can easily make a mistake if he is rushed. It is no use boasting to your friends that you did the whole job on Saturday and Sunday if it is a smoking wreck on Monday.

Check that all nuts and bolts are clean and in good condition, and renew as necessary all spring washers, lock washers and tab washers which may have become damaged or unserviceable during dismantling. A supply of clean engine oil and clean cloths (to wipe excessive clean oil off your hands only!) and a torque spanner are the only things which should be required in addition to all the tools used in dismantling the engine.

35. Crankshaft & Main Bearing - Reassembly

1. Stand the cylinder block inverted on the bench and gather together the bearing caps and new bearing shells, and have the crankshaft alongside lined up in the way in which it will eventually be placed into the cylinder block. Make sure that the oilways in the crankshaft are all quite clear.

2. Make sure that the bearing housings in the cylinder block are perfectly clean and smooth, in preparation for the fitting of the top halves of the main bearing shells. The centre and two end bearing shells have a central groove running through them, whilst the other two are plain. Each bearing shell has an oil hole in it and this must line up with the corresponding hole in the cylinder block. Each shell is notched, and this notch also must line up with the corresponding notch in the cylinder block. Carefully fit each shell into position taking care not to bend, distort or scratch it in any way. When they are in position lubricate them with a liberal quantity of clean engine oil (Photo).

3. Make sure that the crankshaft is the right way round, next pick it up and very carefully lower it square and straight into position on the shell bearings in the crankcase (Photo).

4. The centre and end bearing shell lower halves are also grooved and the other two plain. Again, make sure that the bearing caps are perfectly clean and fit the shells so that the notches in their ends line up and fit snugly into the grooves in the bearing caps. There are no oilways in the bearing caps so that the holes in the bearing shells will not line up with anything (Photo).

5. The crankshaft endfloat is controlled by two semi-circular thrust washers which fit at the sides of the centre main bearing journal. Place these in position (Photo) and slide them round into the gap between the bearing housing and the flange of the crankshaft (Photo), making sure that the grooves in the thrust washers face outwards away from the centre. Once these are in position the endfloat can be checked by pushing the crankshaft as far as it will go in one direction and measuring the gap between the face of the thrust washer and the machined surface of the flange with a feeler blade (Photo). Next arrange all the bearing caps complete with their shells so that you know precisely where each one should go. The front and rear ones are easily identifiable by their particular shape, as is the centre one. The others, two and four, are numbered and should be arranged accordingly. As there is the possibility of a seepage of oil through the end main bearing cap mating faces, it is permissible to put a very thin smear of non-setting jointing compound on to the outside edge of the vertical face where the bearing cap locates in the crankcase. The precise position is indicated in 'Fig.1.8. Location A'.

6. Lubricate the main journals of the crankshaft liberally with clean engine oil and place all the bearing caps in position and fit the bolts. The front main bearing cap has a machined front face and this must line up with the front surface of the cylinder block (Photo). Make sure that this is done with a straight edge before finally tightening down the bolts. When all the caps are settled correctly in position (Photo), tighten the bolts down evenly, using a torque spanner, to the correct torque as given under the specifications (Photo). When this has been done, revolve the crankshaft to make sure that there are no intermittent tight spots. Any signs that something is binding whilst the crankshaft is being revolved indicates that something is wrong and there may be a high spot on one of the bearings or on the crankshaft itself. This must be investigated or a damaged bearing could result.

36. Pistons, Gudgeon Pins & Connecting Rods - Reassembly

1. If new pistons are being fitted to the existing connecting rods, it is assumed that the fit of the new gudgeon pins which will be supplied with the pistons is correct in the small end bush of the connecting rod. There is an oil squirt hole on one side of each connecting rod and this faces the right hand side of the cylinder bores (Photo). Each piston also has an indication on its top surface showing which is the front so that the piston and connecting rod can be assembled properly to ensure that the offset in the piston is in the correct direction.

2. Make sure the piston is sufficiently warm to enable the gudgeon pin to slide easily through the bosses and then place the gudgeon pin half way into the piston, insert the connecting rod the correct way round, and push the gudgeon pin completely home into position (Photo). Fit the circlips into the grooves on each end of the piston to locate the gudgeon pin in position (Photo).

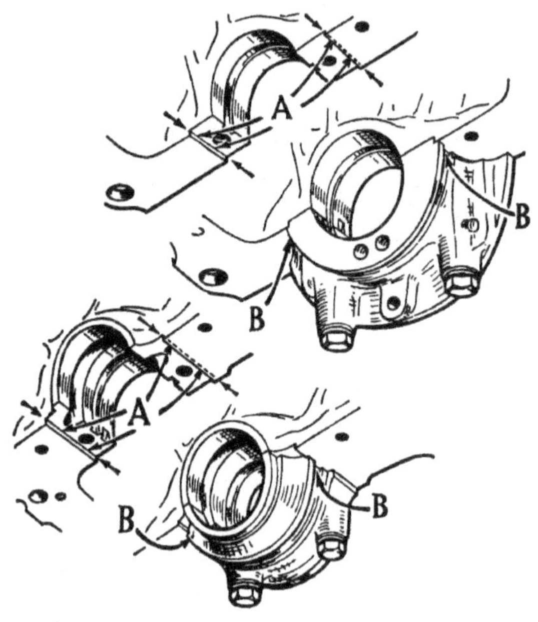

Fig.1.8. MAIN BEARING CAP

A Use Wellseal here to prevent oil seepage

B Use quick setting jointing compound here at ends of the bearing cap to sump cork gaskets

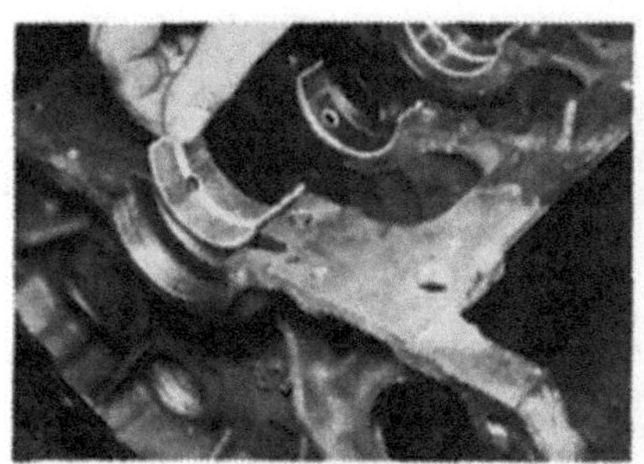

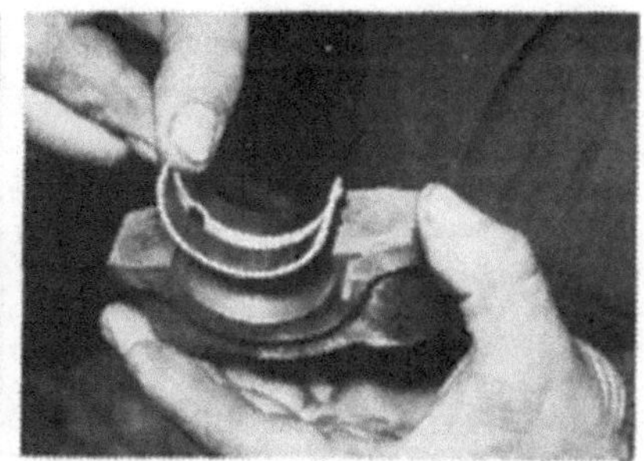

Sections 35.2, 35.3, and 35.4.
Fitting main bearing shells and replacing crankshaft

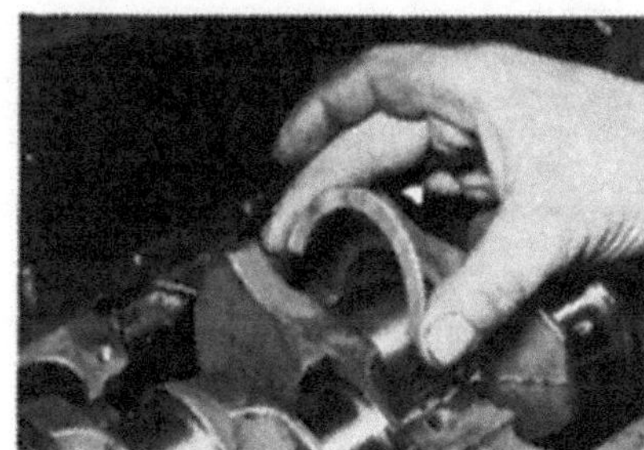

Section 35.5. Fitting thrust washers and checking end float

Section 35.5. Fitting and tightening down main bearing caps

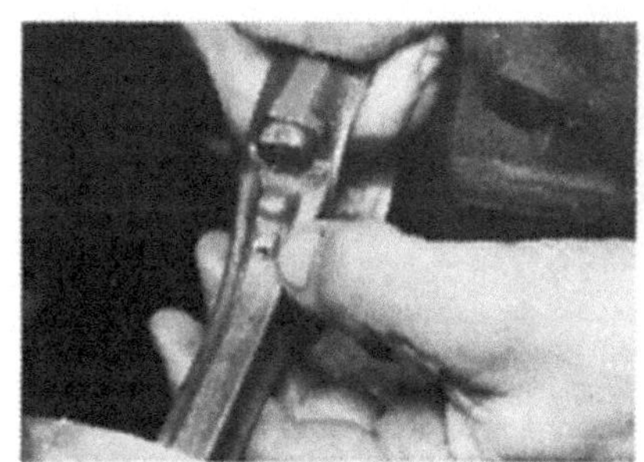

Section 36. Reassembling piston, gudgeon pin and connecting rod

37. Piston Rings - Replacement on Pistons

1. Before fitting new piston rings to the old pistons, make sure the ring grooves in the piston are completely clean and free of carbon deposits. A piece of old, broken piston ring is a useful tool for doing this, but make sure that the sharp edge is not permitted to gouge out any pieces of metal. Check also that the specified gap between the edge of the new piston ring and the groove is correct.
2. All rings must be fitted from the top of the piston (a possible exception to this is the bottom oil control ring which is fitted into the skirt of some pistons which are supplied). To get the new rings into position involves spreading them sufficiently to clear the diameter of the piston itself and then moving them down over the existing grooves into their appropriate positions. Care must be taken to avoid straining them to a point where they could break. A piece of thin shim steel or an old feeler gauge blade is a very useful means of guiding the ends of the rings over the grooves to prevent them inadvertently dropping in, rather than passing over each groove.
3. Before fitting the rings to the piston it is important to check that the end gap matches the cylinder bore into which they will eventually be fitted. Push the rings down the bores using the piston until they are about 2½ inches below the top surface of the cylinder head. Then measure the gap. If the gap is too large you have either got the wrong piston rings or the cylinder bores are worn more than you had anticipated. If the gap is too small then it will be necessary to remove a piece of material from the end of the ring. The gap may be increased to the correct specification by clamping the end of the ring in a vice so that a very small portion of the end projects above the top of the vice. Then use a fine file to take off the material in very small quantities at a time. Do not clamp the ring so that the end being filed projects too far above the vice jaws or it may easily be snapped off while the filing is being done.
4. When every ring has been checked and the gaps made correct the rings should be assembled to the piston to prevent them being mixed up with other rings which will be fitted to other bores. Fit the bottom scraper ring first by placing it over the top of the piston and spreading the ends. Move it down the piston a little at a time, taking care to prevent it from snagging in the grooves over which it will pass. The next ring to be fitted is the lower compression ring and this only goes on one way up. The top edge of the ring will be marked 'top' and this, of course, should go uppermost. Don't be misled into thinking that this means that the ring is the top one on the piston. The top compression ring, which is the last one to go on can be fitted either way up on the piston.
5. When all the rings are in position in their grooves, try and arrange the gaps to be equally spaced around the piston. Obviously, if the gaps of all the rings are in a straight line there will be a much greater tendency for compression to be lost at that point.

38. Pistons & Connecting Rods & Big End Bearings - Reassembly to Cylinder Block & Crankshaft

1. If new piston rings, on either new pistons or the old pistons, are going into the original cylinder bores it is important that the piston ring gaps should be checked before fitting the piston assemblies. This will mean removing the rings from a new piston in order to check them (Section 37.3).
2. In order to assist the bedding in of the new piston rings to the original cylinder bore, it is a good idea to remove the oil glaze which builds up on a bore as an engine becomes more used. This can be done with fine emery cloth, wrapped round a wooden plug of suitable diameter. If the crankshaft is already fitted to the cylinder block, the greatest care must be taken during this operation to keep any carborundum particles away from the bearing surfaces. This will involve masking off the bottom end of each cylinder and taking every precaution to prevent contamination. Careful and thorough cleaning out afterwards will also be necessary, so unless you are perfectly sure that you can do this job safely, it is best not to do it at all.
3. To assist in fitting the piston and rings into the bore it is also useful if the top edge of each cylinder bore is chamfered. This gives a lead for the piston rings to run into the bore when they are compressed. The bottom oil control ring is very fragile and is easily broken if restricted.
4. Tap the piston and connecting rod assembly into the top of the block, making sure that the front of the piston is towards the front of the engine block, and fit a suitable clamp around all the piston rings to compress them into the grooves of the piston. It is possible to improvise a ring compressor out of a suitably sized hose clip, but great care should be exercised if this is done as it is not possible to get it to lie dead flat due to the adjusting screw housing projecting beyond the edge of the clip. This can permit the edge of a piston ring to escape its control and then be trapped against the cylinder block face and consequently break. If a strip of sheet metal is cut from an old tin and used in conjunction with a hose clip this is less likely to happen. With the rings suitably clamped, the piston may then be gently tapped into the bore (Photo).
5. Fit a new shell bearing into the connecting rod half of the big end, making sure that the oil hole and notch in the end of the shell line up with the corresponding hole and notch in the connecting rod. Lubricate the big end journal on the crankshaft with clean engine oil and push the connecting rod down on to the journal. Fit a new shell bearing into the cap, lining up the notch accordingly (there is no oil hole in the cap), and replace it on to the big end studs (Photo). The big end bearing caps will have been marked on removal as noted in the appropriate section so there should be no difficulty in making sure that the same cap goes on to the same connecting rod the right way round. Refit the self-locking nuts which one should not be able to turn with the fingers (if you can they should be renewed), and tighten them down to the correct torque (Photo).
6. If you have had the crankshaft reground and the firm which reground it is not actually assembling the pistons and connecting rods to it, it is a good idea to check the fit of each big end bearing on the crankshaft before actually inserting the pistons into the cylinder block. Then if any high spots are apparent when the bearing is turned on the crankshaft, suitable action can be taken. Defects of this nature are rare but can be caused by poor quality workmanship on the regrinding of the crankshaft, or damage to the mating faces of the big end bearing caps where some previous owner has misguidedly filed them down in an attempt to take up any bearing slackness.

39. Camshaft & Tappets - Replacement in Cylinder Block

1. If the tappets have been removed from the cylinder block, then they should not be replaced until the camshaft has been refitted. If the tappets are still in position in the cylinder block and the engine is out of the car it is best to lie it on its side, pushing the tappets up in their bores so that they will not foul the lobes of the camshaft as it is being inserted into position. It should also be noted that if the engine has been completely dismantled the camshaft should always be refitted before the oil pump.
2. Make sure that all the camshaft bearings are in good condition and perfectly clean. Lubricate them with clean engine oil and then carefully replace the camshaft into the cylinder block (Photo). The main precaution when doing this is to make sure that the hardened steel lobes of the camshaft do not damage the soft metal bearing surfaces through which they have to pass. When the camshaft is fully home the thrust plate should be replaced and secured by the two bolts (Photo). If for any reason the front engine plate has been detached from the block it should now be replaced using a new gasket.
3. To avoid the possibility of the tappets falling out of their locations due to gravity with the engine inverted, it is best to wait until the oil pump and sump have been replaced on the engine and it is, once again, upright. The tappets should be thoroughly cleaned and lubricated with clean oil before replacing them in their appropriate

Section 38.4. Replacing piston/connecting rod assemblies and fitting big ends

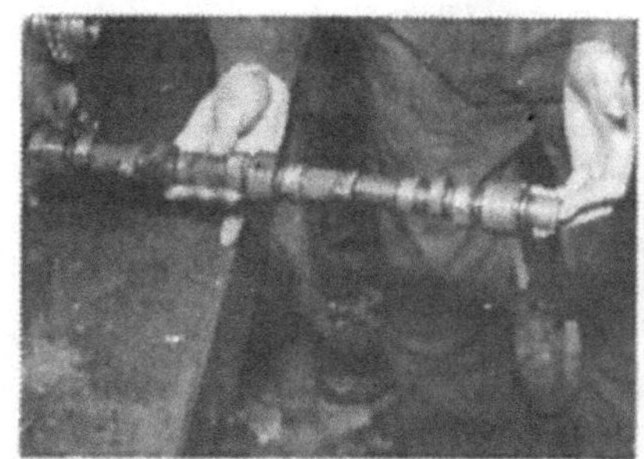

Section 39.2 Refitting camshaft and thrust plate

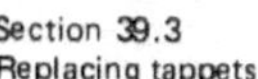

Section 39.3 Replacing tappets

Section 39.4 Refitting tappet chest cover (In these photos the final replacement is shown, after the fitting of the cylinder head and rocker gear)

bores (Photo).

4. Using a new gasket replace the tappet chest cover (Photo) and tighten down the securing bolts evenly (Photo).

40. Timing Chain, Tensioner, Sprockets,& Cover - Replacement

1. Before fitting the timing chain or sprockets, make sure that the front plate has been put back on to the cylinder block if it was removed. If the timing chain is one which is fitted with a detachable connecting link, then the two sprockets may be replaced on their respective shafts independently of the chain, but it is in fact better to assemble the chain to the sprockets before replacing them. It can be a fiddle to get the connecting link fitted otherwise. Also, if the chain is being replaced with the engine in the car there is the possibility of dropping a piece of the link into the aperture where the oil feed pipe comes out, if this happens the front plate has to come off.

2. When fitting the connecting link note that the two keep plates are different thicknesses - the thicker one goes in the centre. Also the open end of the spring clip should be at the trailing end of the link. The chain revolves in a clockwise direction as viewed from the front. So place the two sprockets inside the chain so that a

straight line through the centre of each also passes through the two dimple marks on the edge of the sprockets. These dimple marks should face each other. The keys on the crankshaft and camshaft should be positioned so that they line up with the sprockets' keyways when assembled to the chain (Fig.1.9).

3. The sprockets and chain together should then be placed on the ends of the shafts and pushed forward together until the keyways locate on the keys. Under no circumstances must the camshaft sprocket be driven on by striking. The camshaft could move back and displace the sealing plug at the other end of the block. Draw the sprocket on with a bolt. The crankshaft sprocket may be tapped on.

4. Do not forget to replace the cover mounting stud between the two sprockets if it has been removed. When the sprockets and chain are satisfactorily assembled check that the timing marks are still correctly lined up. Refit the two lockwashers on to the camshaft sprocket mounting bolt and bend the top lockwasher into a flat on the bolt head (Photo).

5. Replace the tensioner arm on to the spindle and refit a washer and new split pin to retain it in position (Photos).

6. Replace the oil slinger disc over the crankshaft with the concave side facing outwards (Photo). The cover may now be refitted using a new gasket (Photo). The tensioner device should be tucked inside the cover and then the cover put on, holding the tensioner in position against the chain. Replace all the securing bolts but do not tighten them up at this juncture (Photo).

41. Crankshaft Pulley Wheel - Replacement

1. The crankshaft pulley wheel is a straight fit on to the end of the crankshaft, the key in the crankshaft engaging in the keyway of the pulley wheel (Photo). There is no oil seal built into the timing cover round the crankshaft pulley wheel, the latter having a scroll groove machined into the boss to return any oil which may try to seep through.

2. If the timing cover has been removed, it should be loosened before the crankshaft pulley wheel is refitted to the crankshaft. This enables the boss of the flywheel pulley to centralise in the aperture of the cover. However, there is a bolt alongside the aperture which must be tightened before the flywheel pulley is finally driven right on, so in the first instance it is best not to push the pulley wheel right home but to centralise the cover, draw the pulley wheel off and tighten up the particular bolt referred to. If one or two other bolts are also nipped up at the same time the remainder can be tightened down whether the crankshaft pulley wheel may be on or off.

3. If the pulley wheel is a tight "' it may be necessary to drive it on using a block of wood (Photo). . he bolt which secures the crankshaft pulley wheel into position may be replaced but it is easier if it is left until the engine is reconnected to the gearbox in the car before it is fully tightened. It is easier to lock the engine so that the necessary torque can be applied.

42. Oil Pump - Replacement

1. The oil pump should not be replaced until the camshaft, crankshaft, pistons, connecting rods and timing chain (but not the cover) have all been reassembled into the block.

2. It is important that the teeth of the oil pump driving spindle should be properly meshed with the skew gear on the camshaft, to enable the distributor drive which also comes from the oil pump driveshaft to be correctly timed. The upper end of the oil pump drive spindle has an offset slot in it which engages into the bottom of the distributor drive spindle, and it is this slot which must be put in the correct position when refitting the oil pump.

3. First of all, it is necessary to put No.1 piston at the top dead centre. This must also be on the compression stroke and not on the exhaust stroke. If you have just finished assembling the camshaft timing chain and sprockets the crankshaft will be in the correct position provided it has not been turned since that assembly was done. The key in the crankshaft to which the flywheel pulley fits is always uppermost at top dead centre on No.1 piston. With the timing marks on the sprockets still lined up, this will mean that No.1 is correctly on the compression stroke TDC.

4. Once the crankshaft is positioned correctly with No.1 piston at top dead centre on compression stroke, the oil pump may be refitted. As the pump is put into position, the spindle will turn due to the curved nature of the gears which mesh together. Initially, therefore, the slot in the spindle must be set so that when it turns it will finish up in the position as shown in Fig.1.10.

5. The mating faces of the pump, and the crankcase where it fits, must be perfectly clean and free from any scratches or burrs. The oil suction pipe, complete with unions, should also be lightly assembled to the oil pump body, as it will not be possible to fit this after the oil pump has been bolted down (Photo).

6. It is best for the engine to be lying on its side when refitting the oil pump as in this way it will be easy to look at the position of the driving slot in the top of the spindle. Tighten the pump mounting bolts and the oil suction pipe unions (Photo).

7. After the oil pump has been satisfactorily replaced but before fitting the sump it is a good idea to check that the distributor will be in the correct position when refitted. To do this, replace the distributor temporarily so that its drive spindle engages in the slot in the oil pump spindle and see that the rotor arm of the distributor lines up with the No.1 plug lead contact when the cap is in position. If, however, the precautions as recommended were taken when the distributor was removed, the position of the driving slot will be known for sure when reassembling the engine. The reason for taking these precautions is that it is possible for the driving dog on the end of a distributor shaft to be in a different location in relation to the rotor arm, and unless this is known a lot of time can be wasted when eventually setting up the ignition timing.

43. Sump - Replacement

1. Before replacing the sump make quite sure that all big end bearing cap nuts are tight, all main bearing cap bolts are tight, and that the oil pump has been replaced and securely tightened down. Fit a new sump gasket to the mating face on the base of the cylinder block, having first made sure that the face has been thoroughly cleaned of all remnants of old gasket and jointing compound.

2. If you have removed the sump baffle plate for cleaning, make sure it is replaced before putting the sump back on the block.

3. Clean off all similar traces of gasket and jointing compound from the mating face of the sump itself. The sump gasket comes in four pieces: two semi-circular cork seals which engage in the grooves of the bearing caps at each end of the crankshaft, and two side gaskets which fit the flanges of the sump pan. Fit the side gaskets first to the crankcase. It is not essential to use a jointing compound although many people prefer to do so as a precaution. However, when fitting the cork seals into the grooves of the bearing caps the ends of the seals should be treated with a quick setting jointing compound where they bear on to the ends of the side gaskets. Carefully place the sump in position over the gaskets and locate all the sump holding bolts into position before tightening them up (Photos).

44. Flywheel - Replacement

1. Before replacing the flywheel to the crankshaft flange, the mating faces must be examined carefully for any signs of dents or burrs and be cleaned up as necessary. All traces of oil and grit must also be removed, and the locating dowel peg should be in position on the crankshaft flange. Offer up the flywheel to the flange squarely and locate it carefully into position without damaging the edges of the

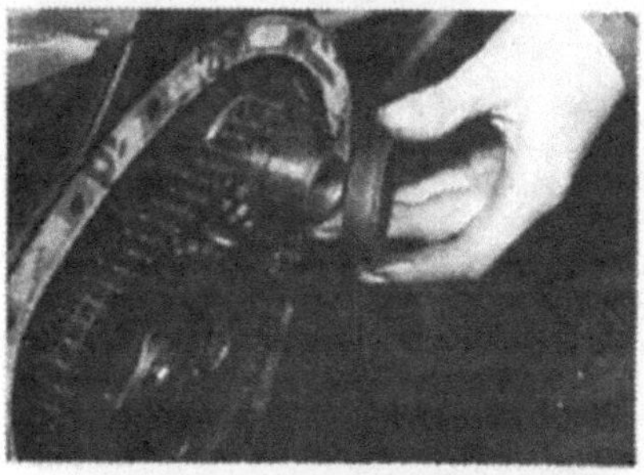

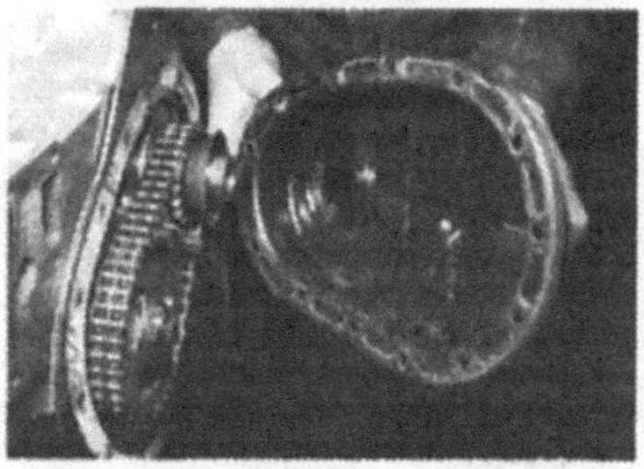

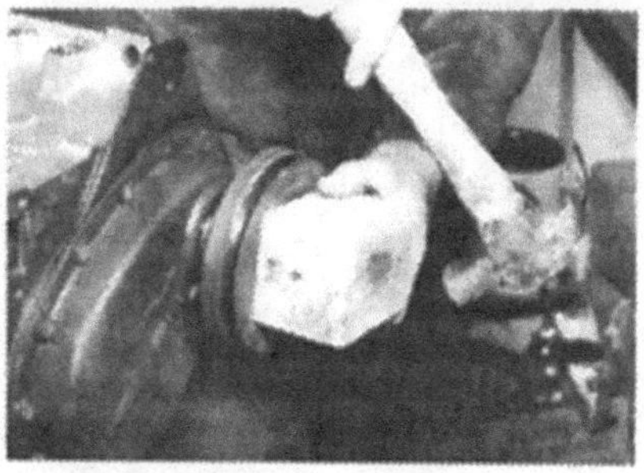

Sections 40 and 41
Final assembly of timing chain cover and crankshaft pulley

Section 42. Oil pump and delivery pipe are secured in position

Section 43.2
Fitting baffle in sump

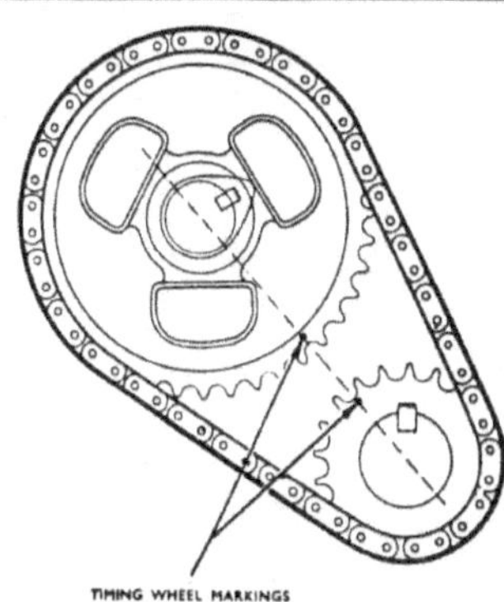

Fig. 1.9 With numbers 1 and 4 pistons at TDC, the shaft keyways and timing chain sprocket marks should be lined up as shown.

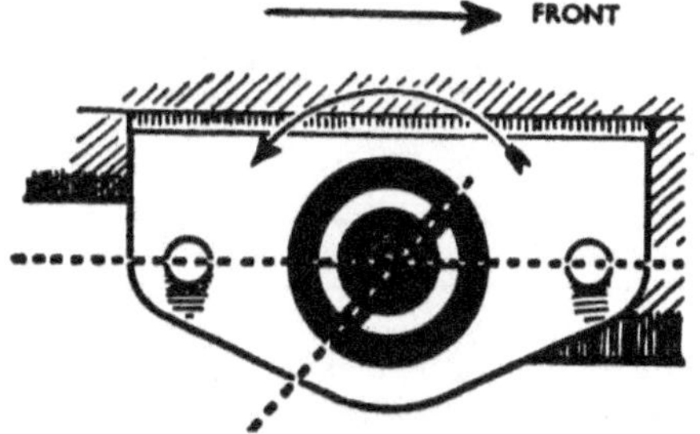

Fig.1.10. With No.1 piston at TDC on compression, this is the correct position for the offset slot in the distributor drive. (See text for possible variations)

mating faces (Photo).

2. Once the flywheel is securely mounted the set bolts should be fitted with new tab washers and progressively tightened up to the specified torque (Photos). If possible, it is a good idea to check the flywheel run-out at the outer edge of the clutch facing. If this exceeds a total of 0.003 inch then it means that the flywheel is not fitted square with the crankshaft and serious vibration problems could result when the engine is running. A micrometer clock gauge will be needed to check this run-out.

45. Valves & Springs - Reassembly to Cylinder Head

1. With the head perfectly clean and having carried out all necessary renewals and renovations as required, lightly lubricate the valve stem for the first valve to be replaced and fit it in the guide (Photo). If the same valves are being used again they should have been kept in order so that they may go back in the same place.

2. Place the spring seating washer over the valve with the lip uppermost, followed by the inner spring, outer spring and collar (Photo). Note that the collars are fitted with sealing rings in their internal bores and these should be renewed if necessary (Photo). The seals are included in the head gasket set.

3. The valve spring compressing tool should then be used to compress the springs sufficiently to enable the split collets to be refitted into the groove in the valve stem (Photo). A little grease may be used to assist holding them in position.

4. Release the spring compressor slowly, watching that the collets do not move out of the groove, and then, when the compressor is removed, hit the top of the valve stem to 'bounce' the spring and verify the assembly is secure.

5. Repeat the procedure for each valve in turn, taking care that each valve is replaced in its correct guide.

46. Inlet & Exhaust Manifolds - Replacement

1. If the engine is removed from the car the manifolds may be replaced on the cylinder head whether the head is fitted or not, except in the case of the H120 engine when the head must be fitted to the block first.

2. A common gasket is used for both inlet and exhaust manifolds and it should be noted that the two outer inlet ports are fitted with steel ring locating inserts. These should be clean and free from carbon or any sign of damage due to heat. Fit them before the gasket (Photo).

3. Put the gasket in position (Photo) and then fit the exhaust manifold followed by the inlet manifold.

4. Tighten down the retaining nuts and bolts evenly and remember to retighten them when the engine has been run for a short time and is warm. If the engine is still out of the car it is probably wiser not to refit the carburettors until it has been replaced in the car.

47. Cylinder Head - Refitting to the Cylinder Block

1. Make sure that the mating surfaces of the head and cylinder block are perfectly clean and flat. Place the gasket in position on the cylinder head. Do not use any sealing compound or grease when fitting it. Make sure it is put in position the right way up. It is marked 'top' on the upper side (Photo).

2. If the tappet chest cover plate has been removed from the block it should now be replaced, with a new gasket fitted, and the bolts done up finger tight into the cylinder block. Make sure the tappets are in position too!

3. Hold the cylinder head over the block, and making sure that the oil feed pipe goes through the centre hole (in line with the pushrod holes), lower the head gently into place over the two studs (Photo).

4. Replace the remaining bolts which hold the tappet chest cover and then tighten all of them evenly. This will ensure that the mating faces of the cover and both the head and block are properly lined up before the head is unmovably tightened down. If a new gasket is not being fitted to the tappet chest cover it may help to guard against possible leaks if the top edge of the gasket is smeared with jointing compound before the head is replaced. This would normally apply only where the engine has not been removed from the car.

5. Replace all the cylinder head bolts and washers and the nuts on to the two studs.

6. All the bolts and nuts should be lightly tightened down equally, and then progressively tightened by about 10 lb ft at a time, in the correct sequence as shown in Fig.1.11, until the correct total torque has been applied (Photo).

7. The length of the two projecting studs will prevent most sockets from reaching the single nut, so the second nut should be locked to it when both may be turned together. The top one may be slackened off by holding the bottom one with an open ended spanner after the full tightening has been completed.

48. Valve Rocker Gear - Reassembly & Refitting to the Cylinder Head

1. The rocker should be fitted to the head after the head has been fitted to the block. Otherwise some of the head bolts are not accessible for tightening with a conventional socket spanner. Also a lot of unnecessary slackening of the rocker adjusters will be necessary in order to refit the pushrods.

2. Replace the pushrods into their appropriate holes and make sure that the lower convex ends engage in the tappets.

3. If the rocker gear has been dismantled reassemble each of the two halves correctly, noting the position of the springs and the standards (see Fig.1.12).

4. When both halves are assembled check that the two centres of the shafts are open ended. These receive the lubricating oil from the centre T-piece which must be next positioned between the two assemblies with the inlet section pointing downwards.

5. Place the union connector over the oil pipe. It will stay put, as the pipe has a small belled out section to prevent it falling through the head (Photo).

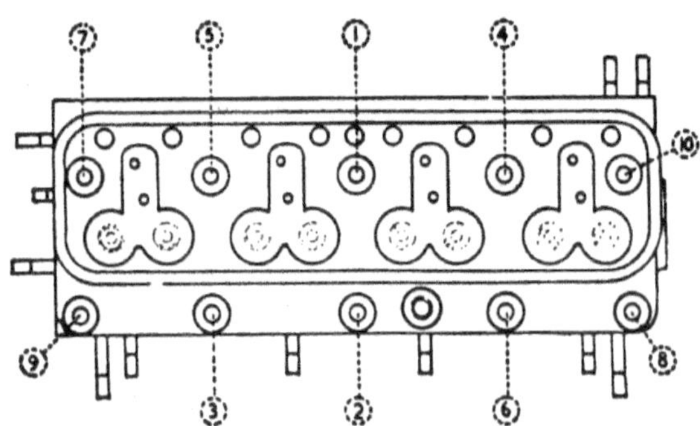

Fig.1.11. Sequence for tightening cylinder head nuts. Slacken in reverse order.

Section 43.3. Fitting and securing aluminium sump

Section 44.1 Fitting flywheel to flange

Section 44.2 Tightening flywheel securing bolts to the correct torque.

Section 45.1. Inserting valves.

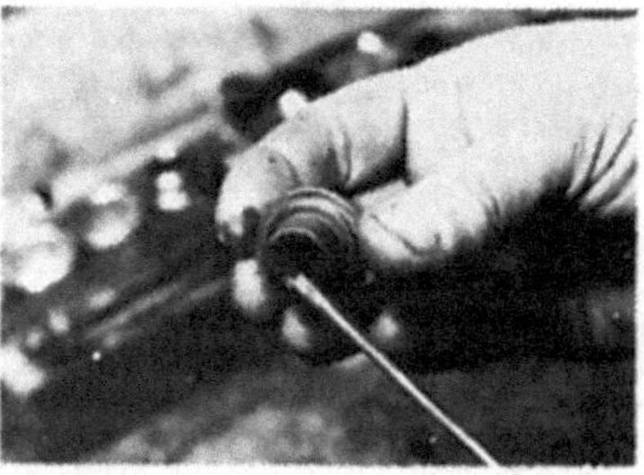

Section 45.2. Assembling valve springs and fittings.

Section 45.3 Compressing valve springs to fit split collets.

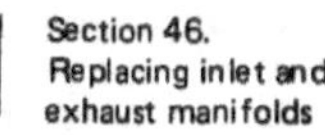

Section 46. Replacing inlet and exhaust manifolds

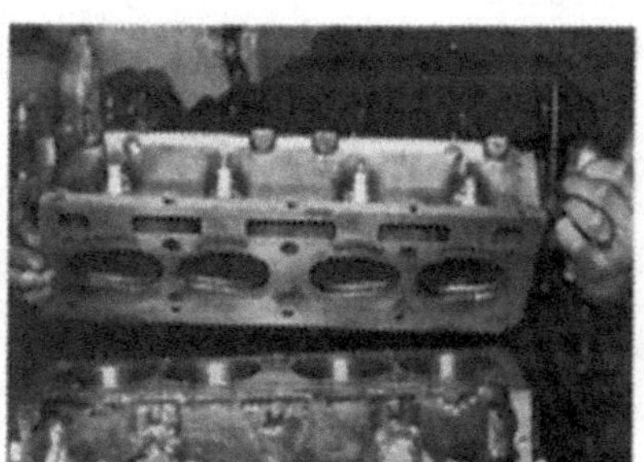

Section 47. Refitting and tightening down cylinder head.

6. The whole assembly should then be picked up as a unit and placed in position so that the oil pipe enters the T-piece and each of the pushrod ends locates into its respective rocker arm adjuster stud. This will probably take a bit of fiddling. Remember also that the assembly will not sit down in position properly as some valves should be in the open position and the pushrods for these will be on the high points of the cams (Photo).
7. Replace all washers and nuts and proceed to tighten them down a small and equal amount each in sequence so as to prevent any distortion caused by the resistance of the springs on the open valves. Check once more that the pushrods are correctly located.
8. When the standards are all seated flat on the head the nuts or bolts should be tightened to the correct torque of 11 lb ft.
9. Tighten the oil pipe union (Photo).

49. Valve Rocker Clearances - Checking & Adjustment

1. The valve rocker clearances are important as they control the amount a vlave opens and when it opens and thus can affect the efficiency of the engine.
2. The clearances should be measured and set by using a feeler blade between the rocker arm and end of each valve stem. This is done when the valve is closed and the tappet is resting on the lowest point of the cam.
3. So that each valve is in the correct position for checking with the minimum amount of engine turning, the procedure and order of checking should follow the sequence given in the following tables. In this table the valves are numbered 1 to 8, starting from the front of the cylinder head. A valve is fully open when the rocker arm has pushed the valve down to its lowest point.

Open Valve	Adjust clearance (hot) Standard	H120
No.8 (exh)	No.1 (exh 0.014 in 0.35 mm)	(0.013 in 0.33 mm)
No.5 (inl)	No.4 (inl 0.012 in 0.30 mm)	(0.013 in 0.33 mm)
No.3 (exh)	No.6 (exh 0.014 in 0.35 mm)	(0.013 in 0.33 mm)
No.7 (inl)	No.2 (inl 0.012 in 0.30 mm)	(0.013 in 0.33 mm)
No.1 (exh)	No.8 (exh 0.014 in 0.35 mm)	(0.013 in 0.33 mm)
No.4 (incl)	No.5 (inl 0.012 in 0.30 mm)	(0.013 in 0.33 mm)
No.6 (exh)	No.3 (exh 0.014 in 0.35 mm)	(0.013 in 0.33 mm)
No.2 (inl)	No.7 (inl 0.012 in 0.30 mm)	(0.013 in 0.33 mm)

If the engine is being assembled on the bench or after the head has been taken off, the gaps should be set 0.002 inch more than those given for clearances (hot) above.
4. Using a screwdriver and spanner first slacken the locknut on the adjusting stud, and then put tne feeler blade, of thickness appropriate to the valve being adjusted, between the rocker arm and valve stem. Slacken the stud adjuster if the gap is too small to accept the blade (Photo).
5. Turn the adjusting screw until the feeler blade can be felt to drag lightly when it is drawn out of the gap.
6. Hold the adjuster with a screwdriver and tighten the locknut. Check the gap once more to make sure it has not altered as a result of locking the stud (Photo).
7. Refit the rocker cover using a new gasket (Photo).

50. Engine Reassembly - Final Stages

1. Before replacing an engine in the car, all those ancillary parts which were removed before the engine was stripped should be replaced. These items were listed in Section 7. One possible exception are the carburettors which project in a somewhat vulnerable way and could be damaged expensively if any mishap occurred.
2. Refit the rocker gear cover, even though it has to be taken off again, as this will protect the rocker gear from damage and dust. Leave the new gasket to be fitted later.

51. Engine - Replacement in the Car

Generally speaking the replacement of the engine is a reversal of the removal procedure but the following points should be borne in mind.
1. If the engine and gearbox have been removed together, they should be reassembled and replaced together. This takes care of the possible difficulties one may encounter fitting the gearbox input shaft into the clutch. It will mean that the propeller shaft may also remain connected. However, it must not be forgotten that the propeller shaft will need to be introduced into the gearbox rear cover before the unit is in its final position, otherwise the propeller shaft will need to be disconnected at the rear axle pinion flange.
2. When lowering the engine into the car make sure first that it is suspended in the correct attitude. It is difficult and possibly dangerous to have to alter the angle of tilt whilst it is suspended.
3. Always lower the engine very slowly and keep a continuous watch, all round it, all through the manoeuvre. It is easy to wrench out wire and pipes due to being in too much of a hurry and not noticing these things when they flip back in the way - as they always seem to do.
4. If the engine will not go where it should, look and find out why. Do not try and force anything.
5. Always fit new oil filter and air filter elements.
6. The following check list should ensure that the engine starts safely and with little or no delay:—

a) Fuel pipes to fuel pump and carburettor - connected and tight
b) Water hoses to radiator and heater - connected and clipped tight
c) Radiator and cylinder block water drain taps shut
d) Cooling system filled up
e) Sump drain plug screwed in tight
f) Oil filter element screwed on tight
g) Oil in sump
h) Oil in gearbox and level plug tight
i) LT wires connected to distributor and coil
j) Sparking plugs clean and tight
k) Valve clearances set
l) HT leads from coil, distributor and spark plugs all connected correctly, and securely
m) Distributor rotor arm fitted
n) Choke and throttle cables connected and controls operating correctly over full range
o) Braided earthing cables from engine to bodyframe secure
p) Starter motor lead securely connected at both ends
q) Fan belt fitted and tensioned
r) Alternator leads connected
s) Oil pressure pipe or sender wire connected
t) Temperature gauge wire connected
u) Battery charged and in good condition and leads securely connected to clean terminals
v) All loose tools removed from engine compartment
w) All jacks and blocks removed.

7. As soon as the engine starts, run it steadily at a fast tick-over for several minutes and look all round for signs of leaks and loose or unclipped pipes and wires. Watch the instruments and warning lights and stop the engine at the first indications of anything nasty!

Section 48. Reassembly and fitting of rocker gear to cylinder head.

Sections 49.4 and 49.6. Checking and adjusting valve rocker clearances.

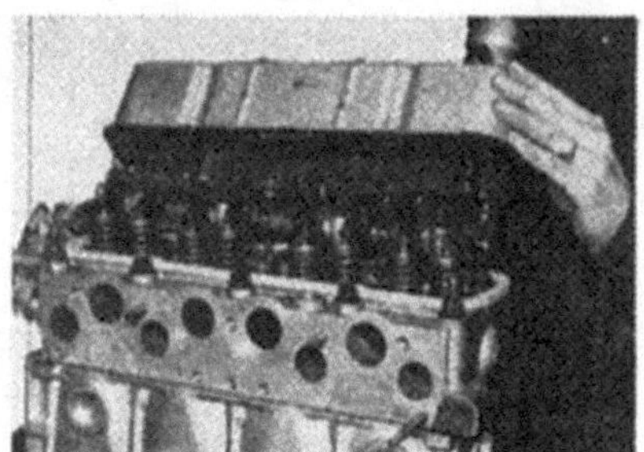

Section 49.7 Refitting rocker cover, with new gasket.

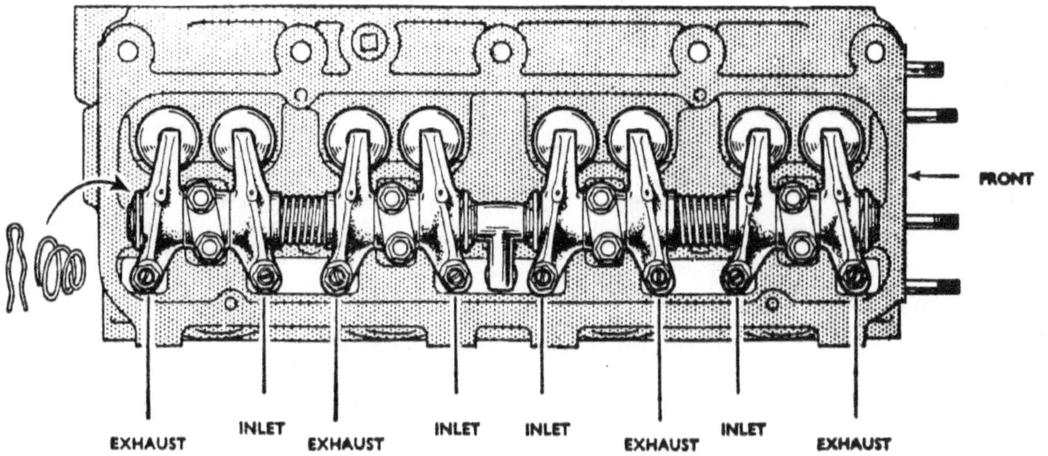

FRONT

EXHAUST INLET EXHAUST INLET INLET EXHAUST INLET EXHAUST

Fig.1.12. Valve and rocker gear layout

Experience shows that faults are usually traced more quickly, and with less frustration, by adopting a systematic approach. However, as owners come to understand their car's individual quirks, they can sometimes go straight to the source of the trouble without more ado. Perhaps the best compromise is to follow an idea if it seems really promising, and then, if results are not immediately forthcoming, follow a system, changing only one factor at a time.

Snap diagnosis is seldom successful when investigating starting and uneven running faults. Poor performance from an engine in terms of power and economy is not usually diagnosed quickly by anyone, however experienced.

The following table gives guidance and refers to key areas for investigation and action.

Symptom	Reason/s	Remedy
Engine will not turn over when starter switch is operated	Flat battery Bad battery connections Bad connections at solenoid switch and/or starter motor	Check that battery is fully charged and that all connections are clean and tight
	Starter motor jammed	Turn the square headed end of the starter motor shaft with a spanner to free it. Where a pre-engaged starter is fitted rock the car back and forth with a gear engaged. If this does not free pinion remove starter
	Defective solenoid	Bridge the main terminals of the solenoid switch with a piece of heavy duty cable in order to operate the starter
	Starter motor defective	Remove and overhaul starter motor
Engine turns over normally but fails to fire and run	No spark at plugs	Check ignition system according to procedures given in Chapter 4
	No fuel reaching engine	Check fuel system according to procedures given in Chapter 3
	Too much fuel reaching the engine (flooding)	Check the fuel system as above
Engine starts but runs unevenly and misfires	Ignition and/or fuel system faults	Check the ignition and fuel systems as though the engine had failed to start
	Incorrect valve clearances	Check and reset clearances
	Burnt out valves Blown cylinder head gasket	Remove cylinder head and examine and overhaul as necessary
	Worn out piston rings	Remove cylinder head and examine pistons and cylinder bores. Overhaul as necessary
Lack of power or excessive fuel consumption	Ignition and/or fuel system faults	Check the ignition and fuel systems for correct ignition timing and carburettor settings
	Incorrect valve clearances	Check and reset the clearances
	Burnt out valves Blown cylinder head gasket	Remove cylinder head and examine and overhaul as necessary
	Worn out piston rings Worn cylinder bores	Remove cylinder head and examine pistons and cylinder bores. Overhaul as necessary
Excessive oil consumption	Oil leaks from crankshaft rear oil seal, timing cover gasket and oil seal, rocker cover gasket, oil filter gasket, sump gasket, sump plug washer	Identify source of leak and renew seal as appropriate
	Worn piston rings or cylinder bores resulting in oil being burnt by engine Smoky exhaust is an indication	Fit new rings or rebore cylinders and fit new pistons, depending on degree of wear
	Worn valve guides and/or defective valve stem seals	Remove cylinder heads and recondition valve stem bores and valves and seals as necessary
Excessive mechanical noise from engine	Wrong valve to rocker clearances	Adjust valve clearances
	Worn crankshaft bearings Worn cylinders (piston slap)	Inspect and overhaul where necessary
	Slack or worn timing chain and sprockets	Adjust chain and/or inspect all timing mechanisms

Chapter 2 Cooling system

Contents

Specifications

Type of system	Pressurised with centrifugal circulation pump, fan and thermostat. H120 fitted with sealed circuit and expansion bottle.
Coolant capacity (with heater)	13.75 pints (16.5 US pints, 7.8 litres)
Thermostat - opening temp	82°C (180°F)
- by-pass port closes at	95°C (203°F)
Radiator type	Two or three row gilled tube
Radiator cap blow off pressure	9 lb sq in (0.63 kg cm^2)
Antifreeze protection to −15°F (−26°C)	25% solution of Castrol Antifreeze
Water pump type	Centrifugal, driven by belt from crankshaft pulley

1. General Description

The engine cooling liquid is circulated round the system on the thermosyphon principle, assisted by a belt driven impeller type pump.

The system is pressurised so that boiling and evaporation will only occur at abnormally high temperatures. The radiator cap valve will lift at a pressure of 8 lb/in^2. The pressure will then drop, as vapour boils off and passes down the overflow pipe, until the valve re-seats. It is therefore important that the radiator cap is one designed for the system and in good condition. Testing equipment is available at most garages.

The circuit also incorporates a thermostatically controlled valve which restricts the amount of water passing through the radiator until the correct engine operating temperature is reached. This assists rapid warming up and keeps the engine at a constant running temperature irrespective of ambient conditions.

The principle of operation is as follows. The water heated by the engine rises out of the cylinder head towards the thermostat which, if cold, is closed. It then diverts via the heater (or heater by-pass pipe if the heater valve is shut) straight to the pump and thence back to the engine.

When the engine warms up a proportion of the warm water will pass via the thermostat valve to the top of the radiator down through which it will pass and cool. The pump will then draw the cold water from the bottom of the radiator and pass it back to the engine (the pump has two inlets). If the engine temperature should rise excessively the thermostat valve will close off the by-pass outlet thus directing all water through the radiator.

Water which may boil off down the radiator overflow pipe passes into a reservoir or expansion bottle, which maintains a level of liquid covering the end of the overflow pipe. Consequently, any liquid exhausted down the overflow is drawn back by the vacuum created when the system cools down. This greatly reduces the need for regular topping up.

The H120 has a fully sealed system.

2. Routine Maintenance

1. The coolant level should be checked at least weekly – more often if indications warrant it - by removing the radiator cap. The level should be just below the bottom of the filler neck. If topping up is required use a soft water (rainwater) if possible. This helps to keep deposits to a minimum.
2. Every 5000 miles, check the fan belt for wear and correct tension and adjust or renew it if needed (Section 10).
3. Every 5000 miles, check specific gravity of antifreeze mixture (if used).
4. The water pump is sealed and need not be touched unless signs of leaking or shaft bearing failure are apparent.
5. In hard water areas removal of deposits using a proprietary chemical de-scaler may be needed from time to time – but not more than annually. A good time to do this is at the change of the seasons when antifreeze may be used.

3. Cooling System - Draining

1. Stand the car level and remove the radiator cap – slowly and with caution if the engine is very hot (and thus likely to boil when pressure is released).
2. Unscrew the drain tap at the bottom of the radiator, and if the coolant is to be re-used because of antifreeze, collect it in a clean container. If the water is to be completely drained from the cylinder

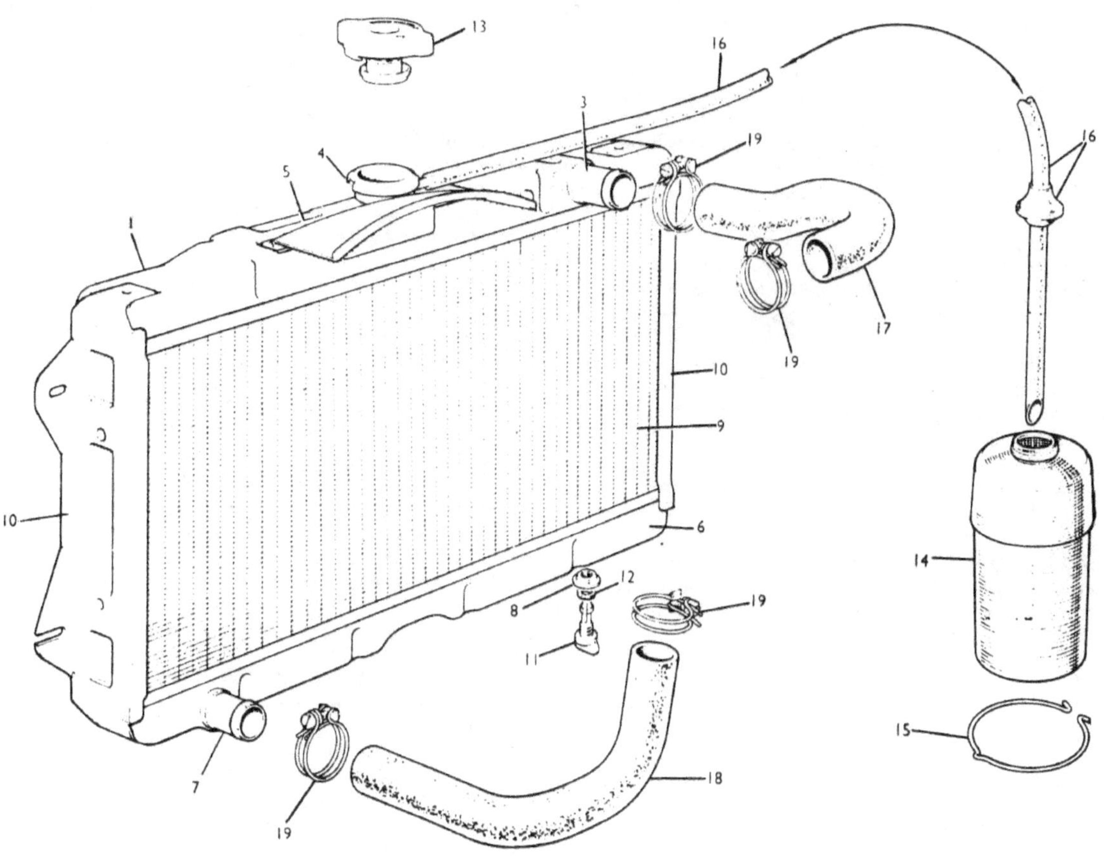

Fig.2.1. RADIATOR, HOSES, AND EXPANSION BOTTLE

1 Top tank
3 Top inlet pipe
4 Filler neck
5 Fan guard
6 Bottom tank
7 Bottom outlet pipe
8 Drain tap boss
9 Core
10 Side strap
11 Drain tap
12 Washer
13 Filler cap
14 Expansion bottle
15 Clip
16 Expansion pipe and cap
17 Top hose
18 Bottom hose
19 Hose clip

block also, the tap on the left side in the centre of the block, beneath the exhaust manifold, should be opened (Photo).

3. When the water has ceased flowing poke the drain tap outlets with a piece of wire to check that no loose sediment is blocking them.

4. Cooling System - Flushing

1. Every so often, particularly in hard water areas, it is a good practice to flush out the system to remove any loose sediment and scale which may have accumulated. The time to do this is when the coolant is being drained or antifreeze added. With the expansion bottle system, however, the need for topping up is very infrequent

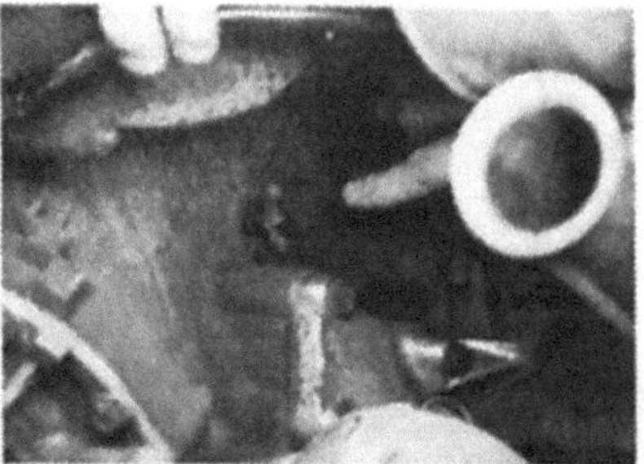

Section 3. Cylinder block drain tap

so that the deposits of lime and so on, from regular additions of new water, are reduced. The need for flushing, therefore, is usually only caused by some other factor, such as a leak which allows air to enter the system and cause oxidisation, or the use of an antifreeze of a type which may cause corrosion.

2. To check the need for flushing, remove the radiator cap and open the radiator drain tap and if the liquid coming out is obviously very dirty and full of solid particles let it run out. If it clears as more runs out and the outflow is in no way restricted then there is no great problem. If, however, constant poking with a piece of wire is needed and the liquid continues very dirty, then obviously a flush out is needed.

3. To flush out, simply leave the radiator and engine block drain taps open, and after removing the radiator cap, run water through the system for about 15 minutes. A hose pushed into the radiator filler pipe is a convenient method. If the taps show signs of blockage keep poking them out. If the blocking is persistent remove the tap completely so that the larger orifice may permit the obstruction to clear itself. In some bad cases a reverse flush may help and this is done by removing the radiator and connecting the hose to the bottom tank so that it flows out of the filler neck.

4. If the radiator flow is restricted by something other than loose sediment then no amount of flushing will shift it and it is then that a proprietary chemical cleaner is needed. Use this according to the directions and make sure that the residue is fully flushed out afterwards. If leaks develop after using a chemical cleaner, a proprietary radiator sealer often cures them, but if not, the radiator has suffered considerable chemical corrosion and the metal is obviously getting very thin in places.

5. Cooling System - Filling

1. Always flush out before refilling.
2. Close both drain taps and fill up slowly. If antifreeze is being used, mix it with the water before putting it in, making up a total quantity about 2 pints less than the capacity of the system. Then top up with water.
3. Run the engine up to normal temperature and then check the level again. If the level was right up to the neck on filling it will have dropped at least ¼ inch and this level should be retained.
4. Check that the heater works. If it does not there may be an air lock in the system. If it does not work efficiently the thermostat may be stuck open.

6. Radiator - Removal, Inspection, Cleaning & Replacement

1. Drain the cooling system as described earlier in Section 3.
2. Slacken the clip and remove the top radiator hose where it connects to the thermostat housing outlet or to the radiator (Photo). Slacken also the clip securing the bottom hose to the radiator and pull off the hose (Photo).
3. The radiator is held by four hexagon headed speed screws. When these are removed the radiator may be lifted out (Photo).
4. Thoroughly clean the exterior of the radiator. It has presumably been removed in order to repair a leak or for further examination of a suspected blockage (except of course as part of a procedure to gain access to something else).
5. As the radiator tanks and connections are made of brass they can be repaired with solder where exterior leaks are accessible. The technique of soldering is not discussed here but suffice it to say that the surfaces to be joined must be thoroughly cleaned, then tinned and the solder able to 'run' in the repair. It is fruitless merely depositing blobs of solder about the place. It would be better to use a resin filler paste which in fact can be used for such repairs in limited applications. Care must also be taken when soldering to localise any heat used. Otherwise the radiator may start to disintegrate where you least want it to. A leak in the internal parts of the honeycomb, if not severe, can be cured with one of the specialist sealers added to the cooling liquid. If severe, professional attention will be needed. Another way, for emergencies only, is to block the whole of the honeycomb in the suspected area with resin filler paste. Old fashioned remedies such as mustard, egg whites and porridge oats added to the water, are not recommended as they have been known to have sinister effects on water pumps and thermostats. There is much less liquid in modern systems and these foodstuffs cannot be digested so readily!

7. Thermostat - Removal, Testing & Replacement

1. If the engine gets too hot or stays too cool; or the heater is inefficient, then the thermostat is probably to blame.
2. Drain out sufficient coolant to lower the level about 4 inches (say a quart), so that no more will be lost when the top radiator hose is next detached from the thermostat housing.
3. Remove the two bolts securing the hose flange to the housing and remove the flange. The thermostat may then be taken out. If it is stuck round the edges carefully clean around the lip with a pointed tool to free it.
4. To test the thermostat, suspend it on a piece of cotton in a pan of water and see how it behaves at the necessary opening temperatures. The valve should start to open within 3°C of the normal operating temperature. Then after another 2 to 3 minutes it should open 3/8 inch (9.5 mm) to the 'by-pass port closed' position. After being once more placed in cooler water it should close within 15 to 20 seconds.
5. If a thermostat does not operate correctly it should be renewed. If one is not immediately available leave the old one out to avoid damage by possible overheating of the engine.
6. Refit the thermostat to its housing carefully and make sure it seats snugly. When refitting the housing flange cover, use a new gasket and sealing compound on both sides. If the mating surfaces are badly pitted it may be necessary to clean them up with a file, but make sure the surfaces remain flat (Fig.2.2).
7. Do not overtighten the securing bolts as the threads in the housing are easily stripped. This is why preparation of the mating surfaces is important to stop leaks.

8. Water Pump - Removal, Dismantling & Replacement

1. If the water pump leaks or the bearing is obviously worn it will need to be removed for renewal or repair.
2. Drain the cooling system and then undo the hoses which are connected to the pump.
3. Slacken the alternator mounting bolts and belt tension adjuster bolt so that the fan belt may be removed.
4. Remove the four bolts that hold the fan and pulley to the pulley centre and take the fan and pulley off (Photo).
5. The pump is held to the block by four larger bolts (do not confuse them with the pump assembly bolts) which should be removed and the pump lifted off (Photos).
6. Before attempting repairs to the pump find out the relative cost of a new bearing assembly, seal and gasket and weigh this against the cost of a complete unit, new or secondhand, and the time factor involved. See also, Section 8.9 below, and Fig.2.3.
7. Begin dismantling by removing the screws securing the impeller

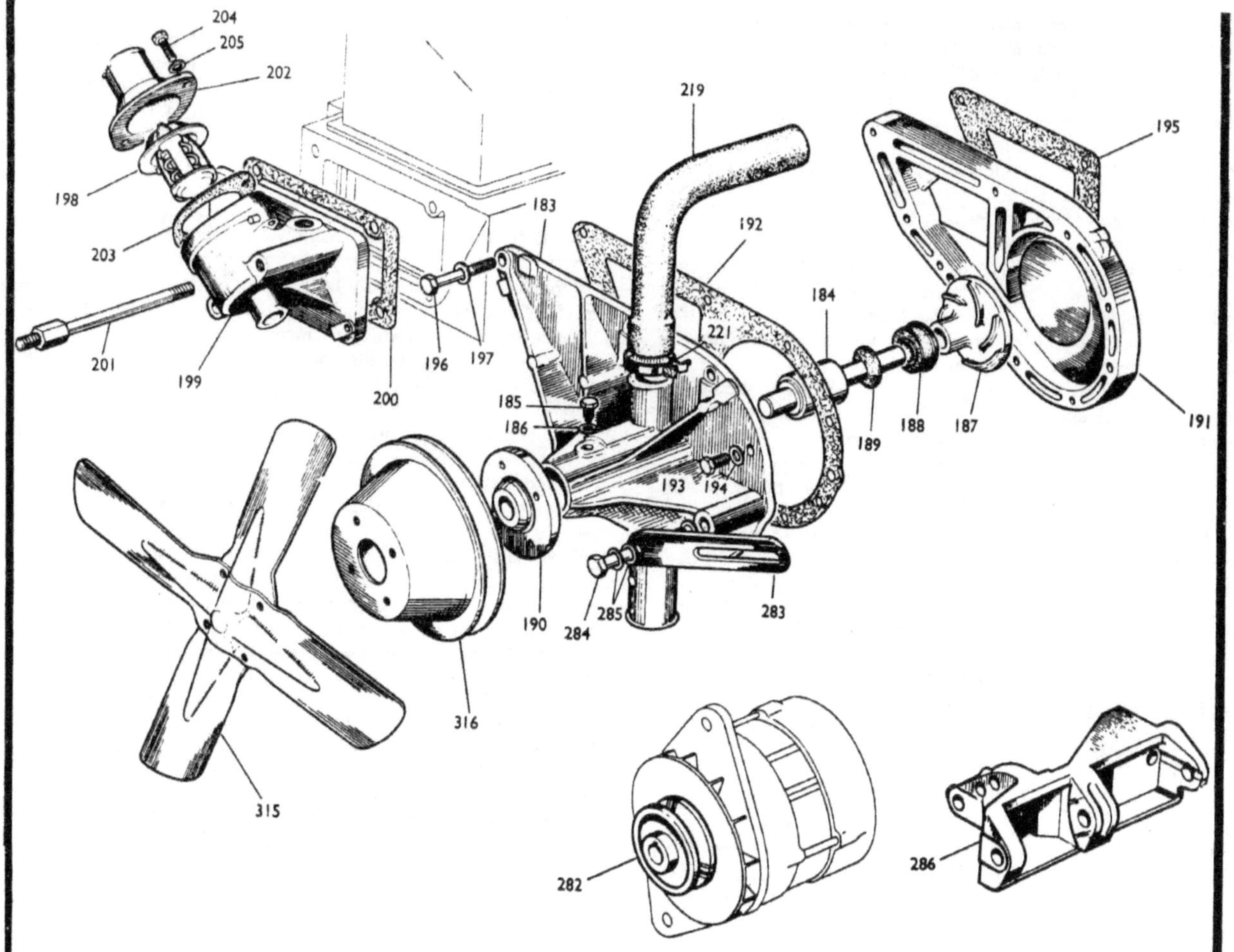

Fig.2.2. EXPLODED VIEWS OF THERMOSTAT AND WATER PUMP

183 Pump body
184 Bearing assembly
185 Locating bolt
186 Washer
187 Impeller
188 Seal
189 Thrower
190 Pulley centre
191 Impeller housing
192 Gasket
193 Bolt
194 Washer
195 Gasket
196 Bolt
197 Washer
198 Thermostat
199 Thermostat housing
200 Gasket
201 Bolt
202 Outlet pipe
203 Gasket
204 Bolt
205 Washer
219 Hose
221 Clip
282 Alternator pulley
283 Adjusting link
284 Bolt
285 Washers
286 Alternator mounting
315 Fan
316 Fan pulley

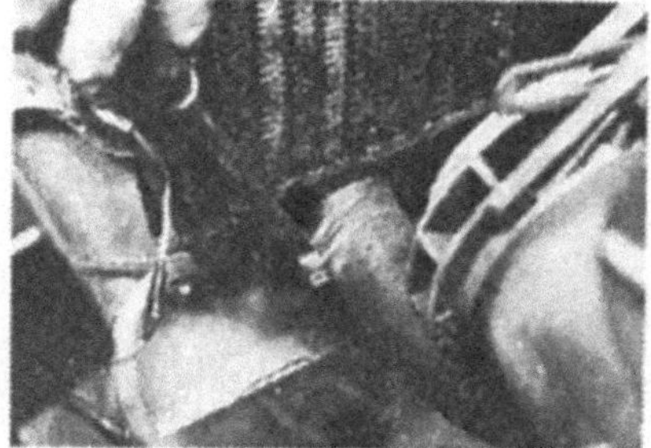

Section 6. Preparing to remove the radiator

housing to the body and separating the two. To remove the bearing and spindle assembly first remove the locating screw and then draw the pulley centre off the spindle with a suitable claw extractor.
8. Warm the pump body in hot water (90°C) in order that the spindle, together with the bearing and impeller, may be pressed out. When this has been done the impeller may be pressed off the spindle. The seal may be removed and replaced when the bearing assembly has been pressed out of the body. The face of the seal is carbon, and both it and the mating face on the body must be perfectly smooth and unscored.
9. Unless one has the use of a proper press, reassembly is tricky. The impeller and pulley centre have to be positioned correctly on the spindle. If pushed on too far or too little the operation of the pump is affected. For this reason repair of the pump should not be undertaken lightly without the proper equipment to hand.
10. When fitting a new seal unit into the pump body it should be smeared with a sealing compound to prevent water seepage. Make sure no traces of sealer get on to the carbon face.
11. Reassembly is a reversal of the dismantling procedure. Heat the body once more when pressing the bearing into position and locate it with the screw whilst it is still warm and movable.
12. Before replacing the pump in the block the mating faces of both the impeller housing and the block must be perfectly clean and free of traces of old gaskets. Fit a new gasket, using jointing compound on both sides, and tighten the bolts evenly to ensure a watertight joint.
13. Refit the fan and pulley, replace the fan belt and adjust the tension. Connect the water hoses and refill the system with coolant. Examine for leaks when cold and also at normal running temperature.

9. Antifreeze

1. Antifreeze liquid added to the coolant is now the accepted protection against cold which can freeze the coolant and crack the block. Even though a heater may be available whilst the car is garaged at night, daytime temperatures when the car is parked outside can be low enough to cause a freeze up! At very low temperatures the bottom of the radiator can freeze up if antifreeze is not used: sometimes this causes the coolant in other parts of the system to boil and blow off as steam, as the ice prevents proper circulation round the engine. Also a small quantity of water will always remain in the block after draining which could freeze and cause damage.
2. Antifreeze has very searching properties and if there are any leaks or were leaks in the system, it will accentuate them and you may soon notice growths of bluish deposits at the offending places. Make sure, therefore, that the cooling system is in good condition before adding antifreeze.
3. Use only antifreeze liquid to BS.3151/3152 which will be an ethylene glycol mixture, specially inhibited to prevent attacks on aluminium alloy components.
4. Mix the required quantity of antifreeze liquid with half the quantity of clean water required to fill the system. Pour this into the flushed out radiator and top up with clean water. Run the engine straight away to thoroughly disperse the antifreeze throughout.
5. The percentages of antifreeze to use (in relation to the total cooling liquid capacity) are given in the table in next column.

Solution strength	Frost protection	Safe pump circulation
25%	−15°F (−26°C)	10°F (−12°C)
30%	−28°F (−33°C)	3°F (−16°C)
35%	−38°F (−39°C)	−4°F (−20°C)
40%	−42°F (−41°C)	−10°F (−23°C)
50%	−53°F (−47°C)	−32°F (−36°C)

10. Fan Belt - Removal, Replacement & Adjustment

1. If the fan belt is obviously badly worn, or stretched so far that it is still too slack at maximum adjustment, it should be renewed. It is wise to carry a spare at all times, as a broken belt means a stopped alternator and water pump. There is a limit to the miles one can do before the battery runs down, especially at night when lights are used.
2. Whether the belt has broken and dropped off, or is being taken off, first slacken the two nuts and bolts on which the alternator pivots and then the bolts underneath which lock the long slotted adjusting brace. Do not slacken any of the bolts more than is necessary to just move the alternator with a little force.
3. Move the alternator so that the fan belt may be removed.
4. Fit a new fan belt over the pulleys and move the alternator out until it is tight. Then tighten the bolts. This will be easier to do if the bolts are tight enough to allow it to move only when levered. Check the fan belt tension by depressing it between the alternator and water pump pulleys. It should not deflect more than ½ inch under 9 lb pressure. Do not overtighten the belt or excessive strain will be put on the alternator and pump bearings.
5. After a new belt has run for a few hundred miles check the tension again as it may have stretched and require re-adjustment.
6. There are no definite rules as regards frequency of checking but it only takes a second every time the oil and water levels are checked.

11. Water Temperature Gauge - Fault Diagnosis & Rectification

1. If no reading is recorded on the gauge when the engine is hot, the fault is in either the gauge, sender unit or wiring. Do NOT remove the wire from the sender unit and short it to earth to check whether a reading can be obtained. This will burn out the windings of the gauge.
2. If the fuel gauge is also not functioning the cause may be that the instrument voltage stabiliser unit is faulty.
3. Otherwise, disconnect the terminal from the transmitter unit (Photo) and insulate the end of the wire so that it will not short accidentally and damage the gauge.
4. Then measure the resistance in ohms, between the transmitter terminal and earth when the engine is cold and again when hot. If there is no difference then it is faulty and should be unscrewed and a new one fitted. If there is a variation in resistance measured then the gauge is probably faulty and will need renewal. Make sure first however, that the wire from sender to gauge is in order. Details of instrument removal will be found in Chapter 10.

NOTE: The section on cooling system fault finding will be found after the illustrations opposite

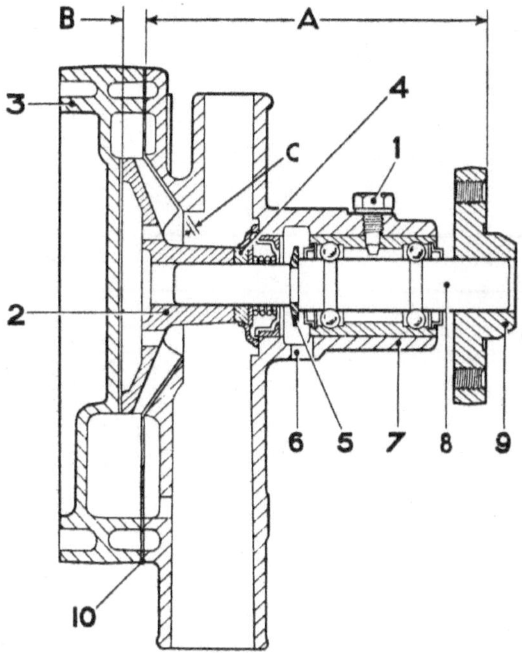

Fig.2.3. SECTIONED VIEW OF WATER PUMP GIVING CORRECT CLEARANCES

1 Bearing locating screw
2 Impeller
3 Impeller bearing
4 Seal
5 Water thrower
6 Drain hole
7 Pump body
8 Bearing assembly
9 Fan pulley centre
10 Gasket

Dimensions
A 4.088 in. (103.8 mm)
B 0.280 in. (7.1 mm)
C 0.010 in. (0.25 mm)

Sections 8.4 and 8.5. Removal and dismantling of water pump.

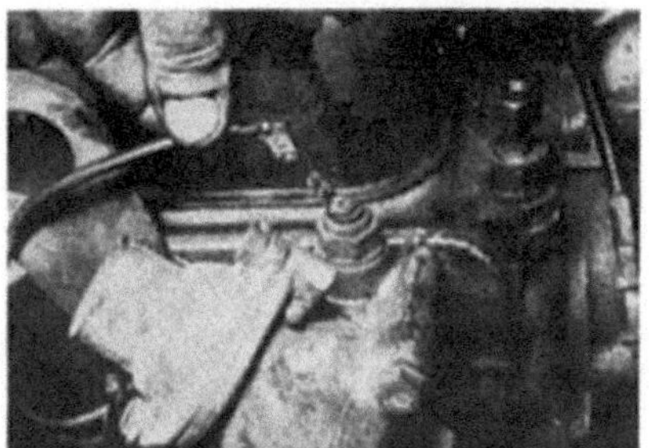

Section 11.3. Detaching lead from temperature gauge sender unit.

12. Cooling System - Fault Finding

Temperature gauges can be a valuable guide to the performance of the car, when related to the weather and other operating conditions. Keen owners always investigate any significant change of temperature which cannot be immediately accounted for, and the following table gives guidance for tracking down probable causes of trouble:

Symptom	Reason/s	Remedy
Loss of coolant but no overheating provided coolant level is kept topped up	Expansion bottle empty	Half fill expansion bottle
	Small leaks in system	Examine all hoses and connections for signs of cracks and leaks when engine is both cold and hot, stationary and running. If no signs, use proprietary sealer in coolant to stop any invisible leaks
Coolant level drops in radiator and expansion bottle fills up	Radiator cap opening pressure too low	Check and fit new radiator cap of correct type
Temperature gauge indicates constant over-heating but no loss of coolant	Radiator cap opening pressure too high	Check and fit new radiator cap of correct type and then diagnose reason for overheating
Overheating and loss of coolant only when overheated	Faulty thermostat	Check and renew if faulty
	Fan belt slipping	Check and adjust
	Engine out of tune due to ignition and/or fuel system settings being incorrect	Check ignition and fuel systems and adjust as required
	Blockage or restriction in circulation of cooling water	Check that no hoses have collapsed Drain, flush out and refill cooling system. Use chemical flushing compound if necessary
	Radiator cooling fins clogged up	Remove radiator and clean exterior as needed
	Blown cylinder head gasket or cracked cylinder head	Remove cylinder head for examination
	Sheared water pump impeller shaft	Remove pump and check
	Cracked cylinder body	Remove engine and examine and repair (if possible)
	New engine still tight	Adjust engine speeds to suit until run in
Engine runs too cool and heater inefficient	Thermostat missing or stuck open	Remove housing cover and inspect

Chapter 3 Fuel system and carburation

Contents

Specifications

Fuel Pump

Type	AC mechanical
Delivery pressure	2¾ – 4¼ lb sq in (0.19 – 0.29 kg cm^2)
Air cleaner	Dry element type

Carburettors

Rapier	Twin Stromberg 150 CDS
Slow running speed	800 – 900 rpm
Main needle size	6R
Needle size 5–10,000 ft	5AC
Needle size 10,000 ft or over	5AD
Spring	Blue
Fast idle adjustment (between screw head and cam)	0.050 in (1.27 mm)
Choke control	Manual
H120	Twin Weber 40 DCOE 34 and 35
Choke tube (large venturi)	30 mm
Auxiliary (small venturi)	4.5 mm
Main jet	100
Idle jet	45 F.4
Pump jet	35
Starting jet	60 F.S.
Emulsion tube	F.14
Air correction jet	140
Float weight	26 gm
Float level setting dimension	8.5 mm
Accelerator pump travel	20 mm
Alpine	Single Stromberg 150 CDS
Slow running speed	750 – 800 rpm
Main needle size	6P
Spring	Red
Choke control	Manual

Fuel Tank

Capacity	15 gallons (18.3 US gals, 68 litres)
Octane requirement	97 minimum (4 star)

1. General Description

A 15 gallon fuel tank is mounted under the rear of the car and from this fuel is drawn by an AC mechanical pump and delivered to the carburettors.

The pump is operated by an arm actuated by an eccentric on the camshaft and is located low down forward on the right hand side of the engine block. The pump incorporates a removable filter screen. In the case of the standard Rapier model, fuel is delivered to twin Stromberg 150 CDS carburettors, whilst on the more powerful H120 engine, twin Weber 40 DCOE carburettors are employed. The Alpine has a single Stromberg 150 CDS carburettor.

The output of the pump exceeds all normal requirements of the carburettor, and the level of the fuel in the carburettor float chambers is regulated by float operated needle valves. When the valve is closed, shutting off the fuel flow, the pump freewheels. The diaphragm is held up by the pressure in the line until such time as the carburettor needle valve opens, allowing the spring action of the pump to resume oscillating the diaphragm and delivering more fuel.

The air taken in through the carburettor is filtered by a renewable paper element or elements.

2. Routine Maintenance

1. Every 5,000 miles, or more frequently in very smoky, foggy, or dusty conditions, remove the air filter element and tap it smartly on a flat surface to dislodge any excess accumulations of dust on the outside. Clean out the interior of the filter housing. DO NOT try to wash, brush, or blow the elements out with compressed air as this could cause damage.
2. Lubricate all moving pivots on the carburettor controls with one or two drops of engine oil from time to time. There is no hard and fast rule about frequency but when you check the engine oil dipstick a drop off the end can be used for this purpose.
3. Every 1,000 miles on Stromberg 150 CDS carburettors, check the level of the oil in the hydraulic damper piston. See Section 6 for details.
4. Every 5,000 miles remove the fuel pump filter cover and examine the filter gauze after lifting it out. Blow through it to clear any particles. Do not use a cloth as strands of cotton or lint must not get into the system.
5. Every 10,000 miles renew the air filter element as described in the following sections.
6. Every 15,000 miles it is beneficial to remove and thoroughly clean the carburettor and float chamber. For procedures refer to the relevant sections in this Chapter.

3. Air Filter Elements - Removal & Replacement

1. With twin Stromberg carburettors (Fig.3.1), unhook the throttle return spring from its small attachment bracket on the back of the air cleaner. Note: If the engine has to be run with the air cleaner removed, connect the throttle return spring to the fuel feed tee piece between the carburettors, to avoid the engine racing up to a speed such that damage could be caused.
2. Where fitted, pull off the crankcase vent pipe on to the air cleaner (Photo).
3. Unscrew the four bolts which hold the air cleaner assembly to the carburettors (Photo). Once these are clear the whole unit may be lifted off (Photo) and separated to give access to the two elements.
4. When reassembling the unit make sure that the sealing rings are intact and correctly positioned. When fitting the elements, they should fit snugly over the locating ridges in the housing.
5. The air intake pipe may be positioned for 'Summer' or 'Winter' conditions by revolving the casing, before the bolts are tightened, so

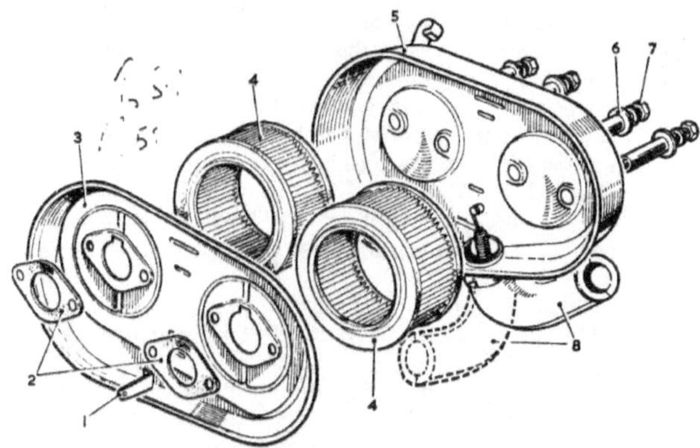

Fig.3.1. Air cleaner used with twin Stromberg CDS carburettors (broken outline of (8) shows winter position)

1 Throttle return spring attachment bracket
2 Air cleaner to carburettor flange gaskets
3 Air cleaner backplate
4 Air cleaner elements
5 Air cleaner casing
6 Distance pieces - four
7 Air cleaner fixing bolts - four
8 Air cleaner intake

Section 3.2. Disconnecting crankcase vent pipe (where fitted)

Section 3.3. Unbolting and removing air cleaner from twin Stromberg CDS carburettors

that the appropriate indication arrows line up. In the winter position the pipe draws air from a heated shroud around the exhaust pipe, reducing the chances of icing up troubles in cold conditions.

6. On H120 models fitted with twin Weber carburettors, the air cleaner is connected to the carburettor air box by means of a flexible tube. Undo the clip holding this tube to the carburettor air box and slide it off (Fig.3.2).

7. Turn the front wheels on to full right lock and then from under the left hand wing undo the two bolts and one nut securing the air cleaner to the body.

8. Remove the air cleaner from the car and undo the central wing nut to separate the two halves. Clean out the body and element as described in Section 2.1 above.

9. On reassembly check the condition of the sealing rings in the cover and the body and ensure the element fits correctly in the body. Replacement is a reversal of the removal procedure, but it is worth putting a little grease on the bolts and nut securing the air cleaner to the body to prevent these rusting in their somewhat exposed position under the wing.

10 The Alpine single element is simply removed and serviced by undoing the two through bolts securing the cover and body to the carburettor flange (Fig.3.3).

4. Stromberg 150 CDS Carburettor - Description & Principle of Operation

1. The Stromberg carburettor is a variable choke design with a single fuel delivery jet. This means that the cross-sectional area of the air intake passage through the carburettor varies according to demands made by the engine. The fuel, which is drawn into the air passage through a jet orifice, is metered by a tapered needle which moves in and out of the jet, thus varying the effective size of the orifice. This needle is attached to, and moves with, the air valve piston which controls the variable choke opening.

2. At rest, the air valve piston is right down, choking off the air supply, and the tapered needle is fully home virtually cutting off the fuel outlet from the jet. For starting, the cold start lever is first pulled, and this sets the cold start device so that fuel may be drawn into the main air passage via an independent passage which is opened up. It also opens the throttle flap a small amount. (On earlier types of Stromberg carburettors the cold start device consisted of mechanically lifting the air valve slightly, thus drawing the needle out of the jet to provide the richer mixture necessary.)

3. As soon as the engine fires the suction from the engine, or manifold depression, is partially diverted to the upper side of the chamber in which the diaphragm attached to the air valve piston is positioned. This causes the valve to rise and provides sufficient air flow to enable the engine to run. As the throttle is opened further, manifold depression is reduced and now it is the speed of air through the venturi which causes the depression in the upper chamber, thus causing the piston to rise further. If the throttle is opened suddenly, the natural tendency of the air valve piston to rise - causing a weak mixture when it is least required (i.e. during acceleration) — is prevented by a hydraulic damper which delays the piston in its upward travel. The air intake is thus restricted and a proportionately larger quantity of fuel to air is drawn through.

4. Under constant speed running conditions the air valve position is balanced by air speed through the venturi, throttle opening and the light pressure of the diaphragm return spring.

5. Stromberg 150 CDS Carburettors - Removal & Replacement

1. Remove the air cleaners as described in Section 3.

2. Unhook the throttle return spring from the air cleaner (Photo).

3. Undo the fuel pipe union between the two carburettors just below the T shaped pipe (Photo).

4. Detach the vacuum pipe from the connection to the mounting flange on the rear carburettor (Photo).

5. Slacken the screws securing the choke inner cables to the carburettor operating levers (Photo), undo the clips over the outer cables and lift the cables away (Photo).

6. Detach the throttle cable from the mounting bracket by undoing the locknut nearest the open end only otherwise the positioning will be upset (Photo). Alternatively, the bracket and cable may be detached together by undoing the bolt holding the bracket to the inlet manifold.

7. Unloop the cable from the throttle lever and take the nipple out of the recess (Photo).

8. The carburettors must be removed as a pair owing to the linkages joining them in the middle. Undo the four nuts holding the carburettors to the manifold. The right hand nut on the front carburettor may prove a little difficult to get at, but it can be removed with a flexible socket, or, as shown in the photo, with a box spanner and tommy bar.

9. The carburettors can now be lifted clear of the engine (Photo).

10. Replacement is a reversal of the removal procedure but take care on the following points.

11. When refitting the choke cables to the carburettors do not clip the outer cable in position until the operating arm has been checked in the fully open position. If the outer cable is clipped in position with the end too far down, the limit of travel of the operating arm will be restricted and result in difficult starting in cold weather.

12. Make sure that the throttle and choke cables are properly secured in their correct positions. If this is not done, variations can result in the amount of movement at the operating levers on the carburettors.

6. Stromberg 150 CDS Carburettor - Setting & Adjustments

1. Before making any adjustments to the carburettor settings make sure that your reasons for the adjustment are sound and that you only do one at a time. Check the result of each adjustment after it is made. The Stromberg carburettor is a finely balanced and relatively delicate instrument and can easily be put off tune.

2. Control settings are important. Make sure the operation of the choke cables moves the levers easily throughout their full range of movement, and return to the closed position when the knob is pushed home. Adjustment can be made by repositioning the inner cables relative to the operating arms at the small clamping screws. The outer cables can be repositioned as necessary where they clip to the brackets on the carburettors.

3. The throttle cable should also be checked for movement throughout its range. Make particularly sure that when the throttle flaps are in the fully open position the position of the accelerator pedal is as far down as it could possibly be, even with the cable disconnected. Otherwise pressure on the pedal will impart severe strain on the cable, and more important, on the throttle spindles and bearings. Adjustment should be made at the point where the end of the outer cable is located in the bracket near the carburettors. Slacken the two locknuts and move the outer cable so that when the accelerator pedal is fully depressed the throttle is just fully open.

4. Referring to Fig.3.4, slow running is adjusted by a screw on each carburettor (1) which regulates the position of the throttle flaps when the accelerator cable is in the fully closed position. The single jet in each carburettor controls fuel mixture throughout the full operational range.

5. If satisfactory slow running or synchronisation cannot be obtained by manipulation of the adjustment screws proceed on each carburettor individually as follows. First remove the air valve piston damper (2) from the top of the carburettor. Insert a thin rod or screwdriver

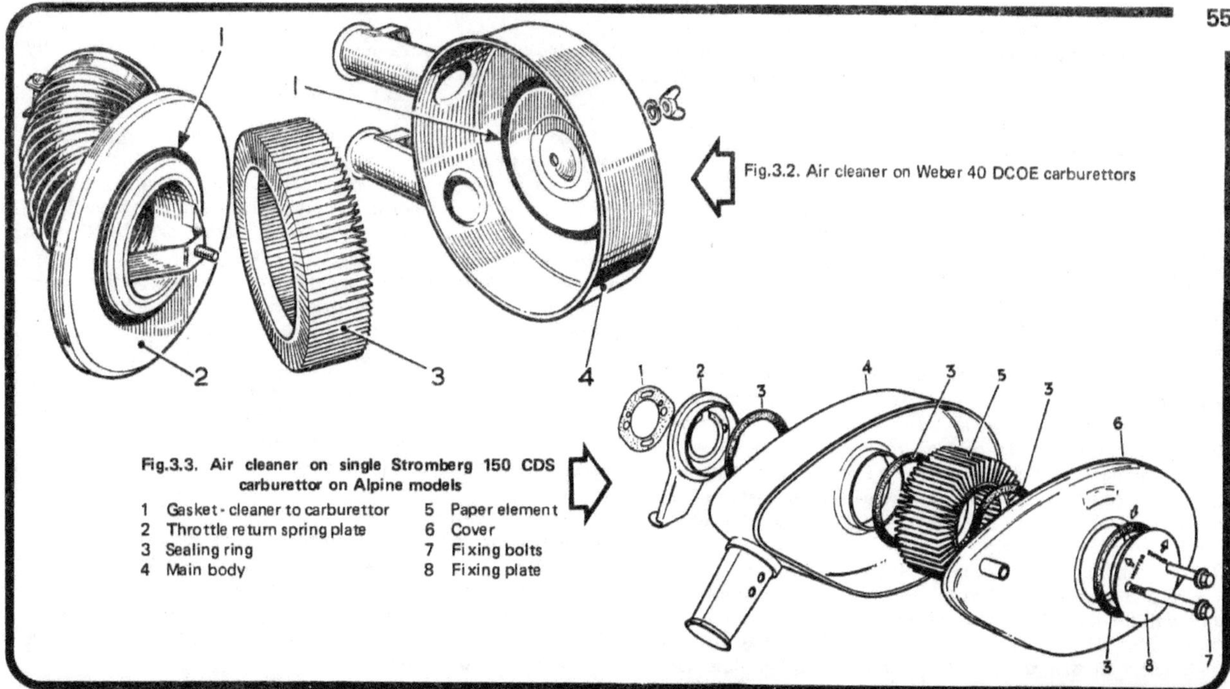

Fig.3.2. Air cleaner on Weber 40 DCOE carburettors

Fig.3.3. Air cleaner on single Stromberg 150 CDS carburettor on Alpine models

1 Gasket - cleaner to carburettor
2 Throttle return spring plate
3 Sealing ring
4 Main body
5 Paper element
6 Cover
7 Fixing bolts
8 Fixing plate

Section 5.2.
Unhooking throttle return spring

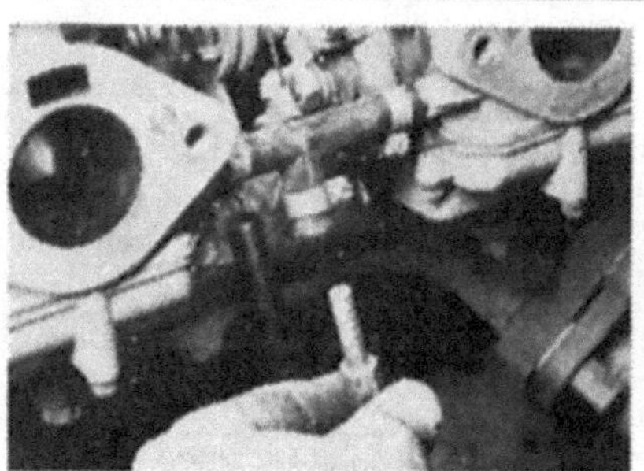

Section 5.3 freeing final pipe union

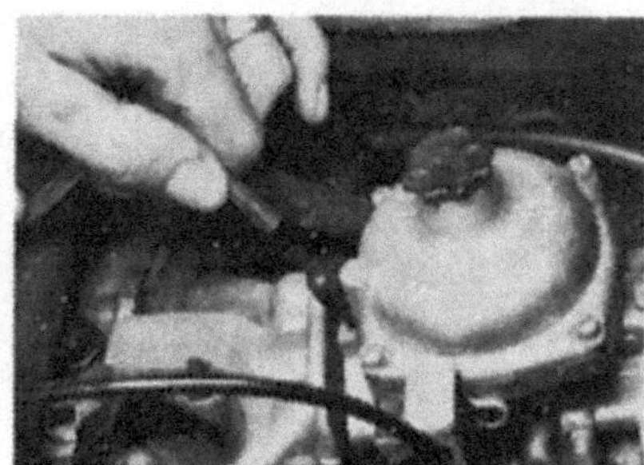

Section 5.4.
Detaching vacuum pipe

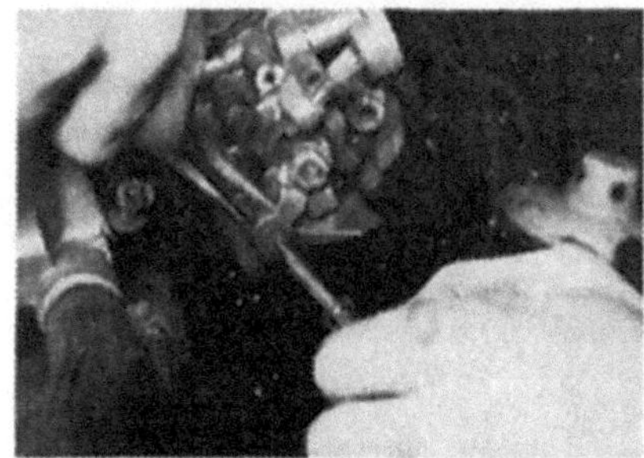

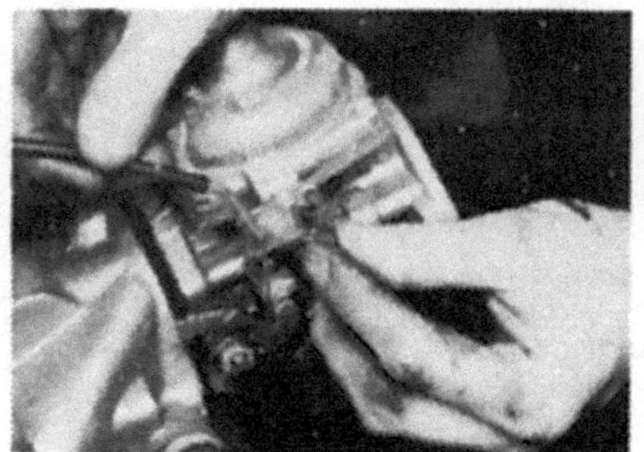

Section 5.5.
Disconnecting choke cables

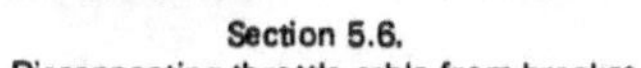

Section 5.6.
Disconnecting throttle cable from bracket

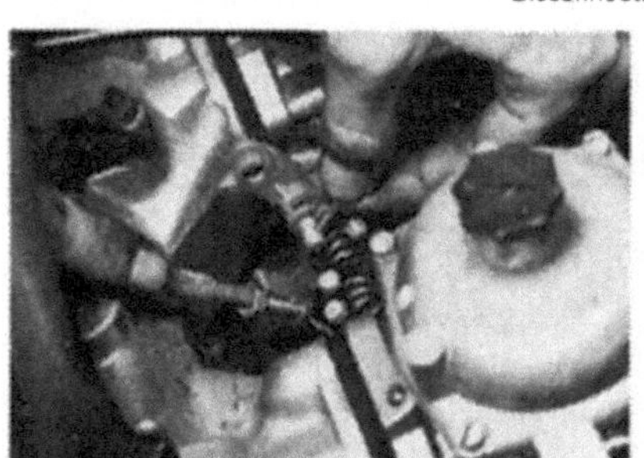

Section 5.7 Unhooking throttle cable from lever on carburettor linkage

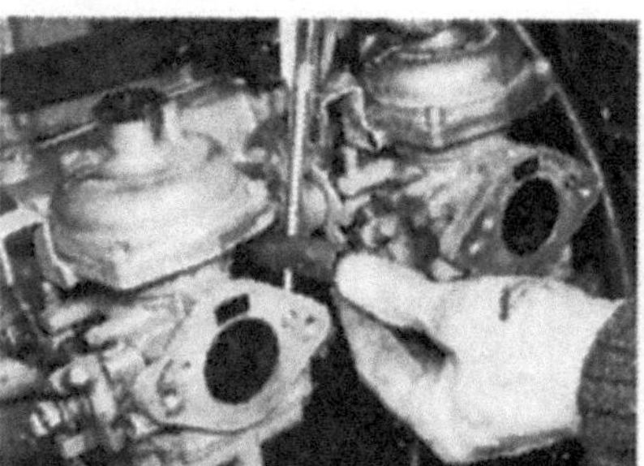

Sections 5.8 and 5.9. Removing the pair together

Section 5. Sequences in removing Stromberg 150 CDS carburettors

into the top and use this to hold the piston down. At the same time turn the jet adjustment screw (5), (N.B. NOT the jet bush retainer) upwards, so that the jet itself eventually touches the air valve piston. This will be felt when the adjusting screw meets resistance. Release the downward pressure on the valve piston and then check that the piston moves freely. This can be done by lifting the pin and letting it fall. An audible 'click' should be heard as the piston hits the jet bridge. (If this does not occur then the jet will need centralising as described later.) Back off the jet adjusting screw two complete turns.

6. Refill the piston damper bore to within ¼ inch (6 mm) of its upper edge with clean engine oil (do not use very low viscosity oils). Refit the damper piston. Run the engine until normal temperature is reached and adjust the throttle stop screw (1) to obtain an idling speed of 700/800 rpm. It is permissible to move the jet adjuster screw not more than ½ turn in either direction in order to achieve the desired smooth running. If no success is achieved it will be necessary to check the needle position in the piston. This involves partial dismantling and is covered in the next Section.

7. The jet will need to be centralised if movement of the piston valve is binding the needle against the side of the jet orifice. The jet is located in a bush which permits it to move up and down when the jet adjusting screw is turned. The bush is locked into position by the jet bush retaining screw and when this is slackened the jet bushing, together with the jet, is free to move laterally. To centralise the jet, first slacken the jet bushing retainer by ½ turn. Then turn the jet adjusting screw so that the jet is level with the bridge face (as described in the previous adjustment). Then tap the jet bushing retainer to assist the jet to find its position round the needle. The jet bushing retainer screw should then be tightened and the piston lifted with the pin and allowed to drop. An audible click indicates that it is falling to the bottom of its stroke without hindrance. Then re-adjust the jet as described for the last adjustment in paragraph 6.

8. In certain cases of excessive fuel consumption or flooding it may be that the floats or needle valve positions need re-setting. For this, dismantling is necessary and the adjustment procedure is incorporated in the next Section.

9. The carburettor is so designed that when the cold start device is used the throttle is automatically opened a specified amount (Fig.3.5). This ensures that the engine speed is kept up; otherwise the rich mixture would stall the engine at low revolutions. The throttle opening is set by the fast idle adjustment screw. The head of this screw bears against the fast idle cam mounted on the cold start device boss. The screw may be adjusted to give the correct gap between head and cam, with the cold start device closed, after slackening the locknut. The clearances are given under 'Specifications'.

10. To ensure that the two carburettors are perfectly synchronised listen with a suitable length of pipe held at the same point on each carburettor intake. A similar hiss should be heard from each one. If a different hiss is heard, slacken off the bolt (1) on the connecting rod between the two carburettors and adjust the slow running adjustment screws (1) on each carburettor until a similar hiss is heard, then re-tighten the clamp bolt (4).

7. Stromberg 150 CDS Carburettor – Dismantling, Inspection & Reassembly

1. Do not dismantle a carburettor unless it is absolutely necessary. This should be only for cleaning at intervals of 15,000 miles or when systematic diagnosis indicates that there is a fault with it. The internal mechanism is delicate and finely balanced, and unnecessary tinkering will probably do more harm than good.

2. Although certain parts may be removed with the carburettor still attached to the engine, it is considered safer to remove it and work over a bench.

3. Having removed the carburettor, take out the piston damper by unscrewing the top cap.

4. Undo the four screws holding the depression chamber cover in position. Mark the edge of the cover and carburettor body so that it may be replaced in the same position. Then carefully lift it off, watching that the diaphragm return spring does not get stretched in the process. The return spring should be carefully detached from its upper and lower seatings and laid to one side. If this spring is kinked, stretched or treated in any way that may affect its pressure when installed, the balance of the carburettor will be upset. Renew it (with one of the correct colour code) if in doubt.

5. Lift out the air valve piston and diaphragm together (Fig.3.8). If the diaphragm shows signs of perforation, cracking or other damage it must be renewed. Remove the four screws and washers by which the retaining ring secures it to the piston. Note also that the diaphragm has tabs on its inner and outer edges that locate into slots in the piston and body of the carburettor. When refitting a diaphragm it is most important that the centre section seats properly on the piston. It is easily dislodged when fitting the retaining ring. With the piston removed it is possible to check that the needle is correctly fitted. The shoulder of the needle should be flush with the face of the piston. If not, it may be reset after slackening the needle locking screw in the side of the piston.

6. The float chamber may be removed next. First unscrew and remove the jet adjusting screw. See that the 'O' ring around it is in good condition. Undo the six screws which hold the float chamber to the carburettor body. The chamber may then be carefully pulled down over the jet bushing retainer. It is not essential to remove the jet and associated parts unless it is being renewed. The resistance to pulling off the float chamber will be the 'O' ring seal which is fitted around the jet bushing retainer. This must be examined for condition.

7. With the float chamber removed, the carburettor may be cleaned with petrol or paraffin (nothing else). Use an air jet where possible to blow out the orifices in the body to the cold start device and the main jet area.

8. When the float chamber is removed the floats may be checked for correct setting. With the carburettor in the inverted position and the needle valve in the closed position the highest point of the float should be 15.5 – 16.5 mm. above the joint face of the body. Both parts of the float should be equal and if necessary the arm that contacts the needle valve may be bent to adjust the float position. If the floats are apparently set correctly and excessive fuel consumption or flooding has been experienced, it is quite possible that the needle valve is worn, so a new one should be fitted. If the needle valve is one which can be separated from its seat, a ridge in the valve face indicates wear.

9. If there is any sign of play between the throttle spindle and the bushes in the body it may be necessary to consider removing the spindle. This can be done after removing the nut holding the throttle operating lever, removing the two screws securing the throttle plate, and drawing the spindle out.

10. Reassembly is a reversal of the dismantling procedure. The float chamber gasket need not necessarily be renewed but it is a good idea to fit three new 'O' rings on the jet, jet bushing and jet bushing retainer. When the diaphragm and piston assembly is replaced make sure the tabs fit the grooves.

11. The jet centralisation and adjustment and fast idle cam clearances may be set before replacing the carburettor on the engine.

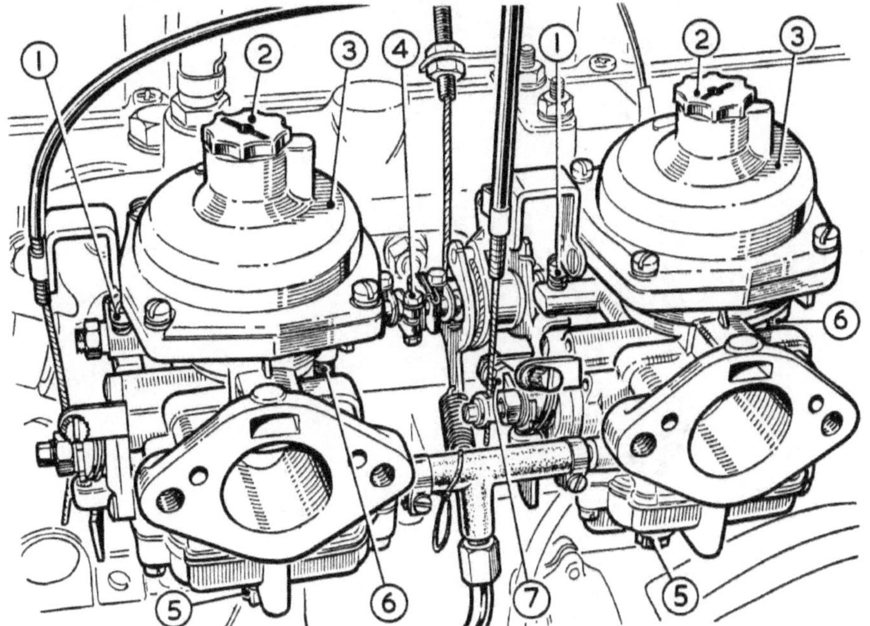

Fig.3.4. THROTTLE SYNCHRONISATION AND JET ADJUSTMENT OF TWIN STROMBERG 150 CDS CARBURETTORS

1 Slow running speed adjustment screw
2 Air valve piston hydraulic damper
3 Depression chamber cover
4 Coupling clamping bolt
5 Jet adjustment
6 Air valve piston lifting pin
7 Fast idle speed adjustment screw

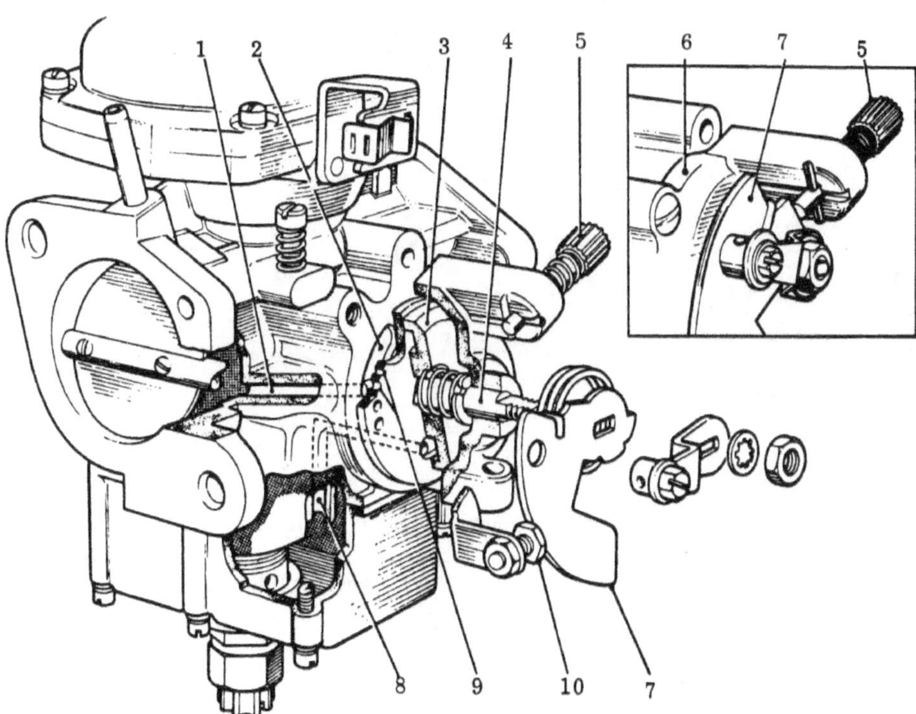

Fig.3.5. COLD START DEVICE ON STROMBERG 150 CDS

1 Drilling for fuel from disc valve
2 Port to fuel feed drilling from disc valve
3 Disc valve
4 Dis valve spindle
5 Two position stop for cold start opening limit
6 Starter device outer housing
7 Fast idle cam
8 Drilling for fuel from float chamber to disc valve
9 Orifices for fuel in disc valve
10 Fast idle adjustment screw

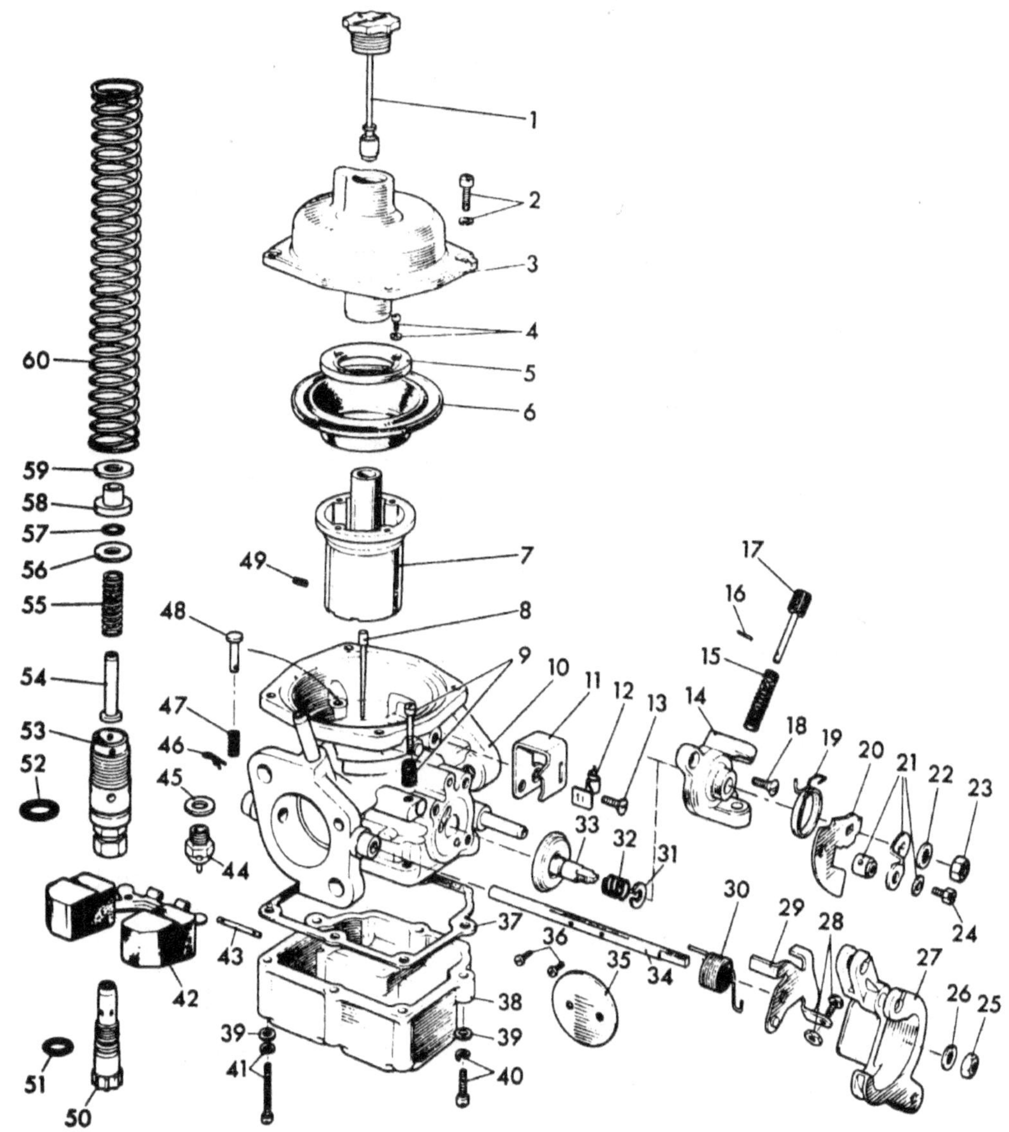

Fig.3.6. SINGLE STROMBERG 150 CDS CARBURETTOR AS FITTED TO ALPINE MODEL

1 Air valve piston damper
2 Screw and spring washer (4)
3 Suction cover chamber
4 Screw and spring washer (4)
5 Diaphragm retaining spring
6 Diaphragm
7 Air valve piston
8 Metering needle
9 Slow running adjustment screw
10 Carburettor body
11 Choke cable bracket
12 Choke cable clip
13 Screw
14 Starter cover
15 Travel stop spring
16 Pin
17 Travel stop
18 Fixing screw (2)
19 Fast idle cam return spring
20 Fast idle cam
21 Lever
22 Washer
23 Nut
24 Screw
25 Nut
26 Washer
27 Guide plate
28 Adjusting screw
29 Stop lever
30 Return spring
31 Spring retainer
32 Disc valve spring
33 Starter assembly disc valve
34 Throttle spindle
35 Throttle valve
36 Throttle valve fixing screws
37 Gasket
38 Float chamber
39 Washer
40 Screw (short) (2)
41 Screw (long) (2)
42 Float assembly
43 Float pivot pin
44 Float valve assembly
45 Valve seat washer
46 Retainer
47 Spring
48 Air valve piston lifting pin
49 Locking screw
50 Jet adjustment
51 'O' ring jet adjustment
52 'O' ring jet bush retaining screw
53 Jet bushing retaining screw
54 Jet
55 Jet spring
56 Washer
57 'O' ring jet
58 Jet and centralising bush
59 Washer
60 Air valve piston return spring

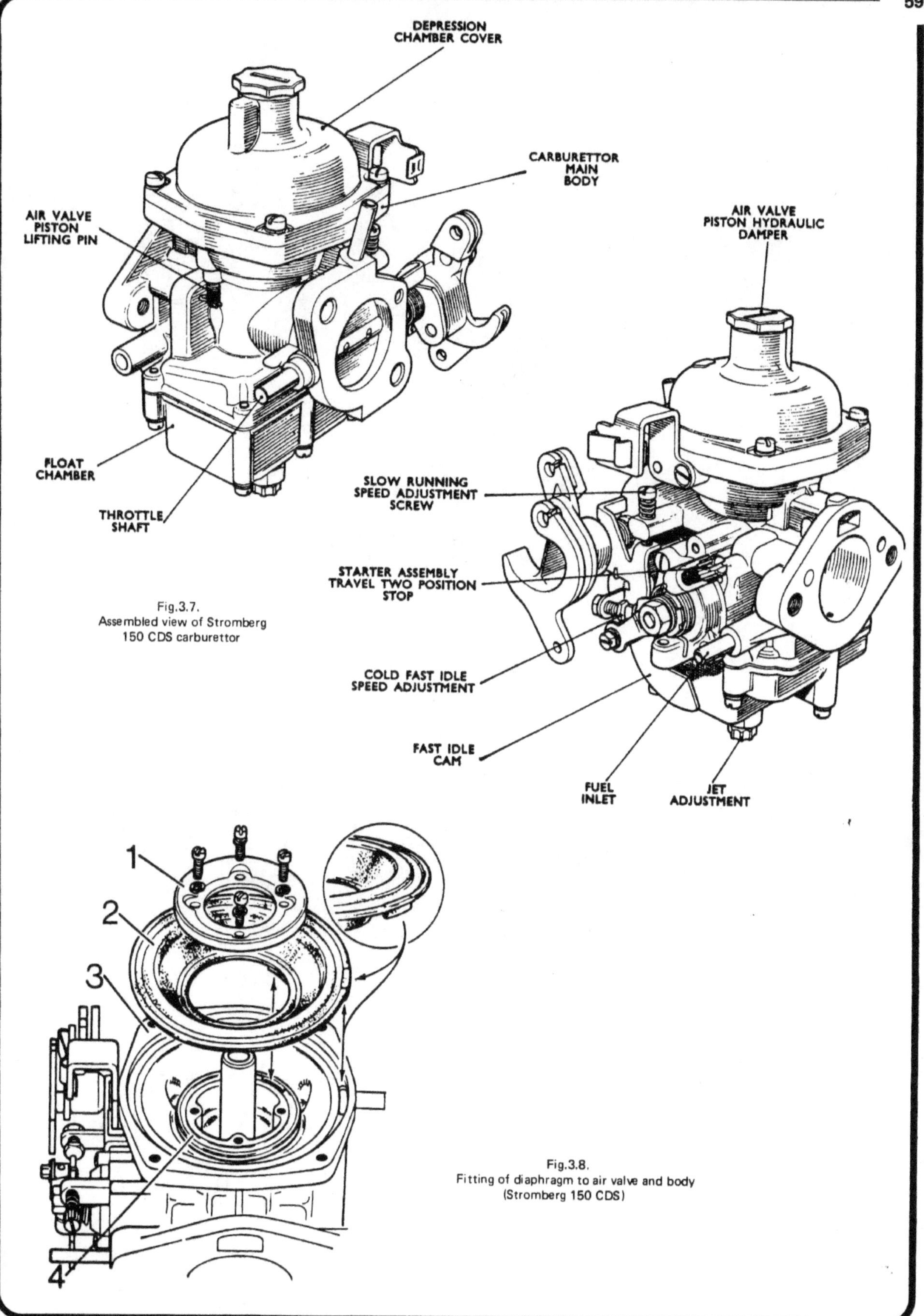

Fig.3.7.
Assembled view of Stromberg 150 CDS carburettor

Fig.3.8.
Fitting of diaphragm to air valve and body (Stromberg 150 CDS)

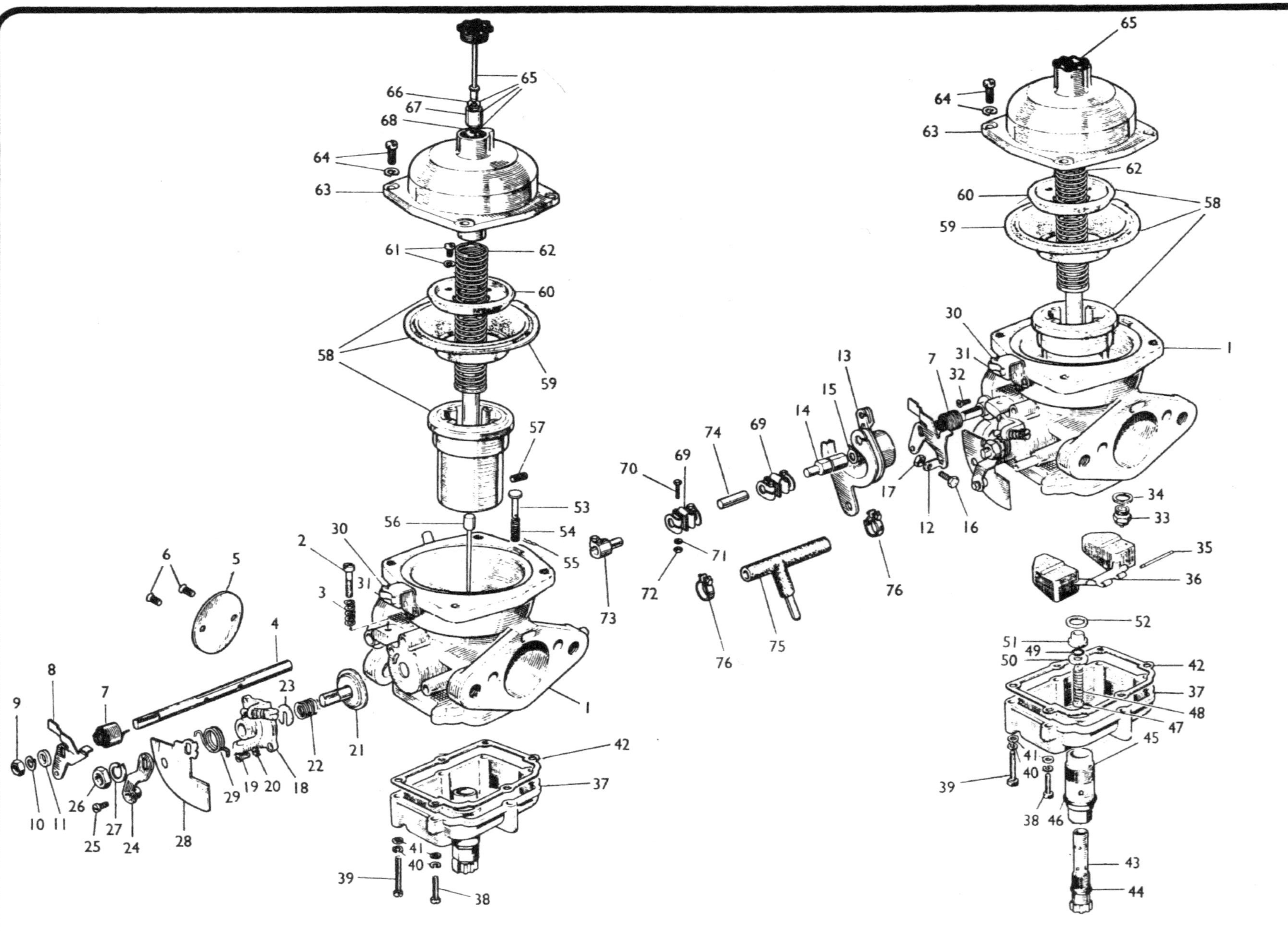

Fig.3.9. EXPLODED VIEW OF TWIN STROMBERG 150 CDS CARBURETTOR INSTALLATION

1 Carburettor body
2 Throttle stop screw
3 Spring
4 Throttle spindle
5 Throttle butterfly
6 Screw
7 Throttle return spring
8 Throttle stop lever
9 Nut
10 Washer
11 Spacing washer
12 Stop
13 Throttle lever
14 Nut
15 Tab washer
16 Fast idle screw
17 Locknut
18 Cover
19 Screw
20 Washer
21 Spindle
22 Spring
23 Washer
24 Starter lever
25 Screw
26 Nut
27 Washer
28 Cam lever
29 Spring
30 Bracket and clip
31 Clip
32 Screw
33 Needle valve
34 Washer
35 Float spindle
36 Float
37 Float chamber
38 Screw
39 Screw
40 Spring washer
41 Washer
42 Gasket
43 Screw
44 'O' ring
45 Screw
46 'O' ring
47 Jet orifice
48 Spring
49 'O' ring
50 Washer
51 Bushing
52 Washer
53 Air valve pin
54 Spring
55 Clip
56 Needle
57 Screw
58 Valve
59 Diaphragm
60 Retaining ring
61 Screw and spring washer
62 Spring
63 Suction chamber cover
64 Screw and spring washer
65 Damper
66 Damper washer
67 Bushing
68 Ring
69 Coupling
70 Screw
71 Washer
72 Nut
73 Sleeve
74 Coupling rod
75 Fuel 'T' piece
76 Clip

NOTE
Information on servicing
WEBER 40 DCOE
carburettors
starts overleaf

8. Weber 40 DCOE Carburettors - Adjustments

1. Before carrying out any adjustments to the Weber carburettors read Sections 6.1 to 6.3 inclusive with reference to carburettor controls.
2. Referring to Fig.3.10, slow running adjustment is controlled by the screw (3) between the two carburettors. Clockwise rotation increases the idling speed and anticlockwise rotation decreases it. If after obtaining the correct idling speed of 1,000 rpm the running appears to be uneven the carburettors will have to be synchronised.
3. Thoroughly warm up the engine, then remove the carburettor air box. Check the tightness of all manifold and carburettor retaining nuts and bolts to ensure there are no air leaks which could cause the uneven running.
4. Screw in the mixture control screws (1) lightly on to their seats then back them off half a turn each. Start up the engine and adjust the throttle stop screw until the engine runs at 1000–1200 rpm.
5. Listen with a suitable length of pipe held at the same point on each air intake. A similar hiss should be heard from each one. If the hiss is different adjust the synchronising screw (2) until a similar hiss is obtained.
6. Listening to the engine very carefully, or with an assistant in the car watching the tachometer, adjust each mixture control screw by no more than 1/12th of a turn at a time until the highest engine speed is obtained as each screw is adjusted. Clockwise movement of the screws weakens the mixture and anticlockwise richens it. If there is no response to these adjustments it indicates that there is an air leak either at the inlet manifold gasket or at the joint between the carburettor and the inlet manifold.
7. Finally adjust the slow running to 1000 rpm with the adjustment screw (3). Short out each spark plug in turn and if the adjustments have been done correctly there should be the same falling off of revs as each plug is shorted out.

9. Weber 40 DCOE Carburettors - Removal & Replacement

1. The operations for removing the Weber 40 DCOE carburettors are much the same as those for removing the Stromberg 150 CDS units described in Section 5, so only brief instruction will be given in this Section.
2. Disconnect the air cleaner hose at the carburettor air box end by releasing the clip (Fig.3.11).
3. Remove the air box from the carburettor by undoing the two long through bolts and nuts.
4. Disconnect the fuel pipe at the T piece between the carburettors and disconnect the throttle operating rod at its upper end at its ball joint with the cable lever.
5. Disconnect both choke cables at the carburettor ends, then remove all eight nuts, spring washer and flat washers holding the carburettors to the inlet manifold, and withdraw the carburettors, still connected together. Note the rubber sealing rings between the carburettors and the manifold.
6. To refit the carburettors reverse the above procedure but carefully note the following points:
7. The rubber sealing rings mentioned above are used to make an air-tight joint between the carburettors and the manifold in conjunction with double coil spring washers under the carburettor flange fixing nuts. This setup gives a certain amount of flexibility to the carburettor mounting which minimises the vibration which can cause excessive aeration of the fuel.
8. The rubber sealing rings can be re-used if they are in good condition, but the coil spring washers should always be replaced by new ones once the carburettors have been removed.
9. The carburettor flange fixing nuts must be tightened evenly so that there is a gap of 0.020 – 0.025 in (0.5 to 0.6 mm) between the spring washer coils when the gaps between the carburettor and inlet manifold flanges are parallel.
10. This can be achieved on the lower nuts by tightening them down until the spring washers are just fully compressed and then undoing each nut a quarter of a turn. This must be done after all the easily accessible nuts have been correctly tightened and the coil gaps set correctly.

10. Weber 40 DCOE Carburettors - Dismantling for Cleaning

1. Do not dismantle the carburettor unless you are absolutely certain that there is a fault within it, as unnecessary tinkering can well upset the fine balance within the instrument.
2. Referring to Fig.3.13, remove the circular cover (9) by undoing the wing nut on its top, and remove the slow running jets (10) and the air correction jets (11).
3. Now remove the two accelerator pump jets (2) and undo the progression hole inspection cover screws (3).
4. Remove the float chamber cover (1) by undoing the five retaining screws and take out the starter jets (16).
5. Undo and remove the fuel filter cover plug (8) from the float chamber cover and take off the gauze filter. Wash it in petrol and dry it with low pressure compressed air if available.
6. Allow the floats to hang down as low as possible and with compressed air blow through the fuel feed hole (7) which is normally covered by the filter.
7. Remove all fuel and any dirt or water that may have accumulated from the float chamber and the well below the main jets which is accessible through the small hole (12).
8. Carefully blow through all the jets previously removed with compressed air. Do NOT under any circumstances use wire or any hard object to clean the jets, as this will enlarge or score them and thereby upset the workings of the carburettor.
9. Having cleaned all the jets, replace them in their locations. Before replacing the float chamber cover it is worth checking that the float level is correct.
10. Fig. 3.14 shows the method of checking the float level and gives dimensional details of a small gauge that needs to be made up.
11. Check that the float can move freely on its fulcrum pin (3). Also examine the float lever (5) for signs of pitting where it contacts the needle valve. If wear is present it must be renewed as it can cause faulty operation of the needle valve.
12. Check that the needle valve body (1) is screwed tightly into its housing and that the pin ball end (4) of the spring loaded damping device in the needle valve is not jammed.
13. Hold the float chamber cover (8) in a vertical position so that the weight of the float allows the float lever to just contact the needle valve. It must not move the ball end of the needle damper pin. In this position both floats should just contact the 8.5 mm steps on the gauge when placed between the cover gasket face and the floats at their highest points. The soldered seams on the floats must not make contact with the gauge.
14. If the float level is found to be incorrect carefully bend the lever tab (5) to correct it. Take care when bending the tab to keep its face at right angles to the needle centre line.
15. Having got the float level correct, check that the total float movement from its level position to its lowest point is 6.5 mm (0.256 in). This is in fact 15 mm (0.591 in) from the gasket face on the cover. This movement, if wrong, can be corrected by bending the lug (2).
16. Once all is correct refit the float chamber cover.

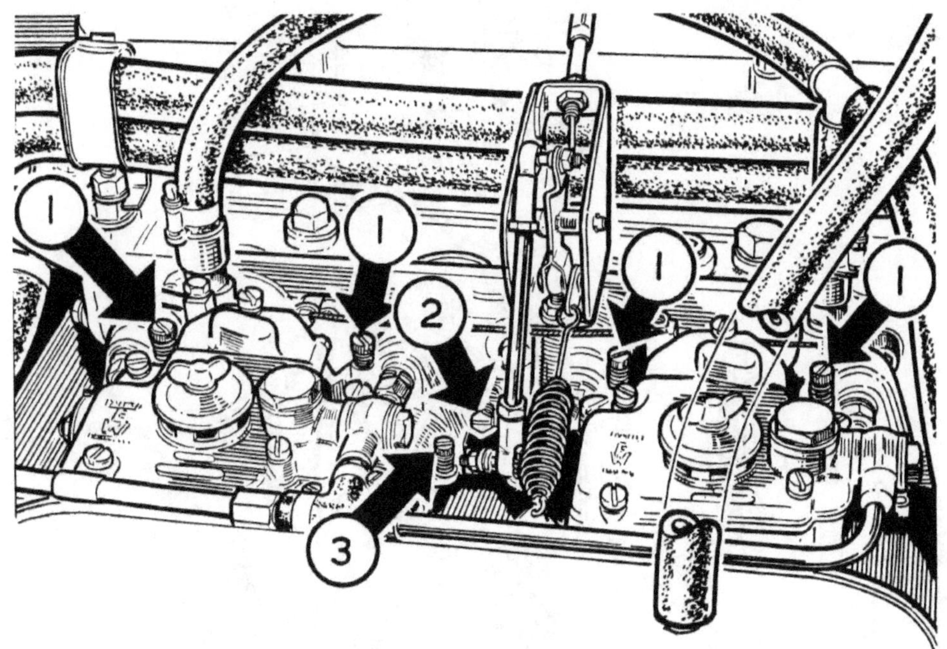

Fig.3.10. SLOW RUNNING AND SYNCHRONISING ADJUSTMENTS ON TWIN WEBER 40 DCOE INSTALLATION

1 Slow running mixture volume control screws
2 Carburettor synchronising adjustment screw
3 Slow running speed adjustment screw

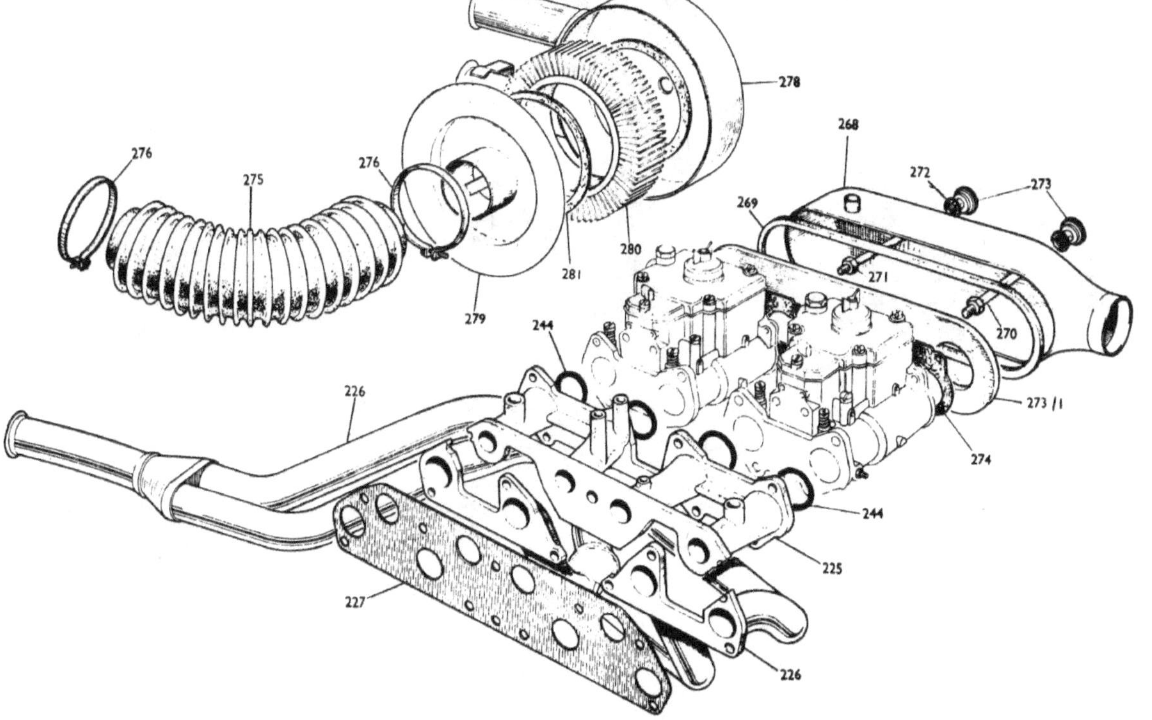

Fig.3.11. AIR CLEANER, MANIFOLDS & AIR BOX FITTED TO H120 MODELS

225 Inlet manifold
226 Exhaust manifold
227 Manifold gasket
244 Sealing rings
268 Air box
269 Gasket
270 Stud
271 Locknut
272 Fibre washer
273 Nut
273/1 Backplate
274 Gasket
275 Air hose
276 Clip
278 Air filter cover
279 Filter body
280 Filter element
281 Sealing ring

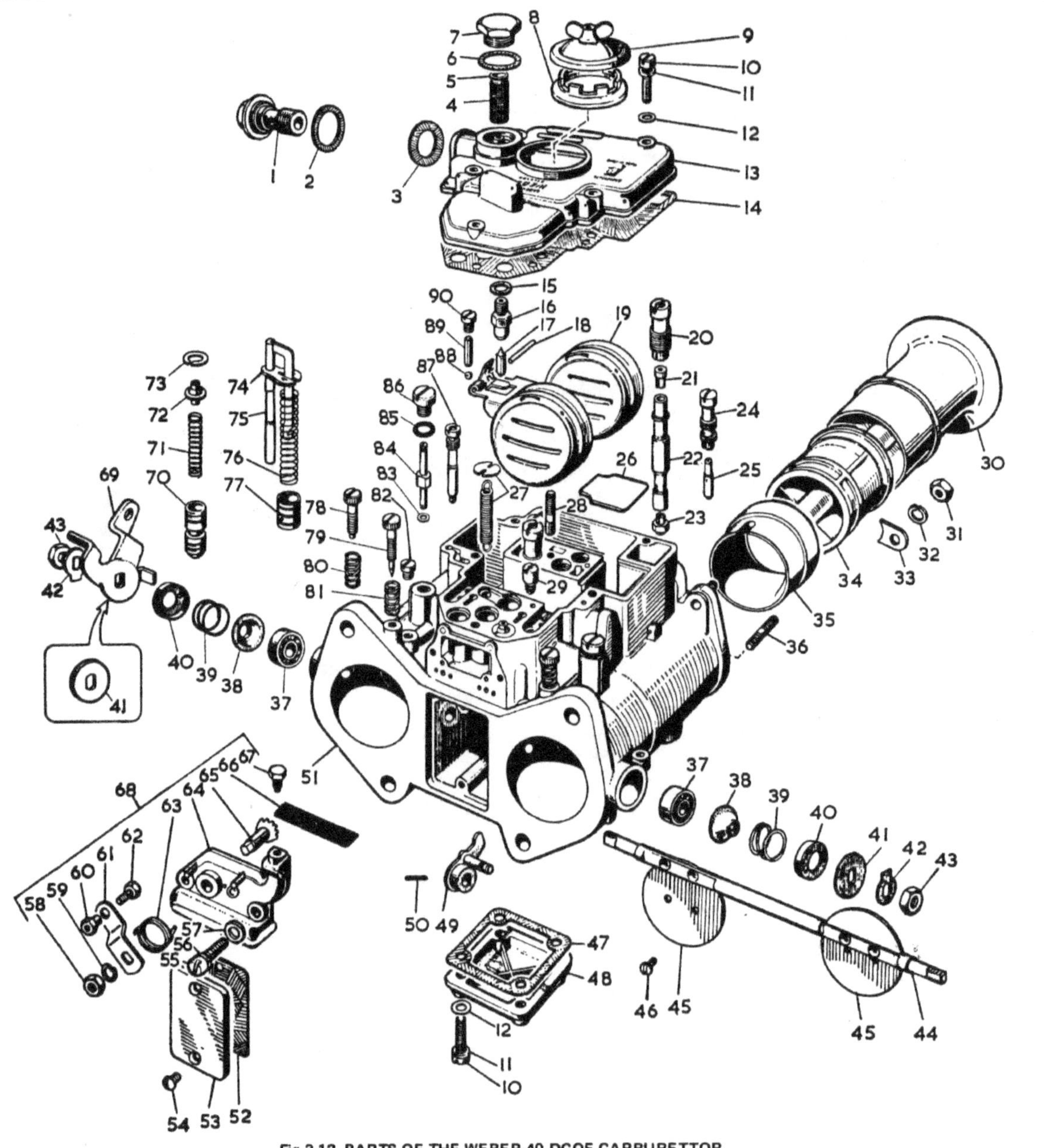

Fig.3.12. PARTS OF THE WEBER 40 DCOE CARBURETTOR

1 Fuel inlet union
2 Washer
3 Washer
4 Filter gauze
5 Bushing
6 Washer
7 Filter cover plug
8 Float chamber air vent
9 Jet inspection cover
10 Screw
11 Spring washer
12 Brass washer
13 Float chamber cover
14 Gasket
15 Washer
16 Needle valve body
17 Needle valve
18 Pin
19 Twin floats
20 Emulsion tube holder
21 Air correction jet
22 Emulsion tube
23 Main jet
24 Slow running jet holder
25 Slow running jet
26 Cover plate
27 Spring and anchorage
28 Stud
29 Accelerator pump inlet valve
30 Air inlet
31 Nut
32 Spring washer
33 Plate
34 Auxiliary venturi
35 Large venturi
36 Stud
37 Bearing
38 Dust cover
39 Spring
40 Cover
41 Distance washer
42 Lock washer
43 Nut
44 Throttle spindle
45 Throttle plates
46 Screw
47 Gasket
48 Cover plate
49 Accelerator pump control lever
50 Pin
51 Carburettor body
52 Gasket
53 Cover plate
54 Screw
55 Screw
56 Spring washer
57 Washer
58 Nut
59 Spring washer
60 Choke cable attachment
61 Starter device operating lever
62 Screw
63 Return spring
64 Cold start device body
65 Starter shaft
66 Gauze
67 Screw
68 Cold start device assembly
69 Throttle lever
70 Starter valve
71 Return spring
72 Spring guide and retainer
73 Spring ring
74 Retainer plate
75 Accelerator pump control rod
76 Return spring
77 Piston
78 Slow running adjustment screw
79 Volume control screw
80 Spring
81 Spring
82 Progression hole cover screw
83 Gasket washer
84 Accelerator pump jet
85 Sealing ring
86 Screw plug
87 Starting jet
88 Ball valve
89 Weight
90 Screw

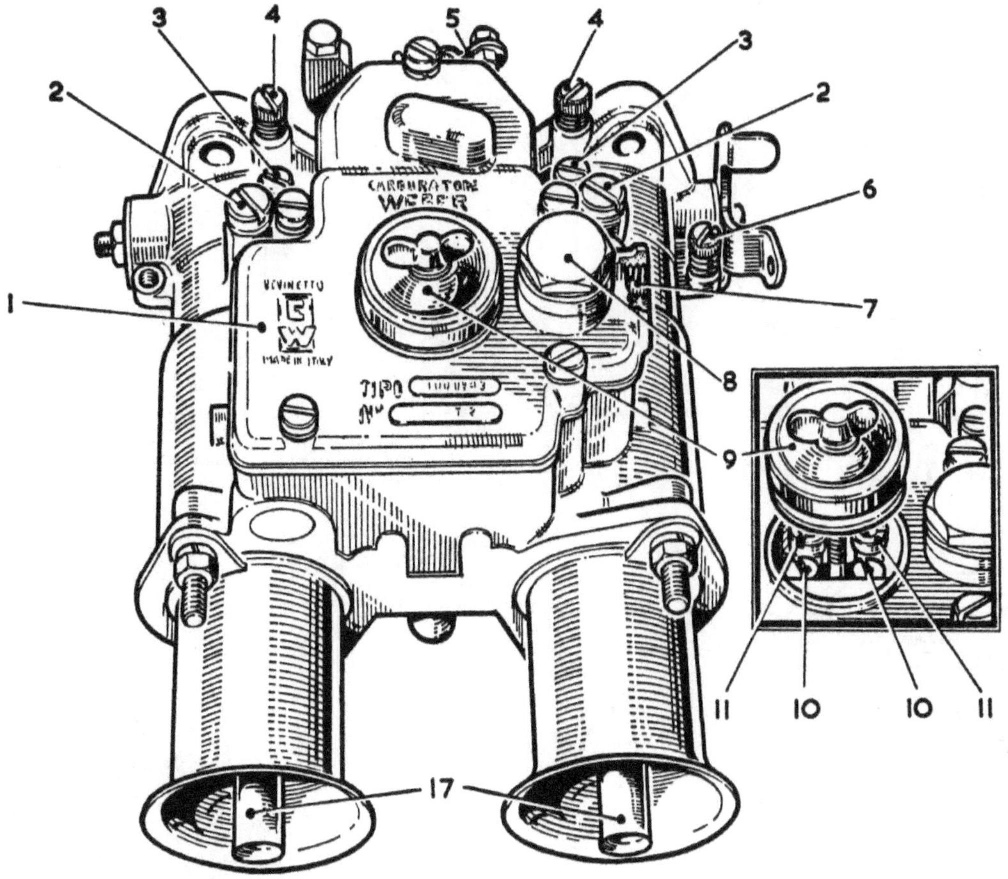

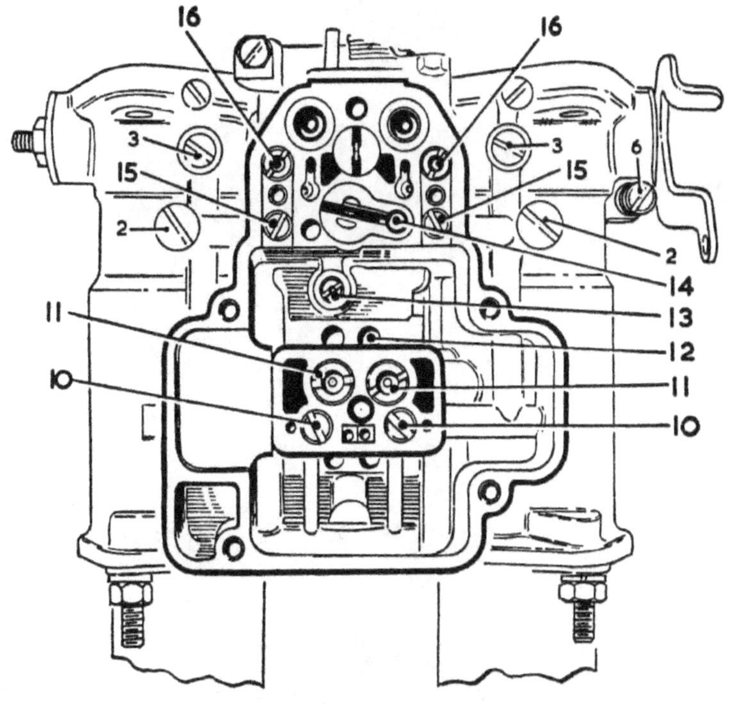

Fig.3.13. Weber 40 DCOE Carburettor: External View With Float Chamber Cover Removed

1 Float chamber cover
2 Accelerator pump jets
3 Progression hole inspection cover screws
4 Slow running mixture volume control screws
5 Cold start device operating lever
6 Slow running speed adjustment screw
7 Fuel inlet
8 Fuel filter cover plug
9 Removable cover for 10 and 11
10 Slow running jet assemblies
11 Main jet-emulsion tube-air correction jet assemblies
12 Feed holes to well below main and slow running jets
13 Accelerator pump inlet valve
14 Accelerator pump
15 Accelerator pump outlet valves
16 Starter jets
17 Small venturi extensions

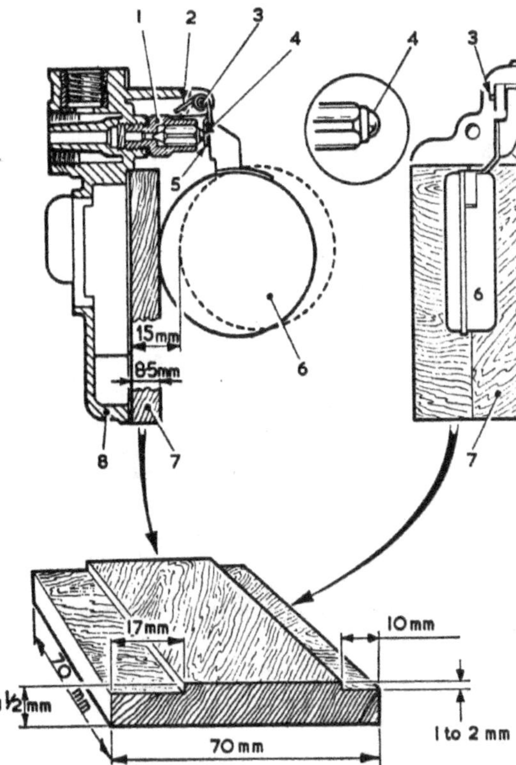

Fig.3.14. Method of checking Weber carburettor float level, and details of gauge required

1 Needle valve body
2 Float lever travel limit stop
3 Fulcrum pin
4 Needle valve - spring loaded damping device end
5 Float lever - tab bent for level adjustment
6 Float
7 Hardwood gauge - used for float level check
8 Float cover assembly

11. Fuel Pump - Removal & Replacement

1. The fuel pump will need removing if it is to be dismantled for overhaul. Disconnect the fuel lines by undoing the union on the inlet side and pulling off the connector pipe on the outlet side (Photo).
3. Undo the two nuts holding the pump flange to the crankcase and take off the pump (Photo). Keep the spacer and gaskets together and do not discard them. If necessary blank off the fuel line from the tank to prevent loss of fuel.
3. Replacement is a reversal of the removal procedure. Make sure that the total thickness of gaskets and spacer is the same as came off (Photo). After starting the engine, check that the fuel line connections are not leaking.

12. Fuel Pump - Inspection, Dismantling & Reassembly

1. First clean the pump exterior thoroughly and mark the edges of the two halves of the body.
2. Undo the cover retaining clip and lift off the cover. The gasket and gauze filter may then be removed.
3. Remove the six screws and washers holding the two halves of the pump together and the top half may then be lifted off.
4. The diaphragm and pull rod should then be pushed down a little against the pressure of the return spring and turned clockwise ¼ of a turn. This will disengage the pull rod from the operating link and the diaphragm may be lifted out.
5. If there are signs of wear in the rocker arm pivot pin, and rocker arm and link bushes, then they should be renewed. They can be taken from the pump body by first clamping the rocker arm in a vice, and then tapping the body away with a soft faced hammer.
6. The valve assemblies should only be removed from the upper body if renewal is necessary. They are staked into the body and are destroyed when levered out.

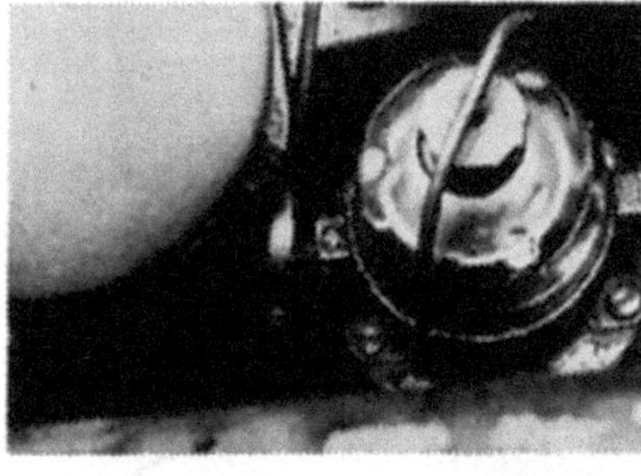

Section 11. Removing and re-installing A.C. fuel pump

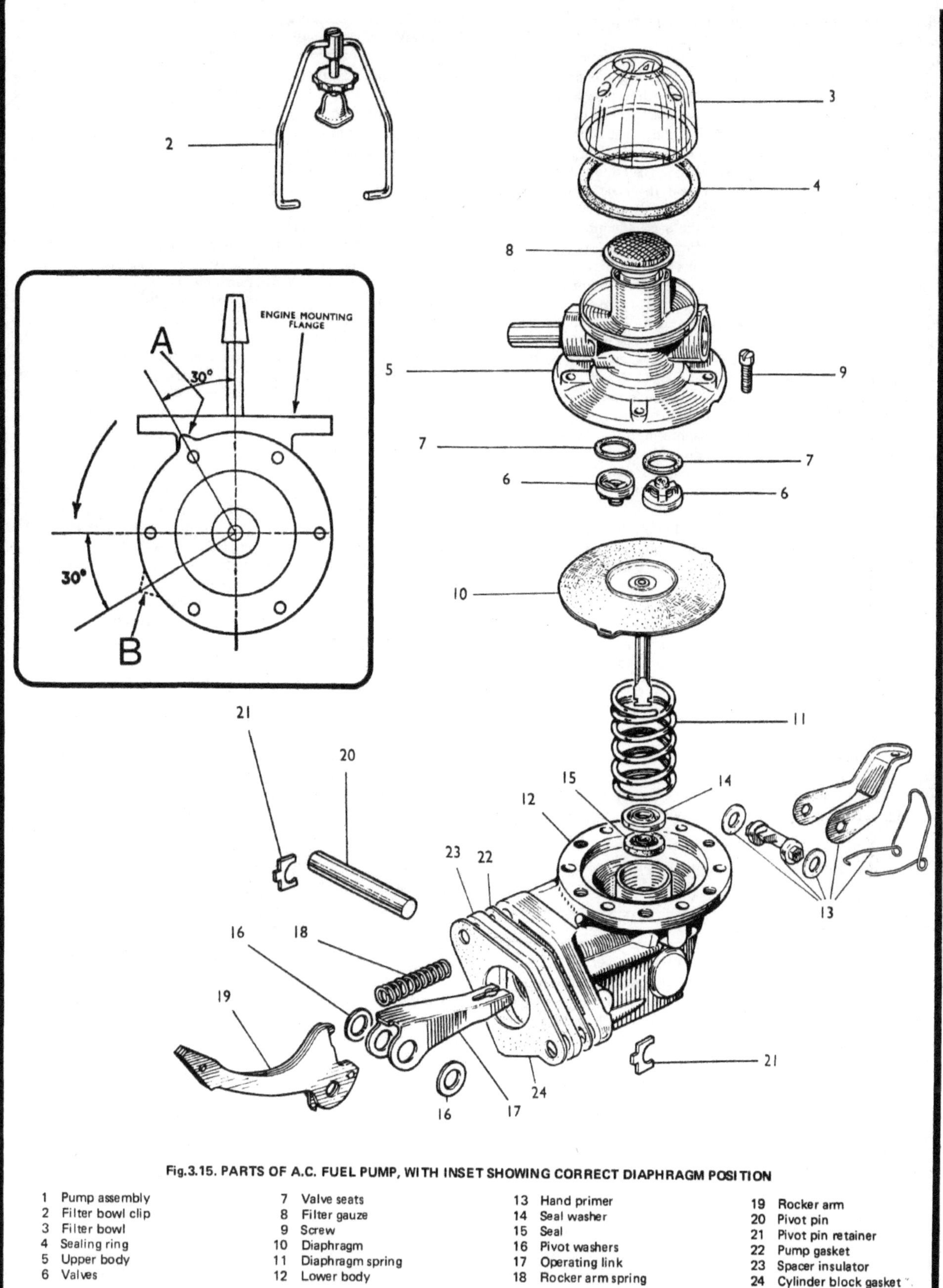

Fig.3.15. PARTS OF A.C. FUEL PUMP, WITH INSET SHOWING CORRECT DIAPHRAGM POSITION

1 Pump assembly
2 Filter bowl clip
3 Filter bowl
4 Sealing ring
5 Upper body
6 Valves
7 Valve seats
8 Filter gauze
9 Screw
10 Diaphragm
11 Diaphragm spring
12 Lower body
13 Hand primer
14 Seal washer
15 Seal
16 Pivot washers
17 Operating link
18 Rocker arm spring
19 Rocker arm
20 Pivot pin
21 Pivot pin retainer
22 Pump gasket
23 Spacer insulator
24 Cylinder block gasket

7. Examine the diaphragm for signs of cracking or perforation and renew if necessary.
8. The oil seal and retainer in the base of the pump (around the pull rod) should be renewed as a matter of course if the diaphragm is also being renewed. They can be levered out with a screwdriver. The new ones should be pressed in carefully, keeping them square.
9. When fitting new valve assemblies to the body, first fit the seating washers and then place the valves, making sure that they are the correct way up according to inlet and outlet. The body will have to be restaked at six (different) places round the edge so that the assemblies are firmly held in their positions. If this is not done properly and leakage occurs between the valve assembly and the seating ring, the pump will not operate efficiently.
10. The rocker arm assembly is refitted to the body by first assembling the link, rocker arm, pivot pin and washers and placing them in position in the pump body. Then locate the spring over the pip on the rocker arm and in the pump body recess. Then tap the pin retainers into the slots in the body so that they are hard up to the pin. The slots should then be staked with a suitable punch so that the retainers are tightly held in position.
11. Place the diaphragm return spring in position in the lower half of the pump. To replace the diaphragm, first fit the stem carefully through the oil seals, then position the diaphragm so that the tab is in the position shown in Fig.3.x. Then press the centre of the diaphragm down which will pass the stem end through the operating link slot. Then, by turning it 90° anticlockwise the stem will hook into position correctly.
12. Fit the upper half of the pump body and line up the mating marks. In order to assemble the two halves and the diaphragm properly, push the rocker arm upwards so that the diaphragm is drawn level. Then place the six screws in position lightly. It is best if the base of the pump is held in a vice whilst the rocker arm is pushed right up to bring the diaphragm to the bottom of its stroke. A short piece of tube over the rocker arm will provide easy leverage. In this position the six screws should be tightened evenly and alternately.
13. Fit a new filter bowl gasket carefully in the groove of the upper body, making sure that it does not twist or buckle in the process. Replace the cover and the retaining clip and screw it down tight.
14. When the pump is reassembled the suction and delivery pressure can be felt at the inlet and outlet ports when the rocker arm is operated. Be careful not to block the inlet port completely when testing suction. If the rocker arm were to be operated strongly and the inlet side was blocked the diaphragm could be damaged.

13. Fuel Gauge - Tank Sender Unit

1. The fuel gauge sender unit is mounted on the side of the tank where the fuel outlet pipe connection is also made. If the gauge does not register, first check that the sender unit, which is a variable resistance, is giving different resistance readings with both a full and empty tank. If not, it should be renewed. If it is, the gauge is faulty.
2. To remove the sender unit, first disconnect the fuel pipe union. Then engage the locking plate lugs with a suitable tool and turn it anticlockwise. The unit can then be lifted out. Take care when replacing that the washer is correctly installed and that both joining surfaces are clean and undistorted.

14. Exhaust & Crankcase Emission Control System

Although no legislation yet exists in the United Kingdom, models in the Sunbeam Arrow range which are exported to North America need to conform to the exhaust emission control regulations for new cars which are in force there.

The purpose of the system is to reduce the amount of hydrocarbons in the form of unburnt fuel and carbon monoxide which are vented to atmosphere by the engine and which contribute to pollution of the atmosphere. This section is intended to give readers an idea of the Rootes system fitted to engines in this range. Different methods are used for different engines. It must also be realised that development of the system is still in its early stages and experience will doubtless evolve modified systems for the future.

Basically the present system needs modified variable choke carburettors - such as the Stromberg 150 CDS - and a modified distributor. Most of the polluting gases reach atmosphere via the exhaust during overrun conditions when the throttle is shut. Normally the exhaust gases excessively dilute the slow running mixture reaching the engine under these conditions and so prevent proper combustion. The modified system uses the manifold depression, which is at maximum on overrun, to operate this. A control valve which in turn operates a throttle by-pass valve permits a proper mixture to reach the cylinders. This, in turn, increases the engine power and so cuts out the overrun engine braking effect. To counteract this an automatic vacuum retard device is fitted to the distributor which retards the ignition 12 crankshaft degrees. The throttle by-pass valve is incorporated as part of the Stromberg CDSE carburettor.

Other refinements on the carburettors are a temperature – controlled valve which weakens the mixture under light load and idling conditions when the engine is hot. Furthermore, the main jet is fixed and the needle is spring loaded to run off-centre in the jet to improve atomisation. The manifold depression has to reach 21 inch Hg. before the system comes into operation. The system cuts out when it drops to 18 Hg, allowing air through the bleed to return the valves to closed positions.

It must be appreciated, of course, that all other aspects of engine condition and tuning settings must be as near perfect as possible to achieve the sought after reduction in emission fumes. Valve clearances, plug gaps, points gap, centrifugal and vacuum automatic advance curves, and static timing are all equally important.

The overall requirement is, therefore, an engine in a very good state of tune at all times. The extra expense of maintaining this is offset by improved performance and fuel consumption, and the knowledge that one is not feeding unwanted elements into the air we breathe.

This manual does not intend to go into any detail on the servicing operations necessary, as the full implications are not yet known of what the owner may or may not be able to do in the tuning and setting up of such a system on his own car.

It is hoped, however, that this brief summary will give readers an idea of what the whole problem is about and will allay any fears, due to lack of knowledge, that the system will be so complex as to be totally beyond their comprehension. This is not so. What is being done, in effect, is to develop the existing carburation and ignition systems to ensure that fuel is more carefully metered in and more thoroughly burnt. Future developments will also incorporate filter systems for even more selective containment of the polluting elements in the exhaust emissions from internal combustion engines.

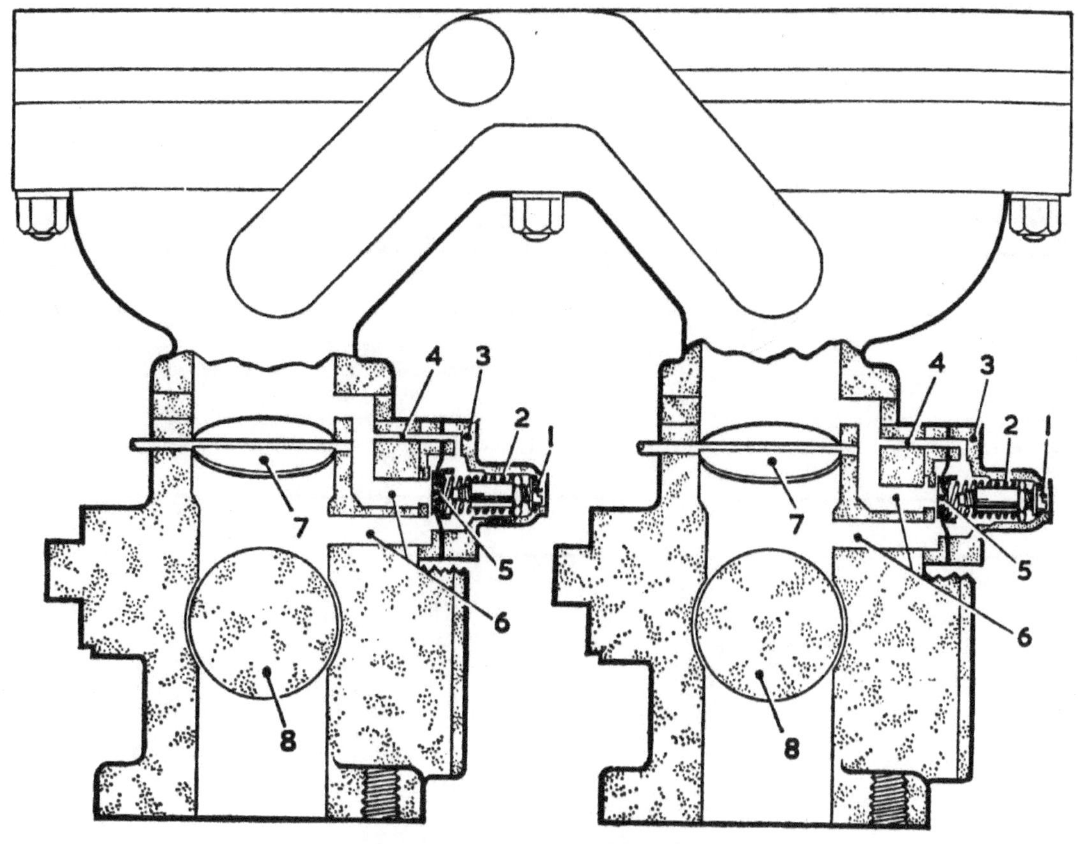

Fig.3.16. EXHAUST EMISSION CONTROL SYSTEM: SCHEMATIC ARRANGEMENT WITH TWIN CARBURETTORS

1 Throttle by-pass valve adjustment
2 Valve return spring
3 Throttle by-pass valve body
4 Vacuum fuel passage
5 By-pass valve and diaphragm
6 By-pass passages
7 Throttle valve
8 Air valve piston

Chapter 4 Ignition system

Contents

Specifications

Spark Plugs

Type	Champion N9Y
Electrode gap	0.025 in (0.635 mm)

Coil

Type	Lucas 11C12 (HA12 on some export models)

Distributor

Type - Standard	Lucas 25D4
- H120	Lucas 23D4
Shaft rotation	Anticlockwise viewed from top
Firing order	1, 3, 4, 2
Contacts gap setting	0.015 in (0.38 mm)
Moving contact spring tension	18 – 24 oz (0.51 to 0.68 kg)
Cam dwell angle	$60^\circ \pm 3^\circ$
Static timing	
- Standard	$6^\circ - 10^\circ$ BTDC
- H120	$6^\circ - 8^\circ$ BTDC

Important Note: The Lucas 23D4 distributor fitted to H120 engines has no vacuum advance mechanism. A mechanical automatic advance mechanism is fitted which cuts in at an engine speed of 500 rpm.

1. General Description

In order that the internal combustion engine with spark ignition can operate properly, it is essential that the spark is delivered at the spark plug electrodes at the precise moment it is required. This moment varies - in relation to the position of the pistons and crankshaft - depending on the speed and loading of the engine. This control of the spark timing is automatic (on early cars the control was manual). When it is realised that at 50 mph approximately 100 sparks per second are being produced then the importance of the need for precise setting is realised. The majority of minor faults and cases of poor performance and economy can be traced to the ignition system.

The principles are as follows. Battery voltage (12 volts) is fed through a circuit which passes through a coil developing high voltage (Fig.4.1).

Without going into electrical principles it is sufficient to say that when the 12 volt circuit is 'made', current is fed into a capacitor (condenser). When the circuit is broken the condenser discharges its current into the low voltage line and a high voltage current is boosted from the core of the coil and along the 'high tension' (HT) lead. This current is delivered to the centre contact of the distributor cap and from there, via the rotor arm, to each of the other four contacts in turn. Each of these is linked by an HT lead to each spark plug.

Obviously the timing of the break in the circuit decides the moment at which the spark is made. The contact points (or breaker points!) are in effect a switch. Not only do they open and close four times for every 2 revolutions of the crankshaft - delivering a spark to the four plugs in turn - they also open earlier or later in relation to the position of the crankshaft/pistons. Ignition advance and retard are the terms used to express this condition and it is measured in degrees - being degrees of angle of any crank on the shaft. Zero degrees is top dead centre, being the highest point of the arc made

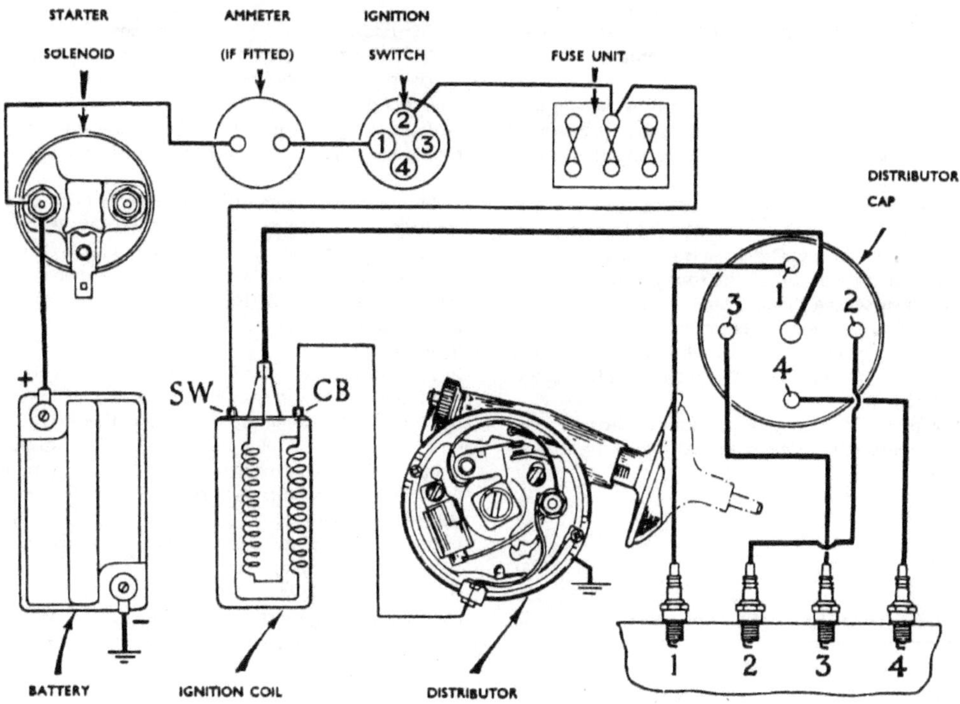

Fig.4.1. Ignition system - showing LT 12 volt primary circuit and HT circuit

by a crank. Timing setting is therefore expressed as so many degrees BTDC (before top dead centre).

In order to vary the ignition timing the contact points mounting plate can rotate a limited amount relative to the centre spindle. This is controlled by the vacuum advance device which works from the suction (depression) in the engine inlet manifold (except on the H120 engine which has no vacuum advance). Secondly, the contact opening cam is able to revolve a certain amount round the centre spindle. This is controlled by spring loaded weights which move out under centrifugal force. When they move out the spindle to cam position is altered.

Timing varies with different engines but normally ranges from the static (at rest) advance of approximately 8° BTDC to 36° BTDC. The vacuum advance device is concerned only with smooth running and economy at the lower engine speeds and part throttle openings. When accelerating and under open throttle conditions the centrifugal control is the only one in operation. The static timing setting is important of course as the two automatic timing advance devices start from this point and consequently if it is incorrect the whole range is affected. The vernier adjustment on the vacuum advance unit alters this static setting entirely - not just for the vacuum advance part.

2. Routine Maintenance

a) Spark plugs (5,000 miles)

Remove the plugs and thoroughly clean away all traces of carbon. Examine the porcelain insulation around the central electrode inside the plug and if damaged discard the plug. Reset the gap between the electrodes to 0.025 in (0.63 mm). Do not use a set of plugs for more than 10,000 miles; it is false economy.

b) Distributor

Every 5,000 miles remove the cap and rotor arm and put one or two drops of engine oil on to the screw beneath the rotor arm, and one drop on the moving contact pivot. Also, a few drops through the aperture in the contact breaker plate, on to the governor weights. Smear the surfaces of the cam itself with petroleum jelly. Do not over lubricate as any excess could get on to the contact point surfaces and cause ignition difficulties.

Every 5,000 miles examine the contact point surfaces. If there is a build up of deposits on one face and a pit in the other it will be impossible to set the gap correctly and they should be refaced or renewed. When the contact surfaces are in order, reset the gap as described in Section 3.

c) General

Examine all leads and terminals for signs of broken or cracked insulation. Also check all terminal connections for slackness or signs of fracturing of some strands of wire. Partly broken wire should be renewed.

The HT leads are particularly important as any insulation faults will cause the high voltage to 'jump' to the nearest earth and this will prevent a spark at the plug. Check that no HT leads are loose or in a position where the insulation could wear due to rubbing against part of the engine.

3. Distributor - Contact Points - Adjustment

1. Remove the distributor cap by unclipping the two leaf springs, one each side of the distributor.
2. Pull off the rotor arm from the cam spindle.

3. First examine the points by carefully levering them apart with a small screwdriver or something similar. If the faces of the circular contacts are pitted or rough then they cannot be properly set and should be removed for renewal or cleaning up.
4. If the faces are clean then turn the engine so that the moving arm of the breaker rests with the follower on one of the four high points on the cam (Fig.4.2). The engine can be turned by engaging a gear and moving the car.
5. Select a feeler blade (0.015 in. (0.4 mm) and place it between the points. If the gap is too great, slacken the fixed point locking screw and move the plate to alter the gap. If the gap is too small the feeler blade may still fit between the points as the spring loaded arm can simply move back. When setting them, therefore, the feeler gauge blade should only be a very light touch on each contact face.
6. Lock the fixed plate screw and recheck the gap. Replace the rotor arm, making sure that the lug in the rotor recess is fully engaged in the slot on the cam spindle.
7. Check the inside of the distributor cap before replacing it and verify that the four contacts are clean and that the centre carbon brush is intact and moves freely.

4. Distributor - Contact Points - Removal & Replacement

1. The contact points will need removal if the surfaces are bad enough to require renewal or re-facing. Generally it is best to renew the contacts completely as re-facing never produces a surface as good as the original (unless done professionally which would cost more than the new ones!) and they will deteriorate again much more rapidly.
2. Remove the distributor cap and rotor arm as described in the previous Section and remove the fixed plate locking screw.
3. Undo the small nut on the terminal post which also secures the end of the spring and lift off the washer and nylon insulating sleeve. The two circular tags from the coil and condenser leads may then be taken off and the spring contact lifted off at the pivot post. The fixed contact can also now be lifted out.
4. Replacement is a reversal of the removal procedure. Modern contact sets are sometimes supplied as a complete assembly which can be fitted and connected as a single unit. If the new points are in separate pieces the assembly on the terminal post is very important. If you did not notice the order in which the pieces came off, the correct order of replacement is - Fixed contact on to the base plate, insulating washer over the terminal post (NOT the pivot post), spring contact, lead connectors on to terminal post, nylon sleeve on terminal post, plain washer and nut. This assembly insulates the spring side of the contacts from earth except when the points are closed.

5. Distributor - Condenser - Testing, Removal & Replacement

1. A faulty condenser causes interruptions in the ignition circuit or total failure. Elaborate testing methods are pointless as the item is cheap to renew.
2. If the contact points become pitted after a relatively small mileage (under 1,000), and if starting is difficult, then it is a good idea to replace the condenser with the points. Another way to check is to remove the distributor cap and turn the engine so that the points are closed. Then switch on the ignition and open the points using an insulated screwdriver. There should be a small blue spark visible but if the condenser is faulty there will be a fat blue spark.
3. To remove the condenser disconnect the lead from the contacts terminal post and remove the crosshead screw securing the condenser mounting bracket to the plate. Fit a new one in the reverse order.

6. Distributor - Removal & Replacement

1. The distributor will need removal if there are indications that the drive spindle is a sloppy fit in the bushes (causing contact gap setting difficulties), or if it is to be dismantled and thoroughly cleaned and checked. It should also be removed before the oil pump is taken out.
2. Before removing the distributor it is helpful to prevent future confusion if the engine is positioned with No.1 piston at TDC on the firing stroke. This can be done by noting the position of the No.1 plug lead in the cap and then turning the engine to TDC so that the rotor is adjacent to the No.1 plug position in the cap. (The cap, of course, will be removed to do this.) For details see Section 8 – 'Ignition Timing'.
3. Detach the plug leads from the spark plugs and the coil HT lead from the distributor cap or coil (Photo). Remove the cap by unclipping the leaf spring clip at each side (Photo).
4. Pull off the LT wire connector at the distributor (Photo) and remove the suction pipe from the vacuum advance unit (Photo).
5. Undo the two bolts securing the flange of the distributor body to the block (Photo). Do not undo the upper clamp bolts or clamp unless the distributor is being renewed. It will keep the timing at least in the right area.
6. Lift the distributor out. Before proceeding any further, note the position of the eccentric slot in the end of the drive shaft inside the distributor mounting recess in the block. This will give a firm timing reference if the oil pump is to be removed.
7. Replacement is a reversal of the removal procedure. Check that the rubber sealing ring between the flange and block is in good condition (Photo). Line up the eccentric tongue on the distributor shaft with the slot in the drive shaft and when the sleeve of the body is being pushed down be prepared to rotate the shaft either way a little so as to engage the drive.

7. Distributor - Dismantling, Inspection & Reassembly

1. If the distributor is causing trouble with the ignition system it is often a good idea to fit a completely new unit. Without the proper test equipment it is difficult to diagnose whether or not the centrifugal and vacuum automatic advance mechanisms are performing as they should. However, play in the shaft bushes can be detected by removing the rotor arm and gripping the end and trying to move it sideways. If there is any movement then it means that the cam cannot accurately control the contact points gap. This must receive attention. (With H120 engine ignore references to vacuum unit.)
2. With the distributor removed, take off the rotor, condenser and contact points as described in Section 4.
3. Unhook the vacuum advance link from the edge of the contact breaker moving plate and then take out the two screws at the edge of the base plate which secure it to the body of the distributor (Fig.4.3).
4. Pull the nylon LT lead terminal from the groove in the side of the distributor and the two plates may then be lifted out.
5. If the shaft is being removed to renew the bushes DO NOT dismantle the centrifugal advance mechanism as it is not necessary. Remove the small circlip from the end of the threaded shank of the vacuum advance vernier adjustment. This will enable the knurled screw to be taken right off. Note the position of the vernier scale on the advance unit. The vacuum unit can then also be withdrawn.
6. Remove the pin securing the offset driving dog with a flat nosed punch, and the shaft complete with cam and centrifugal advance mechanism may be taken out. Note the relative position of the dog offset to the cam rotor slot.
7. To renew the bush first press or drive out the old one from inside the distributor body.

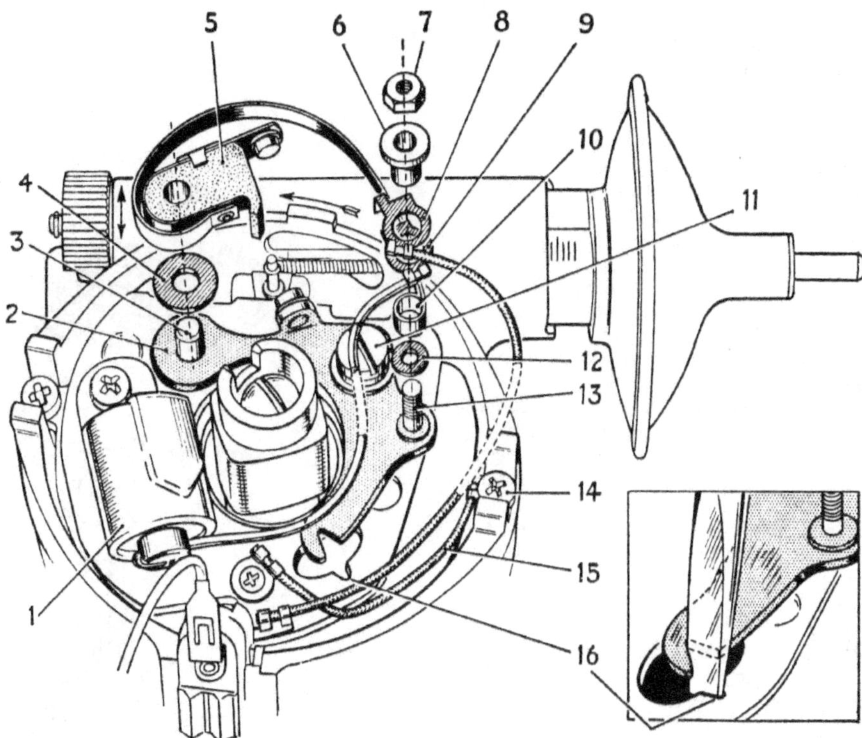

Fig.4.2. PARTLY DISMANTLED VIEW OF CONTACT BREAKER ASSEMBLY

1 Condenser
2 Fixed contact plate
3 Moving contact pivot post
4 Fibre insulating washer
5 Moving contact
6 Nylon insulating sleeve
7 Terminal nut
8 Lead from coil
9 Lead to condenser
10 Moving contact spring eye
11 Fixed contact plate securing screw
12 Fibre insulating washer
13 Terminal post
14 Contact base plate securing screw (and earth wire connection)
15 Earth wire
16 Screwdriver notch for adjustment

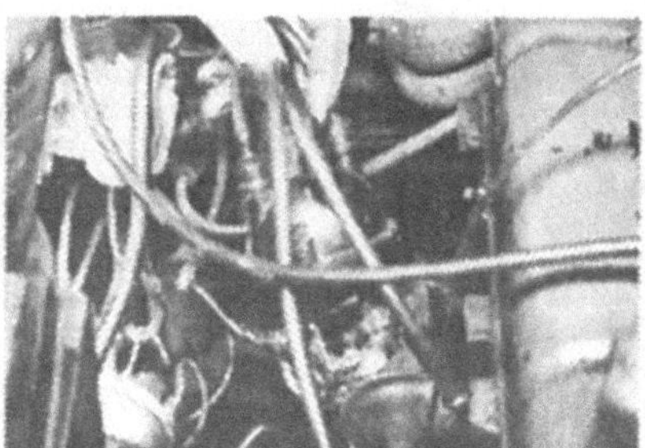

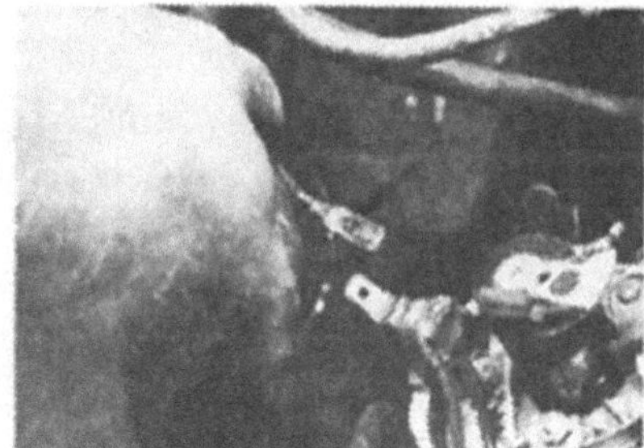

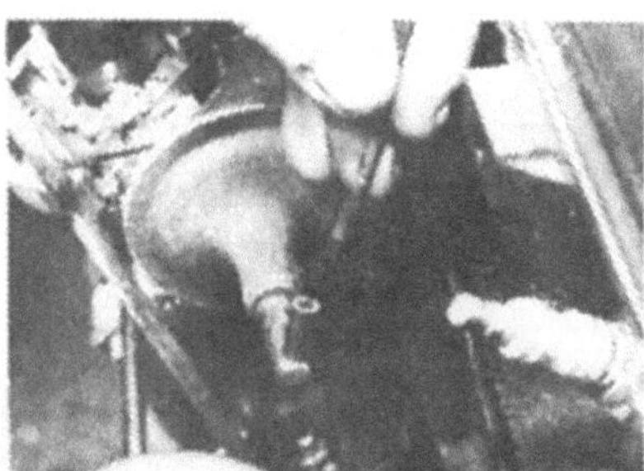

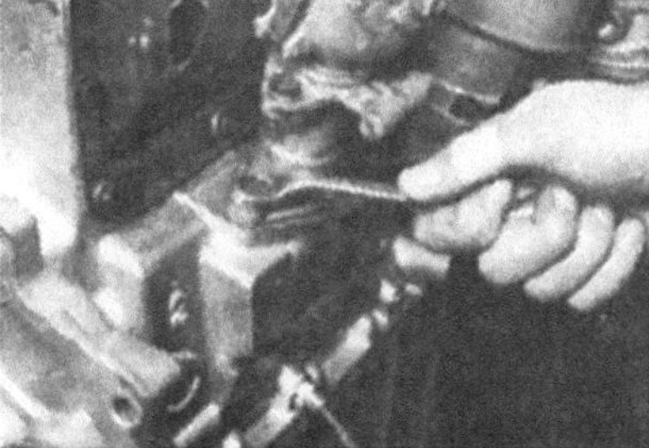

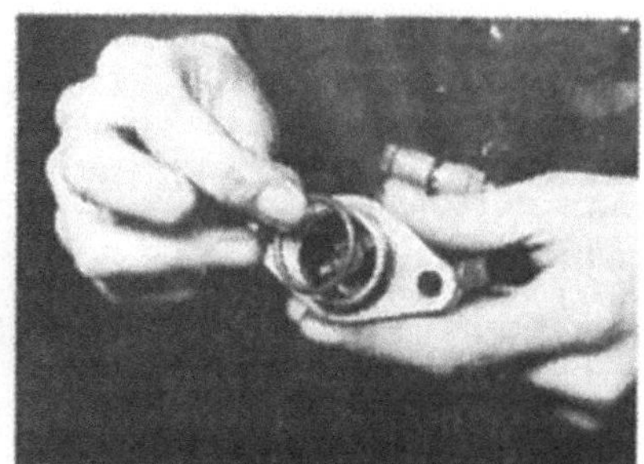

Sections 6.3 and 6.4. Sequence for removing distributor

Section 6.7. Checking condition of 'O' ring

8. The bush is stepped at its lower end for ¾ inch (19 mm). Before fitting a new bush it should be soaked in engine oil for at least 24 hours - or hot oil for 2 hours - before fitting. It is made of sintered copper/iron and retains its lubricant due to porosity. The new bush should be pushed in from the lower end, the small diameter part first. When the shoulder part reaches the body the bush should be pressed in with a shouldered mandrel in a press or vice. Any attempt to drive it in - even using blocks of wood - will almost certainly cause it to break up. The bottom of the bush should be flush with the distributor body and it should protrude very slightly at the top inside.

9. When fitted the bush should be drilled through in line with the shaft oil drain hole in the body. Make sure there are no burrs or loose metal particles anywhere in the bush.

10. Refit the shaft, lubricate with engine oil. If it is tight it will need 'running in' by hand until there are no traces of binding. The bush must not be reamed as this will impair its self lubricating properties. Do not forget the distance collar on the shaft under the action plate.

11. If the centrifugal advance device is to be dismantled, first remove the two springs very carefully so as not to kink, distort or stretch them. Then note the position of the cam rotor arm slot relative to the offset drive dog on the bottom of the shaft, and unscrew the screw in the top of the cam securing it to the shaft. The cam may then be lifted off, followed by the counter weights.

12. Reassembly of the distributor is a reversal of the dismantling process. Take care to see that the cam rotor arm slot is in the same relative position with the driving dog as before and do not stretch the centrifugal springs. Smear the contact breaker base plate with a thin film of oil or grease between it and the moving plate. Make sure the drive dog retaining pin is peened over sufficiently to prevent it working loose.

8. Ignition Timing

1. It is necessary to time the ignition when it has been upset due to overhauling or dismantling which may have altered the relationship between the position of the pistons and the moment at which the distributor delivers the spark. Also, if maladjustments have affected the engine performance it is very desirable, although not always essential, to reset the timing starting from scratch. In the following procedures it is assumed that the intention is to obtain standard performance from the standard engine which is in reasonable condition. It is also assumed that the recommended fuel octane rating is used. It is possible today to have an engine checked on special equipment designed to indicate where different faults may be. These instruments are excellent for indicating what may be wrong with your engine in a variety of areas. They do not, however, compute the full combination of settings needed to get the best possible performance from your particular engine as it is. The final check for ignition timing depends solely on the performance of the car on the road in all the variety of conditions that it meets.

2. The static or datum timing is getting the spark to arrive at a particular position of the crankshaft (see Section 1). Most manufacturers stick to the convention of using No.1 cylinder for this adjustment and the Rapier is no exception. From the specifications we know that the static timing is say, 8° Before Top Dead Centre. The range of 6°–10° given is intentional. No two engines are identical. Neither are the combined operations of their components. So we start in the middle of the possible range.

3. The crankshaft pulley wheel, keyed to the front of the crankshaft, is marked with a series of notches (or lines on those models with damper pulley wheels). A pointer is fitted to the front of the timing gear cover. If the engine is revolved clockwise, TDC on No.1 piston will be achieved when the LAST notch (or line) comes up to the pointer. Do this and then look at the distributor cap and see at which position the HT lead from No.1 spark plug connects. Then remove the cap and see whether the top of the rotor arm is facing the No.1 plug contact. If it is, good! If not then the engine must be

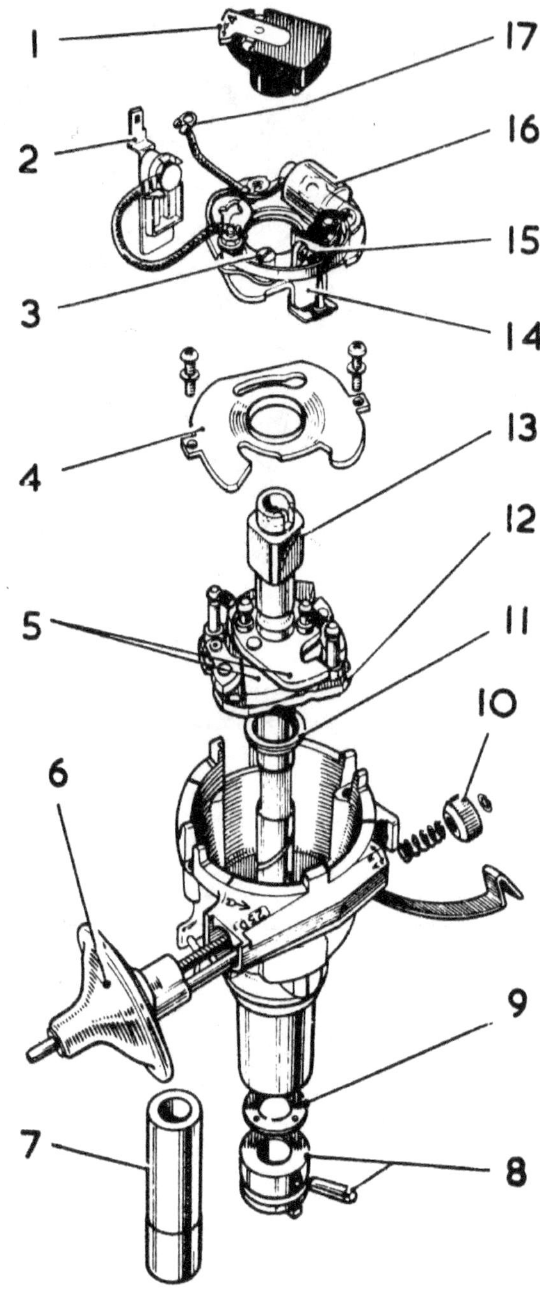

Fig.4.3. EXPLODED VIEW OF DISTRIBUTOR (LESS CAP)

1 Rotor arm
2 LH terminal
3 Fixed contact plate securing screw
4 Contact breaker base plate
5 Centrifugal advance control weights
6 Vacuum advance control unit
7 Bearing bush
8 Dog and pin
9 Thrust washer
10 Vernier adjustment nut
11 Distance collar
12 Action plate
13 Cam
14 Contact breaker moving plate
15 Contacts
16 Condenser
17 CB earth connector

Sections 2 and 9. The condition of spark plugs can be a guide to the state of tune of the engine (see text).

White deposits and damaged porcelain insulation indicating overheating

Broken porcelain insulation due to bent central electrode

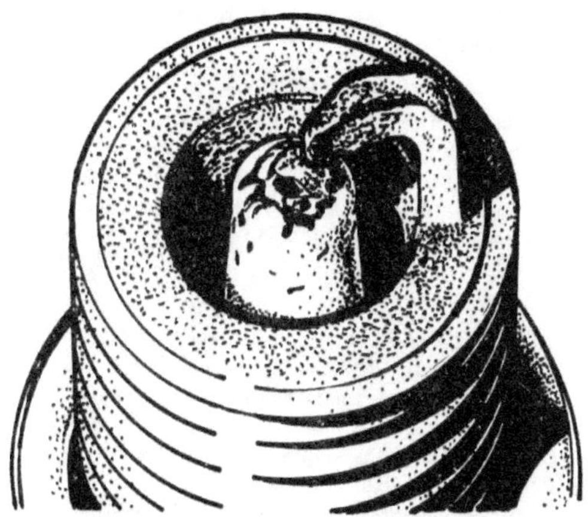

Electrodes burnt away due to wrong heat value or chronic pre-ignition (pinking)

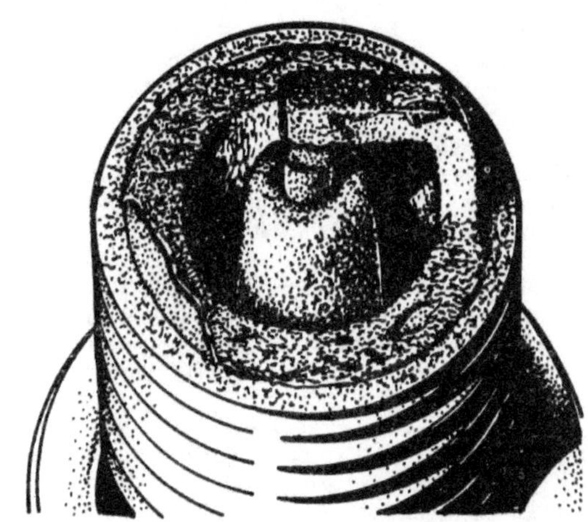

Excessive black deposits caused by over-rich mixture or wrong heat value

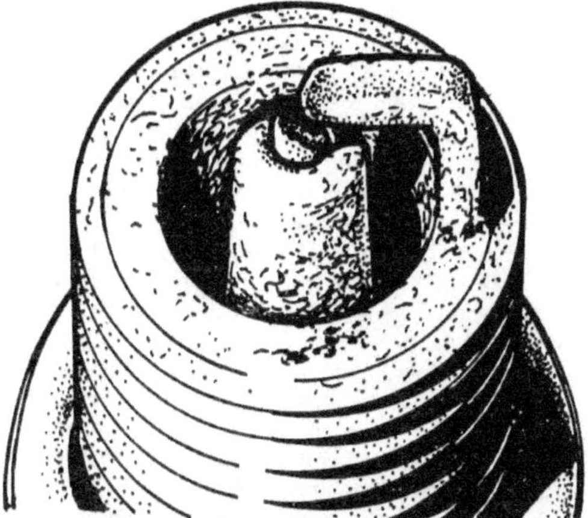

Mild white deposits and electrode burnt indicating too weak a fuel mixture

Plug in sound condition with light greyish brown deposits

turned another complete revolution to the TDC mark again. The rotor arm should then be in the correct position. Should the rotor arm still be way out, check whether the distributor body can be rotated enough to compensate, by slackening the clamp and trying it. It may be possible, with alterations to plug lead lengths. Such a state of affairs usually indicates that the oil pump drive spindle is out of position. With luck it will not have to be repositioned (see Chapter 1 'Oil Pump Replacement').

4. Now the engine should be set at the correct static advance position. Each notch, or line, represents 5^{0} so for 8^{0} advance turn the engine back 1½ notches/lines from the TDC mark (Fig.4.4).

5. As discussed in the opening section the spark is produced when the contact points in the LT circuit open. It is now necessary to slacken the distributor clamping screw so that the body of the distributor may be turned (whilst the rotor spindle stays still). Also the vernier control on the vacuum advance should be set in the centre of the range to give scope for equal fine adjustment either way later. This central position is with two divisions of the scale showing. The distributor should now be turned slightly, one way or the other, so that the contact points are fully open on the cam. The contact gap MUST be set correctly. As it is difficult to see exactly when the points are just closed a means of doing this electrically is necessary. Use a continuity tester or a 12 volt bulb and a jumper lead. If the latter is used, put one lead to the terminal where the coil LT lead joins the distributor and the other to a good earth on the engine block. With the ignition switched on the bulb will now light. Turn the body of the distributor anticlockwise until the light just goes out. Then, lightly holding the rotor arm with clockwise pressure, turn the body clockwise again until the light just comes on again. Then tighten the clamping screw. If desired the correctness of the setting can be checked with a stroboscopic timing light but such a device is not essential for accurate setting of the static timing.

6. The performance of the engine should now be checked by road testing. Make any adjustments by turning the vernier adjustment wheel a measured number of 'clicks' – start by increasing the advance – and road test after each adjustment. One complete revolution of the vernier adjuster is equivalent to a 3^{0} crankshaft movement and 1 division on the scale represents 4^{0} (Fig.4.5).

7. Should the owner wish, he may check the vacuum and centrifugal advance characterisations of the distributor. For this he will need to employ an accurate tachometer and a stroboscopic timing light. Using the table for the degrees of advance at various engine revolutions he may calculate whether the distributor is doing its job properly. It must be remembered that these are ranges of degrees rather than precise figures. If the distributor was seriously wrong then the performance of the car would be noticeably affected. Should the distributor be suspected of malfunction in this respect it would be best to get it tested on the specialised equipment available at some garages or simply fit a new one. Often the cost of thorough checking (which involves removing the distributor if it is to be done very precisely) is not far short of the cost of a new unit.

9. Spark Plugs & HT Leads

1. With the development of modern technology and materials, spark plugs are generally very reliable and require minimal attention. When they are due for checking and cleaning it is good practice to have them thoroughly sand blasted, gapped and checked under pressure on the machine that most garages have installed. They can also be used as good indications of engine condition, particularly as regards the fuel mixture being used and the state of the pistons and cylinder bores. Check each plug, as it is possible that one cylinder condition is different from the rest.

2. Plugs come in different types to suit the particular type of engine. A 'hot' plug is for engines which run at lower temperatures than normal and a 'cold' plug is for the hotter running engines. If plugs of the wrong rating are fitted they can either damage the engine or fail to operate properly. Under normal running conditions a correctly rated plug in a properly tuned engine will have a light deposit of a brownish colour on the electrodes. A dry black sooty deposit indicates an over-rich fuel mixture. An oily blackish deposit indicates worn bores of valve guides. A dry hard whitish deposit indicates too weak a fuel mixture. If plugs of the wrong heat range are fitted they will have similar symptoms to a weak mixture together with burnt electrodes (plug too hot) or to an over-rich mixture caked somewhat thicker (plug too cold). Do not try and economise by using plugs beyond 10,000 miles. Unless the engine remains in exceptionally good tune, reductions in performance and fuel economy will outweigh the cost of a new set.

3. The HT leads and their connections at both ends should always be clean and dry and, as far as possible, neatly arranged away from each other and nearby metallic parts which could cause premature shorting in weak insulation. The metal connections at the ends should be a firm and secure fit and free from any signs of corrosive deposits. If any lead shows signs of cracking or chafing of the insulation it should be renewed. Remember that radio interference suppression is required when renewing any leads.

10. Ignition Faults - Symptoms, Reasons & Remedies

Engine troubles normally associated with, and usually caused by, faults in the ignition system are:

a) Failure to start when the engine is being timed.
b) Uneven running due to misfiring or mistiming.
c) Smooth running at low engine revolutions but misfiring when under load or accelerating or at high constant revolutions.
d) Smooth running at higher revolutions and misfiring or cutting-out at low speeds.

a) First check that all wires are properly connected and dry. If the engine fails to catch when the starter is operated do not continue for more than 5 or 6 short burst attempts or the battery will start to get tired and the problem made worse. Remove the spark plug lead from a plug and turn the engine again holding the lead (by the insulation!) about ¼ inch from the side of the engine block. A spark should jump the gap audibly and visibly. If it does then either the plugs are at fault or the static timing is very seriously adrift. If both are good, however, then there must be a fuel supply fault, so go on to that.

If no spark is obtained at the end of a plug lead detach the coil HT lead from the centre of the distributor cap and hold that near the block to try and find a spark. If you now get one, then there is something wrong between the centre terminal of the distributor cap and the end of the plug lead. Check the cap itself for damage or damp, the 4 terminal lugs for signs of corrosion, the centre carbon brush in the top (is it jammed?) and the rotor arm.

If no spark comes from the coil HT lead check next that the contact breaker points are clean and that the gap is correct. A quick check can be made by turning the engine so that the points are closed. Then switch on the ignition and open the points with an insulated screwdriver. There should be a small visible spark and, once again, if the coil HT lead is held near the block at the same time a proper HT spark should occur. If there is a big fat spark at the points but none at the HT lead then the condenser is done for and should be renewed.

If none of these things happen then the next step in this tale of woe is to see if there is any current (12 volts) reaching the coil (+ terminal). (One could check this at the distributor, but by doing back to the input side of the coil a longer length of possible fault line is bracketed and could save time.)

With a 12v bulb and piece of wire suitably connected (or of course a voltmeter if you have one handy), connect between the + or 'SW' terminal of the coil and earth and switch on the ignition. No light means no volts so the fault is between the battery and the coil via

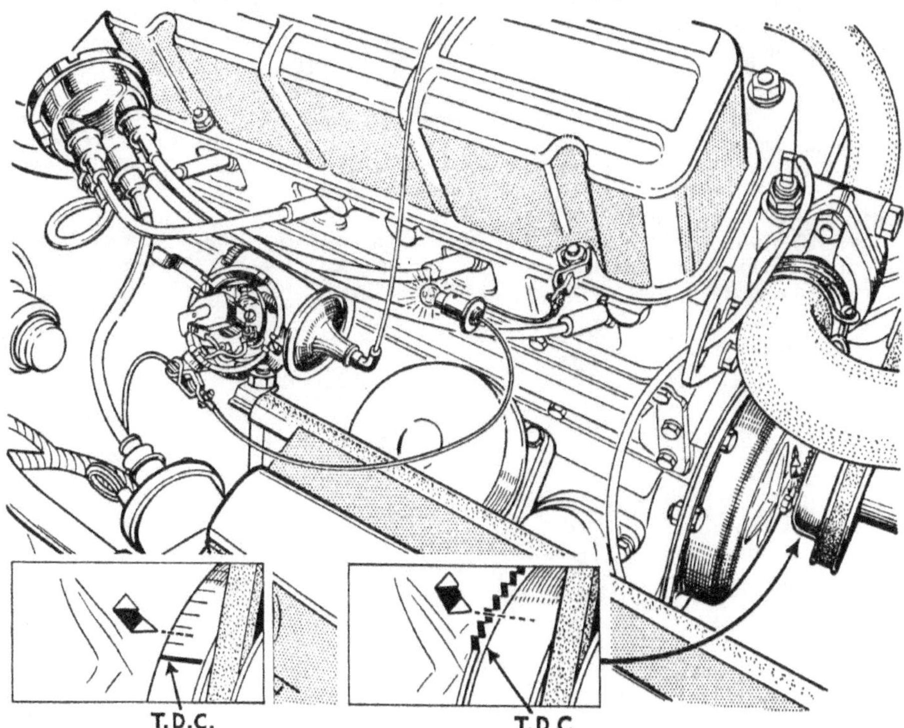

Fig.4.4. Set-up for static ignition timing. The inset drawings show a setting of 8° advance BTDC on the crankshaft pulley wheel scale

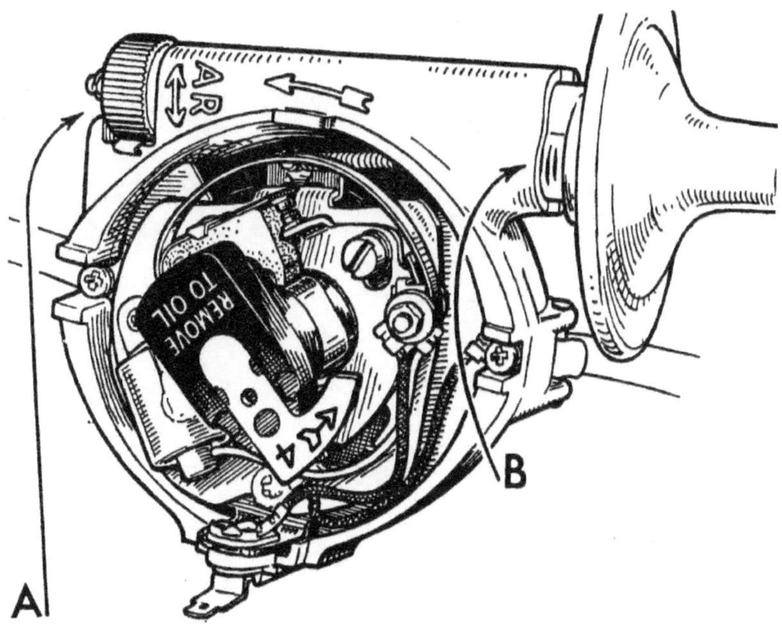

Fig.4.5. Static advance of the ignition is adjusted on the distributor by means of vernier screw A and indicated on scale B (setting illustrated at mid-point of scale, 2 divisions showing)

the ignition switch. This is moving out of the realms of just ignition problems - the electrical system is becoming involved in general. So to get home to bed get a piece of wire and connect the + terminal of the coil to the + terminal on the battery and see if sparks occur at the HT leads once more.

If there is current reaching the coil then the coil itself or the wire from its '–' terminal to the distributor is at fault. Check the '–' or CB terminal with a bulb with the ignition switched on. If it fails to light then the coil is faulty in its LT windings and needs renewal.

b) Uneven running and misfiring should first be checked by seeing that all leads, particularly the HT ones, are dry and connected properly. See that they are not shorting to earth through broken or cracked insulation. If they are, you should be able to see and hear it. If not, then check the plugs, contact points and condenser just as you would in a case of total failure to start.

c) If misfiring occurs at high speed check the points gap, which may be too small, and the plugs in that order. Check also that the spring tension on the points is not too light thus causing them to bounce. This requires a special pull balance so if in doubt it will be cheaper to buy a new set of contacts rather than go to a garage and get them to check it. If the trouble is still not cured then the fault lies in the carburation or engine itself.

d) If misfiring or stalling occurs only at low speeds the points gap is possibly too big. If not, then the slow running adjustment on the carburettor needs attention.

Chapter 5 Clutch and actuating mechanism

Contents

Specifications

Clutch

Type	Borg and Beck diaphragm spring
Operation	Hydraulic
Diameter	
- Standard	7½ inches (19.0 cm)
- H120	8½ inches (21.6 cm)
Spring colour	
- Standard	2 orange/violet and 2 white/light green
- H120	White/light green
Number of springs	
- Standard	4
- H120	6
Thrust bearing	Carbon
Master cylinder bore	5/8 inch (15.875 mm)
Slave cylinder bore	1.1/8 inch (28.585 mm)
Adjustment	On pedal only

1. General Description

All models have a diaphragm spring single plate hydraulically operated clutch. The cover assembly which incorporates the diaphragm spring and pressure plate bolts to the flywheel, sandwiching the friction disc between them. The friction disc has a splined hub which engages with the splined input shaft of the gearbox. The friction material on both sides of the plate is gripped by the cover and flywheel surfaces in much the same way as brake shoes grip the drums, and when the clutch pedal is depressed the pressure plate is pulled off by the diaphragm spring.

The centre section of the friction plate is spring cushioned against the outer part to take up any shock and help ensure a smooth drive take up.

The diaphragm spring is mounted on the shouldered studs between two fulcrum rings and is attached to both pressure plate and cover by tangentially positioned straps. When pressure is applied to the centre of the diaphragm the outer edge moves in the opposite direction, drawing the pressure plate with it.

The friction disc between the pressure plate and flywheel is free floating along the input shaft splines and as it gets thinner with wear so the pressure plate automatically moves forward to take it up under the pressure of the diaphragm spring.

In turn, the travel of the operating lever is compensated by the hydraulic clutch piston moving fractionally further along the cylinder in the rest position. The pressure is applied to the centre of the diaphragm by a carbon-faced thrust ring pivot mounted at the end of the operating lever. No adjustments are necessary.

2. Routine Maintenance

Every 5,000 miles or 3 months (minimum) have a look at the level of the fluid in the reservoir (look at the brake fluid reservoir too!). If the level is slightly down add Lockheed hydraulic fluid to within ½ inch (13 mm) of the top. If the level is well down there must be a reason – probably a leak. Trace the pipe to both ends and if signs of fluid leaking are apparent take the necessary action. Keep the reservoir cap clean and the air vent hole clear. Lubricate the pedal cross shaft bushes with a few drops of engine oil.

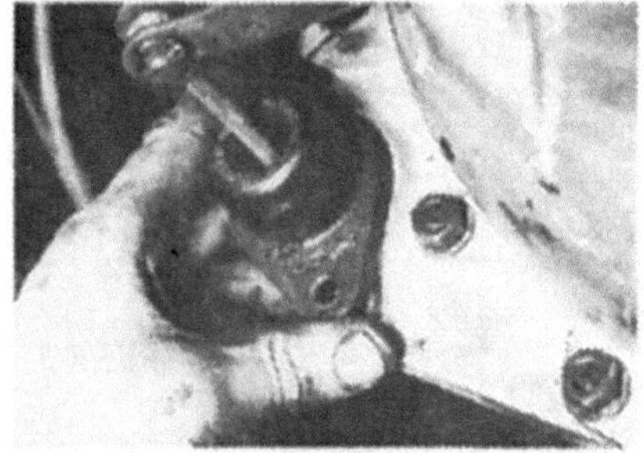
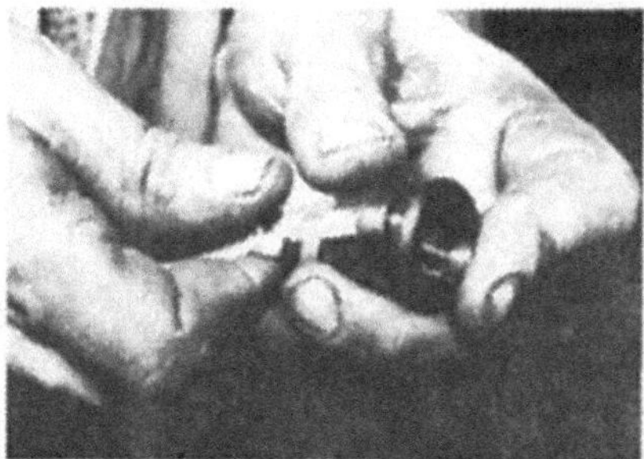
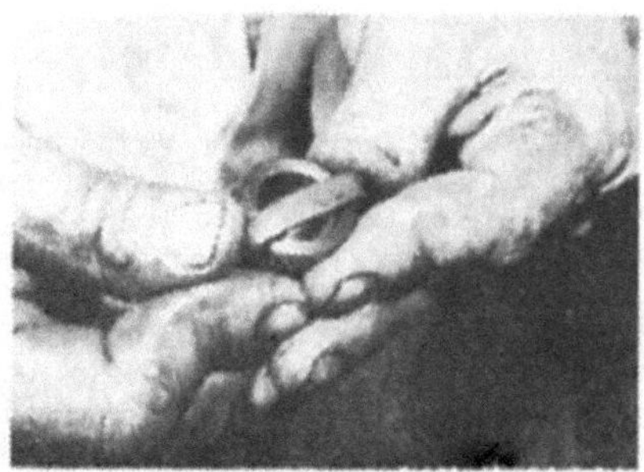
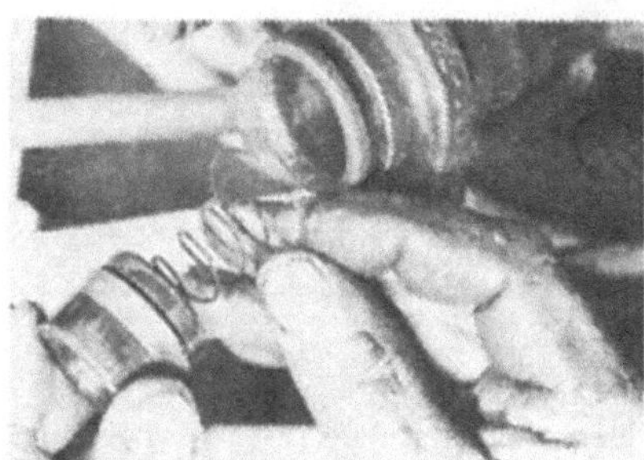
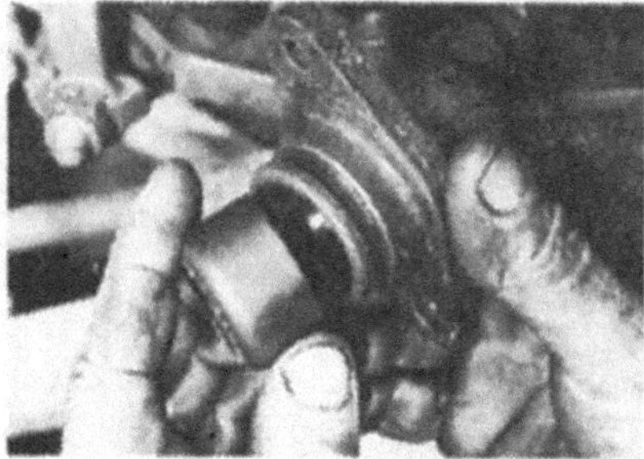
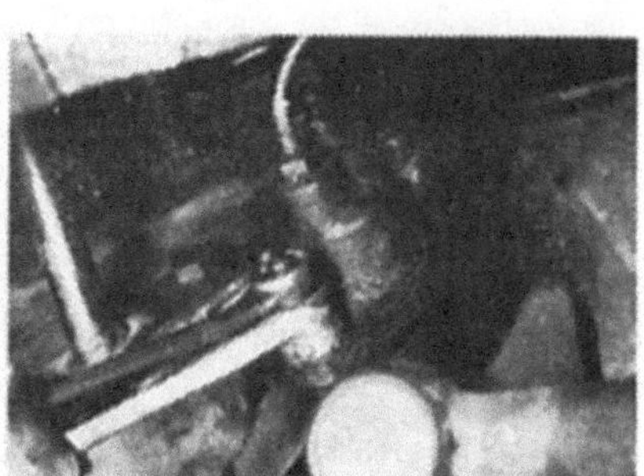

Section 4. Clutch hydraulic cylinder: dismantling, renewal of piston seal, reassembly and refitting.

3. Hydraulic System (Clutch) – Bleeding

1. The need for bleeding the cylinders and fluid line arises when air gets into it. Air gets in whenever a joint or seal leaks, or part of the system has to be dismantled. Bleeding is simply the process of venting the air out again.
2. Make sure the reservoir is filled and obtain a piece of clean 3/16 inch bore diameter rubber tube about 2 to 3 feet long and a clean jam jar. A small quantity of fresh, clean Lockheed hydraulic fluid is also necessary.
3. Detach the cap (if fitted) on the bleed nipple at the clutch cylinder and clean up the nipple and surrounding area. Unscrew the nipple ¾ turn and fit the tube over it. Put about ½ inch of fluid in the jar and put the other end of the pipe in it. The jar can be placed on the ground under the car.
4. The clutch pedal should then be depressed quickly and released slowly until no more air bubbles come from the pipe. Quick pedal action carries the air along rather than leaving it behind. Keep the reservoir topped up.
5. When the air bubbles stop tighten the nipple at the end of a down stroke.
6. Check that the operation of the clutch is satisfactory. Even though there may be no exterior leaks it is possible that the movement of the pushrod from the clutch cylinder is inadequate because fluid is leaking internally past the seals in the master cylinder. If this is the case, it is best to replace all seals in both cylinders.

4. Clutch Operating Cylinder - Removal, Dismantling, Assembly & Replacement

1. The clutch cylinder is fixed to the rear left hand side of the clutch bellhousing flange by two bolts. If it is to be removed for overhaul, first seal the cap of the fluid reservoir with a piece of plastic film (to minimise fluid loss) and undo the pipe where it joins the cylinder. Then remove the two mounting bolts, disengage the pushrod from the piston inside the rubber boot, and lift the unit out (Photo). (If the cylinder is merely being moved out of the way for gearbox renewal the pipe need not be detached.)
2. Remove the rubber boot. If a little air pressure is applied to the fluid inlet it will force the piston out of the cylinder - or it may be possible to shake it out. If the piston is seized, removal may be difficult. Soak the assembly in methylated spirits and if this does not release it buy a new unit. The cylinder bore will almost certainly be damaged anyway.
3. The seal may be removed from the piston by levering it off out of the groove (Photos). Note that the feathered side of the seal faces into the cylinder so that a new seal must be fitted the same way on to the piston. Pistons vary. Some have a flat end into the cylinder, others have two concave ends and the inner end is the one to which the seal groove is nearest. Thoroughly clean the cylinder and piston with methylated spirit or clean hydraulic fluid, and fit a new seal by stretching it over the piston into the groove. The lip faces INTO the cylinder.
4. Refit the piston into the cylinder using a little fluid to lubricate the walls, and make sure the lip of the seal does not get turned back (Photo). Replace the rubber boot so that it locks into the outer groove (Photo). It is quite a good idea to smear a little rubber grease (not ordinary grease) around the end of the piston under the boot.
5. Replacement is a reversal of the removal procedure. Make sure the unit is fitted on the rear side of the bellhousing flange - it is possible to put it on the front! (Photo).
6. Bleed the system as described in the previous section.

5. Clutch Master Cylinder – Removal, Dismantling, Assembly & Replacement

1. The master cylinder and fluid reservoir are a single unit and indications of something wrong with it are if the pedal travels down without operating the clutch efficiently (assuming, of course, that the system has been bled and that there are no leaks).
2. To remove the unit from the car, first seal the cap with a piece of film to reduce fluid wastage whilst dismantling the pipes. Alternatively, the fluid may be pumped out from the clutch cylinder bleed nipple by opening the nipple and depressing the pedal several times.

3. From inside the car remove the split pin and clevis pin which attach the pushrod assembly to the clutch pedal. To do this, it will be necessary to remove the parcel tray, which is held by a screw at each end and plastic buttons to the side panels. When the pushrod is free, remove the spring retainer collar and return spring.
4. From the engine compartment undo the hydraulic union of the pipe outlet from the cylinder and pull the pipe out and to one side. Undo the two bolts holding the whole unit to the vertical face of the bulkhead and take it out.
5. To dismantle the assembly first remove the rubber boot, and then with a pair of contracting circlip pliers remove the circlip from the internal bore of the cylinder. The piston assembly may then be drawn out. The trap valve can be ejected by blowing through the cylinder outlet orifice.
6. Thoroughly clean all the component parts and the cylinder and orifices with methylated spirit or clean hydraulic fluid.
7. Reassembly is a reversal of the dismantling process, using a new trap valve and seal cups as necessary. A complete repair kit will include everything required. Before fitting new seals, however, examine the cylinder bore for any signs of pitting, ridging or scoring. Any such signs mean that the cylinder is unserviceable and should be renewed. This normally means replacement of the whole assembly.
8. It is most important that the seals and washers are assembled into the cylinder in the correct sequence and the right way round. This sequence can be seen from the exploded drawing (Fig.5.1). The main cup seal should have its lip facing the interior of the cylinder, and the dome washer between it and the piston should have the convex surface against the head of the piston. The secondary cup seal should be carefully fitted into the groove at the outer end of the piston, also with its lip facing forward into the cylinder.
9. Finally, ensure that the circlip is fitted securely into the groove and replace the rubber boot.
10. Refit the unit to the car in the opposite order to removal. Refill the reservoir with fresh fluid of the correct specification. It is false economy to re-use the old fluid. Bleed the system as described in Section 3 and then check that the clutch movement is satisfactory and that no leaks are apparent.

6. Clutch Pedal - Removal & Replacement

1. It may be necessary to remove the pedal if the bush and cross shaft are worn so much that operation is affected.
2. To detach either of the two control pedals it is necessary first to withdraw the whole assembly (Fig.5.2).
3. First remove both brake and clutch master cylinders from the car. Then remove the four nuts inside the car, which hold the mounting plate to the bulkhead, and disconnect the bracing bracket from the steering column. The whole assembly can then be lifted out from the engine compartment. Take out the split pin from the cross shaft and the pedals may be removed. Renew the shaft or pedal as necessary. When refitting the pedals and cross shaft make sure the wave washer is correctly placed between the clutch pedal boss and the mounting plate on the cross shaft.
4. The assembly is replaced in reverse order of removal.

7. Clutch - Removal

1. To renew the friction plate or examine the clutch in any way it will first of all be necessary to remove the gearbox (see Chapter 6). If the engine has been removed then the clutch is, of course, accessible. Whether the gearbox is removed or the engine taken out the succeeding operations are the same, although work is easier with the engine out if no pit or ramp is available. If the engine and gearbox have been removed from the car together they will first have to be separated of course.

2. Before removing the clutch cover bolts mark the position of the cover in relation to the flywheel so that it may be put back the same way.

3. Slacken off the cover retaining bolts ½ a turn at a time in a diagonal fashion evenly so as to relieve the pressure without distorting the diaphragm spring (Fig.5.3).

4. When the bolts are removed the friction plate inside will be released and the cover can be pulled off the locating dowel pegs.

8. Clutch - Inspection & Renovation

1. Unfortunately it is not possible to inspect the clutch without going to the considerable trouble of removing the assembly. Consequently, one waits for trouble to develop or makes a decision to check and overhaul it at a specific mileage. Wear of the clutch friction plate very much depends on how the car has been driven. Habitual clutch slipping will obviously cause rapid wear. If it is assumed that the friction disc will need replacement at 35,000 miles and will be worth replacing at 25,000 miles there will be no significant waste of time and money if the work is done. Of course, a history of the car is very valuable for this decision. If, on the other hand, trouble is awaited, action must be taken immediately it occurs; otherwise further more costly wear could occur. Trouble usually comes in the form of slipping, when the engine speeds up and the car does not; or squealing, denoting that the friction material is worn to the rivets; or juddering, denoting all sorts of things (see 'Faults' Diagnosis). Wear on the carbon thrust release ring which presses on to the centre of the diaphragm every time the clutch is operated could also cause squealing if the wear was extreme. If the clutch is not examined when wear is apparent the faces of the flywheel and pressure plate may be severely scored and call for costly replacement.

2. Having decided to dismantle the clutch, first examine the faces of the flywheel and the pressure plate. If these are smooth and shiny you may smile. If they are slightly ridged or scored frown a bit but stay happy in the knowledge that a new friction disc will be enough to regain satisfactory performance. If there is severe scoring, curse mildly and be prepared to buy a new pressure plate assembly and/or flywheel. It is possible to shim the face of the flywheel but engineering advice should be sought. If a new flywheel is obtained it will have to be matched to balance the same as the original. If you hurriedly put the badly scored surfaces back together with a new friction plate you will achieve short-lived results only. After a few thousand miles the same old trouble will recur and judder will always be present in some form or another.

3. The friction plate lining surfaces should be at least 1/32 inch (0.8 mm) above the heads of the rivets, otherwise the disc is not really worth putting back. If the friction lining material shows signs of chipping or breaking up or has black areas caused by oil contamination it should also be renewed. Oil contamination will be confirmed by signs of oil which may be visible on the flywheel or in the bellhousing (on the gearbox). Consideration must be given to curing any such leaks before refitting the clutch assembly. Linings can be obtained for fitting the existing clutch discs but it is hardly worth it. With a new assembly you know that the splines and the disc itself are in good condition.

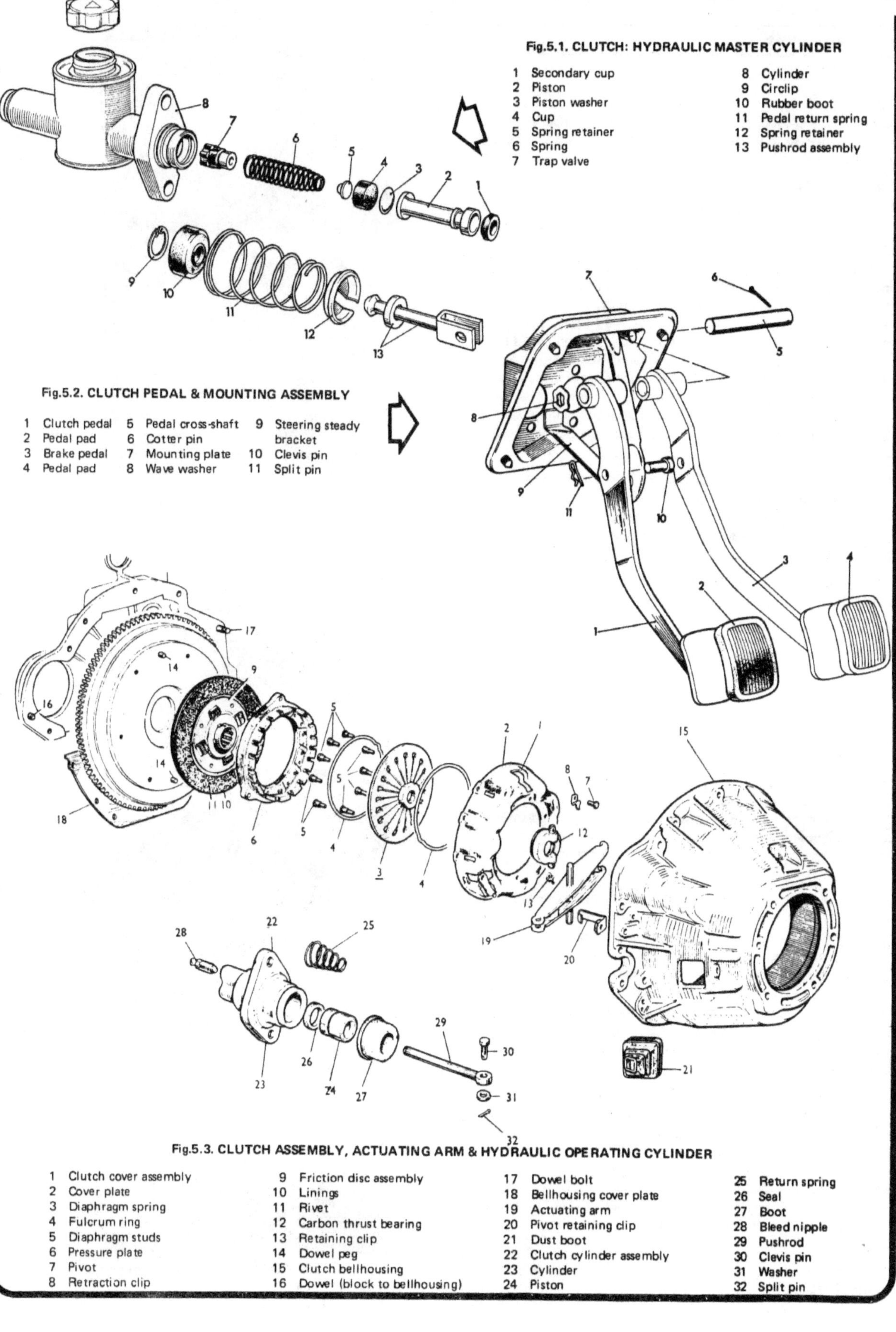

Fig.5.1. CLUTCH: HYDRAULIC MASTER CYLINDER

1 Secondary cup
2 Piston
3 Piston washer
4 Cup
5 Spring retainer
6 Spring
7 Trap valve
8 Cylinder
9 Circlip
10 Rubber boot
11 Pedal return spring
12 Spring retainer
13 Pushrod assembly

Fig.5.2. CLUTCH PEDAL & MOUNTING ASSEMBLY

1 Clutch pedal
2 Pedal pad
3 Brake pedal
4 Pedal pad
5 Pedal cross-shaft
6 Cotter pin
7 Mounting plate
8 Wave washer
9 Steering steady bracket
10 Clevis pin
11 Split pin

Fig.5.3. CLUTCH ASSEMBLY, ACTUATING ARM & HYDRAULIC OPERATING CYLINDER

1 Clutch cover assembly
2 Cover plate
3 Diaphragm spring
4 Fulcrum ring
5 Diaphragm studs
6 Pressure plate
7 Pivot
8 Retraction clip
9 Friction disc assembly
10 Linings
11 Rivet
12 Carbon thrust bearing
13 Retaining clip
14 Dowel peg
15 Clutch bellhousing
16 Dowel (block to bellhousing)
17 Dowel bolt
18 Bellhousing cover plate
19 Actuating arm
20 Pivot retaining clip
21 Dust boot
22 Clutch cylinder assembly
23 Cylinder
24 Piston
25 Return spring
26 Seal
27 Boot
28 Bleed nipple
29 Pushrod
30 Clevis pin
31 Washer
32 Split pin

9. Clutch - Replacement

1. If the original cover is being re-used line up the marks made before removal, and support the friction plate on one finger between cover and flywheel so that the larger boss faces the flywheel (Photo). Friction discs are normally marked 'This side to flywheel'.

2. Locate the cover on the dowel pegs in the flywheel and then place all the cover bolts in position and screw them up lightly by hand.

3. It is necessary to line up the centre of the friction disc with the exact centre of the flywheel. This is easily done if a piece of shouldered bar can be placed in the counter bore at the flywheel centre with the larger diameter supporting the friction disc. If you do not have such a thing, the disc may be lined up by eye if the engine is out of the car. For the man flat on his back on a cold concrete floor with his eyes full of grime it is certainly worthwhile making up some sort of centralising tool from a piece of broom handle or tube to get reasonably accurate positioning. If this is not done great difficulty (and possible damage to the gearbox input shaft) may be experienced when the time comes to refit the gearbox to the engine.

4. With the friction plate centralised the cover bolts should be tightened diagonally, evenly and progressively so that the diaphragm spring will not be distorted (Photo). Remove the centralising tool. Before refitting the gearbox to the engine do not forget to check the clutch thrust release bearing and operating mechanism.

5. Refit the gearbox (Chapter 6) and bleed the hydraulic system if it has been disturbed.

Sections 9.1 and 9.4. Replacing and securing clutch assembly with centralising mandrel in position.

10. Clutch Operating Lever & Thrust Release Bearing - Dismantling, Inspection & Reassembly

1. When the clutch pedal is depressed the hydraulic clutch cylinder piston actuates the lever which pivots in the bellhousing and forces a carbon-faced thrust ring or bearing against the steel boss at the centre of the diaphragm spring. In time the carbon ring will wear away and if this condition is allied to a well worn friction plate difficulty may be experienced in disengaging the clutch due to the limit of piston travel being reached before the diaphragm has been depressed sufficiently. A new carbon thrust ring face projects ¼ inch (6 mm) approximately from the housing and should be renewed if it is significantly less than this.

2. To renew the release bearing the clutch bellhousing and gearbox must be separated from the engine. The bearing is held to the actuating arm by two spring steel clips which, when released, allow it to be drawn off over the gearbox input shaft (Photos). Replacement is a reversal of the removal procedure. Should the release arm require removal the pivot pin clip holding it in position may be released by undoing the nut on the outside of the bellhousing. Do not undo this without supporting the engine and gearbox, as you will not be able to get it back.

3. The appearance of a typically worn carbon thrust ring can be seen in the photograph.

Section 10.2. Removal of thrust bearing and actuating arm.

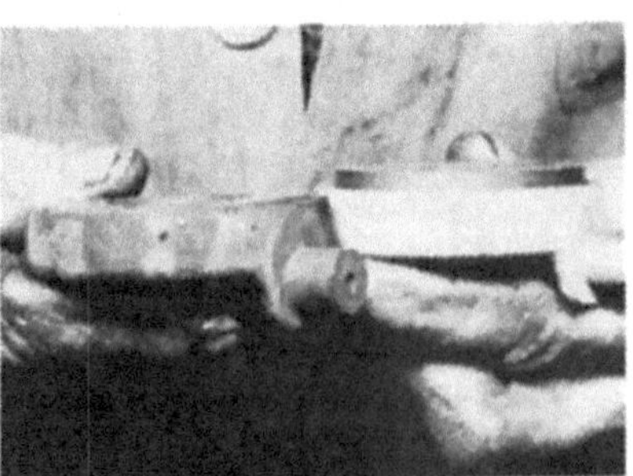

Section 10.3. Comparison of worn and new carbons in clutch thrust bearings.

11. Clutch Faults - Diagnosis & Remedies

1. Provided the clutch is not intentionally slipped excessively, or held out, in gear, at traffic lights, or the pedal used as a footrest, which will wear out the carbon thrust ring more quickly than normal, the only malfunction of the clutch one would expect would be routine wear of the friction plate. This normal wear will become obvious as the clutch starts to slip; that is the engine turns normally but the car fails to accelerate properly or slows down on hills. In such cases the clutch must be examined, and repaired immediately if necessary. Delay could be more costly. The gearbox will have to be taken off for this job.
2. Squealing noises from the clutch (and make sure they are from the clutch and not the fan belt or water pump) are most likely to come from a worn out clutch release bearing. The actual efficiency of the clutch may not be immediately affected but damage could be caused to the thrust boss on the diaphragm if no action is taken. Another reason for squealing could be a worn out or oil contaminated friction plate. In such instances the next symptom one could expect would be clutch slip. Do not wait for that however as the friction plate rivets could be scoring up the flywheel or pressure plate surfaces (see Section 8.2 above). Once again inspection and repair involves gearbox removal.
3. Failure to disengage the clutch when the pedal is fully depressed, (sometimes referred to as 'clutch spin'), can be caused by one or more of several factors. Symptoms are considerable difficulty in engaging any gear at rest - and when a gear is engaged it will be accompanied by a nasty crunch and the car bucking forwards (or backwards!). First check that the hydraulic system is moving the actuating lever when the pedal is depressed. An empty fluid reservoir or visible leaks will indicate that the system is malfunctioning. If the hydraulics are all right then the fault may be due to the friction plate sticking to the pressure plate or flywheel due to rusted splines, which prevent it from floating fore and aft on the gearbox input shaft. This is not unusual if the car has been standing unused for a long time. Try engaging a gear, with the engine stopped and handbrake on; then depress the clutch and try starting the engine. If the clutch is seized solid the engine will not turn over, but if you are lucky and the engine starts and the clutch can be slipped, it should be possible to get it back to normal operation after using it a few times. Rust on the friction faces as well as on the splines will have the same effect and can be cured by the same treatment. If the clutch spin does not eventually disappear completely, then some other defect such as distortion on the pressure faces may be the cause and this will involve dismantling. Thirdly, the cause could be a worn out thrust bearing allied to a well worn clutch plate. Squealing noises, each time the clutch is operated, will be an indication of this, and dismantling will be necessary.
4. Another fault is judder - particularly to be noticed when the clutch is taking up the drive. Although the symptom is noticed when the clutch is operated, the clutch is not necessarily the culprit. Check the condition of the engine mountings - two forward and one under the gearbox. If the engine vibrates and rocks excessively when started up it would indicate that they are spongy or broken. Then check that the universal joints on the propeller shaft are not worn and that the back axle and suspension are secure and free from excessive backlash. Defective rear dampers can also cause drive judder. If diagnosis finally indicates that the fault lies in the clutch it will be caused by wear, contamination, or distortion in one or other of the components, and dismantling will be needed to ascertain for sure what is causing it.

Chapter 6 Gearbox

Contents

Specifications

Gearbox - General

Number of gears	4 forward, 1 reverse
Forward gears	All synchromesh, helical cut
Reverse	Straight cut spur gears
Oil capacity	3½ pints (1.9 litres) 4½ pints (2.5 litres) with overdrive

Gearbox Bearings

Mainshaft	Main bearing - ball - spigot bearing needle rollers (23)
Input shaft	Ball - spigot bearing - oilite bush
Reverse gear	Phospher bronze bush
Layshaft	Needle rollers - 27 at each end

Adjustments

Layshaft	Selective assembly
Layshaft endfloat	0.006 – 0.008 inch (0.15 – 0.20 mm)
First speed wheel endfloat	0.004 – 0.009 inch (0.10 – 0.23 mm)

Ratios

Top	1.000 to 1
Third	1.296 to 1
Second	1.993 to 1
First	3.122 to 1
Reverse	3.323 to 1
Overdrive ratio	0.803 to 1
Pump pressure	480 – 500 lb sq in (33.75 to 35.15 kg cm^2)

Torque Wrench Setting

Gearbox mainshaft nut	80 lb ft (11.0 kg m)

1. General Description

The gearbox is a constant mesh four forward and one reverse speed unit, with synchromesh fitted on all four forward speeds.

The input shaft and mainshaft are mounted in the casing on ball bearings and locate into each other on needle rollers.

The laygear cluster revolves on needle roller bearings on the fixed layshaft; endfloat is controlled by a thrust washer at each end fitted between the casing and the laygear. With the exception of reverse, all gears are helically cut.

Gear selection is by three forks running on three separate rails. The forks are held in their neutral and selection positions by spring loaded detent balls housed in each fork, which engage in grooves in the rails.

The selector lever operates the forks through a remote control which permits a short, positive action lever to be used. Reverse gear selection position is achieved by overcoming a spring loaded plunger which bears on the base of the gear shift lever at the end of the remote control housing.

Overdrive is fitted as standard equipment on the Rapier and Rapier H120 models but is only available as an optional extra on the Alpine. The unit fitted is the Laycock-de-Normanville D Type, giving an increase in propeller shaft speed of 27.67%.

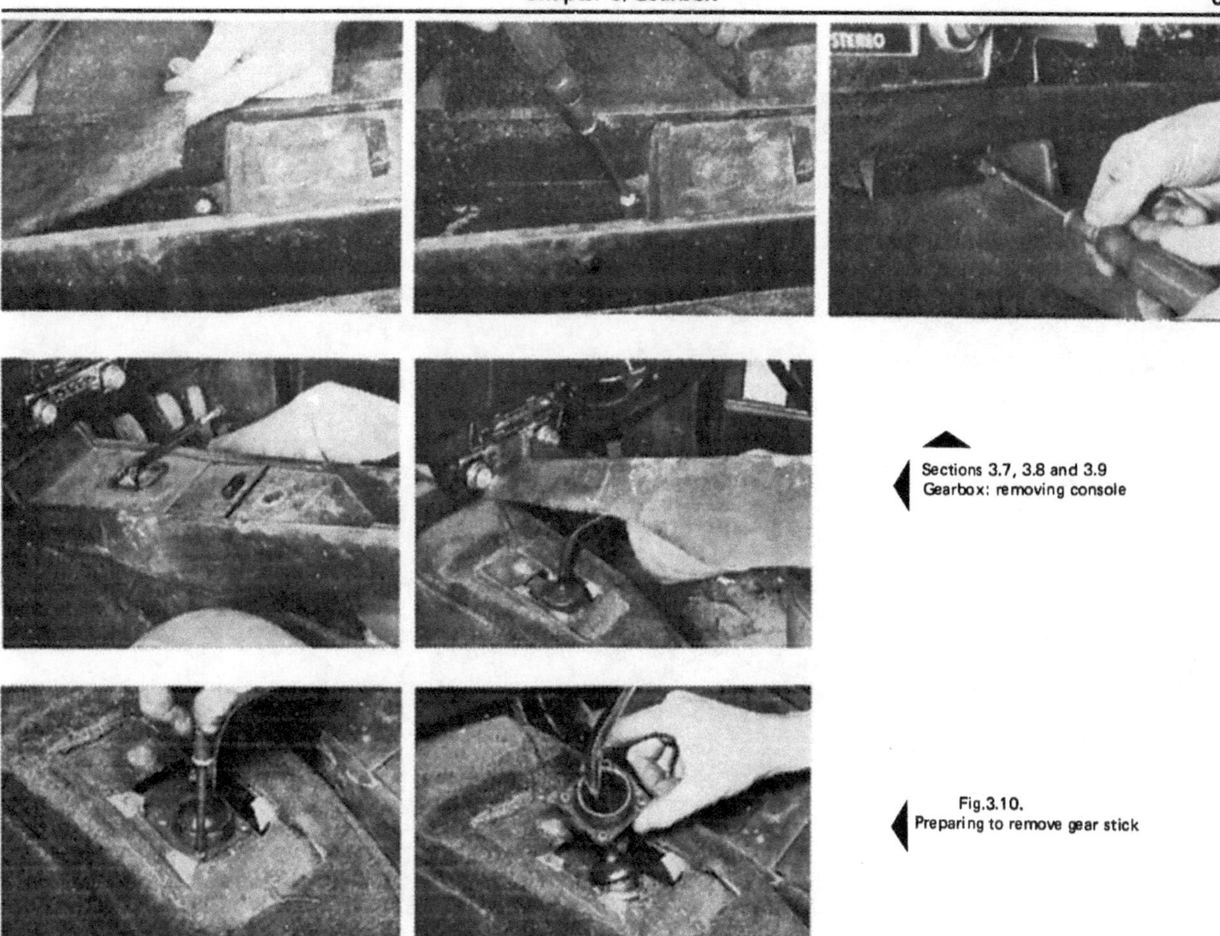

Sections 3.7, 3.8 and 3.9
Gearbox: removing console

Fig.3.10.
Preparing to remove gear stick

2. Routine Maintenance

1. Apart from checking the oil level in the gearbox every 5,000 miles the manufacturers state that draining and refilling with fresh oil is only necessary at intervals of 30,000 miles.
2. To check the oil level in the gearbox, stand the car on level ground and remove the filler and level plug, which is mounted on the right hand side of the gearbox casing. A quantity of the correct specification oil should be added until it overflows from the filler hole. In cold weather it may be necessary to wait a little time for this to be seen. Do not overfill the box in such instances, otherwise additional internal pressure will be built up when running which may burst oil seals or at least force oil past them.
3. To drain and replenish the gearbox oil first run the car for sufficient time to enable the warmth of the engine to transmit to the gearbox and thin the oil down slightly. Then stand the car on level ground and remove both the filler and drain plugs. Allow at least fifteen minutes to drain and then replace the drain plug. preferably with a new washer, and refill with the correct oil to the level plug hole. The overdrive unit has a separate drain plug.

3. Gearbox - Removal & Replacement

1. The gearbox may be removed together with the engine, in which case the instructions to do this are given in Chapter 1.
2. If the gearbox is being removed on its own, time spent on initial preparation work in raising and supporting the car will be amply repaid later. Ideally, of course, the car would be raised on a hoist or ramp, or put over a pit, but as most owners will not have this facility, they must certainly acquire a set of four chassis stands to support the car as high as possible safely. The maximum possible clearance between the car and the ground should be obtained to provide the easiest possible access and manoeuvring space for two people when the gearbox is eventually lowered to the ground.
3. Disconnect the battery leads, drain the cooling system and drain the oil from the gearbox and overdrive (if fitted). Disconnect the top radiator hose from the engine so that when the engine is tilted if will not be strained.
4. Remove the four bolts securing the rear end of the rear portion of the split propeller shaft to the pinion flange, having first made mating marks to ensure reassembly in the same position.
5. Now separate it by the same method from the rear of the centre bearing, again making sure that appropriate mating marks are made.
6. Remove the bolts securing the bearing assembly to its bracket, and with the front half of the propeller shaft still attached pull them out of the gearbox extension having first placed a tray under the extension to catch any escaping oil. Now remove the gearbox drain plug and allow the rest of the oil to drain into the tray or suitable container.
7. Unscrew the knob from the gearlever, then prise up the centre tray from the console (Photo), and undo the four screws under the tray (Photo).
8. Remove the screws and bracing pieces from the front of the console (Photo), then slightly lift the console at the rear and reaching underneath disconnect the cigarette lighter.
9. The console can now be lifted over the gearlever and clear of the car (Photo).
10. Undo the four screws holding the plate at the bottom of the gear stick (Photo) then lift the plate clear (Photo).
11. Now lift the ball disc off the gear stick (Photo), then pull the

Section 3.11. Removing gear stick from gearbox

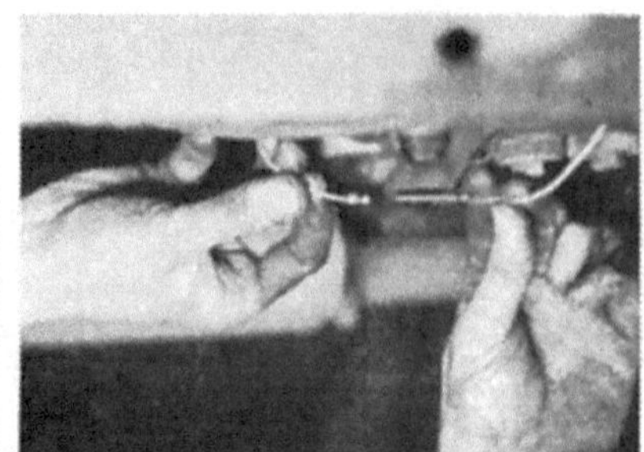

Section 3.12.
Disconnecting reversing light

Section 3.13. Disconnecting speedometer cable

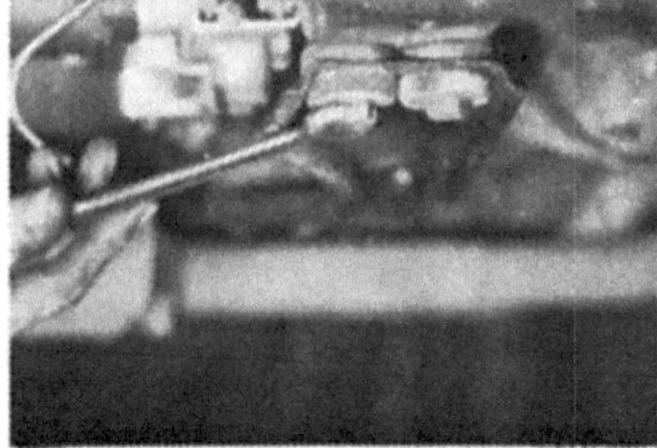

Section 3.17.
Removing gearbox crossmember bolts

Section 4.2.
Removing gearbox top cover

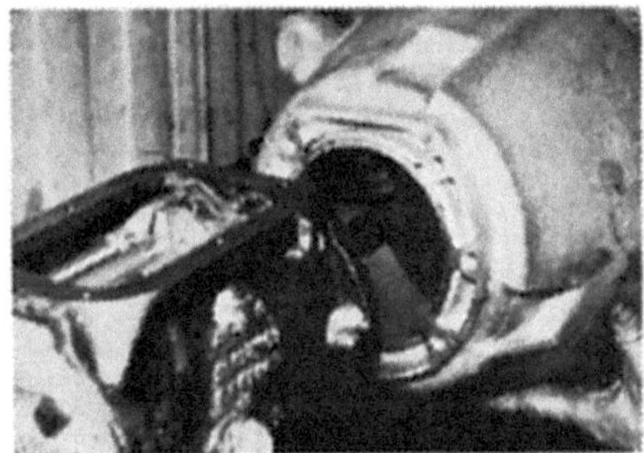

Section 4.3.
Separating gearbox and clutch

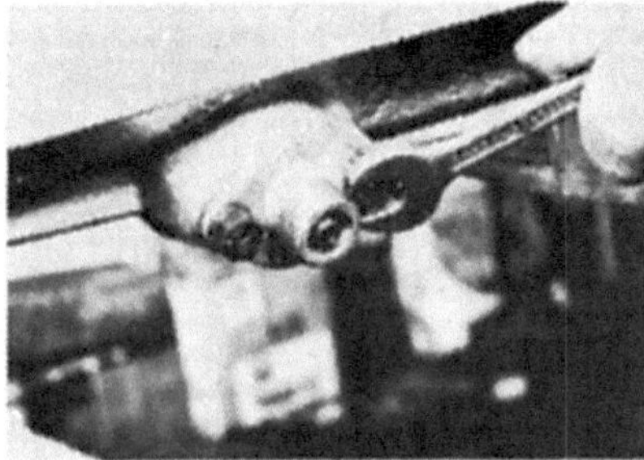

Section 4.4. Removing speedometer drive gear mechanism

complete gear stick and its spring from its location in the gearbox extension (Photo).

12.Moving underneath the car disconnect the reversing light wire at its connector, if fitted, and the overdrive wire (Photo).

13.Unscrew the knurled nut at the end of the speedometer cable where it enters the gearbox extension and pull the cable clear (Photo). Tuck it out of harm's way.

14.It is necessary to detach the centre track rod of the steering gear from the drop arm and slave arm connections. This is so that the bellhousing is not obstructed when the gearbox is drawn back. The centre track rod will still be connected to the outer track rods but it will be possible to drop it the necessary 3 to 4 inches. For details of disconnecting the ball joint pins refer to Chapter 11.

15.Remove the clutch hydraulic cylinder mounting bolts and move the cylinder to one side. The hydraulic system need not be disturbed.

16.Undo and remove the bolts between the sump and the bellhousing, then remove the starter motor bolts and draw the starter forward, clear of the housing. It may rest alongside the engine if tied up with a piece of string to hold it in place.

17.So that the gearbox may be withdrawn from the engine, the engine has to be tilted backwards and this is achieved when the rear supporting crossmember is removed. Before removing this, however, the engine must be supported on a jack which will keep the degree of tilt under control. The head of the jack should be placed as near the rear of the sump as possible. Put a piece of wood between the jack and sump to spread the load. The crossmember may then be removed by undoing the four rubber bushed mounting bolts - two at each end (Photo).

18.Carefully lower the jack so that the engine tilts sufficiently to enable the gearbox to come off when the remainder of the bell-housing bolts are removed. Watch the front of the engine to see that the sump does not foul the anti-roll bar; although when sufficiently tilted the engine may be chocked with wood against the roll bar.

19.The remainder of the bolts holding the bellhousing to the engine may now be removed and the gearbox should be free to move.

20.Two people at least are needed to support the weight of the gearbox. If they are lying underneath the car it is a wise precaution to place some soft padding such as sacks underneath the gearbox. Then, if the weight is suddenly too much, it will not be damaged if it falls a bit quickly! Whatever else may happen do not tilt the gearbox nor heave it from side to side whilst it is still mated to the clutch

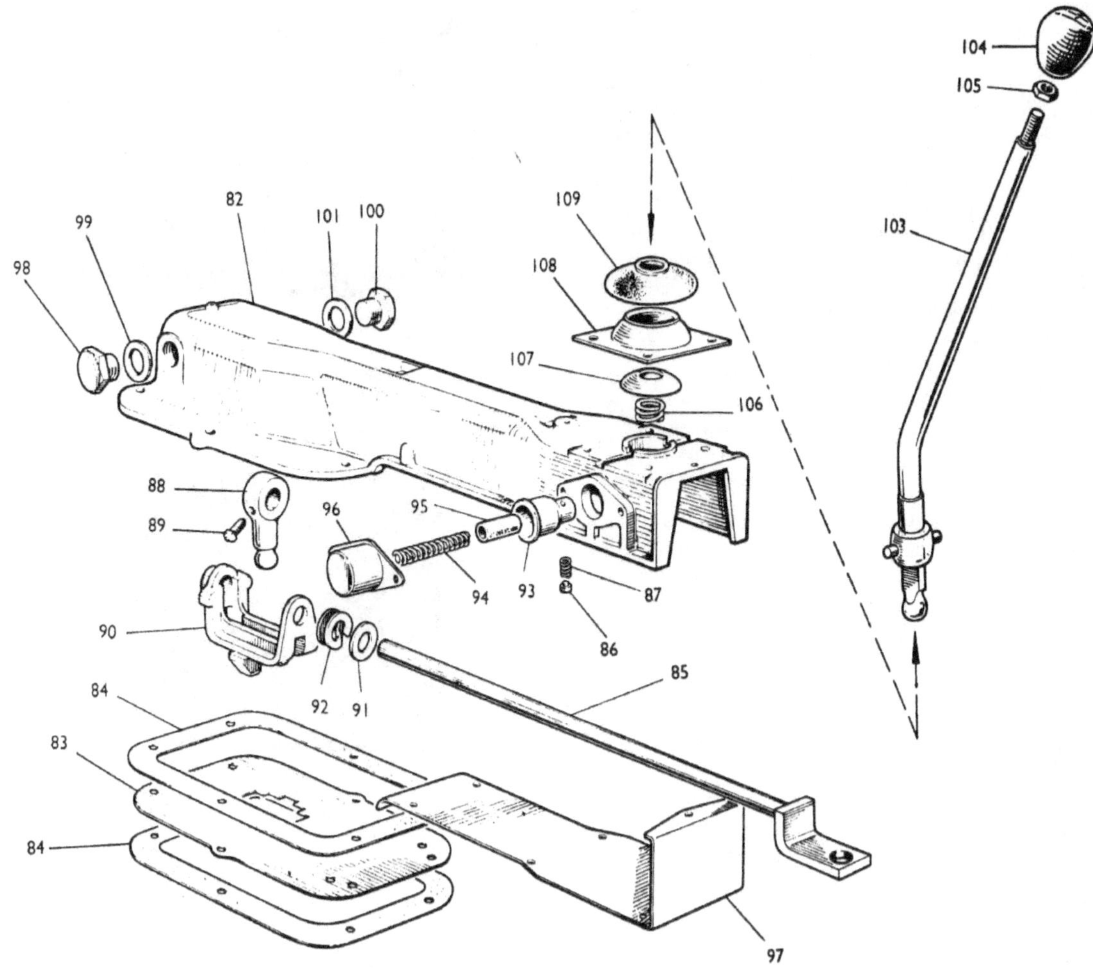

Fig.6.1. GEARBOX: TOP COVER & GEARCHANGE MECHANISM

82	Top cover	91	Washer	100	Plug - overdrive switch hole
83	Oil shield	92	Spring washer	101	Washer
84	Gasket	93	Reverse stop plunger	103	Gear change lever
85	Change shaft	94	Spring	104	Knob
86	Damper pad	95	Rubber sleeve	105	Locknut
87	Spring	96	Retainer	106	Spring
88	Selector lever	97	Closing plate	107	Disc
89	Locking screw	98	Plug-reverse light switch hole	108	Retaining cap
90	Selector safety catch	99	Washer	109	Grommet

assembly. This could cause strain and damage to the gearbox input shaft or clutch cover.

21. Replacement of the gearbox is a reversal of the removal procedure but the following points have to be borne in mind:

a) The clutch friction disc must be properly centred if the clutch assembly has been disturbed (Chapter 5 refers).

b) The propeller shaft should be replaced so that the mating flanges line up in the same position.

c) Do not forget to replace the oil.

4. Gearbox - Dismantling

1. Before any dismantling begins, thoroughly clean off the gearbox exterior with paraffin or a proprietary solvent. This will keep the working area clean and minimise the possibility of dirt and grit being transferred from the exterior to the interior.

2. Next remove the top cover (Fig.6.1), which incorporates the remote change mechanism, by undoing the six bolts which hold it to the top of the gearbox casing (Photo). The oil shield plate underneath should then be lifted off.

3. The clutch thrust release bearing and arm should now be detached as described in Chapter 5. The bellhousing may next be separated from the gearbox casing by undoing the six bolts and washers inside the bellhousing (Photo).

4. Next, remove the mainshaft extension cover, or overdrive unit if fitted. To do this, first remove the two setscrews holding the speedometer drive gear mechanism to the side of the cover (Photo). With these removed the whole assembly may be drawn out (Photo).

5. Then undo the bolts holding the overdrive or extension housing to the rear of the gearbox, and draw it off (Photo). If wished, the mounting crossmember can be removed from it but this is not essential.

6. The selector rails and forks are next to be dismantled and the first thing to note is that the rails must be driven out from the front towards the rear. Also, one should have available dummy selector rails made from 1/16 inch rod (11 mm). These are used to retain the detent balls and springs in the selector forks when the rail proper is driven out. Otherwise the ball could fly out and get lost. Three shafts are needed, 2 x 2.9 inch (73.6 mm) long and one 4.95 inch (125.7 mm) long. On some models the 3rd/4th selector fork (the one on the centre rail) has a long integral boss instead of a spacer tube, and for these two long and one short dummy rail are required. Using the dummy shafts, drive out the selector rails from the front of the casing starting with the reverse selector rail (the left one). Leave the dummies in position after the rails have been driven out and then lift out the selector forks.

7. The next step is to remove the layshaft so that the laygear cluster may be lowered to the bottom of the box. A dummy shaft will certainly be needed for reassembly so it is best to use it also for dismantling. It should be made from ¾ inch (18 mm) diameter bar or tube and be 6½ inches (165 mm) long. A piece of electrical conduit pipe was used on the occasion when the photographs were taken. First remove the bolt and washer holding the locking plate into the groove at the rear of the casing. Using the dummy layshaft drive the layshaft out from the front of the box. Provided the dummy shaft has not been made too long it will fit flush with the ends of the laygear and permit it to drop the inch or so to the bottom of the casing.

8. If the four nuts (or setscrews) holding the front cover to the casing are now taken out, the input shaft, bearing and front cover can all be withdrawn from the casing. The counter bore end of the input shaft houses 23 needle rollers and a spacer ring and these should be taken out now and kept in a suitable container where they will not be lost. The baulk ring on the 3rd/4th synchro hub for 4th gear will now be free to lift off the end of the mainshaft assembly. Ideally, its position should be noted so that the cut-outs will relate to the same hub blocker bars on replacement.

9. The mainshaft assembly is removed through the front of the casing. First remove the two circlips which hold the nylon worm gear for the speedometer in position. Then use the jaw of a large open-ended spanner and a hammer to drive the gear off the shoulder of the shaft rearwards. Remove and retain safely the Woodruff key. To undo the mainshaft nut the shaft will have to be held firm. It can be locked in the box by engaging two gears at once, i.e. sliding the forward hub back on to 3rd gear and the rear hub on to either 1st or 2nd. Alternatively, the shaft can be gripped in the soft metal covered jaws of a vice but help will be needed to support the weight of the casing if this is done (Photo). If a lockwasher is fitted, bend back the tab and with a suitably large spanner undo the nut and take it and the washer off the shaft. The front end of the mainshaft should now be supported with one hand and the shaft driven forward with a mallet through the rear bearing which will remain where it is. As soon as the shaft is free it can be fed through the front of the casing, but 1st gear and its centre bush will have to be slid off the back of the shaft as they are too large to go through the hole. Do not drop them!

10. With the mainshaft assembly removed lift up the laygear from the bottom of the box keeping it horizontal so that the needle rollers in the ends do not fall out unintentionally. Take out also the two thrust washers located one at each end of the laygear, between it and the casing.

11. The mainshaft bearing can now be driven out of the casing from the inside, using a suitable drift.

12. The reverse idler gear and operating lever do not normally need removal as they rarely cause trouble, being comparatively little used. However, if it is necessary a spacer will have to be made. Remove the operating lever and the screw and spindle locking pin from the side of the casing. Then make up a U shaped spacer from some 3/16 flat strip. It should be 5/7 inch (16 mm) long and radiused to fit round the smaller diameter of the idler shaft (See Fig.6.2). The gear can then butt the spacer up to the larger diameter shoulder at the front end of the shaft. Use a brass drift through the rear of the casing placed near the centre of the gear, and drive the shaft forward out of the casing. The gearbox is now completely stripped into main assemblies.

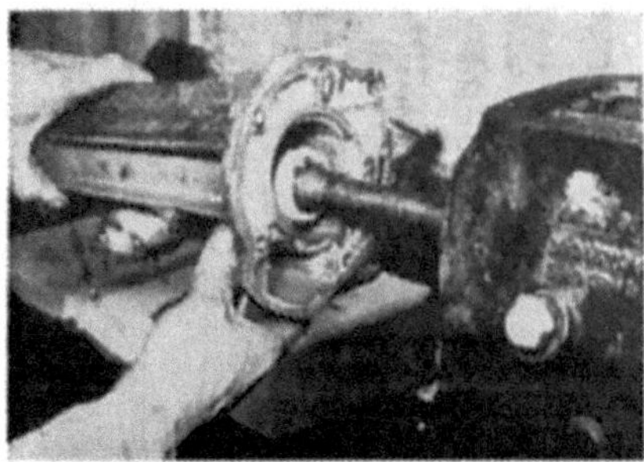

Section 4.5.
Removing gearbox extension housing
(or overdrive if fitted)

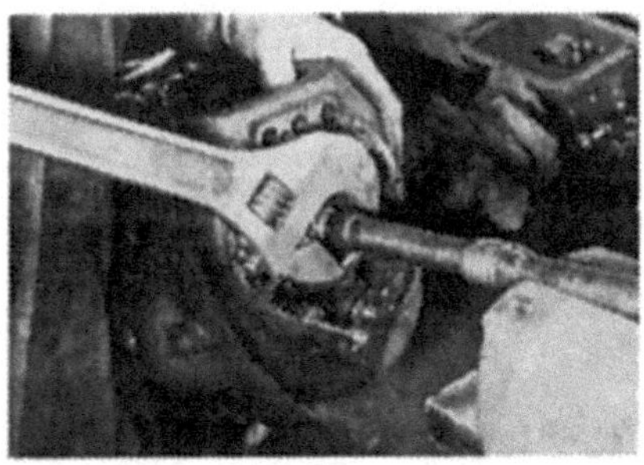

Section 4.9.
Removing gearbox mainshaft

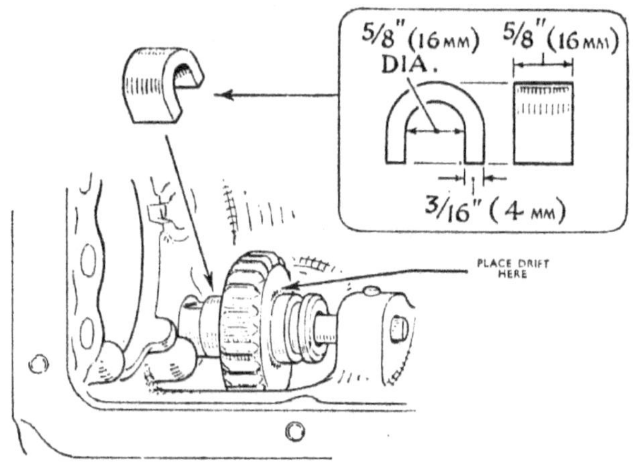

Fig.6.2. Reverse idler gear: dimensions of spacer required to drift out the shaft

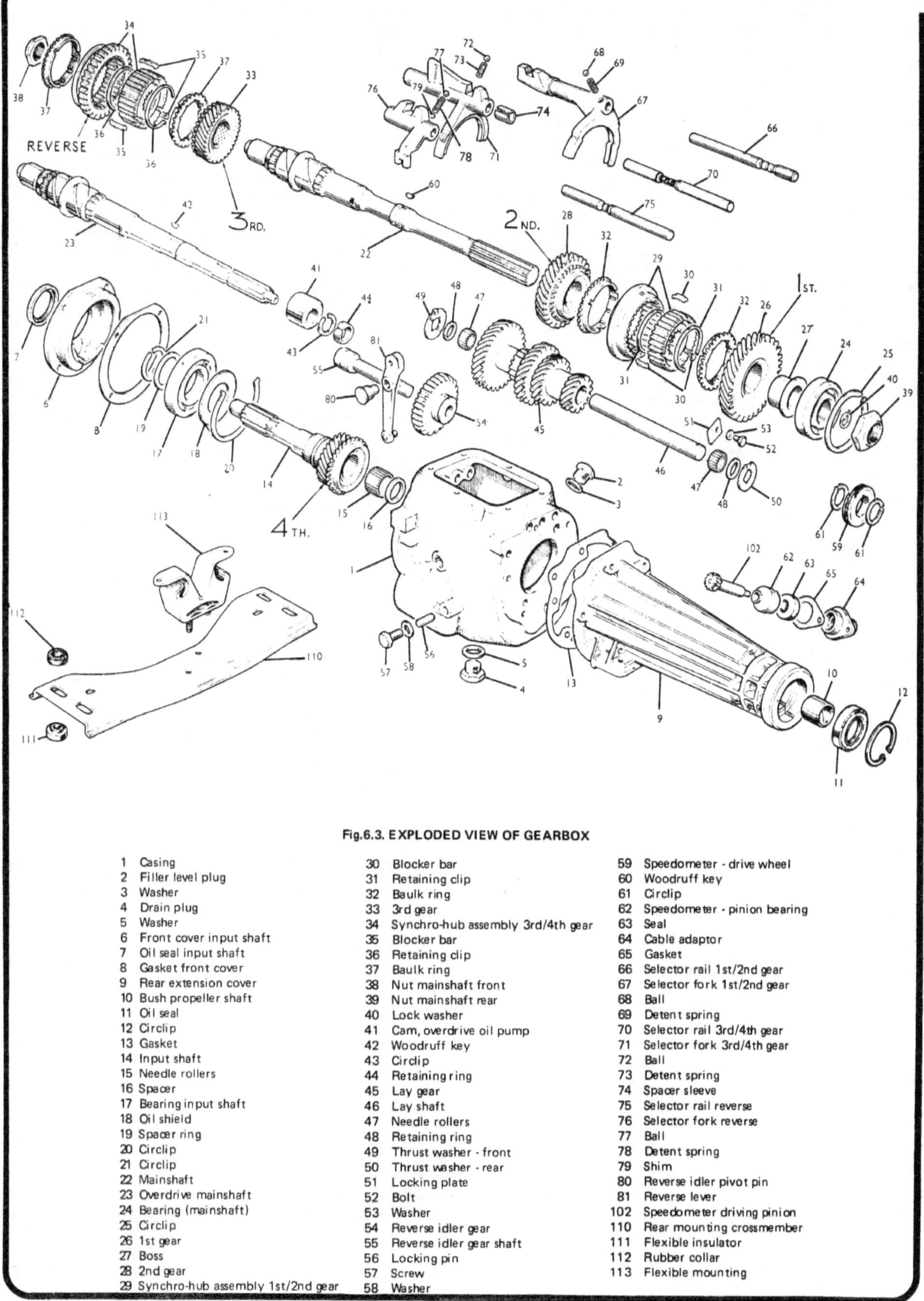

Fig.6.3. EXPLODED VIEW OF GEARBOX

1 Casing
2 Filler level plug
3 Washer
4 Drain plug
5 Washer
6 Front cover input shaft
7 Oil seal input shaft
8 Gasket front cover
9 Rear extension cover
10 Bush propeller shaft
11 Oil seal
12 Circlip
13 Gasket
14 Input shaft
15 Needle rollers
16 Spacer
17 Bearing input shaft
18 Oil shield
19 Spacer ring
20 Circlip
21 Circlip
22 Mainshaft
23 Overdrive mainshaft
24 Bearing (mainshaft)
25 Circlip
26 1st gear
27 Boss
28 2nd gear
29 Synchro-hub assembly 1st/2nd gear
30 Blocker bar
31 Retaining clip
32 Baulk ring
33 3rd gear
34 Synchro-hub assembly 3rd/4th gear
35 Blocker bar
36 Retaining clip
37 Baulk ring
38 Nut mainshaft front
39 Nut mainshaft rear
40 Lock washer
41 Cam, overdrive oil pump
42 Woodruff key
43 Circlip
44 Retaining ring
45 Lay gear
46 Lay shaft
47 Needle rollers
48 Retaining ring
49 Thrust washer - front
50 Thrust washer - rear
51 Locking plate
52 Bolt
53 Washer
54 Reverse idler gear
55 Reverse idler gear shaft
56 Locking pin
57 Screw
58 Washer
59 Speedometer - drive wheel
60 Woodruff key
61 Circlip
62 Speedometer - pinion bearing
63 Seal
64 Cable adaptor
65 Gasket
66 Selector rail 1st/2nd gear
67 Selector fork 1st/2nd gear
68 Ball
69 Detent spring
70 Selector rail 3rd/4th gear
71 Selector fork 3rd/4th gear
72 Ball
73 Detent spring
74 Spacer sleeve
75 Selector rail reverse
76 Selector fork reverse
77 Ball
78 Detent spring
79 Shim
80 Reverse idler pivot pin
81 Reverse lever
102 Speedometer driving pinion
110 Rear mounting crossmember
111 Flexible insulator
112 Rubber collar
113 Flexible mounting

5. Gearbox - Examination of Main Assemblies

1. The gearbox has presumably been dismantled because of one of the faults listed under Fault Finding in Section 10. To rectify faulty synchromesh, gear jumping and other operative faults is usually straightforward enough, although if quietness is also demanded it is virtually impossible to guarantee it without renewing everything. Worn gears will still work but not quietly. Examine the input shaft bearing for signs of sloppiness or roughness - it is usually the first component to wear. In any case it is worthwhile fitting a new one while the box is stripped. Examine the mainshaft bearing similarly.

2. There are four baulk rings, one each side of the two synchroniser hub assemblies, but only one of these (for 4th gear) can be renewed without dismantling the mainshaft. The critical wear occurs in the three cut-outs where the blocker bars engage, and is difficult to judge unless by comparison with a new one. As a general guide it is worthwhile replacing all four baulk rings anyway, and certainly if the synchromesh is at fault.

3. The hubs themselves should be gripped (by hand) and twisted to see if the outer sliding sleeve moves rotationally in relation to the hub. If it does the splines between the hub and sleeve are worn and the whole hub assembly needs renewal.
4. All gears should be examined for signs of chipped teeth and extraordinary wear. They should also be a smooth sliding fit on the shaft and not rock at all.

5. The nose of the mainshaft, which engages in the needle rollers in the counter bore of the input shaft, should be examined for signs of pitting or ridging. If such signs are apparent the only cure is a new mainshaft. Examine the needle rollers also for signs of wear or pitting and renew them all if one looks bad.

6. The layshaft gears should be examined for chipping or extreme wear. The shaft itself may show signs of wear at the ends where the gear runs on the needle roller bearings. If there is severe pitting or ridging then the layshaft should be renewed and new needle roller bearings fitted. The thrust washers at the ends of the laygear should be renewed as a matter of course.
7. The selector mechanism should also have careful examination. Check the forks to see that they are not worn where they guide the hub sleeve. The 3rd/4th selector runs in a groove in the hub and there should be no play between the hub groove and fork. The 1st/2nd selector fork is grooved to engage and land on the hub and here again there should be no play between the two. An impositive 'feel' in gear changing or jumping out of gear could be caused by insufficient pressure being exerted by the detent springs on the balls when engaged in the selector rail grooves. This can be tested by gripping the selector fork in a soft jawed vice and temporarily replacing the appropriate rail. A suitable clamp and hook should be fitted to the end of the rail so that a pull scale can be attached. The force necessary to pull the rail groove across the ball should be between 25–35 lb for forward gears and 40–45 lb for reverse. The spring loading can be varied by adding or removing shims underneath the detent spring in the fork. This effectively tensions or relaxes the spring as necessary. If there are signs of wear on the rails or balls they should be renewed; as should any broken springs, of course.
8. Examine the gear casing for any signs of damage or cracks.
9. To summarize, if the gearbox is being dismantled it is worthwhile renewing the following items as a matter of course; the gaskets are essential.

Input and mainshaft bearings (2)
Baulk rings (4)
Laygear thrust washers (2)
Gaskets including cover oil seals (set)
Circlips and mainshaft nuts.

10. If there are many other components in an obviously tired condition one must weigh up the advantages of replacing many parts (and ending up with a less than perfect gearbox) against obtaining a fully reconditioned unit on exchange.

6. Gearbox - Input Shaft Bearing - Removal & Replacement

1. The bearing is held into the front cover by a large internal circlip, the ends of which fit in a cut-out in the cover. Remove the circlip. If the edge of the cover is carefully supported between vice jaws, gear facing downwards, the shaft can be driven down with a mallet, and the bearing and shaft together will come out of the cover. Next remove the external circlips round the shaft in front of the bearing and the abutment washer behind it. Then support the bearing on the vice jaws, making sure that the gear teeth are not fouling them and drive the shaft out downwards from the bearing. Remove the shield plate from behind the bearing.
2. Refitting the bearing to the input shaft is a reversal of the removal method. Place the shield over the shaft first and then place the shaft into the bearing. Support the bearing on the inner race across the soft clad vice jaws and drive the shaft into it with a mallet. Do not close the vice jaws too far or they will catch the shoulder on the shaft. Make sure the bearing is driven on right up to the limit of the shoulder.
3. The abutment washer comes in one of two thicknesses, 0.054–0.056 inch or 0.058–0.060 inch, and the larger of the two should be fitted, if it will go between the bearing and circlip. A new circlip should also be used.
4. It is wise to renew the front cover oil seal also before refitting the bearing and shaft. Drive out the old one from the inside using a suitable punch. Fit the new one in square so that the flexible lip faces the bearing. The shaft and bearing may now be driven into the cover. One note of caution here. There are occasions when the lip of the oil seal stubbornly refuses to go on to the seal land on the shaft but sticks on the shoulder before reaching it, thus forcing the inner part of the seal back. This is no good as the seal will soon wear out and leak. To guide the lip of the seal on to the land, a tube made up of flexible shim steel will be needed to put round inside the seal and over the shaft land. This can then be withdrawn after the bearing is fully home inside the front cover.
5. Refit the large circlip locking the bearing and shaft into the cover.

7. Gearbox Mainshaft - Dismantling & Reassembly

1. The difficult parts to shift on the mainshaft are the two synchro hub assemblies which are the only items now left to remove. They are a splined press fit on to the shaft. They have to be moved by pressure as opposed to striking. If no press equipment is handy, two long levers with lipped ends (tyre levers) are essential. It is best also to try and avoid dismantling them unless it is absolutely necessary. If they do happen to fly apart, it will be impossible to know where each blocker bar came from and how the splines were mated. It will not mean that the hub is useless but wear will be accelerated when unmatched surfaces come together on reassembly. For those who wish to inspect the hubs in detail, information is given at the end of this Section.
2. Grip the plain section of the tail end of the shaft in the padded jaws of a vice so that the two hub assemblies are tilted upwards. To remove the front nut requires a large socket or tubular spanner. If none is available cut a nick near one of the corners of the nut and undo it with a steel drift and hammer. The locking ring is peened into the groove but this will automatically come away when the nut turns. If this locking ring is seriously chewed up when the nut is removed a new nut should be obtained to ensure safe locking up when reassembled.

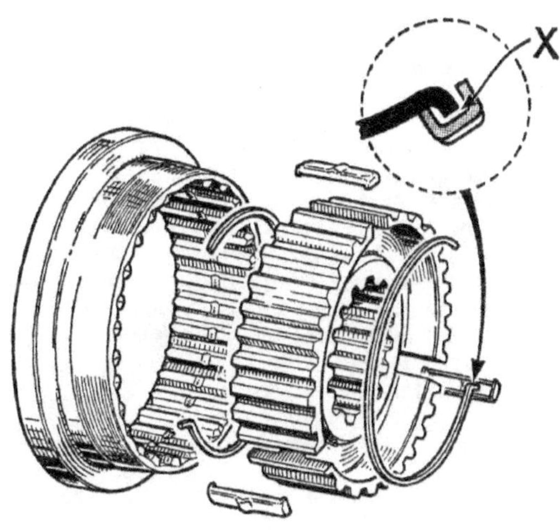

Fig.6.4. Synchro hub (note gap (X) which should exist between the end of the retaining clip and the recess in the blocker bar)

Section 7.3. Removing 2nd and 3rd gears

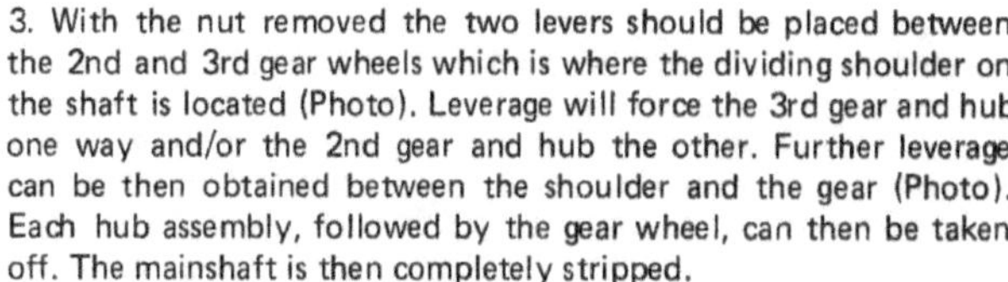

3. With the nut removed the two levers should be placed between the 2nd and 3rd gear wheels which is where the dividing shoulder on the shaft is located (Photo). Leverage will force the 3rd gear and hub one way and/or the 2nd gear and hub the other. Further leverage can be then obtained between the shoulder and the gear (Photo). Each hub assembly, followed by the gear wheel, can then be taken off. The mainshaft is then completely stripped.
4. If a hub assembly is suspected of being worn and is to be dismantled, first mark with a coloured wax crayon or a small dab of paint, the relative positions of the hub and outer sleeve and each blocker bar to its groove in the hub. Then slide the outer sleeve off the hub and the blocker bars and spring circlips will fall free. Then replace the sleeve on the hub. It should slide freely but with no other movement possible. The internal teeth on the sliding sleeve should have flat faces and be free from grooves or ridges. The blocker bars should be identical in length and top profile. The blocker bar circlips should not show signs of wear where they rest on the edges of the bars and the turned over end should not touch the inner face of the bar (see Fig.6.4). If it does, carefully grind a little off. When reassembling the hub fit the circlips so that when viewed from their own side the hooked end is at the anticlockwise tail of the clip. Do not put both hooked ends into the same blocker bar. If a hub is badly worn the whole assembly should be renewed, bearing in mind, of course, the overall condition of the gearbox.
5. Reassemble the mainshaft by first clamping it in a vice by the plain section of the rear end, using soft jaws in the vice (Photo). Third gear should then be placed over the nose of the shaft (3rd gear is the smallest of the three gears on the mainshaft - top gear is on the input shaft). The helical tooth part of the gear abuts the shoulder on the shaft. Then place a baulk ring over the gear cone, making sure that it is the right type (Photo); the two rings on the 3rd/4th hub are different from those on the 1st/2nd hub. The hub assembly is next put on with the selector fork groove of the outer sleeve towards the nose of the shaft. This will be a drive fit on to the splines and two things have to be carefully watched. You do not want the thing to fly apart when putting it on, so when driving it on with a drift hit the centre of the boss only (Photo). At the same time keep an eye on the baulk ring to make sure the three cut-outs line up on the blocker bars of the hub when it is driven fully home.

Section 7.5. Reassembling 3rd/4th hub on mainshaft

6. The large front nut should next be fitted. Strictly speaking, a new one should be used because the old self locking ring will almost certainly line up with the used part once more against the groove. However, it is known for them to be re-used provided the locking ring is not severely disturbed on removal. The nut should be tightened to a torque of 80 lb/ft. and the locking ring staked into the groove. If you have to tighten up using a hammer and drift, use a 2 lb hammer and take it as far as it will go (Photo).

7. Remove the mainshaft from the vice and support it vertically in the jaws, tail end upwards, clamping the nose between soft jaw plates. 2nd gear is fitted next (the middle size of the three), placed with the helical teeth abutting the shoulder. Place a baulk ring over the cone of the gear wheel (Photo). Just like the 3rd/4th hub this one has to be driven on to the splines and thus should be done with the drift against the centre hub only (Photo). Note also that the selector fork land of the outer sleeve is next to the 2nd gear wheel.

8. Gearbox Rear Cover - Removal & Refitting of Oil Seal

1. The rear cover oil seal should be renewed if the gearbox is dismantled and of course must be if it is obviously leaking. It is possible to do this job with the gearbox still in the car, after removing the propeller shaft. First take out the circlip which retains it, if fitted (Photo). There are three ways of getting the old seal out.
2. If you can borrow a proper extractor tool it can be drawn out quite easily with the gearbox on or off the car. If not, then it can be driven out with a long drift against the inside of the seal, provided, of course, that the rear cover is removed from the gearbox (Photo). This may also be done with the gearbox still in the car but will involve removal of the propeller shaft, speedometer drive gear and the rear support crossmember first.
3. The third method is to cut the old seal away from the outside with a cold chisel. This method will require great care to avoid damaging the bore of the case where the seal fits.

4. The new seal should be driven in firmly and square, open side inwards, with a suitably sized drift, such as an old piston (as was used in the photographs).

9. Gearbox - Assembly

1. Before assembly begins, make sure that every part is perfectly clean, including the interior of the casing, and that a supply of clean oil, grease and the necessary new parts and gaskets are available. A proprietary jointing compound should also be handy as all gaskets should be coated with it on fitting.

2. Check first that the endfloat of the laygear is correct. Place the two thrust washers in position so that the pips fit the cut-outs in the casing. Put the laygear (without the shaft) in position between them and measure with a feeler gauge, the gap between the end of the gear and the face of a thrust washer. It should be between 0.006–0.008 inch (0.15–0.20 mm) and if necessary a front thrust washer of a different thickness may be obtained from a Rootes/Chrysler parts store.

3. Fit the mainshaft bearing into the casing before anything else. First the circlip should be fitted into the outer race and the bearing tapped square into the casing. The wider part of the race (the circlip is off centre) goes into the casing (Photo).

4. Begin assembling by fitting the reverse idler gear assembly so that the flat on the smaller end of the shaft will engage with the pin in the interior supporting lug in the casing. Replace the operating lever with the pin in the groove of the gearwheel (Photo).

5. The laygear should now be prepared by fitting the 27 needle rollers into each end, holding them in position with thick grease (Photo). Then put the spacer ring on top of the rollers and put the dummy shaft into position in the gear (Photo). Put the cluster into the gearbox with the larger gear towards the front (Photo) and let it rest on the bottom. At the same time position the thrust washers at each end so that they line up as near as possible with the layshaft holes in the casing. They should be fitted so that the pips locate in the cut-outs in the casing and if smeared with grease they will not move around. In subsequent operations care should be taken not to disturb them. If they move out of line from the shaft holes too far it may be impossible to position them again when the time arrives to fit the layshaft, and that is one of the last things to be done.

6. The mainshaft can now be put into the casing from the front, tail end first. Get first gear with its centre boss and baulk ring ready (Photo), and when the end of the mainshaft is inside the box put the baulk ring on first, cut-out side towards the hub, followed by the gear wheel and boss (Photo). The gear wheel cone side goes towards the baulk ring and the flange of the boss is towards the tail end of the shaft. The mainshaft can then be put through the bearing in the casing.

7. The whole gearbox should now be carefully positioned over the vice jaws so that the mainshaft bearing is supported by the jaws and the rear of the mainshaft points downwards. The shaft is then driven downwards with a mallet and at the same time an eye must be kept on the 1st/2nd synchro hub and 1st gear baulk ring. As the gap between the gear and rear bearing diminishes the baulk ring must be positioned so that the three cut-outs line up with the blocker bars in the hub. If the fit of the shaft into the bearing is not too tight the final positioning may be done more easily with the gearbox horizontal once again on the bench (Photo). (Watch that the bearing is not inadvertently driven back out of the casing!)

8. The mainshaft locking nut can now be fitted. First fit the lock-washer and then run the nut up to it. Check once again that the first gear baulk ring is properly located and that the bearing circlip is fully up to the casing. Do not tighten the nut fully at this stage.

9. The gearbox is now ready to receive the input shaft assembly. First place the spacer ring over the nose of the mainshaft with the chamfered edge inwards, followed by the last of the four baulk rings which goes on to the front of the 3rd/4th hub. The three cut-outs should engage with the blocker bars. A little dab of grease will help to hold it in position until the input shaft is fitted.

10.The counter bore of the input shaft should be smeared with thick grease and the 23 needle rollers put into position. Then place a new gasket in position on the cover, having smeared it on both sides with jointing compound to ensure an oil tight seal. The assembly should then be located on the nose of the mainshaft engaging the front cover over the four studs in the casing. The flat on the front cover should be horizontal at the upper edge so that the oil drain hole in the casing is at the lower edge. Replace the nuts and tighten them up fully.

11.Now is the time to fit the layshaft. First make sure that the thrust washers are in position, and then carefully turn the box upside down so that the laygear drops into mesh with the mainshaft gears and input shaft. Make final adjustments to the position of the thrust washers, and then insert the layshaft from the rear of the gear casing, plain end leading. Carefully tap it through the laygear, driving the dummy shaft ahead. Do not pull the dummy shaft out ahead of the layshaft. If a single needle roller were to move out of position it could be a considerable fiddle getting it back into position again. As soon as the layshaft is home, line up the locking slot so that the

Section 7.6.
Fitting large front nut to mainshaft

Section 7.7. Fitting 2nd gear hub assembly

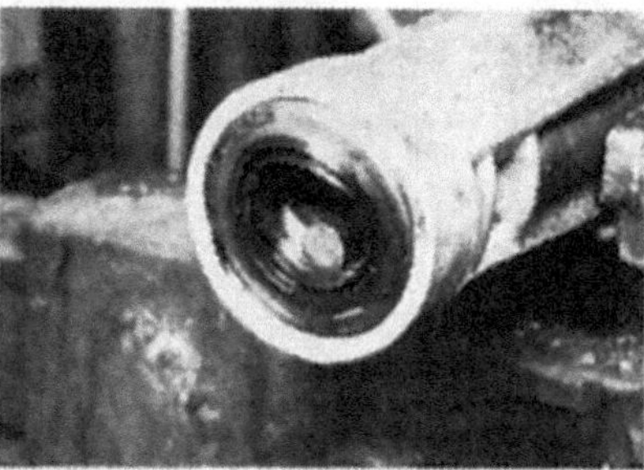

Sections 8.1 and 8.2. Removing rear cover oil seal

Section 8.4.
Applying new rear cover oil seal

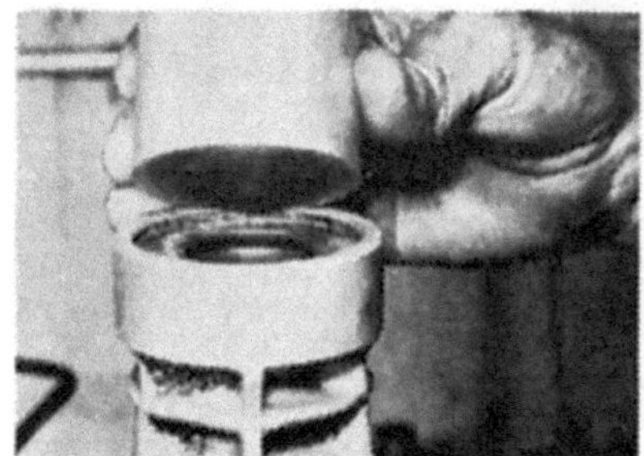

Section 8.4.
Driving in new rear cover oil seal

Section 9.3.
Fitting mainshaft bearing in casing

Section 9.4.
Assembling reverse idler gear in position

Section 9.5. Fitting needle roller bearings, dummy layshaft into laygear and into gearbox casing

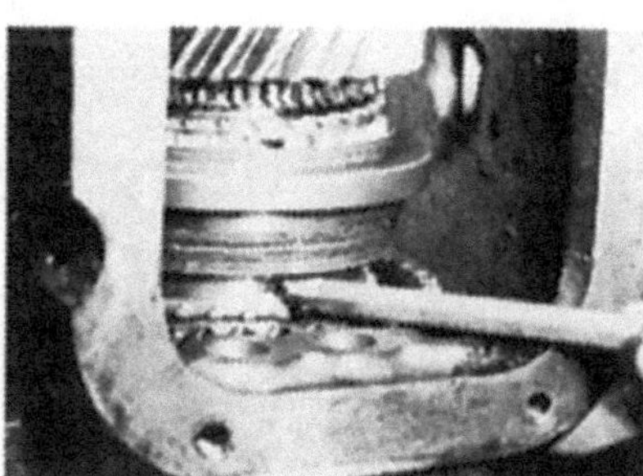

Sections 9.6 and 9.7. Fitting mainshaft and lining up baulk rings and synchro hubs

locking plate and bolt can be fitted and tightened.

12.The mainshaft nut can now be tightened to 80 lb ft of torque. If a suitable torque spanner is not available, full force on a 129 shifter will be adequate (Photo). The mainshaft can be locked, whilst tightening the nut, by locking both synchro hubs on to two gears at the same time. Otherwise the mainshaft should be manoeuvred so that it can be clamped in the vice whilst the weight of the gearbox is still supported properly. Move the hubs to neutral when finished. Punch the lockwasher on to a flat of the nut when fully tightened (Photo). Give the mainshaft a spin to ensure that everything is revolving freely and smoothly.

13.Next refit the speedometer drive gear inner circlip and Woodruff key. Drive on the gear with an open ended spanner jaw and fit the second circlip (Photos).

14.The selectors are fitted next. Provided dummy rails have been used no difficulty need be experienced. First fit the 1st/2nd selector fork in position (this is the one with the groove in the fork), then the 3rd/4th fork, and finally the reverse selector, fitting the small forked arm over the pin on the reverse operating lever.

15.The rails are fitted next, starting with the 1st/2nd gear selector rail. This is the one with the three detents nearest the end of the rail, and should be tapped in from the rear of the casing with the long plain section leading. The dummy rail will be driven ahead (Photo).

16.The 3rd/4th gear selector rail goes next in the centre. This rail has three detents nearer the centre than the 1st/2nd rail, and should be pushed in with the shorter plain section first. As soon as it is through the casing fit the sleeve over the end (if there is one) and then continue driving it through the fork. Once again the dummy rail will be driven ahead of it (Photo).

17.Finally insert the reverse selector rail, this being the one with only two detents. The shorter plain section goes in first, from the rear of the casing.

18.When all rails are fitted the ends should be flush with the casing. With the gears in neutral the cut-outs in the tops of the forks should line up with each other (Photo).

19.For those who have decided not to use dummy rails the appropriate shims and springs should be placed in the hole in the fork. The ball can then be held to the end of a suitable rod with a blob of grease (Photo) and put into position (Photo), and pressed down whilst the rail proper is moved forward to trap it (Photo). A steady hand and some patience are needed here, and it must also be remembered that if a ball, with a blob of grease attached, is dropped into the box, it might just stick in an awkward place and be very difficult to shake out. If this should happen, remove the springs and shims from the forks before inverting the box, and if necessary use a quantity of paraffin to flush it out.

20.Next fit a new gasket on to the mating face of the rear cover, having treated it with jointing compound on both sides, and offer up the cover to the casing (Photo). Replace the bolts and tighten them up (Photo).

21.There are two gaskets for the top cover, one above and one below the splash shield. Treat both with jointing compound before fitting them and the splash shield into position and replacing the top cover. Refit the top cover bolts and tighten them down evenly (Photos).

22.It is a good idea at this stage to refit the gear lever into the top cover remote control extension, so that the selection of gears can be checked. Check that the reverse stop plunger and spring are well greased and tight, and that the selector lever and screw are absolutely tight on the gearshift shaft.

23 Replace the clutch bellhousing (Photo) and clutch operating lever and thrust bearing.

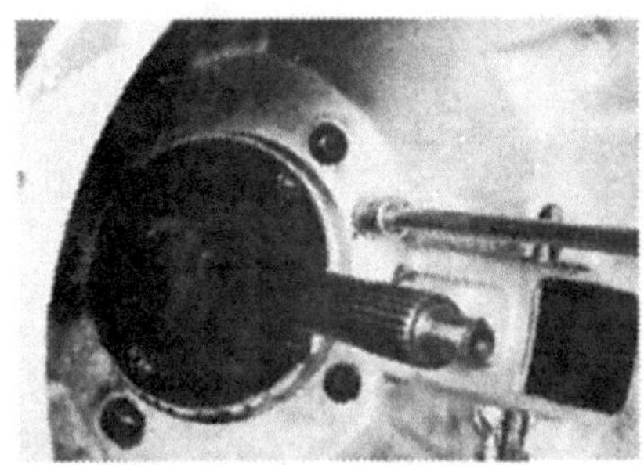

Section 9.23.
Replacing clutch bellhousing, operating lever and thrust bearing

10. Gearbox - Fault Finding

Faults in the gearbox can range from small buzzing noises and minor snags in engaging gears to serious faults such as loud howling whines, vibrations or great difficulty in remaining in or getting into gears in general. For serious faults the only thing to do is remove the gearbox and have a look, or just renew it unseen with a reconditioned or secondhand unit. For minor faults, other than those which can be positively identified as coming from the base of the gear lever which can be easily got at, it is more a matter of how long the fault or

Fault Finding Chart – Gearbox

Symptom	Reason/s	Remedy
Sloppy gear lever and rattles	Worn ball joint and pins or loose reverse stop plunger	Minor - can be repaired with gearbox in position
	Loose selector lever in top cover over gearbox	Serious - loose locking screw could drop in gearbox
Ineffective synchromesh on one or more gears	Worn baulk rings. Worn blocker bars	Minor - can go on for many miles
Jumps out of one or more gears	Weak detent springs Worn selector forks Worn engagement dogs Worn synchro hubs	Depends on how many gears involved and whether driving safety is affected
Whining, roughness, vibration, allied to other faults	Bearing failure and/or overall wear	Major - could break up and lock transmission which is dangerous
Noisy and difficult gear engagement	Clutch not operating correctly	

Section 9.12. Tightening and locking mainshaft nut

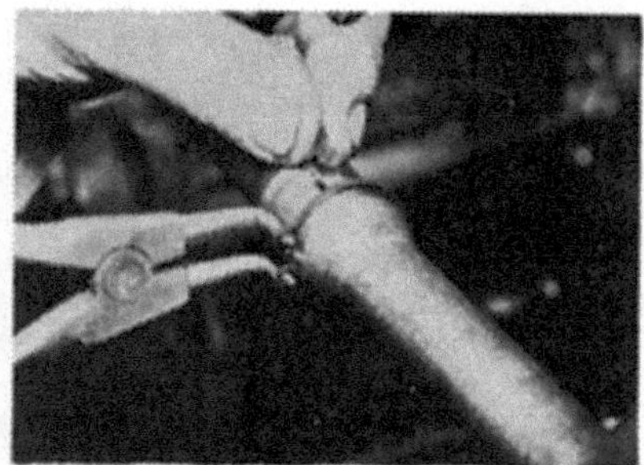

Section 9.13.
Fitting speedometer drive inner circlip and Woodruff key

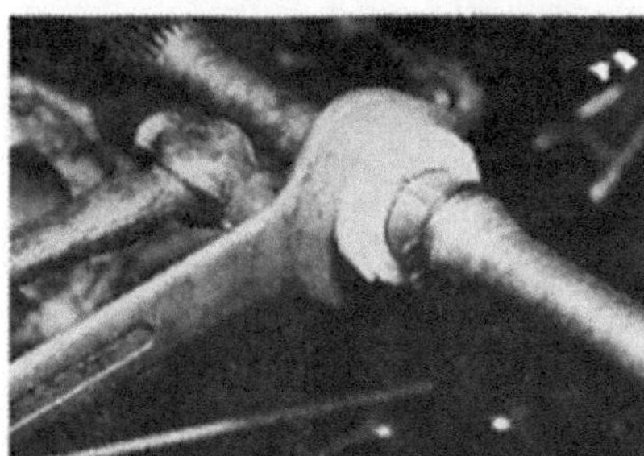

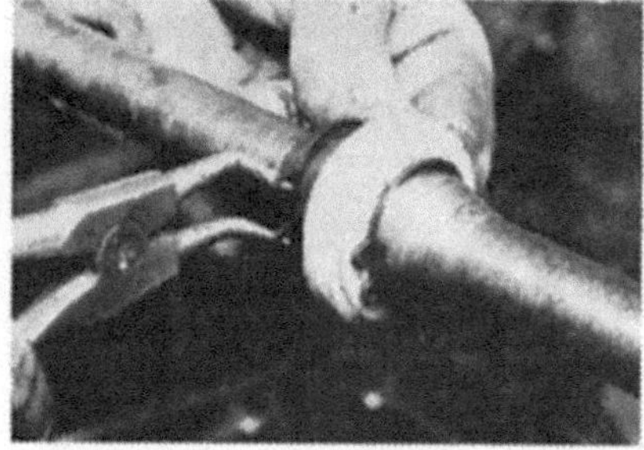

Section 9.13. Driving on speedometer gear and fitting second circlip

Section 9.15.
Fitting 1st/2nd gear selector rail

Section 9.16.
Fitting 3rd/4th gear selector rail

Section 9.18.
All selector rails fitted and fork cutouts all lined up in neutral gear position

Section 9.19.
Fitting parts to selector forks

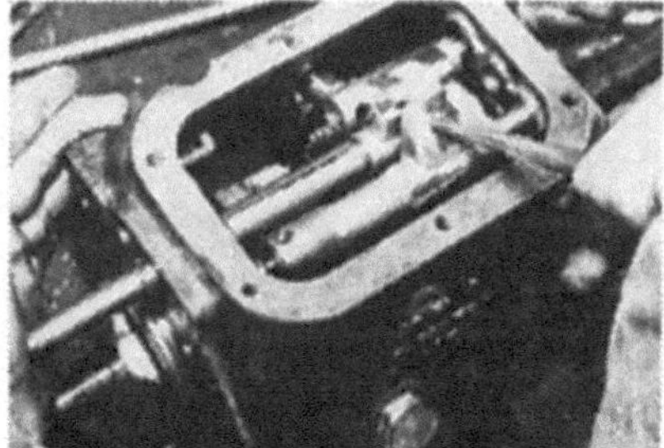

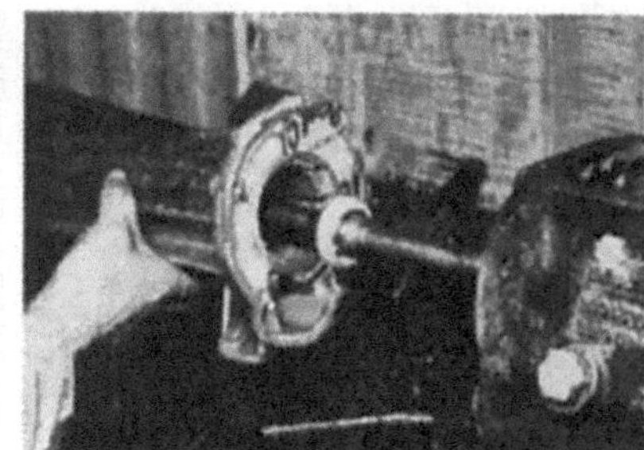

Section 9.19. Fitting parts to selector forks

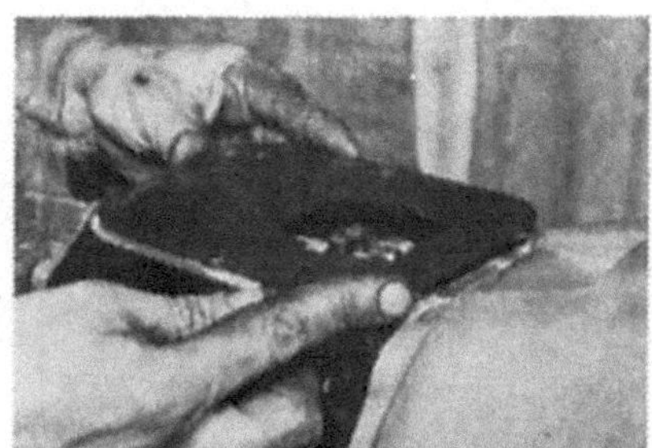

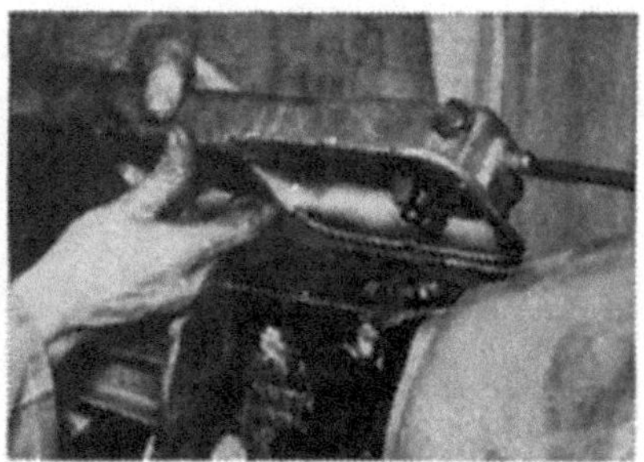

Section 9.20. and 9.21. Fitting new gearbox gaskets

irritating noise can be tolerated before doing something about it. Once something starts to wear to a noticeable degree other things may also start to deteriorate rapidly.

Unfortunately, the amount of trouble to rectify a minor fault will be the same as for a major one - removal and dismantling of the gearbox. One may save something on the cost of spares required but even this is open to doubt as accurate diagnosis can only be made when the gearbox is stripped. Some faults can go on for thousands of miles without getting noticeably worse or affecting anything else - a worn baulk ring for example. Failure of a bearing on the other hand could wreck the whole assembly in a few hundred miles. The list of faults and causes is intended to give the owner some help and guidance in deciding when to take action in the light of the degree of seriousness. All the faults require removal and dismantling of the gearbox except where stated.

11. Overdrive - General Description

The overdrive unit is attached to the extension on the rear of the gearbox by eight studs and nuts, and takes the form of a hydraulically operated epicyclic gear. Overdrive operates on third and fourth speeds to provide fast cruising at lower engine revolutions. The overdrive 'IN–OUT' switch on the right of the steering wheel actuates a solenoid attached to the side of the overdrive unit. In turn the solenoid operates a valve which opens the hydraulic circuit which pushes the cone clutch into contact with the annulus when overdrive is engaged (Fig.6.5 and 6.6).

Attached to the end of the extended gearbox mainshaft are the inner components of a unidirectional clutch. The hydraulic pressure which enables the overdrive clutch to be engaged is provided by a hydraulic pump operated by an eccentric cam on the front of the mainshaft.

Behind the cam is a steady bearing with a plain phospher-bronze bush carried in the main housing. Next to this is the sun wheel of the epicyclic gear which is carried on a Clevite bush. The planet carrier and unidirectional clutch come next and are mounted on splines cut in the mainshaft. The smaller diameter portion of the end of the mainshaft turns in a needle roller bearing fitted inside the larger diameter output shaft.

Two roller bearings mounted in the rear of the overdrive casing support the output shaft. A ball bearing housed in a flanged ring is held to the cone clutch member. A bolt at each of the four corners of the flange pass through one of the four clutch return springs by which the ring, together with the clutch cone, is held against the annulus.

The pressure of the springs prevents free-wheeling on overrun, and they are also strong enough to handle reverse torque. Also attached to the bolts are two bridge pieces which rest against two hydraulic operating pistons working in cylinders cast in the main casing.

The sun wheel and pinions are case hardened and the annulus heat treated. The pinions have needle roller bearings and run on case hardened pins. The gearteeth are helical. The outer ring of the unidirectional clutch is pressed into the annulus. The clutch is of the caged roller type and is loaded by a round wire lock type spring.

The overdrive unit works in the following way. Under normal running conditions with the overdrive switched out the cone clutch is held against the centre annulus by the four clutch return springs, so locking the sun wheel to the annulus. In this way the complete gear train rotates together as a solid unit giving direct drive.

On switching in the electrically operated solenoid, the centre rod moves inwards, operating the linkage mechanism which lifts a tube, so raising the ball valve off its seating against the pressure of the spring which normally holds the ball in place.

With the ball valve lifted, oil under pressure is free to travel along the drillings in the casing to the two operating cylinders. The pistons are pushed forward against the two bridge pieces which move the clutch cone into contact with the cast iron brake ring sandwiched between the main and tail casings. This brings the sun wheel to rest and allows the annulus to overrun the unidirectional clutch and so give an increased speed to the output shaft.

When the overdrive is switched out the rod in the centre of the solenoid moves outwards, allowing the valve tube to drop and the ball valve to return to its seat. Oil from the two cylinders is then free to return through the centre of the tube to the bottom of the overdrive casing. To ensure direct drive is re-engaged smoothly the cylinders are emptied slowly because of a small restrictor jet in the base of the valve tube. The oil is then free to flow round in open circuit.

The oil for the hydraulic system is supplied by a pump which is pressed into the main housing and held by a grub screw. The pump supplies oil through a non-return valve to a relief valve, in which a piston moves back against a compression spring, until the correct pressure is obtained when a hole in the relief valve is uncovered. Excess oil from the relief valve is then led through drilled passages to an annular groove in the mainshaft steady bush. Radial holes in the shaft feed oil through axial drillings to the needle roller bearings, thrust washers and unidirectional clutch.

The overdrive is normally a very reliable unit and trouble is usually due to either the solenoid sticking, a fault in the hydraulic system due to dirt or insufficient oil, or incorrect solenoid operating lever adjustment.

12. Overdrive - Removal & Replacement

1. It is not necessary to remove the overdrive from the car in order to attend to the following: the hydraulic lever setting; the relief valve; the non-return valve; the solenoid and the operating valve.
2. If the unit as a whole requires overhaul it must be removed from the car together with the gearbox, as described in Section 3 of this chapter.
3. Before separating the overdrive from the gearbox, remove the top cover and remote control assembly as described in Section 4, paragraph 2.
4. Undo the eight nuts from the ¼ inch (6.35 mm) diameter studs (noting the extra length of one of the studs), to separate the main overdrive casing from the gearbox rear extension. Carefully pull the overdrive off the end of the mainshaft.
5. To mate the overdrive and gearbox, start by placing the overdrive in an upright position and then line up the splines of the clutch and planet carrier by eye, turning them anticlockwise only, with the aid of a long thin screwdriver.
6. Under normal circumstances if everything is in line the gearbox mainshaft should enter the overdrive easily. If trouble is experienced do not try and force the components together but separate them and re-align the components. Place the gearbox in top gear while refitting.
7. As the mainshaft is fed into the overdrive gently, rotate the input shaft to and fro to help in feeling the mainshaft into the splines. At the same time make certain that the lowest portion of the cam on the mainshaft will rest against the pump. Also take care, as the gearbox extension and overdrive come together, that the end of the mainshaft enters into the needle roller bearing in the tail shaft.
8. The remainder of the replacement procedure is a straightforward reversal of the removal sequence.

13. Overdrive - Dismantling, Overhaul & Reassembly

1. All numbers in brackets in this section refer to Fig.6.6. Unscrew the operating valve plug (54) and take out the spring (38), plunger (39) and ball (40).
2. Undo the nuts (26) from off the bolts (19) then remove the two bridge pieces (25). If wished the two operating pistons (52) can now be pulled out of their cylinders in the main casing assembly (71).

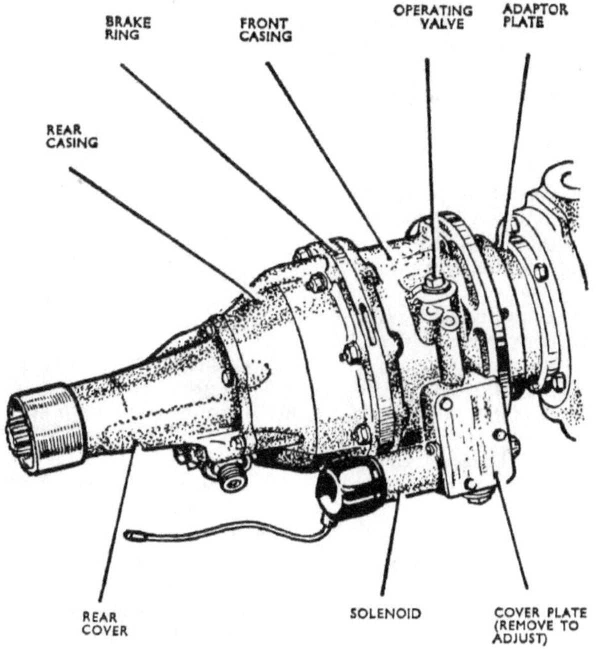

Fig.6.5. General view of the overdrive unit

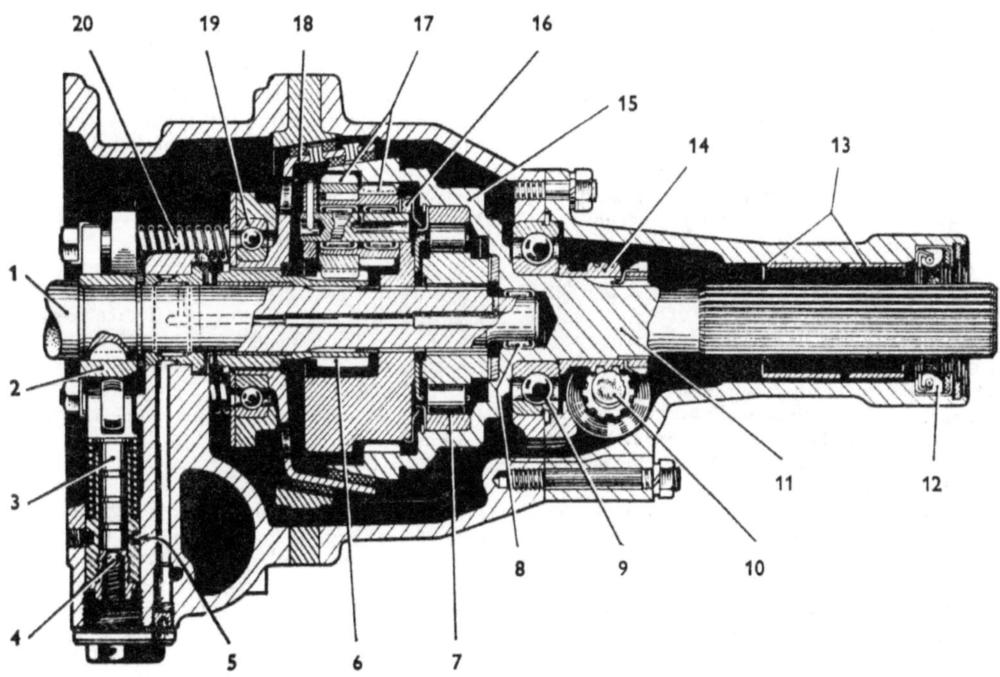

Fig.6.6. A SECTIONAL VIEW OF THE OVERDRIVE UNIT

1 Input shaft
2 Pump cam
3 Oil pump
4 Pump valve
5 Pump inlet
6 Sunwheel
7 Unidirectional clutch (splined to input shaft)
8 Spigot bearing
9 Rear bearing
10 Speedometer pinion
11 Output shaft (integral with annulus)
12 Oil seal
13 Support bushes
14 Speedometer wheel
15 Annulus
16 Planet carrier
17 Planet wheel
18 Cone clutch
19 Clutch thrust bearing
20 Clutch spring

3. Cut the locking wire (if fitted) on the non-return relief valve plug (59); undo the plug and remove the spring (47) and ball (46). The non-return valve body (48) can then be unscrewed from the pump body (50). Undo the grub screw (45) and pull the pump body (50) from the casing (71).

4. Undo the eight nuts and spring washers a turn at a time from the studs (70) which hold the main casing assembly (71) to the rear casing (73). As the nuts are undone the pressure of the springs (28) will gradually be released. Take off the main casing (71) together with the brake ring (72) and pull the four clutch springs (28) off their guide bolts (19). Remove the clutch (18) together with the sun wheel assembly (17).

5. It is likely that the brake ring (72) will stick to the casing (71). To separate the ring, gently tap it on its flange with a soft faced hammer.

6. To free the sun wheel (17) from the centre of the clutch assembly (18) release the circlip (24) on the splined end of the sun wheel and push out the sun wheel (17).

7. Remove the large circlip (23) with a pair of circlip pliers, and pull the bearing housing (20) complete with thrust bearing (21) off the clutch assembly (18).

8. Lift out the planet carrier (16) from the annulus (7). Removal of the unidirectional roller clutch is not recommended unless the rollers are thought to be chipped or worn, but if it is wished to do so, take off the circlip and brass retaining washer in front of the clutch.

9. As the inner member (11) is removed the roller bearings (10) will fall out. Gather them together carefully. On no account should the outer bearing ring be removed as it is expanded into the annulus.

10.If it is wished to renew the roller bearing (9) in the centre of the annulus (7), carefully lever it out or use an extractor if available.

11.To remove the combined output shaft and annulus (7) from the rear casing, first undo the locking screw to free the speedometer pinion and bush (80), then remove the tailshaft casing (75) from the rear casing (73) by undoing the six retaining nuts. When sliding off the tailshaft casing take care not to damage the oil seal (78) and bush (76).

12.Remove any shims (4) between the tailshaft cover and the annulus main bearing (6). Remove the circlip (5) from round the bearing (6) and remove the annulus (7) and bearing (6) by driving them forward into the rear casing (73).

13.To remove the rear bearing (6), knock back the lockwasher (2), undo the locknut (1) and slide off the speedometer drive gear (3) and the bearing (6).

14.Thoroughly clean all component parts and then examine them carefully. Check that the oil pump plunger and pin are not worn and that the spring has not contracted. Examine the O rings from the operating pistons and renew them if worn or if they are becoming hard, and check that the cylinder bores are free from score marks and wear. Check the ball bearings for roughness when turned and for looseness between the inner and outer races. Examine the splines for burrs and wear, and the rollers of the clutch for chips and flat spots.

15.Renew the clutch linings if they are burnt or worn, and carefully examine the main and rear casings for cracks or other damage. Renew the steady bush if it is worn, and examine the gear teeth for cracks, chips and general wear. Examine the sealing balls for ridges which will prevent them seating properly and check the free length of the springs.

16.Assembly of the unit can commence after any damaged or worn parts have been exchanged and new gaskets and seals obtained. Start by fitting the rear bearing (6) with its circlip groove to the rear over the output shaft. Drive the bearing with a piece of pipe into its correct position against the locating shoulder behind the annulus.

17.Fit the speedometer gear (3), the lockwasher (2) and the locknut (1). Now fit the annulus assembly (7) into the rear casing (73) and fit the circlip (5) into its groove in the bearing (6).

18.The bearing (6) is located at the rear by the tailshaft cover (75) and a shim or shims (4) is fitted into the recess in the cover to ensure a snug fit with a correct end float of the output shaft of 0.005 to 0.010 inch.

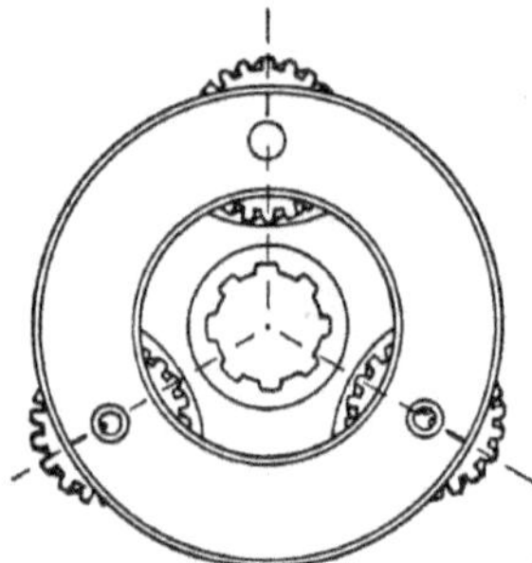

Fig.6.8. Line up etched lines on planet wheel and planet carrier before fitting to sunwheel

19.If it was necessary to fit a new bearing, note that four different thicknesses of shim are available. Shims can be obtained in the following sizes:--

0.090 in (2.28 mm) 0.095 in (2.41 mm), 0.100 in (2.54 mm) and 0.105 in (2.67 mm)

20.Refit the tailshaft cover (75) and secure it with the six nuts. Insert the speedometer drive and pinion (80) and secure it with its washer and locking screw.

21.Reassemble the components of the unidirectional clutch, holding the rollers (10) in place in the cage (13) with grease prior to fitting the inner member (11). Ensure that the circlip (12) is fitted in such a way that it pushes the rollers up the ramp on the inner member (11). Do not omit to replace the thrust bearing (8). Finally fit the retaining plate (14) and circlip (15) in place.

22.Turn each of the planet gearwheels so the line etched on one tooth of each of the gearwheels lines up with one of the three corresponding lines on the periphery of the planet carrier (see Fig. 6.8). Insert the sun wheel (17) into the carrier to keep the planet gearwheels in the correct positions, and carefully fit the complete sun wheel and carrier assembly to the annulus. When fitted, the sun wheel can be withdrawn. Note that the sun wheel can now be inserted or removed as frequently as required, but if the planet carrier is removed from the annulus, the carrier gear wheels will have to be reset as described at the beginning of the paragraph.

23.Slide the splined end of the sun wheel (17) into the centre of the clutch assembly and secure the sun wheel with the circlip (24). If the thrust bearing was removed for renewal press the new bearing (21) into its housing (20). Insert the four bolts (19) into the housing, threaded ends facing forwards, and fit the bearing and housing assembly over the centre of the clutch assembly (18). Lock the bearing and housing in place on the clutch with the bearing retaining circlip (23) which fits in a groove on the clutch.

24.Carefully fit the clutch and sun wheel assembly to the planet carrier in the annulus. Refit the retainer plate (22) and clutch springs (28) over the bolts (19).

25.Coat the mating faces of the main casing (71) and rear casing (73) with jointing compound, and offer up the rear casing to the brake ring and front casing. Slide the four bolts (19) through their holes in the main casing and replace and tighten down a turn at a time the nuts and washers which hold the casings together.

26.Fit the rubber O rings (55) to the two operating pistons (52) and with the pistons generously lubricated with oil slide them into their cylinders in the housing, so the spigoted ends face the front of the overdrive assembly. Slip the two bridge pieces (25) over the ends of the four bolts (19) and refit the nuts and washers (26,27) and tighten them down.

26.Replace the oil pump body, smaller end first, into the centre hole at the bottom of the casing, making sure that the oil inlet faces the rear. Gently tap it into position until the groove lines up with the grub screw hole. Fit and tighten the grub screw.

27.Refit the component parts of the relief valve, operating valve, and non-return valve in the order shown in Fig.6.7, and do up the three plugs. If fitted, lock the plugs together with wire. Assembly is now complete.

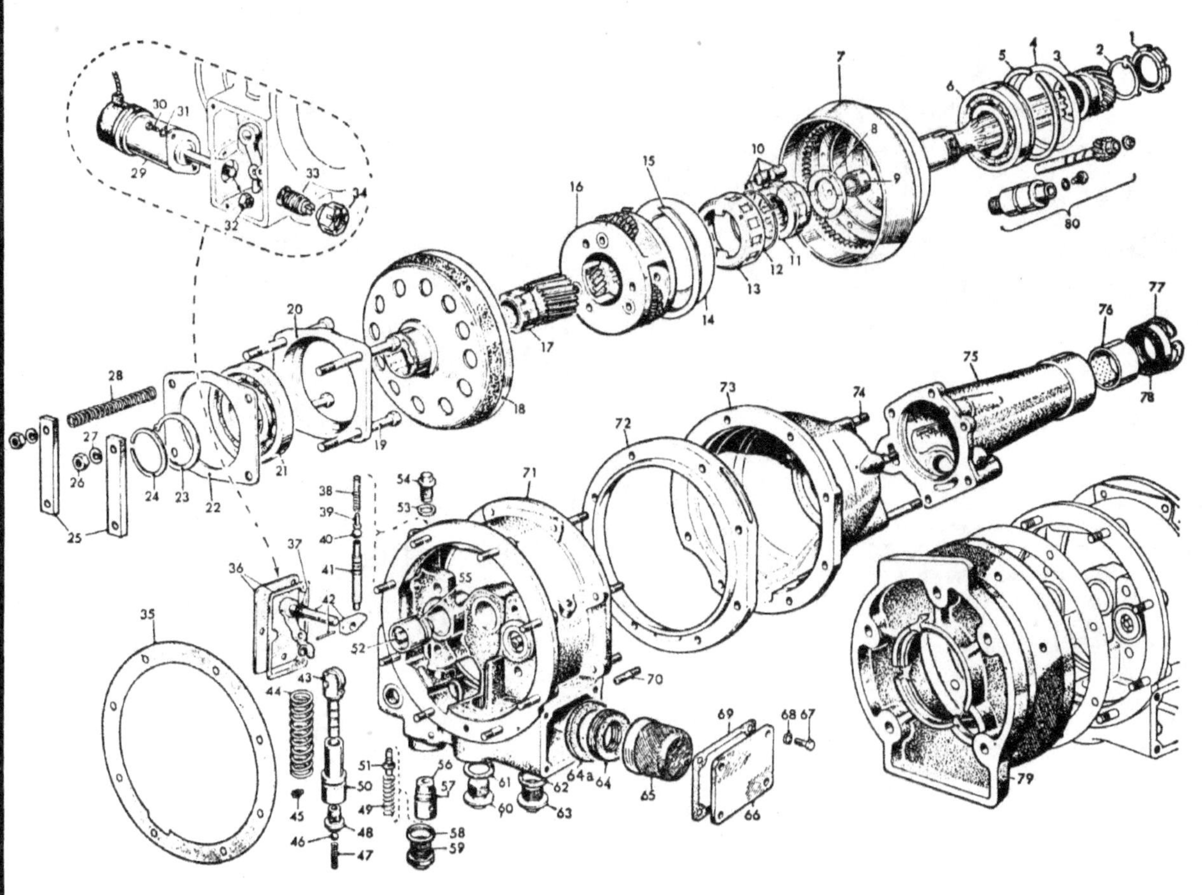

Fig.6.7. EXPLODED VIEW OF THE OVERDRIVE UNIT

1 Locknut
2 Tabwasher
3 Speedometer wheel
4 Shim
5 Circlip
6 Rear bearing
7 Annulus
8 Thrust washer
9 Mainshaft bearing
10 Rollers)
11 Ratchet) Free
12 Circlip) wheel
13 Roller cage)
14 Retaining plate
15 Circlip
16 Planet carrier with wheels
17 Sunwheel
18 Clutch cone
19 Bolt
20 Bearing housing
21 Bearing
22 Retainer plate
23 Circlip
24 Snap ring)
25 Bridge plates) Clutch
26 Nut) release
27 Tab washer)
28 Spring
29 Solenoid
30 Set screw
31 Washer
32 Nut-solenoid to valve lever
33 Stop pad) Solenoid and valve
34 Locknut) lever adjustment
35 Joint ring
36 Valve lever cover
37 Sealing ring-operating shaft
38 Spring)
39 Plunger) Operating valve
40 Ball)
41 Operating valve
42 Operating lever assembly
43 Plunger
44 Spring
45 Pump body retaining screw
46 Ball
47 Spring
48 Valve body
49 Spring
50 Pump body
51 Plunger
52 Operating piston
53 Washer
54 Plug
55 Piston ring (rubber)
56 Relief valve body
57 Rubber ring
58 Washer
59 Plug
60 Cover plug
61 Washer
62 Washer
63 Drain plug
64 Ring magnets
64a Sealing ring
65 Filter
66 Filter cover plate
67 Set screw
68 Washer
69 Filter cover plate joint
70 Stud - front to rear casing
71 Front casing
72 Brake ring
73 Rear casing
74 Stud - rear casing to rear cover
75 Rear cover
76 Bush
77 Circlip
78 Rear oil seal
79 Gearbox adaptor
80 Speedometer drive assembly

Fig.6.9. Checking the adjustment of the operating plunger

14. Overdrive Operating Lever - Adjustment

1. If the overdrive does not engage, or will not release when it is switched out, providing the solenoid is not at fault, the trouble is likely to be that the operating lever is out of adjustment. Adjustment can be made without removing the overdrive.
2. Undo the three bolts and washers holding the solenoid cover plate in position, to give access to the operating lever and solenoid plunger.
3. Procure a short length of mild steel rod of 3/16 inch (4.76 mm) diameter. Switch the ignition on, put the car in top gear, and flick the actuating switch to the overdrive position.
4. If the 3/16 inch rod can now be passed through the hole 'A' in the operating arm (see Fig.6.9) into the hole in the casing, adjustment is correct.
5. If the solenoid does not move the arm far enough for the rod to be inserted into the hole in the casing, or if it moves the arm too far, hold the solenoid plunger from turning by means of the two flats machined on its shank, and pressing the plunger tightly into the solenoid, screw the self locking nut 'B' in Fig.6.9 in or out until the 3/16 inch test rod can be pushed fully home into the hole in the casing.
6. Operate the switch several times, checking with the test rod to ensure adjustment is correct. Measure the current consumed by the solenoid which, with the operating arm correctly set, should be 2 amps. If a reading of about 17 amps is obtained this shows that the solenoid plunger is not moving sufficiently to switch to the holding coil from the operating coil. If very fine adjustment will not remedy this condition, fit a new solenoid and plunger.

15. Overdrive Relief, Non-Return & Operating Valves – Removal, Inspection & Replacement

1. Access to the relief and non-return valves located in the bottom of the overdrive is gained after removing the engine steady rod and bracket from the rear crossmember. Drain the oil from the gearbox and overdrive.

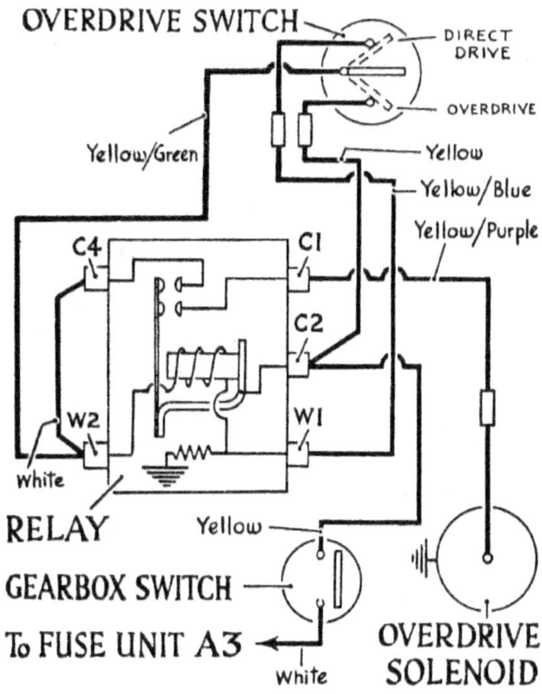

Fig.6.10. Overdrive circuit diagram

2. Cut through the locking wire, unscrew the plugs and remove and clean the components. Note that the valve cap and non-return valve body are unscrewed from the pump, and that the relief valve body is removed with circlip pliers.
3. Examine the seatings for pits or chips, and the balls for wear and ridges. The steel ball in the non-return valve is very hard and if the ball is undamaged and the seating is suspect tap the ball firmly into its seat with a soft metal drift.
4. Reassembly is a straightforward reversal of the removal sequence. Do not omit to fit the copper washer on the relief valve between the cap and main casing, and hold the non-return valve ball to its spring with petroleum jelly during refitment.
5. Access to the operating valve can only be gained after removing the remote control assembly from inside the car. Undo the plug and check that the ball is lifted 1/32 inch when the solenoid is actuated. Failure to move points to a fault in the solenoid or operating arm.
6. The ball can be removed with a magnet and the valve with a piece of 1/8 inch wire. Check the ball and seat and clean out the small hole in the side of the valve tube. Check if the oil pump is working by jacking the rear of the car off the ground and placing the car in top gear. Engage overdrive and with the engine running watch if oil is being pumped into the valve chamber. Replacement is a reversal of the removal procedure.

Chapter 7 Propeller shaft and universal joints

Contents

Specifications

Type	Two piece tubular, supported by rubber insulated steady bearing Universal joints sealed, needle roller bearings

1. General Description

Engine power is transferred from the engine to the rear axle and wheels through the gearbox and a two piece tubular propeller shaft supported in the centre by a rubber insulated steady bearing which is bolted to the underframe. Fitted at each end of the rear portion, and at the front end of the front portion, are universal joints which allow for vertical movement of the rear axle. Each universal joint comprises a four legged centre spider, four needle roller bearings and two yokes.

Fore and aft movement of the rear axle is absorbed by a sliding spline in the front of the propeller shaft which slides over a mating spline on the rear of the gearbox mainshaft. A supply of oil from the gearbox lubricates the splines. The universal joints are pre-packed with grease on assembly and should require no further attention.

2. Routine Maintenance

No specific maintenance is necessary. Examine the universal joints from time to time for signs of wear and check the security of the flange nuts and bolts and the centre bearing mounting bolts.

3. Propeller Shaft - Removal & Replacement

1. As the two piece shaft with its centre bearing is rather an unwieldy object it is better to remove the rear portion of the shaft first.
2. Jack up the rear of the car, or position the rear of the car over a pit or ramp.
3. If the rear wheels are off the ground, place the car in gear and put the handbrake on, to ensure that the propeller shaft does not turn when an attempt is made to loosen the four nuts securing the propeller shaft to the rear axle.
4. The propeller shaft is carefully balanced to fine limits and it is important for it to be replaced in exactly the same position as it was in, prior to removal. Scratch a mark on the propeller shaft and rear axle flanges, also on the flanges at the front end of the rear portion, to ensure accurate mating when the time comes for reassembly.

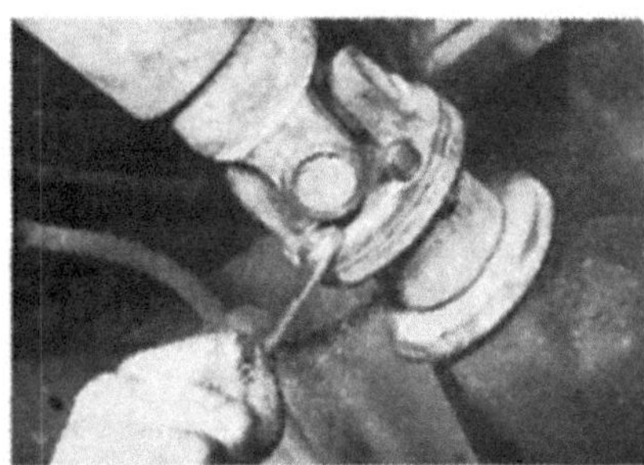

Section 3. Removing flange coupling bolts and withdrawing sliding splined sleeve

5. Unscrew the four self locking nuts, bolts and securing washers which hold the flanges together at either end (Photo), and lower the rear portion from the car.
6. Place a can or tray under the rear of the gearbox or overdrive extension to catch any oil that may leak out when the front of the propeller shaft is drawn out.
7. Undo the bolts holding the centre bearing assembly to its mounting bracket and draw it to the rear, complete with the front portion of the propeller shaft (Photo).
8. Replacement of the propeller shaft is a reversal of the above procedure. Make sure that the mating marks made on the rear portion line up correctly.

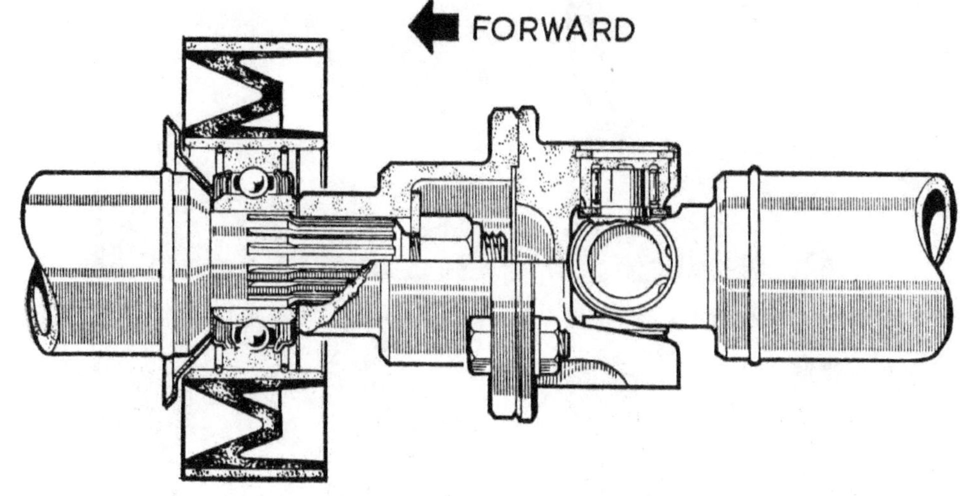

Fig.7.1. Cutaway view of the centre bearing assembly

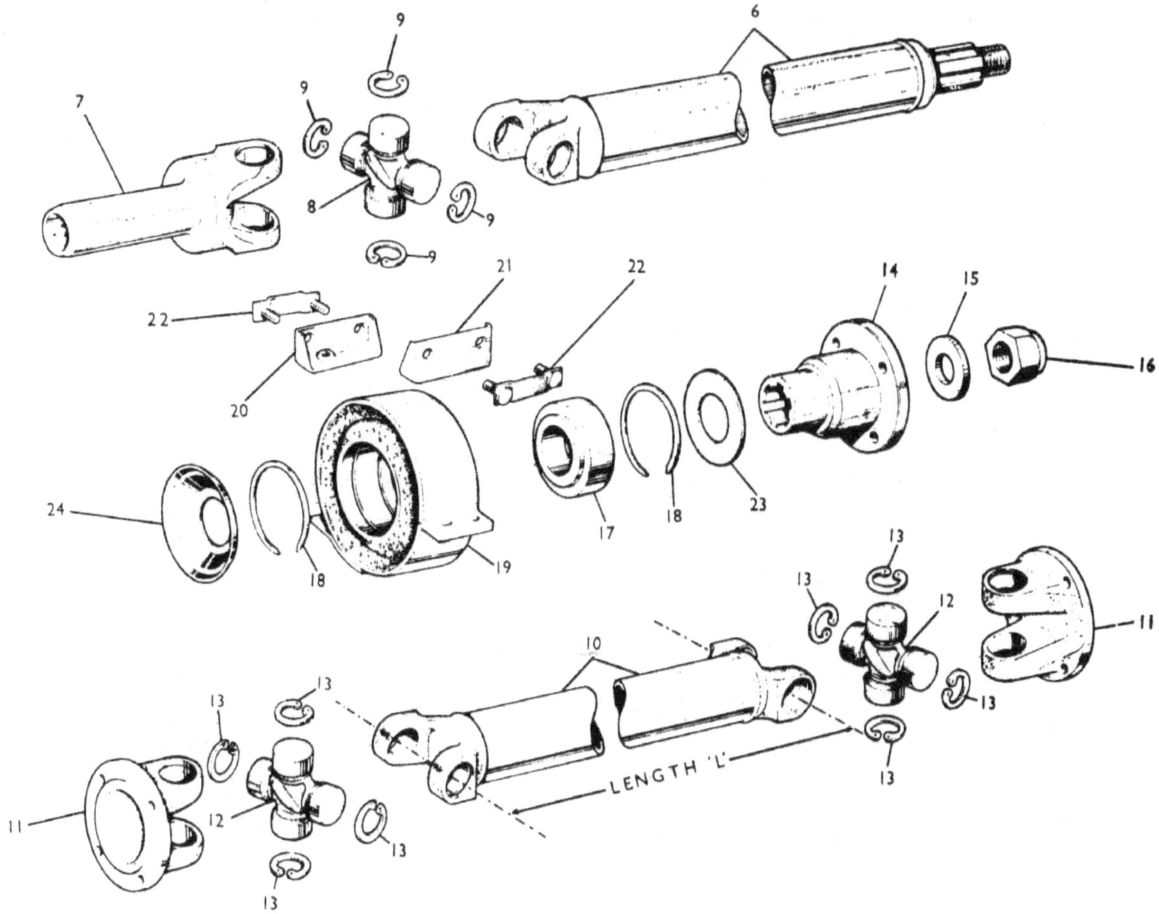

Fig.7.2. EXPLODED VIEW OF THE TWO PIECE PROPELLER SHAFT AND CENTRE BEARING ASSEMBLY

6 Front portion shaft
7 Sleeve and yoke
8 Spider
9 Circlips
10 Rear portion shaft
11 Flange
12 Spider
13 Circlips
14 Coupling
15 Washer
16 Self-locking nut
17 Centre bearing
18 Circlip
19 Bearing housing
20 Bracket
21 Bracket
22 Plate and studs
23 Dust shield
24 Water shield

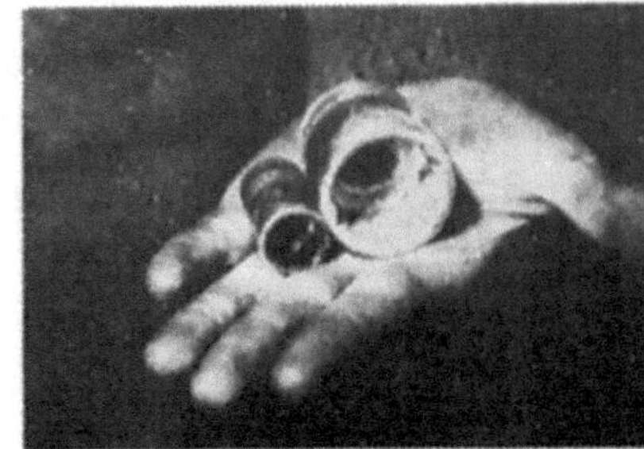

Section 5. Removing needle roller bearings, using sockets as drifts between the vice jaws

4. Universal Joints & Splines - Inspection & Repair

1. Wear in the needle roller bearings is indicated by vibration or 'clunks' in the transmission, particularly when the drive is being taken up or when going to over-run. (Backlash in the rear axle has the same effect, so check that also, if symptoms occur.)
2. It is easy to check the needle roller bearings whilst the propeller shaft is still in position. Try to turn the shaft with one hand and grip the flange or sleeve on the other side of the joint with the other hand. There should be no movement between the two. If there is any, the bearings will need renewal.
3. The splines of the sliding sleeve should be a smooth sliding fit on the gearbox mainshaft, and no trace of rotational backlash should be apparent. If there is any serious backlash the repair could be costly as both the gearbox mainshaft and the sleeve may need renewal (although a new sleeve only may suffice). Any significant signs of ridging on the outer surface of the sleeve may be the cause of oil leaks from the rear of the gearbox and a new seal may not be sufficient to rectify the trouble. Much depends on the degree of wear apparent and the owner will have to decide whether a new sleeve is worthwhile.

5. Universal Joints - Dismantling & Fitting New Bearings

1. Clean away all traces of dirt from the whole assembly and then remove the circlips which hold each set of needle roller bearings in position. If the circlip is tight, tap the face of the bearing cup inside it which may be jamming it in its groove (Photo).
2. The bearing should come out if the edges of the yoke ears are tapped with a mallet. If, however, they are very tight, it should be possible to shift them by pressing them between the jaws of a vice, using two distance pieces. Two different size socket spanners (Photos) are ideal, and it will be possible to force one out sufficiently far to enable it to be gripped by another suitable tool (pliers or vice again) and drawn out (Photo). Take care not to damage the yokes. If the bearings have seized up or worn so badly that the holes in the yokes are oval, then a new yoke will be needed - and if this is on the propeller shaft then that will have to be acquired too, as the whole assembly is balanced and parts are not supplied separately.
3. New bearings will be supplied with new seals and circlips. Make sure the needles are correctly in position and the cup 1/3 full of grease. Put the gaskets and retainers on the four journals of the spider. Each cup may then be tapped through the yoke on to the spider journal. Fit all four on one joint before putting the circlips in position and make sure everything moves freely.

6. Centre Bearing - Removal & Replacement

1. Mark the coupling and the front half of the propeller shaft to ensure the shaft goes on to the same splines in the rear coupling on reassembly.
2. Undo the self-locking nut holding the front portion of the propeller shaft in the rear coupling, then withdraw the shaft and remove the water shield from the front of the bearing housing and the dust seal from the rear.
3. Remove the circlips from their grooves in the bearing housing from either side of the bearing; then press out the bearing.
4. To replace the bearing, fit one of the circlips in its groove, press the bearing up to it, then fit the other circlip to lock it in position. Both sides of the bearing should now be packed with a waterproof sealing compound.
5. Reassembly from now on is a direct reversal of the removal procedure.

Chapter 8 Rear axle

Contents

Specifications

Type	Semi floating, hypoid bevel gears
Oil capacity	1.75 pints (2.1 US pints, 1 litre)

Ratios	**Rapier/Alpine**	**H120**
Final drive	4.22	3.89
Overall ratios:		
Overdrive top	3.39	3.12
Top	4.22	3.89
Overdrive third	4.39	4.05
Third	5.47	5.04
Second	8.42	7.75
First	13.18	12.14
Reverse	14.03	12.92
Speed per 1000 rpm (direct top) mph	15.6	17.29

Pinion Bearing Preload	
New bearings	6–12 lb in (0.07 – 0.14 kg.m)
Used bearings	4–8 lb in (0.05 – 0.09 kg.m)
Differential side bearing preload:	
Shims added	0.002 in (0.05 mm)
Pinion to crownwheel backlash	0.005 – 0.009 in (0.13 – 0.23 mm)

Torque Wrench Settings	
Pinion nut	110 lb ft (12.4 Kg.m)
Axle shaft nut	180 lb ft (24.8 Kg.m)
Crownwheel set bolts	48 lb ft (6.6 Kg.m)
Differential bearing cap nuts	53 lb ft (7.3 Kg.m)
Differential housing to casing	10 lb ft (1.4 Kg.m)

1. General Description

The rear axle is of the semi-floating type incorporating a hypoid crownwheel and pinion with a two pinion differential. The crownwheel and pinion and differential are mounted as an assembly in the differential carrier and this is bolted to the front of the banjo type axle housing. This means that the axle does not have to be disturbed in order to remove and examine the differential and final drive.

2. Routine Maintenance

1. Every 5,000 miles remove the level plug located in the right hand horizontal web of the differential casing. The oil should be level with the bottom of the threads in the hole and in order to see this the use of a hand mirror will help. Top up with the recommended oil as required.

2. Every 30,000 miles remove the level/filler plug and drain plug after a run, when the axle should be a little warmer than normal, and drain the oil out. Refill with 1¾ pints of the recommended oil. If wished, the recommended amount of a proprietary grade of molybdenum disulphide may be added as an aid to wear reduction and reducing friction.

3. Check that the breather plug is clear when checking the oil level.

3. Half Shafts, Bearings & Oil Seals - Removal & Replacement

1. The half shafts may be withdrawn without disturbing the differential gear. They are removed in order to renew the bearings or oil

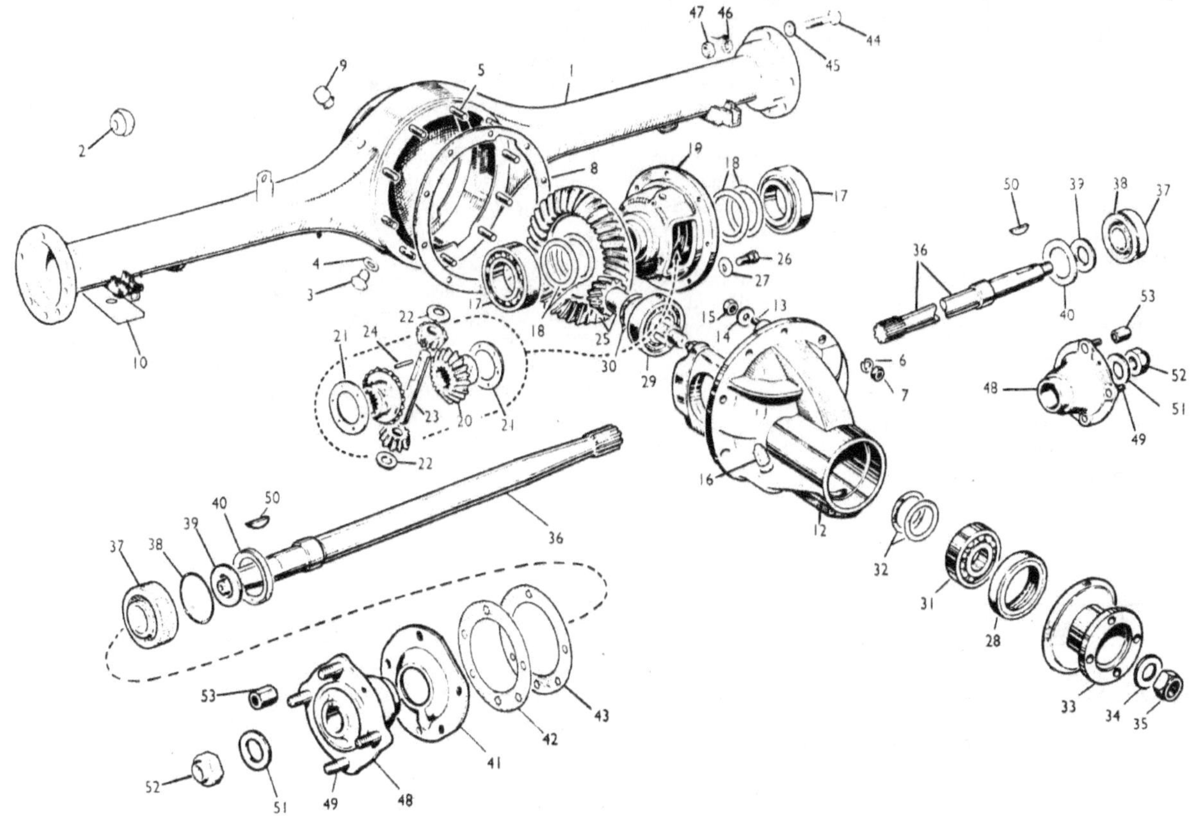

Fig.8.1. EXPLODED VIEW OF REAR AXLE

1 Axle casing
2 Bearing-brake rod steady bracket
3 Drain plug
4 Washer
5 Stud
6 Spring washer
7 Nut
8 Gasket
9 Breather plug
10 Taper wedge
11 Differential assembly
12 Differential housing
13 Stud - side bearing
14 Washer
15 Nut
16 Oil level plug
17 Differential side bearing
18 Shims
19 Differential case
20 Differential pinion assembly
21 Thrust washer-side wheel
22 Thrust washer - pinion
23 Cross pin
24 Lock pin
25 Crownwheel and bevel pinion
26 Crownwheel bolt
27 Tab washer
28 Oil seal
29 Inner pinion bearing
30 Shim
31 Outer pinion bearing
32 Shims
33 Coupling flange
34 Washer
35 Self locking pinion nut
36 Half shaft and sleeve
37 Bearing
38 'O' ring
39 Inner sludge guard
40 Outer sludge guard
41 Oil catcher
42 Gasket (0.006 in)
43 Gasket (0.010 in)
44 Screw
45 Washer
46 Spring washer
47 Nut
48 Hub
49 Wheel stud
50 Woodruff key
51 Plain washer
52 Self locking nut
53 Wheel nut

seals or if the differential is to be removed. Read the whole of this Section before starting work.

2. Jack up the car at the rear and support it firmly on proper stands. Remove the rear wheels, free the handbrake and remove the brake drums, as described in Chapter 9.

3. Remove the clevis pin from the handbrake linkage and disconnect the hydraulic brake pipe from the wheel cylinder (Chapter 9).

4. Remove the nuts and bolts securing the oil catcher plate and brake backplate to the axle casing flange. The half shaft hub, bearing and backplate are now held in position as an assembly by the fit of the outer race of the bearing into the axle casing. Ideally the use of a proper impact hammer removal tool is needed to draw the assembly out. This consists of a flange which bolts to the wheel studs and to which is fitted a long shaft extension with a sliding weight on it. The sliding weight is hit against a flange at the extremity of the shaft and this draws the axle out. Whatever you do, this principle - of attaching a suitable bracket and striking point to the wheel studs - must be followed. No part of the axle assembly itself must be struck. A sustained pull is also quite ineffective and will probably only result in heaving the car off the stands. So get something suitable organised in advance or you will be wasting your time. One possibility is to use an old wheel rim bolted to the studs and then strike it from the inside with something suitably heavy. The success or otherwise of this method depends on access and the ability to get a good swing at it. Whatever method is used the car should be firmly supported.

6. It is essential that proper facilities are also available if the bearing/oil seal is to be renewed. The bearing has to be drawn off the outer end of the shaft. First, therefore, the hub has to be removed. It is held by a nut on to a keyed taper at the end of the shaft. A proper puller to get this off is essential, otherwise the end of the shaft may be damaged. The bearing may then be pulled off, also using a suitable tool which can bear on the end of the shaft and pull against the inner race of the bearing. A keen owner may be able to make up a suitable puller, but the time and effort involved should be weighed against the advantage of handing the shaft to someone with the necessary equipment for fitting a new bearing.

7. Behind the bearing is a very tight fitting sleeve round the shaft. This serves to grip the bearing inner race against the hub. When the bearing is removed, therefore, the sleeve has to be moved approximately 1/32 inch (1 mm) towards the outer end of the shaft so that when a new bearing is pressed on, the hub will finally be drawn up against

the bearing and the bearing will force the sleeve back. The force needed will be sufficient to grip the inner race of the bearing. It will be seen, therefore, that to attempt this work with nothing more than a hammer, chisel and hope will be almost certainly doomed to failure.

8. When fitting the new bearing (having first moved the sleeve into position on the shaft), make sure that the inner sludge guard is fitted to the shaft first, and that the oil seal which is incorporated in the bearing faces inwards. The bearing should be pressed on until the sludge plate is just held between the inner race and sleeve on the shaft - no further. Then put the backplate and dust cover in position, followed by the hub. When the hub is drawn on with the nut the bearing will be finally moved into position as required. The nut needs tightening to 180 lb ft.

9. When replacing the half shaft, the splines at the inner end should first pick up the splines in the differential side gears. Then enter the bearing into the axle casing recess until the outer edge of the race is nearly flush with the casing. Then bolt up the backplate evenly, which will draw the bearing completely into position.

10. Reconnect the hydraulic pipe and handbrake linkage, refit the brake drum and bleed the brakes.

4. Differential Carrier - Removal & Replacement

1. Jack up the car and support it on stands as for half shaft removal. Drain the oil from the back axle by removing the filler plug and drain plug. The half shaft should then be removed sufficiently far for the inner ends to disengage from the differential side pinions. The propeller shaft should then be dismantled from the rear axle pinion flange. It is not necessary to draw it out from the gearbox provided it can be conveniently rested out of the way on one side.

2. Undo the ten nuts and washers holding the differential carrier to the casing. The whole unit can then be drawn forward off the studs and taken out.

3. When replacing the assembly ensure that the mating faces are perfectly clean and free from burrs. A new gasket coated with sealing compound should also be used. Otherwise refitting is a reversal of the removal operation.

5. Differential, Crownwheel & Pinion - Overhaul

1. At some point in the life of a rear axle an owner is faced with the need to cure either severe backlash or an unacceptable whine or noise level. Such symptoms usually indicate worn bearings coupled with worn gears to a varying degree. Due to the fact that rebuilding and setting up a differential assembly is a specialised job, calling for training and experience, any owner contemplating such work should first seriously consider the relative economics of obtaining parts and rebuilding (with the possibility of an unsuccessful result), compared with obtaining a complete assembly, either new or secondhand from a breaker. This manual does not, therefore, detail the step-by-step procedures of assembly.

2. Dismantling is no problem at all. The specifications and exploded drawing should enable someone with experience to get on with it. If the pinion oil seal is leaking a new one may be fitted after first removing the pinion nut and flange. The old seal may be dug out with a pointed tool, taking care not to damage the casing. The new one should be sealed with compound on the outside and pressed on the inner lip. These oil seals rarely fail and if one does then it is likely that the pinion bearings have also failed. In such cases the fitting of a new seal would be a waste of time.

6. Rear Axle - Removal & Replacement

1. Removal of the rear axle should be a rare occurrence; the most likely reason is if the differential unit has gone and a replacement assembly obtained from a breaker is being fitted complete, rather than just the differential assembly.

2. Jack up the rear of the car and support the body under the side frame, allowing the axle and springs to hang free. Remove the wheels.

3. Disconnect the propeller shaft (Chapter 7) and the dampers at their lower mountings only (Chapter 11).

4. Disconnect the handbrake linkage at both hubs and from the bracket on the axle casing (Chapter 9). Also disconnect the hydraulic flexible brake hose coupling at the union with the rigid pipe (not at the three-way connector). Protect the ends of the fluid lines from dirt.

5. Remove all the 'U' bolts clamping the axle to the springs and then withdraw the axle from one side between the springs and the body.

6. When refitting the axle make sure it is correctly located with the correct spring seats and clamps in position (see Chapter 11), and tighten the 'U' bolt nuts to the correct torque of 35 lb ft. Reconnect the handbrake linkage and hydraulic lines. Finally, bleed the hydraulic system.

Chapter 9 Braking system

Contents

Specifications

Type	Lockheed hydraulic
Servo	Lockheed Type 6
Diameter and lining width	
Front	Discs 9.6 in (24.4 cm)
Rear	Drums 9.0 in (22.9 cm) Lining width 1.75 in (4.5 cm)

Lining Material

	Standard	Dual Braking
Front pads	Don 222 or Ferodo 2430F	Mintex M.78
Colour code	RRYY BWWWB	RGRGR
Total area	20 sq in (129.0 cm^2)	15.6 sq in (100.6 cm^2)
Rear shoes	Don 24	Don 202
Colour code	–R–RRR	RRR
Total area	59.4 sq in (382.2 cm^2)	55.7 sq in (359.2 cm^2)
Min.pad thickness	1/8 in (3 mm)	1/8 in (3 mm)
Master cylinder bore	3/4 in (19.05 mm)	13/16 in (20.63 mm)
Rear wheel cylinder bore	3/4 in (19.05 mm)	15/16 in (23.81 mm)
Caliper cylinder bore	2.1/8 in (53.975 mm)	2.1/8 in (53.975 mm)
Max. disc run-out	0.004 in (0.10 mm)	0.004 in (0.10 mm)

Torque Wrench Settings

Disc to hub	32 lb ft (4.4 Kg.m)
Caliper to stub axle carrier	60 lb ft (8.3 Kg.m)
Backplate to axle casing	17 lb ft (2.3 Kg.m)
Bleed screws	6 lb ft (0.8 Kg.m)
Union nuts (male)	7 lb ft (0.9 Kg.m)
Union nuts (female)	9 lb ft (1.2 Kg.m)

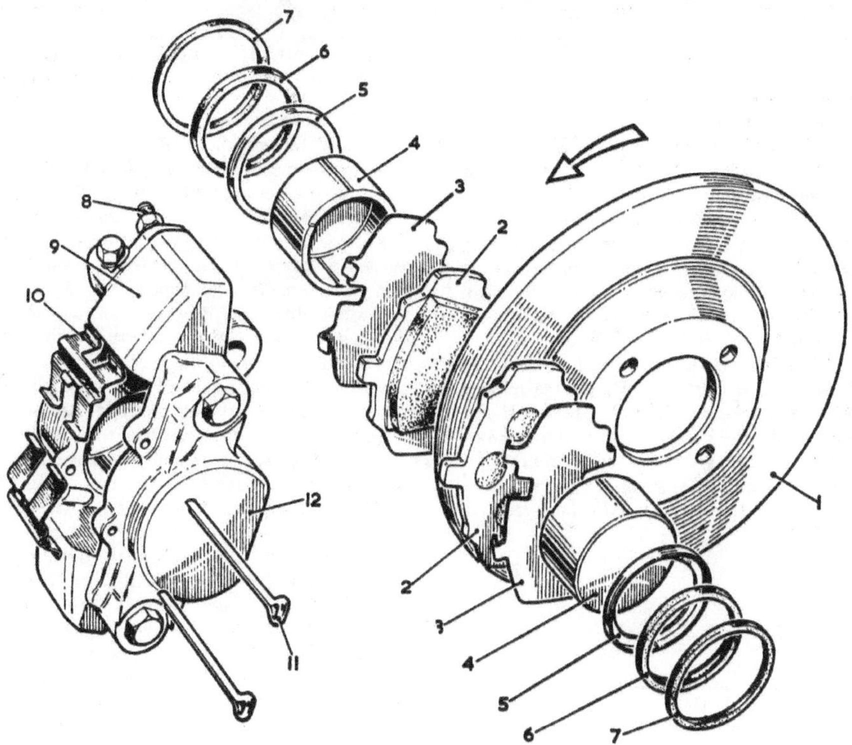

Fig.9.1. EXPLODED VIEW OF EARLY MODEL DISC BRAKE (WITH SHIMS)

1 Disc
2 Brake pads
3 Anti-squeal shims
4 Pistons
5 Dust seal retainer
6 Dust seals
7 Fluid seals
8 Bleed nipple
9 Inner half of caliper
10 Steady springs
11 Split pins
12 Outer half of caliper

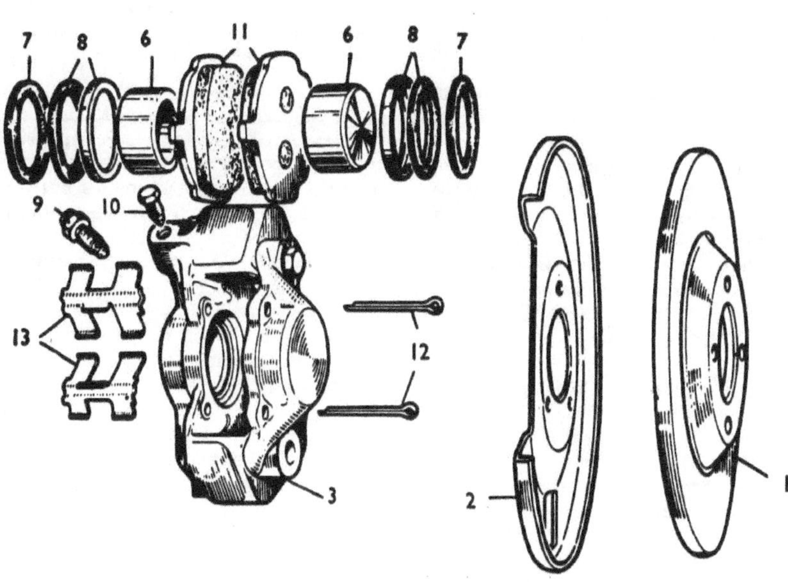

Fig.9.2. EXPLODED VIEW OF LATER TYPE DISC BRAKE (WITHOUT SHIMS)

1 Disc
2 Splash shield
3 Caliper body
6 Piston
7 Fluid seal
8 Dust seal and retainer
9 Bleed nipple
10 Plug
11 Pads
12 Split pin

1. General Description

All models are fitted with Lockheed disc brakes at the front and drum brakes and shoes at the rear. All are hydraulically operated by the foot pedal and the independent handbrake operates the rear drum brakes only by an independent mechanical linkage.

No adjustment to the brakes is necessary as the pistons for the disc pads move forward automatically (without retracting) as the pads wear. The hydraulic fluid in the system is automatically increased from the reservoir as the capacity increases when the pistons move forward. The rear brake shoes are automatically adjusted by a mechanical ratchet which restricts retraction as the linings wear.

The retraction of the pistons which force the pads against the discs is a fractional distance and is governed only by the minute distortion of the fluid seal in the bore of the cylinder. The rear shoes, however, are spring retracted, and the override ratchet device holds them closer to the drums as the linings wear. The ratchet is operated and takes up as needed, each time the brakes are applied.

A Lockheed type 6 servo unit is incorporated in the system to assist braking.

2. Routine Maintenance

1. Every week remove the hydraulic fluid reservoir cap, having made sure that it and the area around it are clean, to prevent any dirt getting into the system, and check the level of the fluid which should be just below the bottom of the filler neck. Check also that the vent hole in the cap is clear. Any need for regular topping up, regardless of quantity, should be viewed with suspicion, and the whole hydraulic system carefully checked for signs of leakage.
2. Every 5,000 miles the brake pads and shoes should be examined to check the thickness of friction lining material remaining. Rear shoe linings should be renewed when the material has almost reached the level of the rivet heads. If the rivets ever rub on the drums they will cause scoring and reduced braking efficiency. The disc pads should be renewed at a minimum thickness of 1/8 inch (3 mm). If inner and outer pads show signs of wearing at different rates, do not interchange at the same wheel. To equalise wear, transpose the pads in pairs from one side of the car to the other, as they are designed to operate in one direction only. (Transposing is not possible on all models.) At the same time as friction material is examined the hydraulic pipes and unions should be examined for any signs of damage or corrosion. Brake lining wear varies according to driving style but no set of disc pads should be expected to last more than 15,000 miles. The rear brake shoe linings will probably last half as long again. Make sure the handbrake functions properly at all times.
3. Every 10,000 miles remove the air filter from the servo unit and clean or renew it.
4. Every 25,000 miles it is good policy to renew all hydraulic cylinder seals and all flexible hoses, as a matter of routine. Any repair work in the interior should also, of course, be attended to. It is recommended that brake fluid be renewed every 18 months.
5. If you have just acquired a secondhand car it is strongly recommended that all brake drums, pads, shoes and discs are thoroughly examined for condition and wear immediately. Even though braking efficiency may be excellent the friction materials could be nearing the end of their useful life and it is as well to know this without delay. Similarly, the hydraulic cylinders, pipes and connections should be carefully examined for leaks or chafing. Faults should be rectified immediately. It should be remembered that three year old cars will be subject to safety tests and that apart from safety, which is paramount, defects in the system, even though they may not yet affect stopping power, will possibly cause the vehicle to fail the test.

3. Disc Pads - Removal, Inspection & Replacement

1. If the brake pads have worn down to a friction material thickness of 1/8 inch (3 mm) they should be renewed as soon as possible. In order to check pad thickness, jack up the car and remove the wheel. The edge of the pad will then be visible in the caliper which is mounted on the forward side of the disc. If one pad is worn on one side of the disc more than the other (this often happens - the inner pad wears faster), it was in order in some early models to change them over; provided, of course, neither had reached the minimum permissible thickness. However, later models and replacement discs are handed. (The pads are identified by a rectangular cut away portion in the trailing edge of the plate.) These pads cannot be moved to the other side of the same disc although they can be moved to the same position on the other disc.
2. To remove the pads depress the steady springs to relieve the pressure on the split pins and draw out the split pins. If the pads are then rotated upwards a little they can be eased out of the caliper.
3. When fitting new pads it will be necessary to ease the pistons back into their bores to accommodate the thicker material. First examine the fluid reservoir because when the pistons move back the level will rise and it should not be allowed to overflow. Then move the pistons back by exerting steady pressure with a flat blade between piston head and disc. At the same time check that the anti-squeal cutout portion of the piston crown is across the line of disc rotation on the lead inside, i.e. upwards in this instance. If it is not, rotate the piston carefully until it is. Where the later type pads are fitted, without shims, the cutout of the piston should be approximately angled at 25° from a line across the direction of disc travel (Fig.9.3).
4. When the gap is wide enough for the pads to go in, lead in the top edge first and then hold the front lug and rotate the pad downwards so that it fits snugly in position. The shim plates (if used) should be slipped in between the pads and the pistons; later models and new pads have no shims. Place the steady springs in position with the longer legs facing each other and refit the split pins, spreading the ends a little to keep them in position.
5. Operate the brake pedal until firm pressure is felt. Then rotate the wheel to ensure that no binding is taking place (although the pads may noticeably just touch the disc). Always fit new pads of the correct specification and if a different type must be used make sure both front wheels are fitted.

4. Discs - Inspection, Removal & Replacement

1. Brake discs rarely give trouble but very severe use in unusually wet or dirty conditions may cause distortion or scoring. If they do not run true the performance of the brakes can be seriously affected. The amount of 'out-of-true' or runout should not exceed 0.004 inch (0.1 mm).
2. To check the discs jack up the car and first make sure that the hub bearing is in good condition. It may be necessary to tighten the bearing nut to eliminate any play which could exist due to the particular positions of the castellations of the nut and the split pin.
3. If a dial gauge micrometer is mounted against the surface of the disc while turning it, the amount of runout can be measured. After checking re-adjust the hub bearing (Chapter 11). If the disc is heavily scored or damaged it should be renewed.
4. A damaged disc should only be reground as a last resort if no replacement is available. It will cost about the same if done properly. A maximum of 0.010 inch (0.25 mm) may be removed from each side, each side must be ground off equally and the maximum runout between mounting and rubbing faces is 0.002 inch (0.05 mm). Rubbing faces must be parallel to 0.001 inch (0.025 mm).
5. To remove a disc, first take off the caliper assembly as described in Section 9. It is not necessary to disturb the hydraulics. Then remove the hub (and disc with it) as described in Chapter 11 for renewal of front wheel bearings.

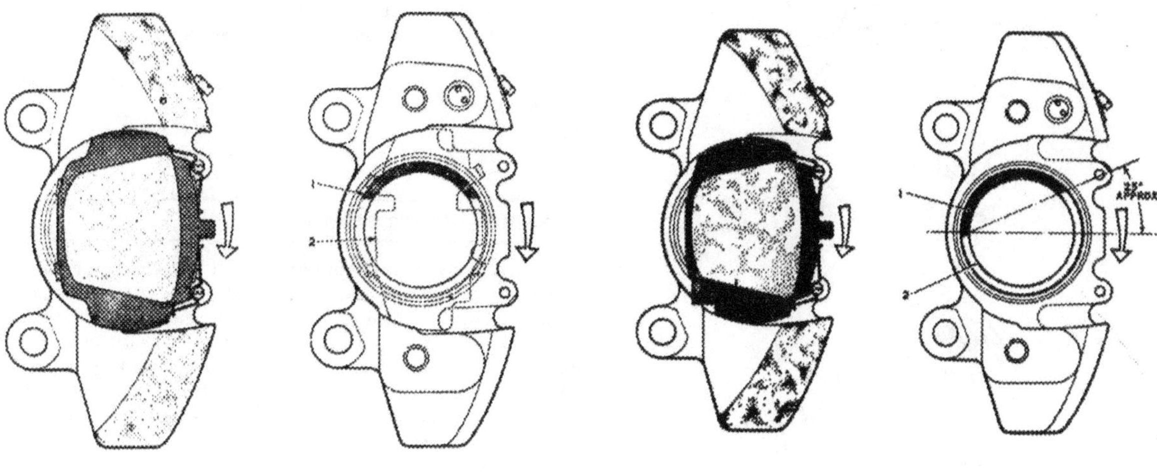

Disc pads with shims

New type disc pads without shims

Fig.9.3. Correct locations of disc pads and piston cutouts on earlier design of disc brakes

6. The disc may then be removed from the hub, by undoing the four bolts and washers.
7. Fitting a disc is the reverse procedure, being careful to ensure that the mating faces of the disc and hub are perfectly clean and free from burrs or high spots. In the case of a new disc, wash off the protective coating first. Tighten the bolts evenly to the specified torque of 32 lb ft.
8. Replace the hub, adjust the bearing and refit the caliper. If the previous pads are being used, allow time for bedding in before full braking efficiency is achieved.

5. Brake Drums & Shoes - Removal, Inspection & Replacement

1. Jack up the car and remove the roadwheel. Block the front wheels and release the handbrake.
2. The drum is located over the four wheel studs and is positioned by a single countersunk screw into the hub which should be removed. The drum may then be pulled straight off the studs. If it seems stuck fast it will be due to binding at the roots of the wheel studs. A little easing fluid and a tap with a mallet on the edge should shift it. Do not hit the drum with a hammer as it is brittle and could easily fracture. It sometimes happens that very badly scored and worn drums can 'mesh' their grooves into the surfaces of the brake linings to such an extent that the drum cannot be pulled off; the automatic adjuster being inaccessible for release. On later models the mechanism can be reached and released by drilling a 5/16 inch hole at a radius of 2.55 inch - opposite the locating screw. This is really rather a waste of time if the drum is to be renewed anyway. If you cannot actually break the drum to pieces with a hammer without risk of damaging the hub then cut it off - or cut nicks in it and try splitting it with a cold chisel. If you cut into the shoes inside as well it does not matter as they are going to need renewal too.
3. With the drum removed brush out any dust and examine the rubbing surface for any signs of pitting or deep scoring. The surface should be smooth and bright but minor hairline scores are of no consequence and could have been caused by grit or brake shoes with linings just worn to the rivets. A drum that is obviously badly worn should be renewed. A perfectly satisfactory replacement can often be obtained from a breakers yard. It is no economy having drums turned up on a lathe (unless you can have it done for nothing!). Also, as the radius is altered if the rubbing surfaces are machined out, standard shoes will not match properly until a lot of bedding in has taken place and re-radiused the linings.
4. The brake shoes should be examined next. There should be no signs of contamination by oil and the linings should be above the heads of the rivets. If the level is close (less than 1/32 inch) it is worth changing them. If there are signs of oil contamination they should be renewed also and the source of oil linkage found before it ruins the new ones as well.
5. To remove the shoes (having of course, removed the drum) first detach the steady posts from the centre of each shoe. This can be done by holding the head with one pair of pliers and rotating the dished, slotted washer 90° so that it unlocks from the post and comes off with the spring behind it.
6. Next note which holes the pull-off springs fit into in the shoes. Then lift the head of each brake shoe (the end not on the hydraulic piston) against spring tension out of its slot on the backplate. This will relieve some of the tension and the other ends of the shoes can be similarly lifted out at the cylinder end.
7. Before fitting new shoes check that the wheel cylinder is free to move in the backplate slot (early models) and that the backplate is not distorted and is securely bolted on. (If it has to be taken off first, take out the halfshaft as described in Chapter 8.) Also see that the hydraulic piston moves freely and that there are no fluid leaks. Be careful not to let the piston come right out of the cylinder or it will be necessary to bleed the brakes after it is put back.
8. To refit the shoes first arrange them as shown in the drawing with the retractor springs hooked into the correct holes. The double coil spring goes next to the cylinder with the hook ends outwards in the two end holes in the shoes. The other spring fits with the hook ends outwards also but using the next to last hole in the trailing end of the leading shoe. (A leading shoe is one where the leading end in relation to the drum rotation is where the piston force is applied.) The tappet should be screwed fully into the adjuster wheel to ease assembly. When the shoes are in position the adjuster wheel can be

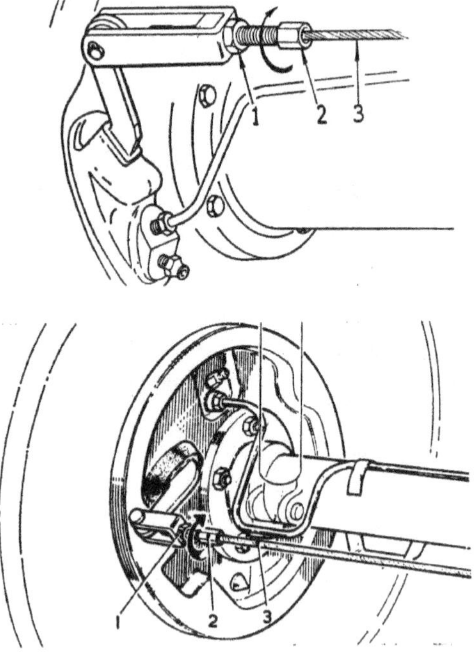

Adjusters
1 Locknut
2 Adjuster unit
3 Cable, inner

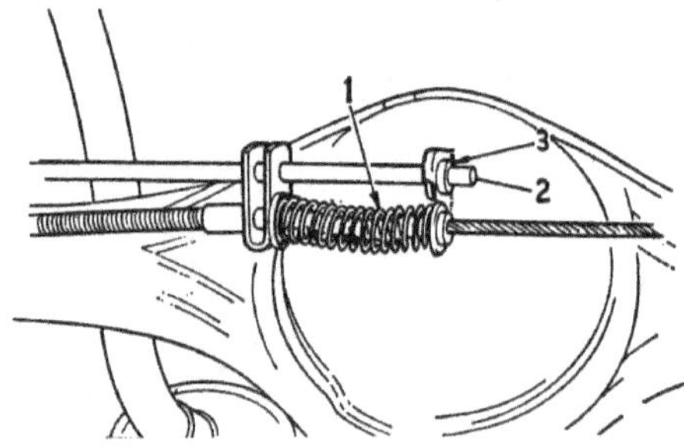

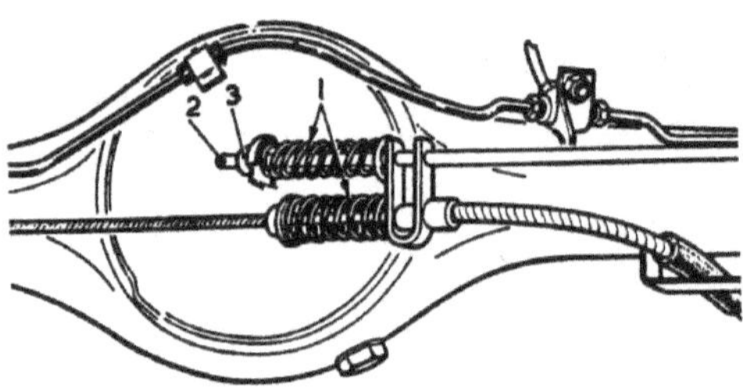

Compensators
1 Return spring
2 Operating rod
3 Rod bearing

Fig.9.4.
Handbrake linkages and adjusters (early and later designs)

rotated to expand the shoes just far enough to allow the drum to be refitted. Replace the steady pins, springs and lockwashers. Centralise the shoes so that the drum will go on easily.

9. When the drum has been replaced operate the brakes to check that they do not bind. It is possible for light binding to occur initially, in which case they should be checked again after a few miles motoring.

6. Handbrake - Adjustment & Cable Renewal

1. There is rarely any need to touch the handbrake as the automatic adjustment of the rear brake shoes also adjusts the handbrake operation. The only need for adjustment is when the cable stretches unduly, or after fitting a new one. The principle of operation is simple. The inner cable runs to one wheel and the reaction of the outer cable when tension is applied is transferred to the other wheel by a rod. The mounting is on the differential cover of the rear axle. The end of the inner cable is connected to the brake wheel lever by a clevis on an adjuster screw. By slackening the locknut the adjuster can be screwed into the clevis, thus shortening the cable and taking up any excessive handbrake lever travel (Fig.9.4).

2. Due to the rear brake shoes being self adjusting, care must be taken to avoid over tensioning the handbrake cable otherwise the brakes may bind on. When adjustments are being carried out, therefore, follow the correct procedure to ensure that this cannot happen. First jack up the rear wheels so they are both off the ground together. Make sure the front wheels are securely chocked. Set the handbrake lever off and then lift it one notch on the ratchet. Slacken the cable adjuster and pump the footbrake to make sure that automatic adjustment is fully taken up. (On early models, make sure also that the wheel cylinders are sliding freely in the backplate, and return to rest normally after pulling on the operating lever.) Then disconnect the clevis from the lever by removing the clevis pin and alter the screwed adjuster until it can be refitted without moving the lever or without pulling on the cable to give any tension. Refit the clevis. After operating the hand lever a few times to settle the linkage, the lever should travel six to eight notches before the brakes are fully on.

3. To fit a new cable it is first necessary to remove the handbrake lever. This is attached to the door sill by two bolts. Remove these, taking care to keep the distance pieces safely as they are essential to correct positioning. The end of the cable is then accessible and can be detached by removing the clevis pin. The other end is detached similarly and the outer cable is released from the brake rod by compressing the spring and releasing the spring retainers from round the cable. Replacement is a reversal of this process and the handbrake should be adjusted as previously described.

7. Hydraulic Fluid Pipes - Inspection, Removal & Replacement

1. Periodically, and certainly well in advance of the MOT test if due, all brake pipes, connections and unions should be completely and carefully examined. Fig.9.7 shows the composition of all such pipes and unions in the system.

2. Examine first all the unions for signs of leaks. Then look at the flexible hoses for signs of fraying and chafing (as well as for leaks). This is only a preliminary inspection of the flexible hoses as exterior condition does not necessarily indicate interior condition which will be considered later.

3. The steel pipes must be examined equally carefully. They must be thoroughly cleaned and examined for signs of dents or other percussive damage, rust and corrosion. Rust and corrosion should be scraped off and, if the depth of pitting in the pipes is significant, they will need replacement. This is most likely in those areas underneath the car body and along the rear axle where the pipes are exposed to the full force of road and weather conditions.

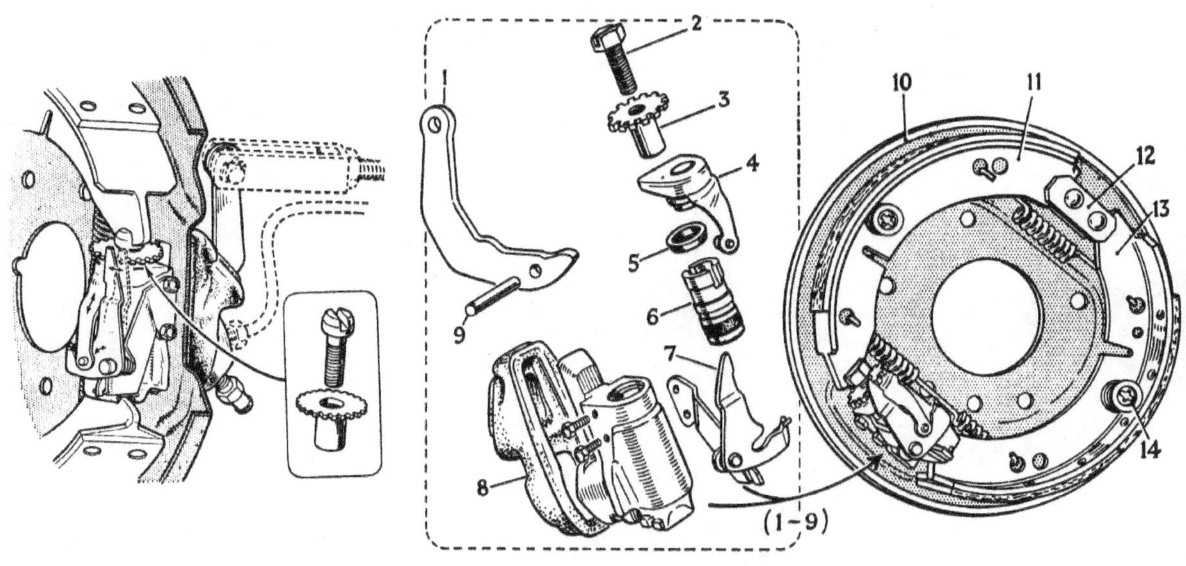

Fig.9.5. VIEWS OF SELF-ADJUSTING MECHANISMS FOR REAR BRAKES (EARLY SLIDING CYLINDER TYPE)

1 Wheel cylinder lever
2 Tappet
3 Adjuster wheel
4 Outer piston and pressing
5 Seal
6 Seal and inner piston
7 Adjuster pawl
8 Rubber dust cover
9 Pivot pin
10 Backplate
11 Leading brake shoe
12 Fixed abutment
13 Trailing brake shoe
14 Steady post

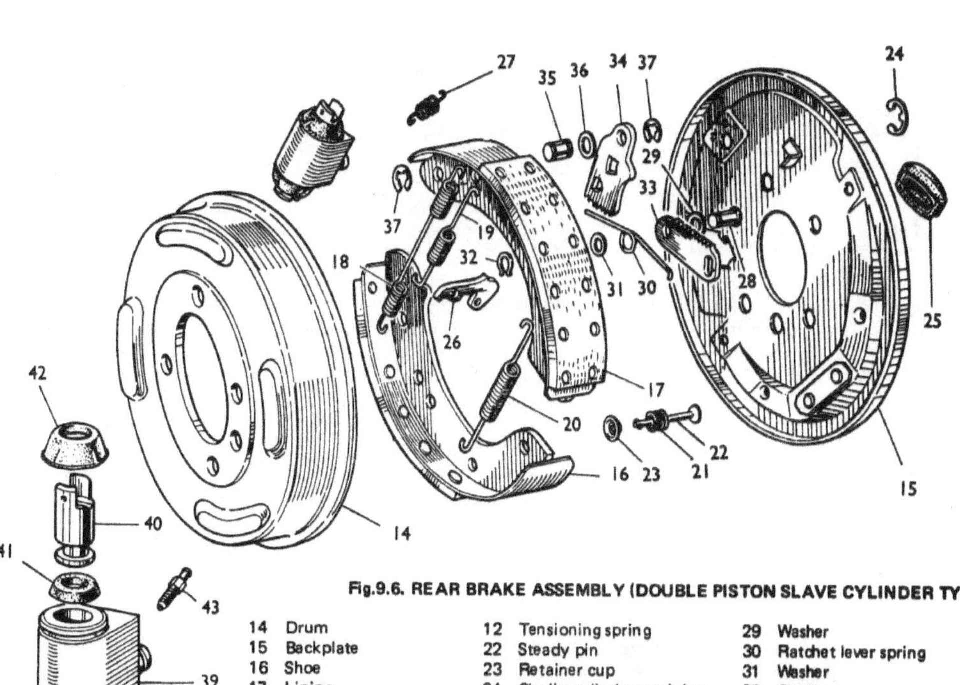

Fig.9.6. REAR BRAKE ASSEMBLY (DOUBLE PISTON SLAVE CYLINDER TYPE)

14 Drum
15 Backplate
16 Shoe
17 Lining
18 Retractor spring
19 Retractor spring-handbrake lever
20 Retractor spring
12 Tensioning spring
22 Steady pin
23 Retainer cup
24 Circlip-cylinder retaining
25 Rubber boot
26 Handbrake lever
27 Shoe to piston link spring
28 Clevis pin - lever pivot
29 Washer
30 Ratchet lever spring
31 Washer
32 Circlip
33 Lower ratchet lever
34 Upper ratchet lever
35 Pivot pin - upper lever
36 Washer
37 Circlip
38 Wheel cylinder assembly
39 Wheel cylinder
40 Piston
41 Seal
42 Boot
43 Bleed nipple

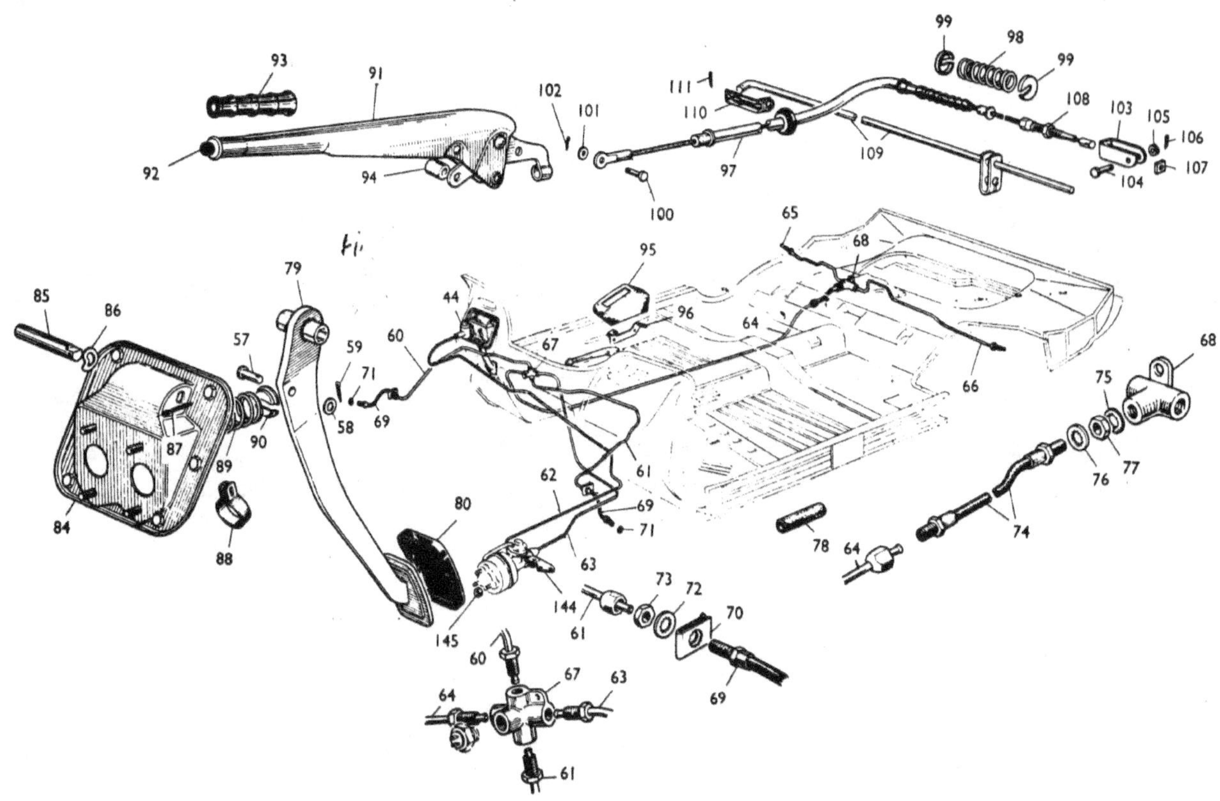

Fig.9.7. LAYOUT & CONNECTIONS OF BRAKE CONTROLS & PIPES

57 Clevis pin - brake pedal
58 Washer
59 Split pin
60 Pipe 4 way to RH hose front
61 Pipe-4 way to LH front hose
62 Pipe - master to servo
63 Pipe - servo to 4 way
64 Pipe - 4 way to rear hose
65 Pipe-3 way to RH rear cylinder
66 Pipe-3 way to LH rear cylinder
67 4-way connector
68 3-way connector
69 Flex. hose LH front
70 Lockplate
71 Gasket
72 Lockwasher
73 Nut
74 Flex. hose - rear
75 Gasket
76 Lockwasher
77 Nut
78 Sleeve
79 Brake pedal
80 Pedal rubber
84 Pedal bracket
85 Pivot pin
86 Wave washer
87 Split pin
88 Clip to steering column
89 Pedal return spring
90 Spring retainer
91 Lever assembly-handbrake
92 Ratchet release knob
93 Handgrip
94 Spacer tube
95 Cover
96 Retainer for cover
97 Cable assembly
98 Cable return spring
99 Spring retainer
100 Clevis pin
101 Washer
102 Split pin
103 Clevis
104 Clevis pin
105 Spring washer
106 Split pin
107 Nut
108 Locknut
109 Actuating rod
110 Lever/rod clip
111 Split pin
144 Bracket
145 Mounting stud spacer

4. If any section of pipe is to be removed, first of all take off the fluid reservoir cap, line it with a piece of polythene film to make it air tight and screw it back on. This will minimise the amount of fluid dripping out of the system when the pipes are removed.

5. Rigid pipe removal is usually quite straightforward. The unions at each end are undone and the pipe drawn out of the connection. The clips which may hold it to the car body are bent back and it is then removed. Underneath the car exposed unions can be particularly stubborn, defying the efforts of an open ended spanner. As few people will have the special split ring spanner required, a self-grip wrench (Mole) is the only answer. If the pipe is being renewed new unions will be provided. If not then one will have to put up with the possibility of burring over the flats on the union and use a self-grip wrench for replacement also.

6. Flexible hoses are always fitted to a rigid support bracket where they join a rigid pipe, the bracket being fixed to the body frame and/or suspension unit. The rigid pipe unions must first be removed from the flexible union. Then the locknut securing the flexible pipe to the bracket must be unscrewed, releasing the end of the pipe from the bracket. As these connections are usually exposed they are more often than not rusted up and a penetrating fluid is virtually essential to aid removal (try 'Plus-Gas'). When undoing them, both halves must be supported as the bracket is not strong enough to support the torque required to undo the nut and can easily be snapped off.

7. Once the flexible hose is removed examine the internal bore. If clear of fluid it should be possible to see through it. Any specks of rubber which come out, or signs of restriction in the bore, mean that the inner lining is breaking up and the pipe must be replaced.

8. Rigid pipes which need replacement can usually be purchased at any local garage where they have the pipe, unions and special tools to make them up. All that they need to know is the pipe length required and the type of flare used at the ends of the pipe. These may be different at each end of the same pipe.

9. Replacement of pipes is a straightforward reversal of the removal procedure. It is best to get all the sets (bends) in the pipe made preparatory to installation. Also, any acute bends should be put in by the garage on a bending machine otherwise there is the possibility of kinking them and restricting the bore area and fluid flow.

10.With the pipes replaced, remove the polythene from the reservoir cap and bleed the system as described in Section 13.

8. Hydraulic Wheel Cylinders (Rear) - Inspection & Repair

1. If it is suspected that one or more of the wheel cylinders is malfunctioning, jack up the suspect wheel and remove the brake drum as described in Section 5.
2. Inspect for signs of fluid leakage around the wheel cylinder and if there are any, proceed as described in paragraph 5.
3. Next get someone to press the brake pedal very gently a small amount. Watch the wheel cylinder and see that the piston moves out a little. On no account let it come right out or it will need reassembly and bleeding. On releasing the pedal pressure make sure that the retraction springs on the shoes move the piston back into position without delay. If the piston moves satisfactorily make sure also that the cylinder body is free to slide endways in the slot in the backplate. If it is seized, it will mean that only one brake shoe is being applied.
4. If there is a leak, or the piston does not move (or only moves very slowly under excessive pressure), then the rubber piston seals will need renewal at least.
5. Seal the reservoir cap and remove the brake shoes as described in Section 5.
6. Disconnect the brake fluid pipes where they enter the cylinder and plug the ends of the lines to minimise loss of fluid.
7. Remove the split pin and clevis pin from the handbrake operating link and the rubber dust cover.
8. The cylinder is retained by two 'U' shaped clips and these can be drawn out by inserting a pointed instrument in the base of the 'U'. On later models the cylinder is fixed and has a double piston, each operating one end of both shoes (Fig.9.5 and 9.6).
9. Then pull out the piston, complete with seal and the spring. Examine the piston and cylinder for signs of wear or scoring and if there are any the whole assembly must be renewed. If they are in good condition only the seal needs renewal. Pull the old one off the piston and thoroughly clean the whole assembly using clean hydraulic fluid or methylated spirit.
10. Fit the new seal to the piston so that the lip faces away from the centre of the piston.
11. Lubricate the components in hydraulic fluid before reassembly which is carried out in the reverse order. Make sure the lip of the seal on the piston enters the cylinder first.
12. When refitting the cylinder to the backplate the handbrake link must be positioned correctly.
13. Reconnect the handbrake cable and hydraulic pipes and replace the brake shoes and drum as described in Section 5. Bleed the hydraulic system as described in Section 13.

9. Disc Calipers - Inspection, Removal & Repair

1. Any indications of fluid leaks or piston seizures in the front brake calipers will mean that they have to be removed for repair.
2. Jack up the car and remove the wheel and brake pads as described in Section 3.
3. To facilitate piston removal depress the brake pedal now to force them out as far as they can go up to the disc.
4. Seal the fluid reservoir cap with polythene sheet and disconnect the hydraulic pipe union from the body of the caliper.
5. The caliper is held to the stub axle by two bolts. Do not under any circumstances loosen the other bolts as these hold the two halves of the caliper together. The caliper can then be lifted away.
6. Provided the pistons are not seized they can be drawn out by hand but in any case if some air pressure can be applied to the fluid inlet it will make things easier. If one piston is very tight try using methylated spirits to ease it. If drastic measures are necessary try and confine any damage to the piston rather than the caliper body.
7. Remove the dust seals and retaining rings from the annular grooves in the cylinder bores and then pull out the piston fluid seals from their grooves.
8. Examine the pistons and bores for signs of wear and scores. If there are signs of wear the whole assembly will probably need replacement.
9. The cylinders and pistons should be thoroughly cleaned in fluid or methylated spirits and care taken to avoid contamination by dirt or mineral oils.
10. Before reassembly lubricate the parts with hydraulic fluid and begin by placing the piston seal in the cylinder in its groove and inserting next the bellows so that its outer lip engages in the top cylinder groove. Then fit the dust seal and retaining ring making sure that they fit flush and square. The piston should be inserted carefully after lubricating with fluid or special disc brake lubricant. On pistons with anti-squeal cutouts make sure these are correctly positioned as mentioned in Section 3.
11. The caliper may now be refitted to the stub axle. Tighten the bolts to a torque of 60 lb ft.
12. Replace the pads and shims as described in Section 3, reconnect the hydraulic pipe and bleed the system as described in Section 13. Replace the wheel and road test the car.

10. Master Cylinder - Removal & Replacement

1. If the disc caliper pistons and rear wheel hydraulic cylinders are in order and there are no leaks elsewhere, yet the brake pedal still does not hold under sustained pressure then the master cylinder seals may be presumed to be ineffective. To renew them the master cylinder must be removed.
2. Disconnect the master cylinder pushrod from the brake pedal by removing the clevis pin.
3. Unscrew the hydraulic pipe union and push the pipe to one side.
4. Remove the two nuts and washers holding the master cylinder to the bulkhead and lift the unit away. Empty the contents of the reservoir into a clean container.
5. Replacement is a reversal of the removal procedure, after which the braking system must be completely bled.

11. Master Cylinder - Dismantling, Overhaul & Reassembly

1. Unless there are obvious signs of leakage any defects in the master cylinder are usually the last to be detected in the hydraulic system.

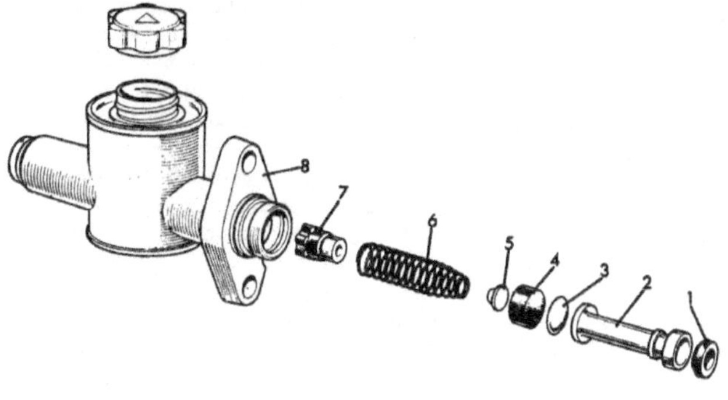

Fig.9.8.
Exploded view of master cylinder

1 Secondary cup seal
2 Piston
3 Piston washer
4 Primary cup seal
5 Spring retainer
6 Return spring
7 Trap valve
8 Cylinder body

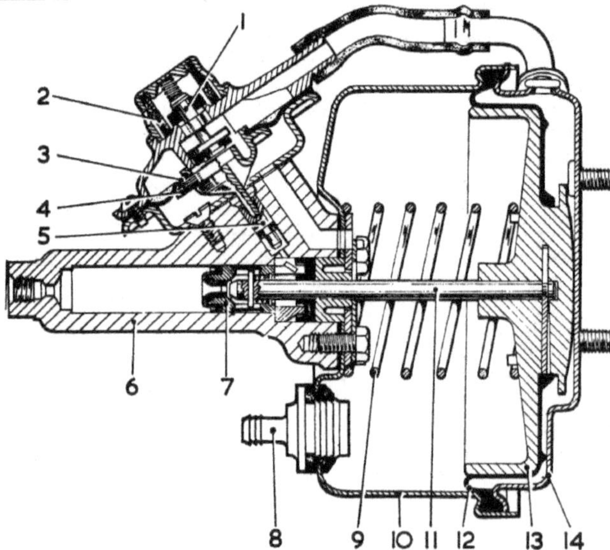

Fig.9.9.
Cross section of Lockheed Type 6 servo unit

1 Air valve and air valve return spring
2 Air filter
3 Air valve diaphragm
4 Air valve diaphragm support
5 Air valve piston
6 Slave cylinder
7 Slave cylinder piston
8 Vacuum connection and non-return valve
9 Servo return spring
10 Servo shell
11 Pushrod
12 Servo rubber
13 Piston
14 Servo end cover

2. Before assuming that a fault in the system is in the master cylinder the pipes and wheel cylinders should all be checked and examined as described in Sections 7 and 8.
3. Remove the master cylinder from the car as described in the previous section.
4. Dismantle and reassemble the unit as described for the clutch master cylinder in Chapter 5; also, see Fig.9.8.

12. Servo Unit - Removal, Overhaul & Reassembly

1. The servo unit, fitted to some cars, is an additional source of power boost to the hydraulic system for brake application. It uses the vacuum from the inlet manifold on a larger diameter diaphragm. This drives a piston in an intermediate hydraulic slave cylinder, thus supplementing the pressure applied on the foot pedal. If the servo unit should fail, the hydraulic system will still be open to permit pressure from the master cylinder to reach the wheel cylinders. If the servo unit needs removal for any reasons, it must be remembered that no braking will be available, other than from the handbrake, unless a direct hydraulic line is made between the master cylinder and the four way connector.
2. The servo is mounted low down on the left hand wing valance panel. To remove it, first disconnect the battery and remove the carburettor air cleaner. Loosen the clamping bolt on the bracket clip at the slave cylinder end and disconnect the vacuum pipe from either the inlet manifold or the servo. Seal the master cylinder reservoir cap with polythene sheet to minimise fluid loss and then disconnect both the hydraulic pipes at the servo slave cylinder. Try to cap the pipe ends with something to keep out dirt and keep in the fluid. Undo the nuts holding the shell and mounting bracket to the bodywork and lift the unit out.
3. Before dismantling the unit make sure the exterior is perfectly clean and prepare an equally clean work bench on which to work. A complete repair kit, which includes diaphragms and seals for the air valve, vacuum piston and hydraulic piston, should be obtained in advance (see Fig.9.10).
4. Grip the servo unit in a well padded vice by the slave cylinder body with the air valve uppermost.
5. Remove the rubber pipe from the end cover connection.
6. Undo the screws securing the plastic air valve cover and lift off the cover assembly complete, which comprises the filter and valve. If the air valve is suspect a new assembly which is part of the complete repair kit will have to be obtained (these individual parts cannot be obtained separately).
7. The dome containing these items is a snap fit into the air valve cover.
8. Remove the rubber diaphragm and its plastic support, and the three valve housing securing screws will then be revealed. Undo these and take off the housing and joint washer.
9. To get the air control valve piston out of its cylinder will require a low pressure inside the slave cylinder. This can be done by blocking one of the two hydraulic fluid unions on the slave cylinder with a finger, and applying air pressure from a foot pump to the other. When it is out, remove the rubber cup from the piston (for replacement).
10.The non-return valve which is mounted in a rubber grommet can be pushed out by thumb pressure. Remove the grommet also.
11.It is now necessary to remove the end cover from the main servo shell. This is a twist fit bayonet type of connection and to remove it calls for an anticlockwise twist as far as the stops in the cover will permit; when it will come off. Although there is a special tool for this (C2030), one can achieve the same result by drilling three holes in a plate to which the vacuum shell can be bolted, and then clamp the plate in the vice and twist the cover off.

12.Put the unit back into the vice as before. To remove the diaphragm it is not necessary to free the retaining key from the pushrod. Turn the diaphragm support so that the retaining key points downwards. Then supply light fluctuating pressure to the backplate against the main return spring and the retaining key will drop out.

13.Hold on to the diaphragm support and take it and the diaphragm and the return spring from the servo shell.
14.The bolts holding the servo shell to the slave cylinder are now exposed. Bend back the locking plate tabs from the bolt heads and remove the bolts, locking plate and abutment plate.
15.The shell can now be taken from the slave cylinder. Retrieve the washer between the two.

16.The pushrod can now be drawn from the slave cylinder together with piston assembly.
17.Slide the bearing cup and spacer off the pushrod noting the order and position in which they came off.

18.Prise the rubber seal off the slave piston.
19.If the rod is to be detached from the piston the following action will be required but a new retaining clip will be needed. It should not normally be necessary to separate them. Open up the retaining clip by twisting a small screwdriver in the join and this will expose the connecting pin which can be pushed out. This disconnects the slave piston from the connecting rod. This unit is now completely dismantled.
20.Examine all rubber cups and seals for wear and replace as necessary. If the air valve unit is in good condition and it is only necessary to clean the filter, blow it through with a tyre foot pump. Do not use any cleaning fluids or lubricants on the filter.
21.Wash all slave cylinder components in clean hydraulic fluid, and remove any deposits from the slave cylinder walls in the same way. If the slave cylinder is scored then it must be replaced.
22.Reassembly must be done in very clean conditions as a single speck of grit in the wrong place can cause total malfunction. It is best to wash your hands, get new clean cloths and lay out all the components on a sheet of clean white paper. Five minutes' extra attention now could save you another complete dismantling operation later.
23.Use clean hydraulic fluid as a lubricant when reassembling the hydraulic components.
24.If the piston and pushrod were separated push the rod into the rear of the piston against the spring until the connecting pin hole is

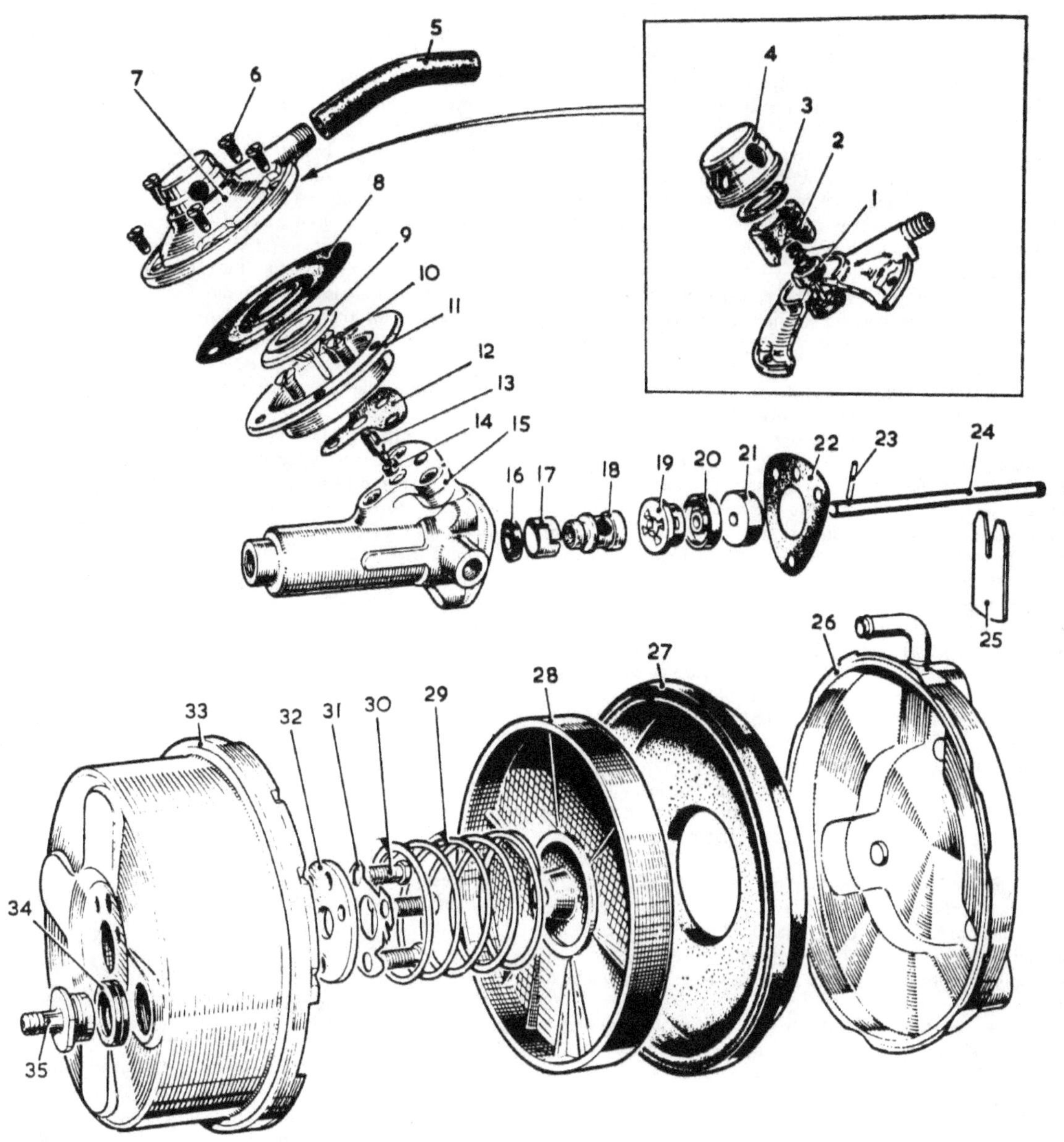

Fig.9.10. EXPLODED VIEW OF LOCKHEED TYPE 6 SERVO UNIT

1 Air valve and air valve return spring
2 Air filter
3 Sorbo washer
4 Air valve cover dome
5 Connecting hose
6 Air valve cover fixing screws
7 Air valve unit cover
8 Air valve diaphragm
9 Air valve diaphragm support
10 Air valve fixing unit securing screws
11 Air valve unit lower housing
12 Joint - air valve unit to slave cylinder
13 Air valve piston
14 Air valve piston rubber cup
15 Slave cylinder
16 Slave piston rubber seal
17 Retainer for connecting pin (23)
18 Slave cylinder piston
19 Plastic spacer
20 Rubber cup
21 Plastic bearing
22 Joint - slave cylinder to servo shell
23 Retainer pin - piston (19) to pushrod (24)
24 Pushrod
25 Retaining key-pushrod (24) to diaphragm support (28)
26 End cover
27 Servo rubber diaphragm
28 Diaphragm support
29 Servo return spring
30 Bolts - slave cylinder to servo shell
31 Locking plate
32 Abutment plate
33 Servo shell
34 Rubber seal mounting - vacuum non-return valve
35 Vacuum connection and non-return valve - plastic

open. Fit the pin followed by the retaining clip. It is important to ensure that the clip fits snugly in its groove. Any protrusions will score the cylinder wall.

25.Refit the rubber seal to the slave piston using only the fingers, ensuring that the lips of the seal face away from the pushrod.

26.Lubricate the cylinder bore (with hydraulic fluid only) and insert the piston. Then replace in correct order over the pushrod the spacer cup and bearing into the mouth of the slave cylinder. Ensure that each item placed into the cylinder has its sealing lips neither bent or turned back and that each is bedded individually in turn.

27.The servo shell is now already in the reverse order as given in paragraph 10. If the locking plate has been used more than once before (i.e. if the servo has already been twice dismantled) a new one should be fitted. Tighten the bolts evenly to a torque figure of 17 lb ft and tap up the locking plate tabs.

28.To replace the diaphragm, support and spring, pull out the pushrod as far as possible. Fit the spring and diaphragm support, ensuring that the spring ends are correctly located over the abutment plate and the diaphragm support boss.

29.Press the diaphragm support over the pushrod with the key slot facing upwards, and when the groove in the pushrod and the slot in the diaphragm are lined up insert the key.

30.Ensuring that the support and diaphragm are quite clean and dry fit the diaphragm to the support, gently stretching the inner edge to ensure that it seats properly in the groove of the support.

31.Smear the outer edge of the diaphragm with disc brake lubricant (not grease or hydraulic oil). This prevents it from binding when the lid cover is refitted to the servo shell.

32.If no service tool is available fix the end cover on to the vehicle mounting bracket (if you did not leave it there when taking it off), using the normal mounting units. Offer up the servo unit to the end cover so that when twisted clockwise the pipe will line up with the elbow on the end cover when the turn is completely up to the stops.

33.With the unit back on the bench replace the non-return valve and its mounting grommet.

34.To replace the air valve assembly first fit the rubber piston cup to the spigot of the piston ensuring that the lips face away from the spigot shoulder. Lubricate the cup with a little hydraulic fluid and insert it into the slave cylinder, taking care that the lips do not get bent back.

35.Fit the joint washer and valve housing to the slave cylinder using the three securing screws.

36.Fit the diaphragm support into the diaphragm and make sure that the inner ring fits snugly into the groove in the support. Then place the spigot of the support into the hole in the air valve piston. Use no lubricants.

37.Line up the screw holes in the diaphragm and the valve housing.

38.If the air filter and dome have been removed now is the time to snap the complete assembly back into the air valve cover.

39.Place the valve cover over the diaphragm so that the projections in the cover engage the slots in the diaphragm. Replace all five securing screws finger tight. Tighten them down firmly, but not overtight, in a progressive pattern roughly North, South, East, West. This tightening sequence is important as the air valve must seat evenly and precisely. Any leak renders the whole servo inoperative.

40.Refit the rubber pipe from the valve cover port to the end cover elbow.

41.Replacement of the unit on the car is a reversal of the removal procedure. Keep all pipes well clear of the exhaust. Bleed the hydraulic system in the normal manner when reconnected, and test without delay.

13. Hydraulic System - Bleeding

1. The system should need bleeding only when some part of the system has been dismantled which would allow air into the fluid circuit; or if the reservoir level has been allowed to drop so far that air has entered the master cylinder.

2. Ensure that a supply of clean non-aerated fluid of the correct specification is to hand in order to replenish the reservoir during the bleeding process. It is advisable, if not essential, to have someone available to help, as one person has to pump the brake pedal while the other attends to each wheel. The reservoir level has also to be continuously watched and replenished. Fluid bled out should not be re-used. A clean glass jar and a 9–12 inch length of 1/8 inch internal diameter rubber tube that will fit tightly over the bleed nipples is also required.

3. Bleed the front brakes first as these hold the largest quantity of fluid in the system. Dual braking systems require a different procedure; see Section 17.11.

4. Make sure the bleed nipple is clean and put a small quantity of fluid in the bottom of the jar. Fit the tube on to the nipple and place the other end in the jar under the surface of the liquid. Keep it under the surface throughout the bleeding operation.

5. Unscrew the bleed screw ½ turn and get the assistant to depress and release the brake pedal in short sharp bursts when you direct him. Short sharp jabs are better than long slow ones becasue they will force any air bubbles along the line ahead of the fluid rather than pump the fluid past them. It is not essential to remove all the air the first time. If the whole system is being bled, attend to each wheel for three or four complete pedal strokes and then repeat the process. On the second time around operate the pedal sharply in the same way until no more bubbles are apparent. The bleed screw should be tightened and closed with the brake pedal fully depressed which ensures that no aerated fluid can get back into the system. Do not forget to keep the reservoir topped up throughout.

6. When all four wheels have been satisfactorily bled depress the foot pedal, which should now offer a firmer resistance with no trace of 'sponginess'. The pedal should not continue to go down under sustained pressure. If it does there is either a leak or the master cylinder seals are worn out.

14. Brake Pedal - Removal & Replacement

Should the brake pedal pivot shaft become excessively sloppy due to wear in the pivot shaft there could be a lot of lost motion between the initial movement of the pedal and application of the brakes. This is not a satisfactory state of affairs. To remove the pedal and shaft assembly follow the procedures as laid down for the clutch pedal in Chapter 5, Section 6.

15. Stop Light Switch

The stop light switch is a pressure operated contact mounted in the hydraulic system on the face of the fourway connector. If the brake lights do not work when the pedal is depressed check first that the bulbs are all right. Then remove both leads from the terminals on the switch and touch them together. With the ignition switched on the brake lights should now work. If they do not the switch is faulty and should be unscrewed and a new one fitted. Bleed the hydraulic system afterwards.

16. Dual Braking System - Description

1. Models for the North American market have to be fitted with dual braking systems to meet the safety laws. It is possible that the law or the manufacturers may decide that the same feature is also necessary for the British market. The dual braking system consists of two separate hydraulic circuits which are operated from a tandem master cylinder. Should there be a break in one circuit with consequent loss of pressure it means that there is still the other remaining to halt the car. Obviously both the two circuits operate both front and rear brakes. All dual brake system models are fitted with servo assistance to the front wheel circuit only.

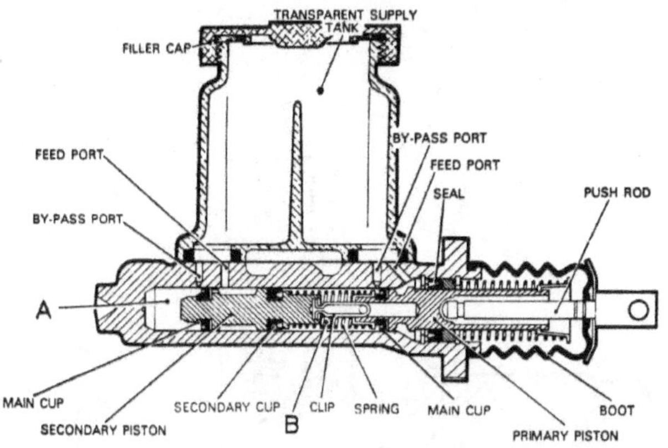

A Rear brake fluid chamber
B Front brake fluid chamber

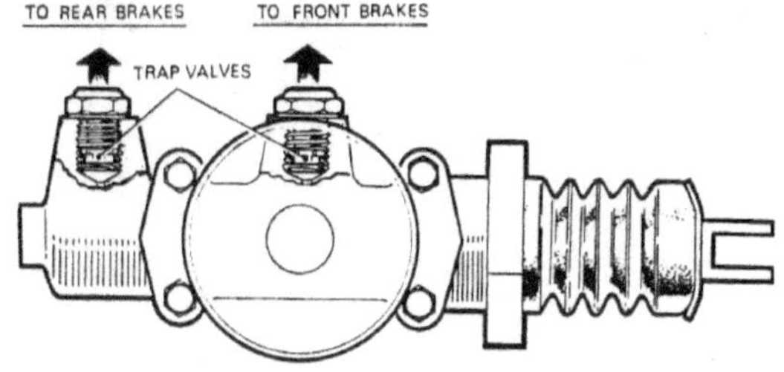

Fig.9.11.
Cross sectional views of tandem master cylinder

2. In addition, a pressure failure switch is incorporated into the hydraulic circuit so that immediate indication is given of the failure of one circuit. It consists of a double ended piston held in central balance in a cylinder, between the opposing pressure of each hydraulic circuit. Should one pressure differ from the other the piston will move and operate a switch which lights an indicator on the instrument panel. The same light is operated by a switch on the handbrake also - which helps to indicate that the electrics are working properly.

17. Tandem Master Cylinder & Pressure Failure Switch - Removal, Overhaul & Replacement

1. The cylinder is disconnected by undoing the hydraulic pipe unions and unscrewing the two mounting bolts, in a manner similar to a conventional cylinder. Before attempting to dismantle the unit it is essential to have a complete repair kit available. Special circlip pliers are also needed. The conventional variety will not reach the circlips in the bore of the cylinder (see Fig.9.11).
2. Remove the rubber boot and pushrod, and place the cylinder in a soft-jawed vice with the bore mouth upwards. Push down the spring retainer and this will reveal a 'Spirolox' locking ring in a groove in the cylinder wall. Carefully hook this out using a small screwdriver, pushing the end in an anticlockwise direction. Then remove the retainer and spring.
3. Remove the first circlip and then pull off the nylon bearing and cup seal from the primary piston. This will involve moving the piston up and down in the bore. Then remove the plain washer.
4. The second circlip is now accessible and should be removed. The piston assembly and stop washer can now be drawn out of the cylinder.
5. To fit new seals the pistons will have to be separated. This can be done by compressing the spring between them and punching out the pin from the end of the primary piston which hooks into the loop from the secondary piston.

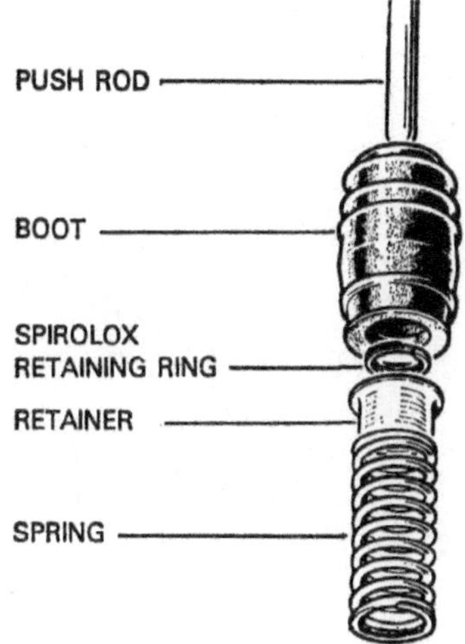

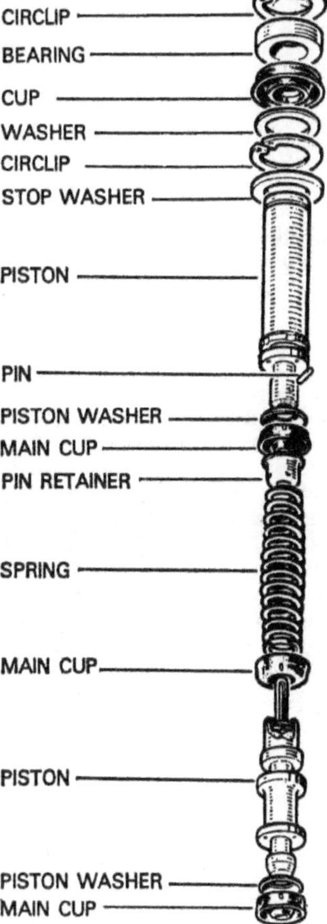

Fig.9.12.
Exploded view of piston assembly (tandem master cylinder)

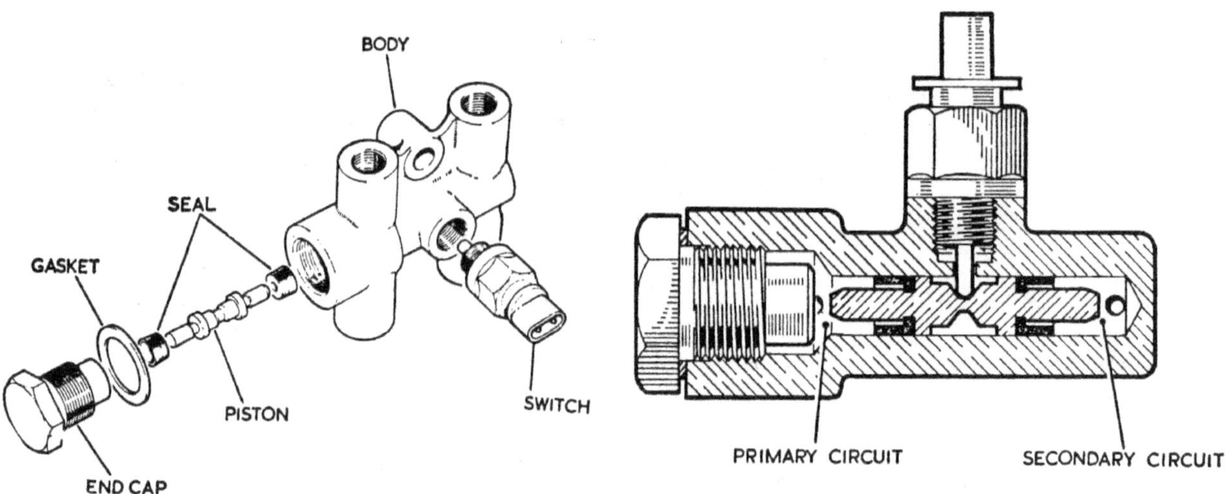

Fig.9.13. Cross sectional and exploded views of pressure switch

6. Apart from the cup already taken out, there are three main cups and two piston washers fitted to the pistons. Note carefully how these are fitted and where, before pulling them off. The odd one out is in fact that on the rear end (the connecting link end) of the secondary piston. The internal bore is larger and there are no dimples in the lip.

7. Maintaining scrupulous cleanliness, fit the new cups and washers in position and reassemble the pistons. Examine carefully the bore of the cylinder which should show no signs of scoring or damage. The cups on the secondary piston should have their lips pointing towards the end of the piston, and the washer behind the head cup should have the concave side against the seal cup. The same applies to the washer behind the cup of the primary piston (see Fig.9.12).

8. When reassembling the pistons to the cylinder make sure the lips of the cups are not turned back. The stop washer should be put over the end of the primary piston (when it is in the bore), and the piston assembly pressed down until the circlip groove is revealed. Make sure the circlip fits securely. After assembly coat the inside and beaded edges of the rubber boot with special rubber grease and insert the pushrod into the boot and the rear of the piston. Then fit the boot over the cylinder with the small hole facing away from the supply tank.

9. If the trap valves are to be taken out of the two outlet pipe unions in the cylinder, first carefully remove the adaptor fittings and discard the copper gaskets which must be renewed each time they are taken out.

10. The seals of the pressure equalising switch may need renewal and this is simply done. First unscrew the switch and withdraw it. Then undo the end cap and pull out the piston. The seals may then be removed (see Fig.9.13).

11. To bleed the hydraulic system on a dual braking system requires a slightly different approach from normal because the pressure equalising switch has to be balanced in a central position. Ensure first that there is no residual vacuum in the servo by operating the brake pedal several times. Do not restart the engine. Begin bleeding with the rear brakes, and if the rear brake system only has been opened then a bleed valve on the front system will also have to be opened at the same time to permit fluid to be released. After finishing the rear brakes, bleed the front. If the pressure warning light should remain on (handbrake off!) after completing the bleeding, open a rear bleed nipple and apply light pressure to the brake pedal. Immediately the light goes out close the bleed valve and then release the pedal. If the light should stay on, even after one complete down stroke of the pedal, close the bleed valve at the end of the pedal stroke and then do the same thing at one of the front brakes. If the warning light flashes on and off intermittently when the brakes are applied then there is a pressure variation between the two systems which must be fully investigated.

18. Fault Finding - Braking System

Before diagnosing faults from the following chart, check that any braking irregularities are not caused by:–

1 Uneven or incorrect tyre pressures
2 Incorrect 'mix' of radial and cross-ply tyres
3 Wear in the steering mechanism
4 Defects in the suspension and dampers
5 Misalignment of the body frame

Symptom	Reason/s	Remedy
Pedal travels a long way before the brakes operate	Automatic adjuster on rear shoes not functioning	Check and repair rear brake automatic adjusters
	Disc pads or linings excessively worn	Inspect and renew as necessary
Stopping ability poor, even though pedal pressure is firm	Linings, pads, discs or drums badly worn or scored	Dismantle, inspect, and renew as required
	One or more caliper pistons or rear wheel cylinders seized, resulting in some pads/shoes not pressing against discs/drums	Dismantle and inspect cylinders and repair or renew as necessary
	Brake pads or linings contaminated with oil	Renew pads or linings and repair source of oil contamination
	Wrong type of pads or linings fitted (too hard)	Verify type of material which is correct for the car and fit it
	Brake pads or shoes incorrectly assembled	Check for correct assembly
Stopping ability still fair, but needing noticeably heavier pedal pressure than before	Servo unit (where fitted) not functioning	Check and repair as necessary
Car veers to one side when brakes are applied	Brake pads on one side are contaminated with oil	Renew pads and repair source of oil contamination
	Hydraulic pistons in caliper are partially or wholly seized on one side	Inspect caliper pistons for correct movement and repair as necessary
	A mixture of pad materials used between sides	Standardise on types of pads fitted
	Unequal wear between sides caused by partially seized hydraulic pistons in brake calipers	Check pistons and renew pads and discs as required
Pedal feels spongy when the brakes are applied	Air is present in the hydraulic system	Bleed the hydraulic system and check for any signs of leakage
Pedal feels springy when the brakes are applied	Rear brake linings not bedded into the drums (after fitting new ones)	Allow time for new linings to bed in
	Master cylinder, brake caliper or drum backplate mounting bolts loose	Tighten mounting bolts as necessary
	Severe wear in rear drums causing distortion when brakes are applied	Renew drums and linings
Pedal travels right down with little or no resistance and brakes are virtually inoperative	Leak in hydraulic system resulting in lack of pressure for operation of wheel cylinders	Examine the whole of the hydraulic system and locate and repair the source of the leak(s). Test after repairing each and every leak source
	If no signs of leakage are apparent the master cylinder internal seals are failing to sustain pressure	Overhaul the master cylinder. If indications are that seals have failed for reasons other than wear, all the wheel cylinder seals should be checked also and the system completely replenished with the correct fluid
Binding, juddering, overheating	One, or a combination of causes given in the foregoing sections	Complete and systematic inspection of the whole braking system

Chapter 10 Electrical system

Contents

Specifications

Battery

Type	Lucas D9 or D11/13
Capacity at 20 hr.rate	D9 - 40 amp. hr. D11/13 - 50 amp. hr.
Voltage	12 volt
Earthed terminal	Negative (–)

Alternator Type	Early Models	Later Models
	Lucas 16 AC	Lucas 16 ACR
Output DC (nominal)	34 amps	34 amps
Rotor coil resistance	4.3 ohms	4.3 ohms
Brush length new	0.5 in (12.7 mm)	0.5 in (12.7 mm)
Renew at	0.2 in (5 mm)	0.2 in (5 mm)
Brush spring tension	7–10 ozs	9–13 ozs
Control box type	8TR	8TR
Rectifier pack model	4DS5	4S5

Starter Motor	Inertia Drive	Pre-engaged Drive
Type	M35G–1	M35G
Drive	'SB'	4SD roller clutch
Lock torque	8.2 lb ft @ 370 amps	8.6 lb ft @ 280 amps
Running current - no load	45 amps @ 9,500-11,000 rpm	60 amps @ 5,500-6,000 rpm
Minimum brush length	5/16 inch (7.9 mm)	5/16 inch (7.9 mm)
Brush spring tension - new	30–34 oz	
- used	25 oz minimum	

Fuses	3, each of 35 amps
No. 1 protects	Ancillary circuits other than those controlled by ignition switch
No. 2 protects	Circuits controlled by ignition switch
No. 3 protects	Side and tail lamp circuits

Windscreen Wiper Motor

Type	Lucas 15W
Normal light running current	1.5 amps
Normal final gear speed	46–52 rpm
High speed running current (light)	2.0 amps
High speed final gear speed (light)	60–70 rpm

Light Bulbs (all 12 volt)

	Lucas reference	Rating
Headlamp	Lucas F575 sealed beam	
Outer	Unit No 2A	50/37½W
Inner	Unit No 1A	50W
Front and rear indicator) Reversing lamp)	382	21W
Rear number plate) Side lamp) Boot lamp) Glove box)	989	6W
Stop and tail	380	21/5W
Interior courtesy	254	6W (festoon)
Instrument illumination	987	2.4W
Warning lights and clock	Phillips 12829	2W

1. General Description

The electrical system is 12 volt and apart from the ignition which is dealt with in Chapter 4, the main items are:–

a) Battery – lead/acid, 12 volt, negative earth.
b) Alternator driven by the fan belt, with a voltage and current regulator.
c) Electro-mechanical starter motor. One of two types is fitted. One throws a pinion into engagement with the flywheel ring gear as soon as the motor shaft starts to revolve. The other first engages the pinion with the flywheel ring gear, by means of a solenoid, and then power is switched to the motor itself.

The battery provides starting power and a reserve, should the loading of the equipment exceed the output of the alternator. This rarely happens. When the alternator is not fully loaded the extra current available is used to charge the battery. When the battery is fully charged and the load demand is light the output of the alternator is regulated so that overcharging does not damage the battery.

2. Battery - Removal & Replacement

1. The battery is situated at the front right hand side of the engine compartment.
2. Disconnect the earth lead (negative) from the terminal by unscrewing the centre screw and twisting the terminal cover off. Do not use any striking force or damage could be caused to the battery. Then remove the positive lead in the same way.
3. Slacken off the nuts holding the battery clamp stays until the assembly can be disengaged sufficiently to lift the battery out.
4. Lift out the battery, keeping it the right way up to prevent spillage of the electrolyte.
5. Replacement is a reversal of this procedure. Replace the positive lead first and smear the terminal posts and connections beforehand with petroleum jelly (not grease) in order to prevent corrosion.

3. Battery - Maintenance & Inspection

1. Check the battery electrolyte level weekly by lifting off the cover or removing the individual cell plugs. The tops of the plates should be just covered with the liquid and if not, add distilled water so that they are just covered. Do not add extra water with the idea of reducing the intervals of topping up. This will merely dilute the electrolyte and reduce charging and current retention efficiency. On batteries fitted with patent covers, troughs, glass balls and so on, follow the instructions in the handbook or marked on the cover of the battery to ensure correct addition of water.
2. Keep the battery clean and dry all over by wiping it with a dry cloth. A damp top surface could cause tracking between the two terminal posts with consequent draining of power.
3. Every three months remove the battery and check the support tray clamp and battery terminal connections for signs of corrosion - usually indicated by a whitish green crystalline deposit. Wash this off with clean water to which a little ammonia or washing soda has been added. Then treat the terminals with petroleum jelly and the battery mounting with suitable protective paint to prevent the metal being eaten away. Clean the battery thoroughly and repair any cracks with a proprietary sealer. If there has been any excessive leakage the appropriate cell may need an addition of electrolyte rather than just distilled water.
4. If the electrolyte level needs an excessive amount of replenishment and no leaks are apparent it could be due to overcharging as a result of the battery having been run down and then left to recharge from the vehicle rather than an outside source. If the battery has been heavily discharged for one reason or another it is best to have it continuously charged at a low amperage for a period of many hours. If it is charged from the car's system under such conditions the charging will be intermittent and greatly varied in intensity. This does not do the battery any good at all. If the battery needs topping up frequently, even when it is known to be in good condition and not too old, then the voltage regulator should be checked to ensure that the charging output is being correctly controlled. An elderly battery, however, may need topping up more than a new one because it needs to take in more charging current. Do not worry about this provided it gives satisfactory service.

5. When checking a battery's condition a hydrometer should be used. On some batteries where the terminals of each of the six cells are exposed a discharge tester can be used to check the condition of any one cell also. On modern batteries the use of a discharge tester is no longer regarded as useful as the replacement or repair of cells is not an economic proposition. The tables below give the hydrometer readings for various states of charge. A further check can be made when the battery is undergoing a charge. If, towards the end of the charge, when the cells are meant to be 'gassing' (bubbling), one cell appears not to be, then it indicates that the cell (or cells) in question is probably breaking down and the life of the battery is limited.

4. Battery - Charging & Electrolyte Replenishment

1. It is possible that in winter time when the load on the battery cannot be recuperated during normal driving time (from a dynamo), external charging may be desirable. This is best done overnight at a 'trickle' rate of 1–1.5 amps. Alternatively a 3–4 amp rate can be used over a period of four hours or so. Check the specific gravity in the latter case and stop the charge when the reading is correct. Most modern charging sets reduce the rate automatically when the fully charged state is neared. Rapid boost charges of 30–60 amps, or more, may get you out of trouble or can be used on a battery that has seen better days anyhow. They are not advisable for a good battery that may have run flat for some reason.
2. Electrolyte replenishment should not normally be necessary unless an accident or some other cause such as contamination arises. If it is necessary, then it is best to first discharge the battery completely and then tip out all the remaining liquid from all cells. Then acquire a quantity of mixed electrolyte from a battery shop or garage according to the specifications in the table below. The quantity required will depend on the type of battery but 3–4 pints should be more than enough for most. When the electrolyte has been put into the battery, a slow charge - not exceeding one amp - should be given for as long as it is necessary to fully charge the battery. This could be up to 36 hours.

Specific gravities for hydrometer readings - (check each cell)

Electrolyte temperature 60°F (15.6°C)

	Climate below 80°F (26.7°C)	Climate above 80°F (26.7°C)
Fully charged	1.270–1.290	1.210–1.230
Half charged	1.190–1.210	1.130–1.150
Discharged completely	1.110–1.130	1.050–1.070

Note:– If the electrolyte temperature is significantly different from 60°F (15.6°C) then the specific gravity reading will be affected. For every 5°F (2.8°C) it will increase or decrease with the temperature by 0.002.

5. Alternator - Description & Maintenance

1. The alternator is a generator capable of producing alternating current which is rectified into direct current so that it may be used in the car electrical system to charge the battery. Its main advantage is that it is lighter, more robust and has a much higher output at low engine revolutions than the more common D.C. dynamo. Incorporated in the charging circuit there are also:–

a) A relay to switch the energising current to the field winding when the ignition switch is turned on.
b) A sealed control unit.
c) Warning lamp control unit.

Of these, only the sealed control unit is capable of being adjusted, but it is considered that the average keen owner is best advised to leave it alone.

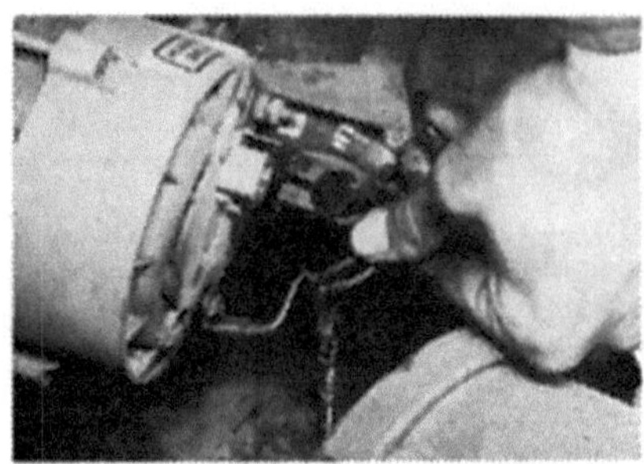

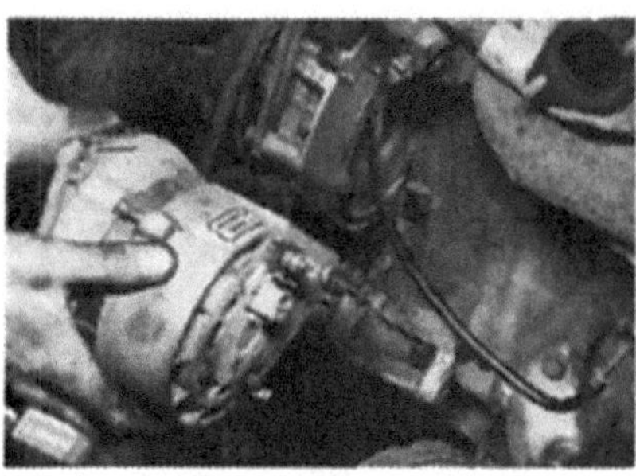

Section 6
Disconnecting and removing the alternator

2. Maintenance is minimal. Both bearings, one ball and one needle roller, are sealed, and the only items subject to any wear are the slip ring carbon brushes, but this is minimal. Otherwise the only regular attention needed is to make sure that the ventilation holes in the slip ring end cover are kept clear and that, as in the case of a dynamo, the fan belt tension is maintained correctly.

6. Alternator - Removal & Replacement

1. Disconnect the battery leads and pull off the terminal connections on the rear of the alternator (Photo).
2. Slacken the two alternator retaining bolts and the nut on the sliding link, and move the alternator in towards the engine so that the fan belt can be removed.
3. Remove the nut from the sliding link bolt (Photo), then remove the two lower attachment bolts. The alternator is then free to be lifted away from the engine (Photo).
4. Replacement is a reversal of the above procedure. Do not fully tighten down the retaining bolts and the nut on the sliding link until the fan belt has been correctly tensioned.

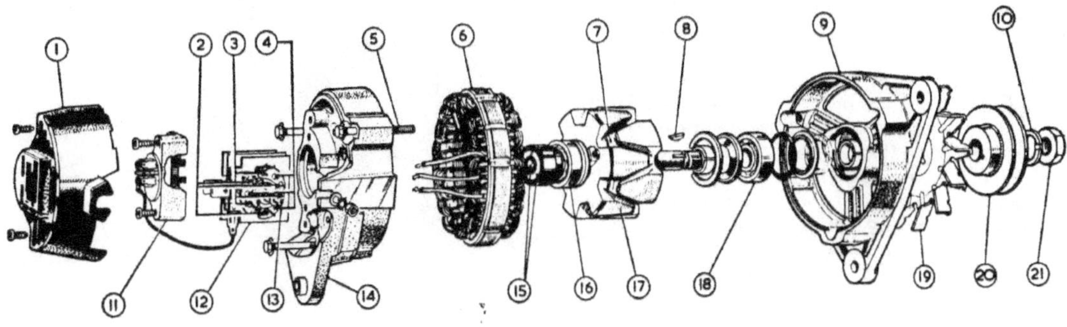

Fig.10.1. EXPLODED VIEW OF TYPE 16AC ALTERNATOR

1 Cover
2 Live side output diodes
3 Earth side output diodes
4 Field diodes
5 Through bolts
6 Stator
7 Field winding
8 Shaft key
9 Drive end bracket
10 Spring washer
11 Brush box moulding
12 Rectifier pack
13 Rectifier assembly bolt
14 Slip ring end bracket
15 Slip rings
16 Slip ring bearing
17 Rotor
18 Drive end bearing
19 Fan
20 Pulley
21 Nut

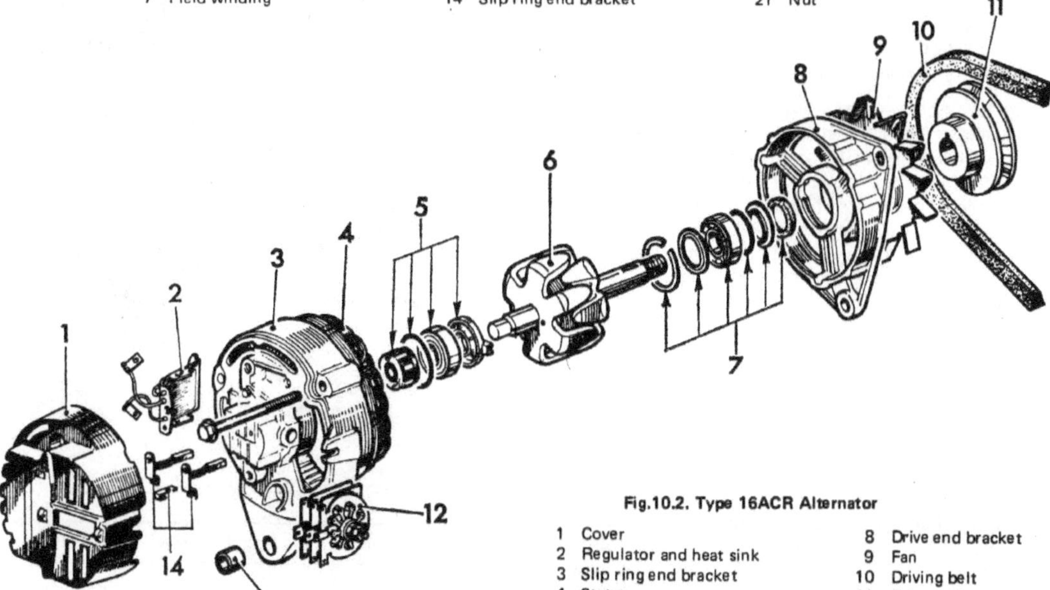

Fig.10.2. Type 16ACR Alternator

1 Cover
2 Regulator and heat sink
3 Slip ring end bracket
4 Stator
5 Slip ring end bearing set
6 Rotor and field winding assembly
7 Drive end bearing set
8 Drive end bracket
9 Fan
10 Driving belt
11 Drive pulley
12 Rectifier
13 Distance bush
14 Brush set

7. Alternator - Dismantling & Reassembly

1. The keen owner should only dismantle the alternator if he has verified that it is in fact faulty. Even then he should only dismantle it with the limited intention of examining the slip ring brushes which can be easily renewed.
2. Remove the shaft nut, spring washer, pulley and fan, and then mark the drive end bracket, starter laminations and slip ring end cover so that they can be reassembled the same way. Then undo the three through bolts and take out the end bracket and rotor (Fig.10.1 or 10.2).
3. At the other end remove the terminal nuts and washers, insulators, brush box screws and 2BA bolt.
4. The stator and heat sink assembly may then be taken out.
5. The brushes are held in by tongues at the root of each field terminal blade and can be removed by closing up the tongues. Check the brushes are at least the specified minimum length of 0.2 inch (5 mm). Renew them if necessary, checking that they slide freely in their holders. Clean the faces of the slip rings with a petrol-moistened cloth while the opportunity presents itself.
6. Reassemble the alternator in the reverse order, and if the brushes have been renewed test the output. If the alternator is still not serviceable it should be exchanged for another unit.

8. Starter Motor - General Description

1. The starter motor is mounted on the clutch bellhousing on the left hand side of the engine. It is secured by two bolts. It has four field coils and four commutator brushes, two of which are earthed. When the motor spins the drive pinion is thrown forward on a spiral

spline to engage with the flywheel ring gear which is then turned. When the engine fires the overrun of the flywheel throws the pinion back out of mesh. (For the pre-engaged type of starter, see Section 13.)

2. A starter motor is not normally looked at until it goes wrong. However, it is worthwhile giving a periodic check - say, every 5,000 miles. This can be done by sliding back the band in order to expose the commutator and brush gear. If an air jet can be used to blow out the dust so much the better. Any signs of dust should be cleaned off with petrol on a cloth and the commutator can be wiped dry with a non-fluffy cloth. Make sure that the connections are perfectly clean and tight. It will also be possible to see if any of the brushes are badly worn.

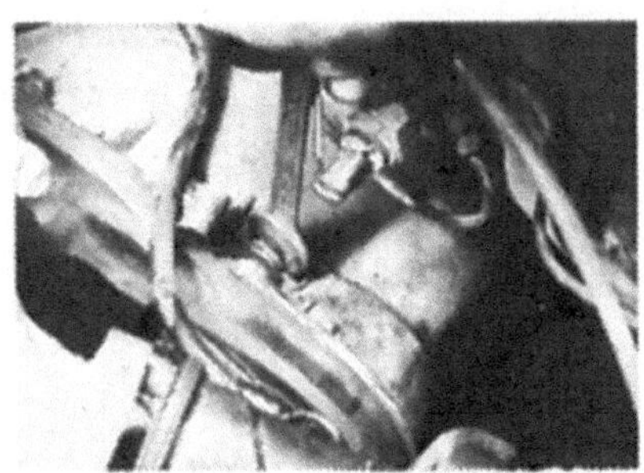

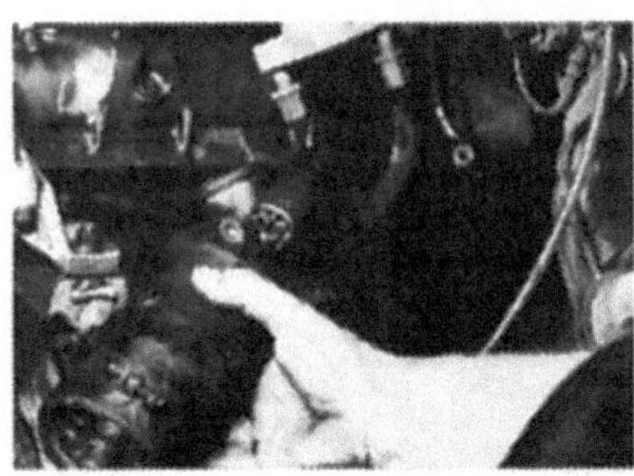

Section 10
Disconnecting and removing the starter motor

9. Starter Motor Circuit - Testing

If the starter motor fails to turn the engine when the switch is operated there are four possible reasons why:–

a) The battery is no good.
b) The electrical connections between switch, solenoid, battery and starter motor are somewhere failing to pass the necessary current from the battery through the starter to earth.
c) The solenoid switch is no good.
d) The starter motor is either jammed or electrically defective.

To check the battery, switch on the headlights. If they go dim after a few seconds the battery is definitely unwell. If the lamps glow brightly, next operate the starter switch and see what happens to the lights. If they go dim then you know that power is reaching the starter motor but failing to turn it. Therefore, check that it is not jammed by fitting a suitable spanner over the squared end of the shaft and making sure it turns easily. If it is not jammed the starter will have to come out for examination. If the starter should turn very slowly go on to the next check.

If, when the starter switch is operated, the lights stay bright, then the power is not reaching the starter. Check all connections from battery to solenoid switch to starter for perfect cleanliness and tightness. With a good battery installed this is the most usual cause of starter motor problems. Check that the earth link cable between the engine and frame is also intact and cleanly connected. This can sometimes be overlooked when the engine is taken out.

If no results have yet been achieved turn off the headlights, otherwise the battery will go flat. You will possibly have heard a clicking noise each time the switch was operated. This is the solenoid switch operating but it does not necessarily follow that the main contact is closing properly. (N.B. if no clicking has been heard from the solenoid it is certainly defective.) The solenoid contact can be checked by putting a voltmeter or bulb across the main cable connection on the starter side of the solenoid and earth. When the switch is operated, there should be a reading or lighted bulb. If not, the solenoid switch is no good. (Do not put a bulb across the two solenoid terminals. If the motor is not faulty the bulb will blow.) If, finally, it is established that the solenoid is not faulty and 12 volts are getting to the starter then the starter motor must be the culprit.

10. Starter Motor - Removal & Replacement

1. Disconnect the battery to prevent accidental short circuits.
2. Remove the main cable from the terminal post on the starter motor (Photo).
3. Undo the two bolts – one above and one below, holding the motor to the bellhousing (Photo). It may then be drawn out (Photo). In the photographs the exhaust pipe is disconnected from the manifold but this is not necessary to remove the starter.
4. Replacement is a reversal of the removal procedure. Make sure that the main terminal is away from the engine, i.e. do not fit the starter the wrong way up.

11. Starter Motor - Dismantling, Repair & Reassembly

1. Grip the motor in a vice if possible, and remove the band cover over the brush gear.
2. Using a piece of stiff hooked wire pull back each of the four carbon brush springs and lift each brush from its holder (Fig.10.3).
3. Unscrew the two through bolts and the commutator end bracket may then be taken off. The pinion end bracket complete with armature and drive assembly may then be removed from the yoke.
4. Before proceeding further, it is advisable to check that both the armature and field coils are in order. There is no point in renewing bearings and brushes if the guts of the motor are useless.
5. To test the armature is not difficult but a voltmeter or bulb and 12 volt battery are required. The two tests determine whether there may be a break in any circuit winding or if any wiring insulation is broken down. Figs. 10.4 and 10.5 show how the battery, voltmeter and probe connectors are used to test whether (a) any wire in the windings is broken, or (b), whether there is an insulation breakdown. In the first test the probes are placed on adjacent segments of a clean commutator. All voltmeter readings should be similar. If a bulb is used instead it will glow very dimly or not at all if there is a fault. For the second test any reading or bulb lighting indicates a fault. Test each segment in turn with one probe and keep the other on the shaft. Should either test indicate a faulty armature the wisest action in the long run is to obtain a replacement starter motor altogether.

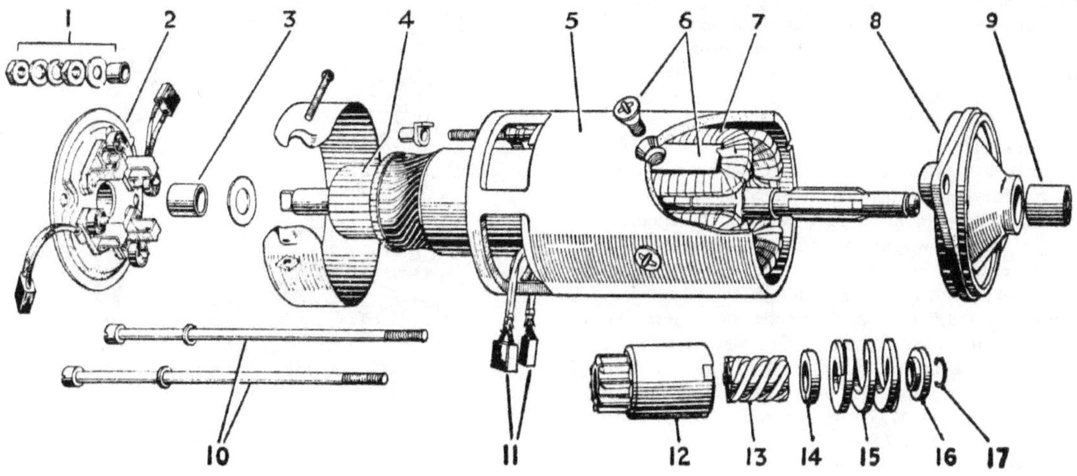

Fig.10.3. EXPLODED VIEW OF INERTIA–TYPE STARTER MOTOR

1 Terminal nuts and washer
2 Commutator end bracket
3 Bearing bush
4 Commutator
5 Yoke
6 Pole shoes and screws
7 Field coils
8 Drive-end bracket
9 Bearing bush
10 Through bolts
11 Insulated brushes
12 Pinion and barrel assembly
13 Screwed sleeve
14 Buffer washer
15 Main spring
16 Shaft collar
17 Jump ring

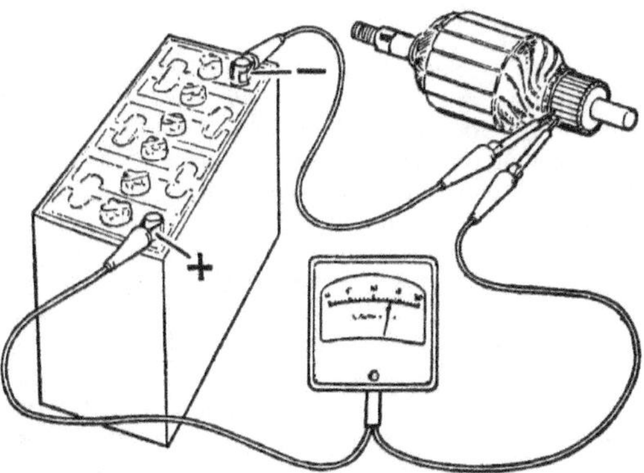

Fig.10.4.
Testing starter motor armature for open circuit

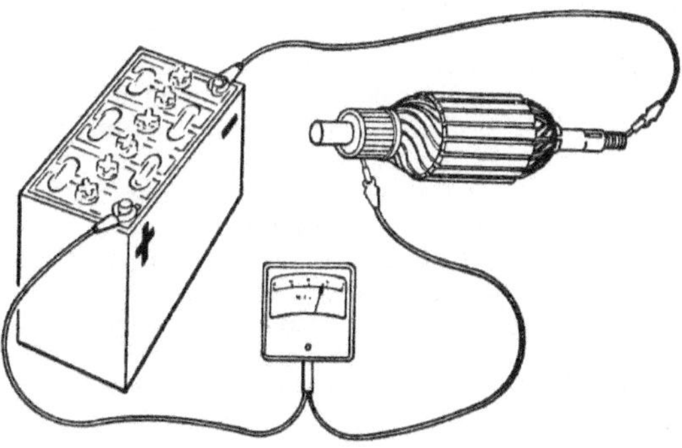

Fig.10.5.
Testing starter motor armature for insulation of windings

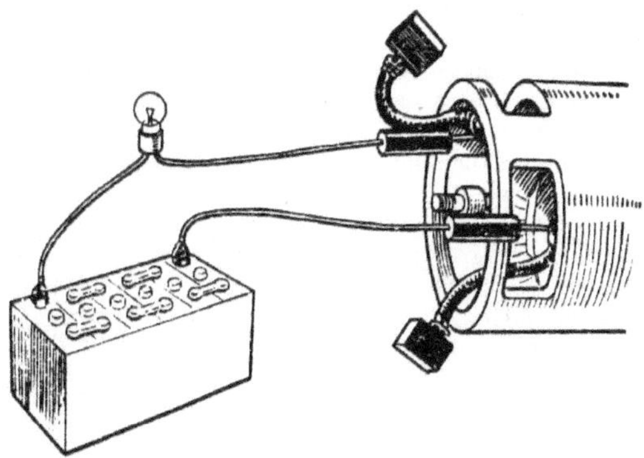

Fig.10.6
Starter motor field coil continuity test

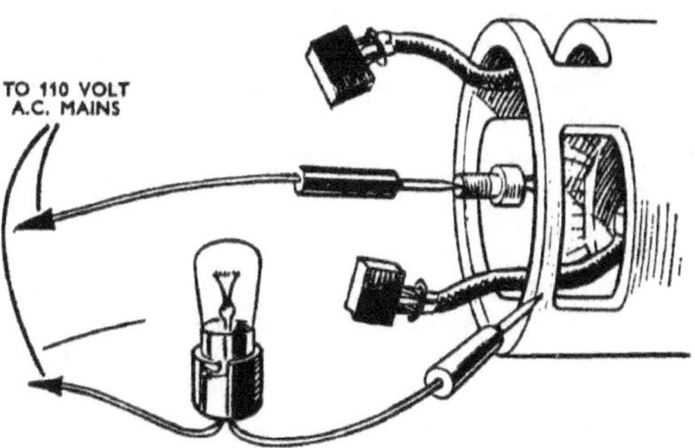

Fig.10.7
Starter motor field coil insulation test

6. To test the field coils for continuity is also straightforward (Fig. 10.6). A 12 volt bulb and battery connected in series can be applied with prods to the connections of the field coil brushes. The bulb should light. This, however, only indicates continuity - the insulation could be in a poor state even so and to test this with surety requires a voltage of more than 12–110 volts to be exact - and this calls for a transformer (Fig.10.7). If you have been able to rig up 110 volts (A.C. will do), wire a 110 volt bulb (a 220 volt will do) into the circuit and prod between the field coil terminal and the yoke of the motor. If the lamp lights (or glows dimly with a 220 volt bulb) then the insulation is broken down and the field coils need renewal.
7. If either the armature or field coils are in need of renewal it is recommended that a complete exchange unit be obtained.
8. If both armature and field coils are in order then check that the bearing bushes are not worn. If they are they may be renewed. To renew the bush in the driving end plate will require the starter pinion assembly to be removed first, in order to withdraw the shaft. This is explained in Section 12. If the carbon brushes are below the minimum length of 5/16 inch (7.9 mm) they should also be renewed.
9. The two brushes attached to the end cover (not insulated) can be unsoldered, and new ones clipped in and re-soldered to the terminal eyelets. The other two brushes connected to the field coils need a little care and attention. Originally they have been resistance brazed to aluminium end tags of the coils. Aluminium cannot be soldered so the old leads must be cut, leaving sufficient copper (at least 1/8 inch/3 mm) to solder the new leads onto. The insulation must also be in perfect condition because no part of the connecting wire must touch the yoke. When soldering the flexible lead make sure that no solder runs along the braid. This would reduce its flexibility and possibly cause it to fracture.
10. Reassembly of the starter motor is a reversal of the dismantling process. The brushes are replaced in the holders after the end cover has been replaced, but before this is done each brush should be checked in its holder to ensure it slides smoothly and freely. Wipe the surfaces with a petrol-dampened cloth if sticking occurs, and if more than this is needed the sides may be smoothed with a very fine file. Before putting the end cover in place make sure that the brushes are so arranged that they can be easily hooked into position and that their leads are not trapped. Remember also that the springs should all be conveniently ready. It ought not to be possible to fit the brushes into the wrong brush boxes, but it is worth noting that the two fixed to the end plate only go into holders to which they are attached at the base. (The other two holders are insulated from the end plate.)

12. Starter Motor Drive Pinion - Dismantling, Repair & Reassembly

1. Persistent jamming or reluctance to disengage indicates that the starter pinion assembly needs attention. The starter motor should first of all be removed.
2. With the starter motor removed, thoroughly clean with petrol the drive pinion, taking care to keep any liquid from running into the motor. If there is a lot of dirt to clean off, this could be the sole trouble. The pinion should move freely in a spiral movement along the shaft against the light spring and return easily on being released. To do this the spiral splines must be completely clean and free of oil. (Oil merely collects dust and gums up the splines.) Both springs should be intact. The larger one acts as a shock absorber when the moving pinion engages the stationary flywheel ring gear.
3. Should either spring be broken, or the spiral splines be badly worn, preventing the pinion from moving smoothly, it will be necessary to remove the starter and drive from the shaft. This requires the heavy spring to be compressed so that the jump ring which locates in a groove round the shaft inside the shaft collar can be removed. This calls for either a special tool or a device to be made up which will enable the spring to be compressed between the jaws of a vice. Such a device has to be very robust to overcome the strength of the spring so unless you have some suitable metal available it would be advisable to borrow one.
4. With the jump ring removed the components of the drive assembly can be removed from the shaft. Renew any parts as necessary, noting that if the pinion is renewed the spiral splined sleeves should also be renewed. Reassembly is a reversal of the dismantling procedure, once again requiring the services of the device to compress the buffer spring.

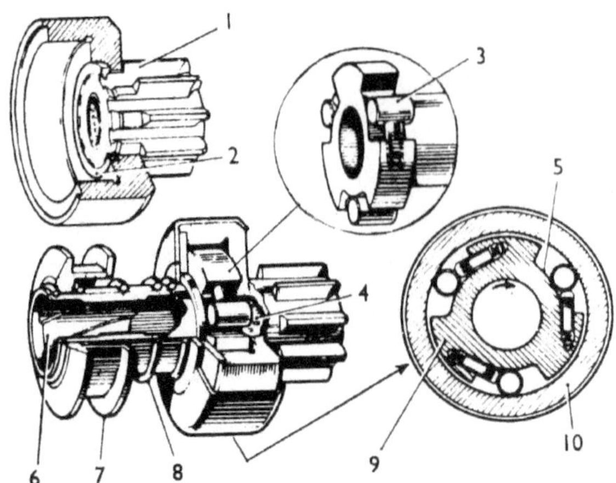

Fig.10.8. Pinion and roller clutch of pre-engaged type starter motor

1 Alternative construction (pinion pressed and cleat-ringed into driven member)
2 Soft metal cleating ring
3 Spring loaded rollers
4 Bush
5 Cam tracks
6 Driving sleeve
7 Operating bush
8 Engagement spring
9 Driving member
10 Driven member (with pinion)

13. Pre-Engaged Starters - Description, Maintenance & Testing

1. The motor part of the pre-engaged starter is no different from the inertia type. The difference is in the method of engaging the driving pinion with the flywheel ring gear. The starter solenoid switch, in addition to making the electrical connection, now also operates a lever which moves the pinion into mesh with the ring gear just before the power is switched to the motor. This results in quieter operation and reduces much of the shock loading on the starter motor. To prevent the engine driving the starter, should the pinion stick, the drive is through a one-way roller type clutch (Fig.10.8). Also, the pinion is spring loaded, so that in the event of an exact abutment of gear teeth preventing engagement the solenoid will still continue and make power contact and the pinion will move into engagement automatically as soon as the shaft moves. The operating lever, which connects the solenoid plunger to the pinion, pivots on an eccentric pin so that the pinion engagement may be set correctly in relation to the switch contacts.
2. Maintenance and testing procedures are the same as for the other type of starter but, of course, in this case the solenoid switch is mounted on the starter motor casing itself.

14. Pre-Engaged Starters - Removal & Replacement

Removal and replacement is the same as for the inertia type with the additional requirement that the two feed wires to the solenoid need pulling off the Lucar connections.

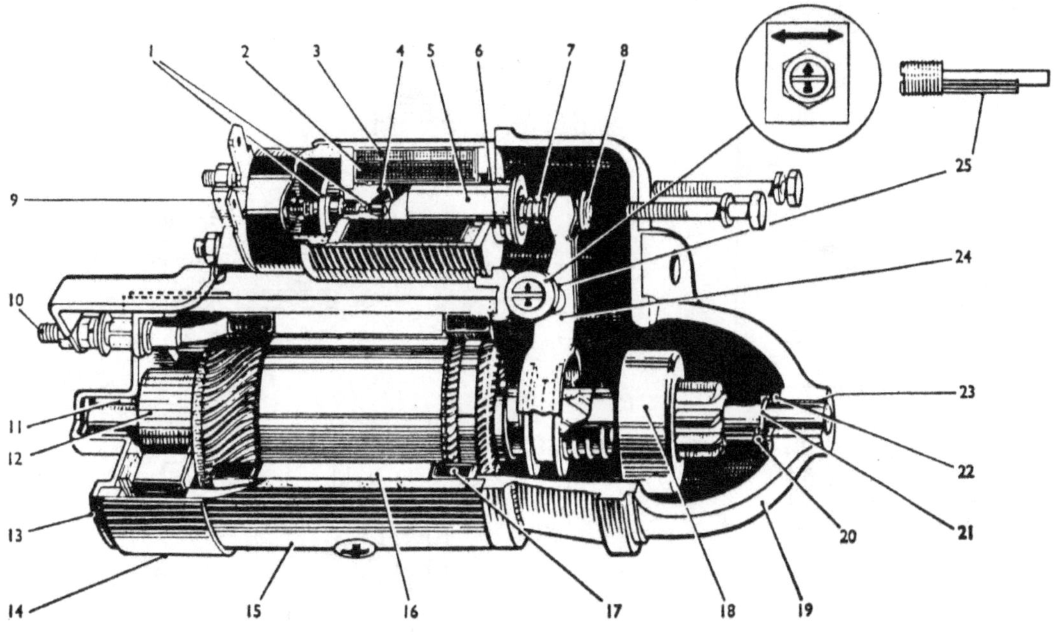

Fig.10.9. CUTAWAY VIEW OF PRE-ENGAGED TYPE STARTER MOTOR

1 Spindle and moving contact assembly
2 Series winding
3 Shunt winding
4 Core
5 Plunger
6 Pinion retraction spring
7 Lost motion spring
8 Sliding collar
9 Solenoid unit
10 Main terminal
11 Bronze bush
12 Commutator
13 Commutator end bracket
14 Band cover
15 Yoke
16 Pole shoes
17 Field coils
18 Roller clutch
19 Drive end bracket
20 Thrust collar
21 Jump ring
22 Thrust washer
23 Bronze bush
24 Engaging lever
25 Eccentric pivot pin

15. Pre-Engaged Starters - Dismantling & Reassembly

1. Having removed the starter motor from the car the solenoid unit may be removed after disconnecting the link cable to the motor from the main terminal (Fig.10.9).
2. The solenoid plunger can be then disengaged from the lever in the drive end bracket.
3. Take off the brush gear band cover and lift out the two insulated brushes from their holders. Then remove the two through bolts which hold both end covers to the yoke.
4. Take the end bracket off the commutator and then slacken the locknut on the eccentric pivot bolt and unscrew the pivot bolt from the drive end bracket.
5. The armature can now be removed from the drive end bracket and the engaging lever after that. Note which way round the lever goes.
6. If the thrust collar on the armature shaft is depressed a small jump ring is revealed. Remove this and the collar and the drive unit can be drawn off. The driving pinion and clutch are a single assembly but can be separated from the grooved operating bush by pushing back the bush to reveal another jump ring. This can be removed, thus releasing the bush from the spindle.
7. Checking of the armature field coils and subsequently bearing bushes and brushgear should be carried out as described in Section 15.
8. Reassembly is a reversal of the removal procedure. All the components of the drive pin and bearings should be liberally greased on assembly. Adjustment of the eccentric pin may be necessary. The best way is to connect a 6 volt supply between the small terminal of the solenoid and the solenoid casing. This will draw in the plunger as far as the springs, which the low power will not permit it to overcome. If the pinion is held back lightly (towards the armature) to take up any lost motion, the gap between the end of the pinion and the thrust collar should be 0.010 inch (0.28 mm). The eccentric pin should be moved to achieve this. The arrow head on the pivot bolt should point only towards the arrowed arc marked in the bracket, as the adjustment range is through 180° only.

16. Fuses

A fuse unit is mounted on the bulkhead and contains three circuit fuses and two spares. The connections are made to the back of the fuse panel by Lucar connectors and reference to the wiring diagram shows the relevant circuit connections.

17. Direction Indicator Flasher Circuit - Fault Tracing & Rectification

1. The unit which causes the lights to flash intermittently is contained in a three inch long cylinder clipped under the dashboard. It has three terminals at one end.
2. If the flashers fail to work properly first check that all the bulbs are serviceable and of the correct wattage. Then check that the nuts which hold the lamp bodies to the car are tight and free from corrosion. These are the means by which the circuit is completed and any resistance here could affect the proper working of the coils in the flasher unit.
3. If there is still no success, bridge the 'B' and 'L' terminals on the flasher unit. When the switch is operated the lights should go on (on the appropriate side) and stay on. If they do, the flasher unit is

COLOUR CODE			
R	RED	P	PURPLE
Y	YELLOW	W	WHITE
G	GREEN	B	BLACK
U	BLUE	L	LIGHT
N	BROWN		

ABBREVIATIONS	
R.H.	RIGHT HAND
L.H.	LEFT HAND
SPEEDO'	SPEEDOMETER
THERMO'	THERMOMETER

SYMBOLS	
	SNAP CONNECTOR
	PLUG AND SOCKET CONNECTOR
	EARTH THROUGH CABLE
	EARTH THROUGH UNIT

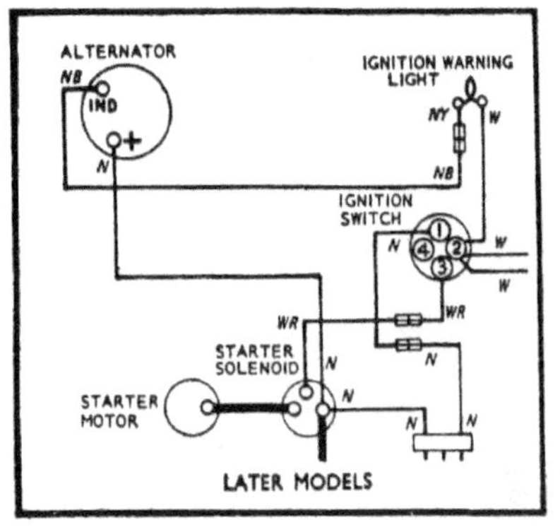

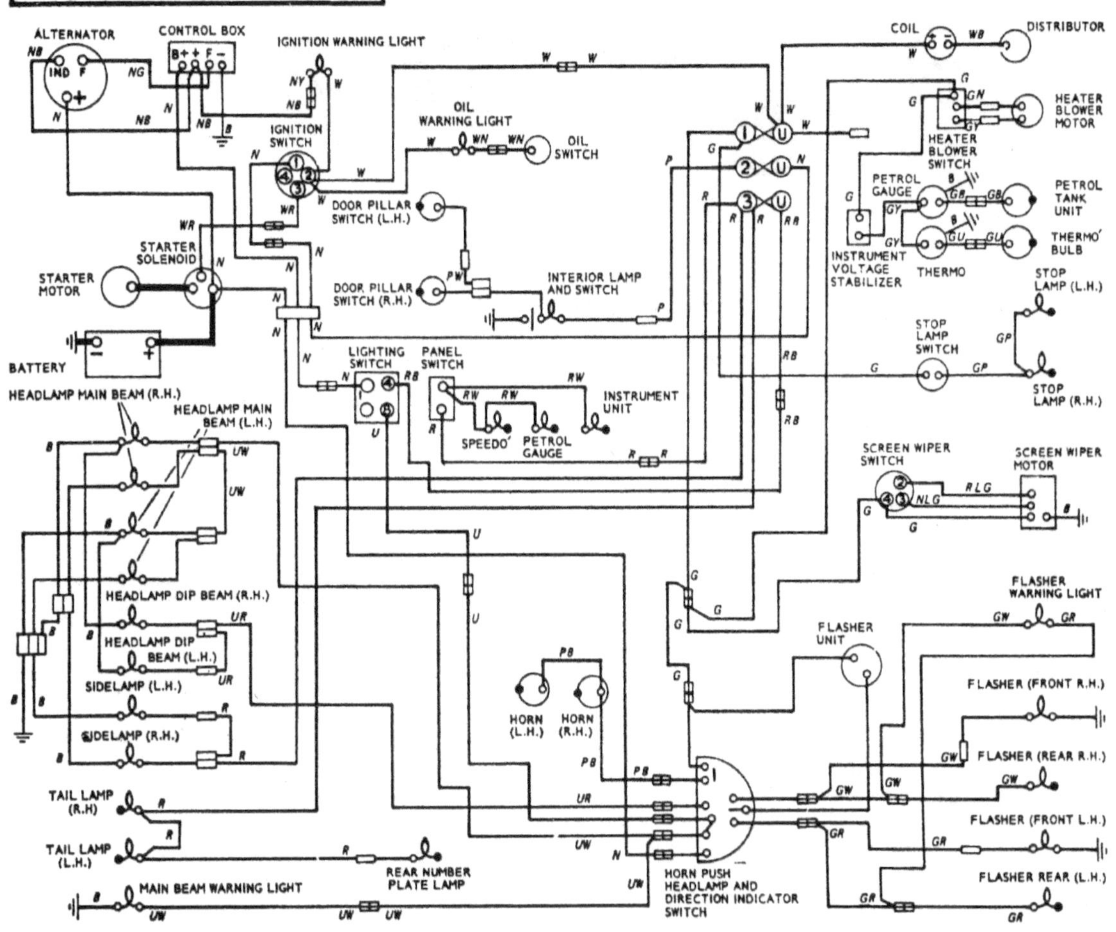

Snap connectors

Quan.	Location
4	Front of left hand wing valance
4	Front of right hand wing valance
1	Behind bumper adjacent to rear number plate
2	Under facia at centre
1	Under facia at left hand side
2	Under facia at right hand side
2	Under bonnet near centre of bulkhead
1	Rear of right hand wing valance

Plug and socket connectors

Plug and socket connectors are shown individually on this wiring diagram, but on the vehicle they are in four separate units under the facia panel

Fig.10.10. WIRING DIAGRAM FOR THE ALPINE

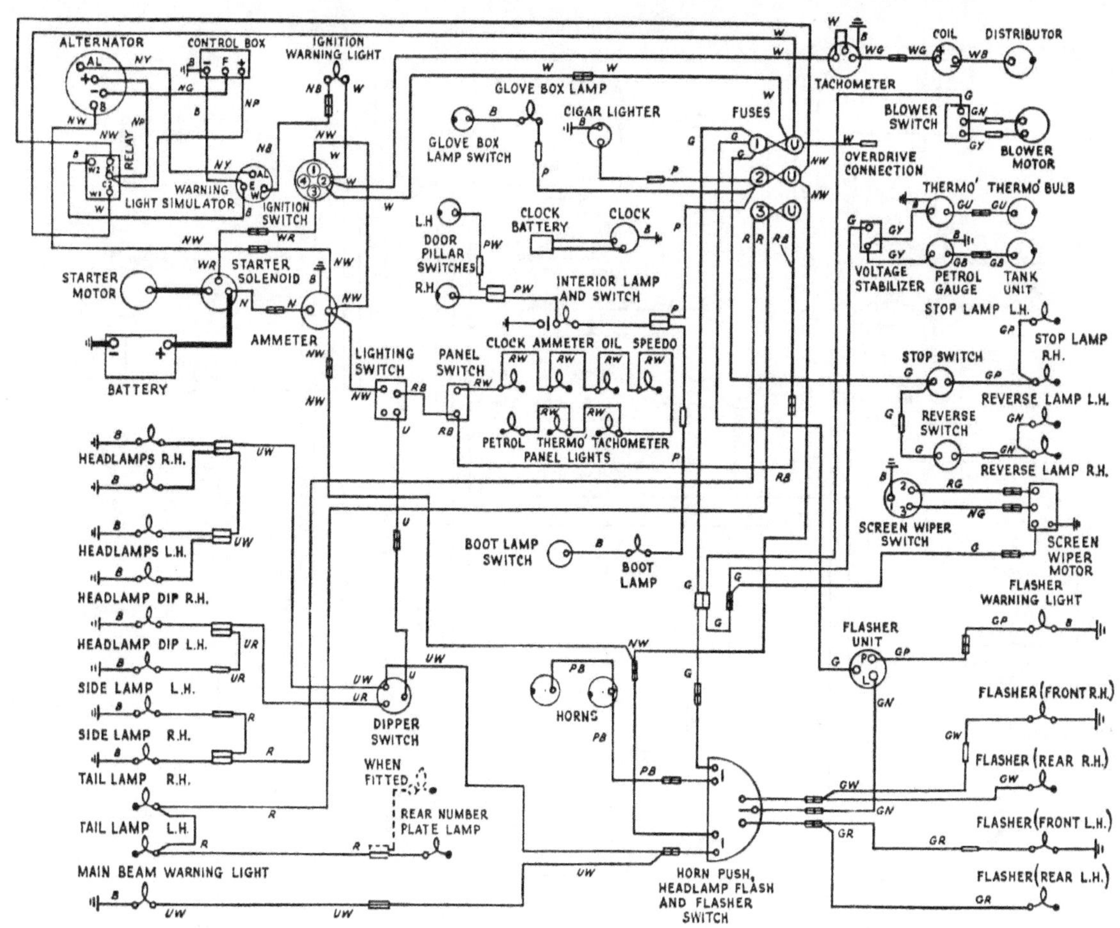

COLOUR CODE			
R	RED	N	BROWN
Y	YELLOW	P	PURPLE
G	GREEN	W	WHITE
U	BLUE	B	BLACK
L/G	LIGHT GREEN		

SYMBOLS	
- - - - - - - - -	ADDITIONAL WIRING (EXPORT MODELS)
—▭—	SNAP CONNECTOR
—▭▭—	PLUG AND SOCKET CONNECTOR
—B—⏚	EARTH THROUGH CABLE
——●	EARTH THROUGH UNIT

ABBREVIATIONS	
R.H.	RIGHT-HAND
L.H.	LEFT-HAND
THERMO'	THERMOMETER
SPEEDO'	SPEEDOMETER

Snap connectors

Quan.	Location
4	Front of left hand wing valance
4	Front of right hand wing valance
1	Behind bumper adjacent to rear number plate
3	Under facia adjacent to blower motor
1	Under facia at left hand side
2	Under facia at right hand side
1	In console on floor tunnel near gear lever
2	Under bonnet near centre of bulkhead
1	Adjacent to lamp in luggage compartment
1	Adjacent to glove box
1	Rear of right hand wing valance

Plug and socket connectors

Plug and socket connectors are shown individually on this wiring diagram, but on the vehicle they are in four separate units under the facia panel

Fig.10.11. WIRING DIAGRAM FOR RAPIERS FITTED WITH TYPE 16AC ALTERNATORS (UP TO, BUT EXCLUDING, CHASSIS NO.341005608)

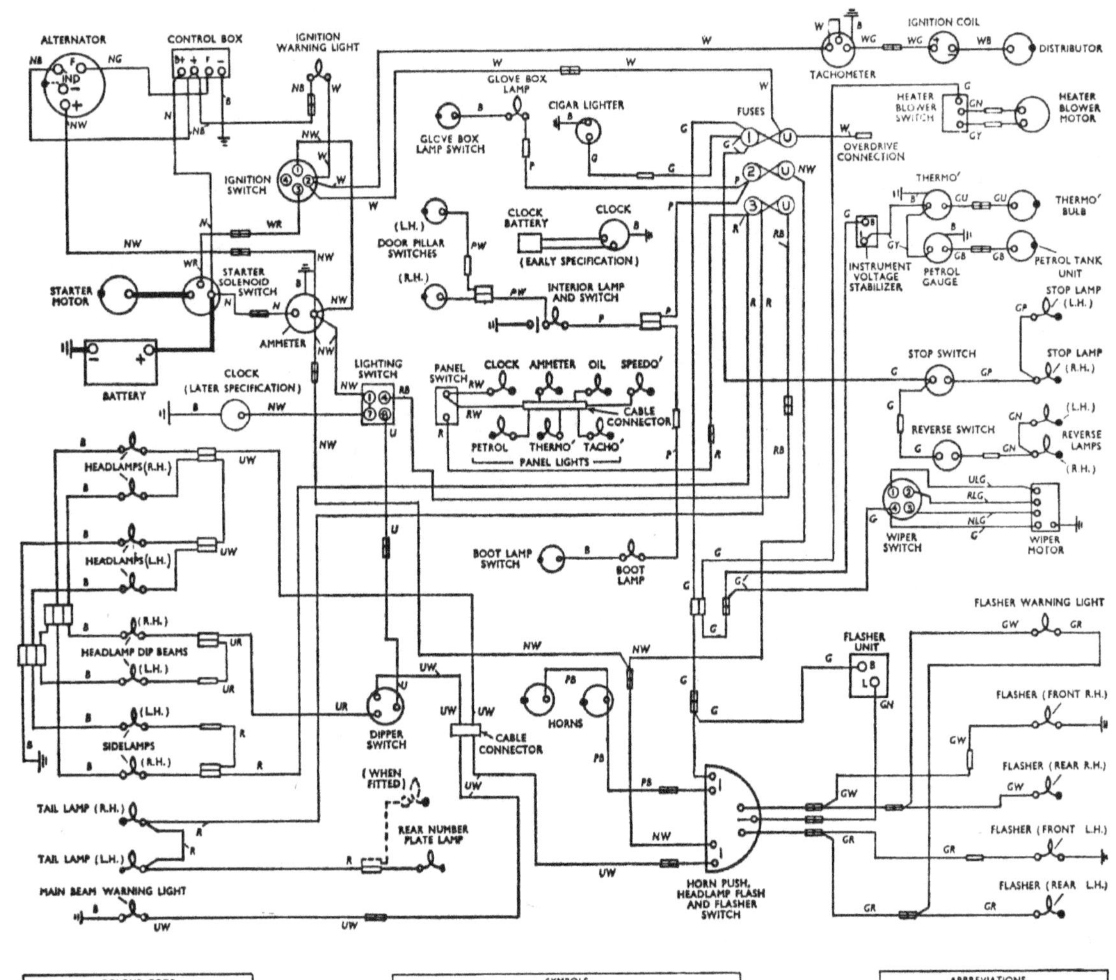

COLOUR CODE			
R	RED	P	PURPLE
Y	YELLOW	W	WHITE
G	GREEN	B	BLACK
U	BLUE	L	LIGHT
N	BROWN		

SYMBOLS	
— — — —	ALTERNATIVE WIRING FOR EXPORT MODELS
	SNAP CONNECTOR
	PLUG AND SOCKET CONNECTOR
	EARTH THROUGH CABLE
	EARTH THROUGH UNIT

ABBREVIATIONS	
R.H.	RIGHT-HAND
L.H.	LEFT-HAND
SPEEDO'	SPEEDOMETER
THERMO'	THERMOMETER
TACHO'	TACHOMETER

Snap connectors

Quan.	Location
4	Front of left hand wing valance
4	Front of right hand wing valance
1	Behind bumper adjacent to rear number plate
3	Under facia adjacent to blower motor
1	Under facia at left hand side
2	Under facia at right hand side
2	In console on floor tunnel near gear lever
2	Under bonnet near centre of bulkhead
1	Adjacent to lamp in luggage compartment
1	Adjacent to glove box
1	Rear of right hand wing valance
1	In luggage compartment adjacent to left hand tail lamp
1	In luggage compartment adjacent to right hand tail lamp

Plug and socket connectors

Plug and socket connectors are shown individually on this wiring diagram, but on the vehicle they are in four separate units under the facia panel

Fig.10.12. WIRING DIAGRAM FOR RAPIERS FITTED WITH TYPE 16AC ALTERNATOR (FROM CHASSIS NO.341005608 ON)

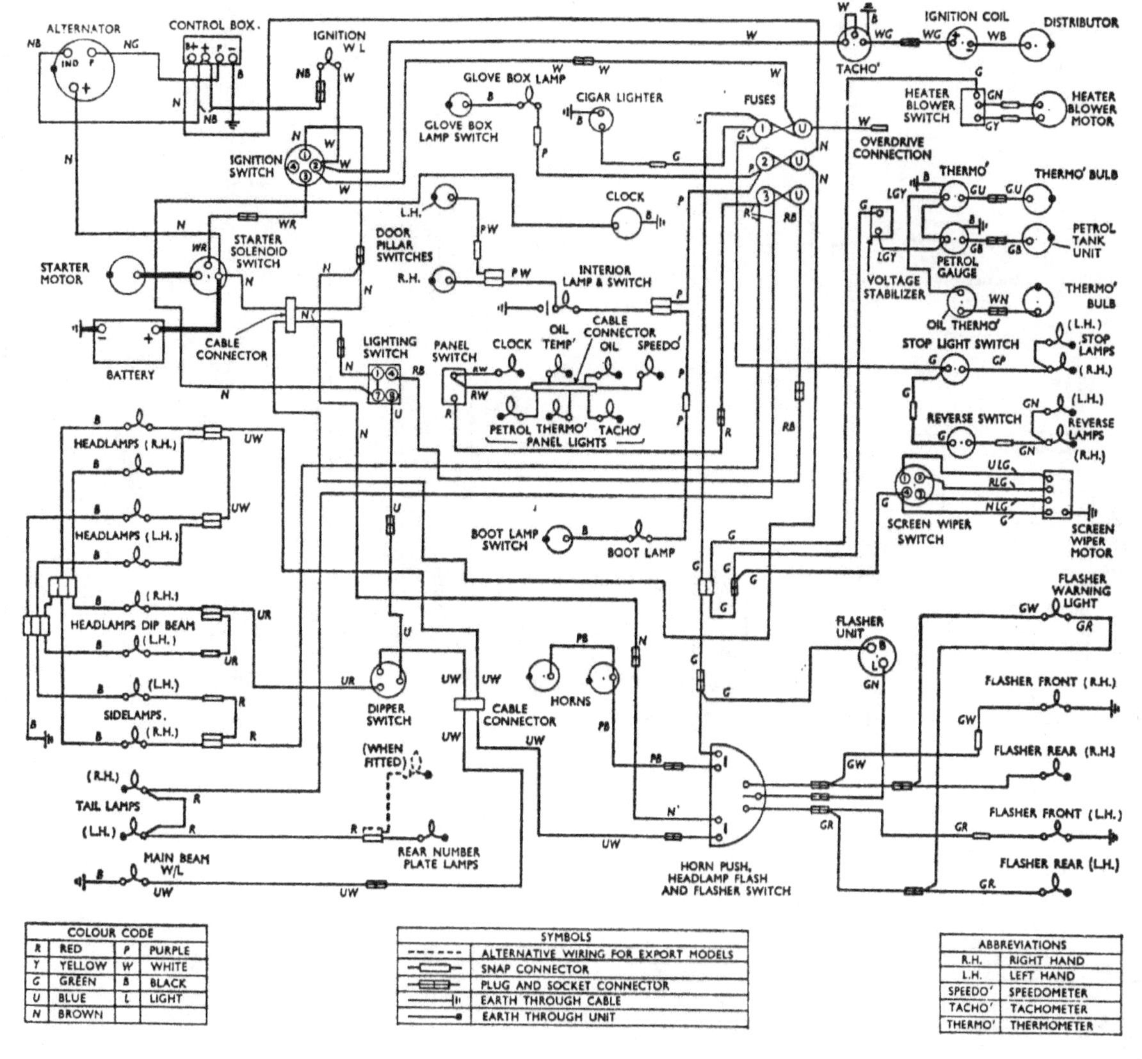

COLOUR CODE			
R	RED	P	PURPLE
Y	YELLOW	W	WHITE
G	GREEN	B	BLACK
U	BLUE	L	LIGHT
N	BROWN		

SYMBOLS	
- - - - - -	ALTERNATIVE WIRING FOR EXPORT MODELS
	SNAP CONNECTOR
	PLUG AND SOCKET CONNECTOR
	EARTH THROUGH CABLE
	EARTH THROUGH UNIT

ABBREVIATIONS	
R.H.	RIGHT HAND
L.H.	LEFT HAND
SPEEDO'	SPEEDOMETER
TACHO'	TACHOMETER
THERMO'	THERMOMETER

Snap connectors

Quan.	Location
4	Front of left hand wing valance
4	Front of right hand wing valance
1	Behind bumper adjacent to rear number plate
3	Under facia adjacent to blower motor
1	Under facia at left hand side
2	Under facia at right hand side
2	In console on floor tunnel near gear lever
2	Under bonnet near centre of bulkhead
1	Adjacent to lamp in luggage compartment
1	Adjacent to glove box
1	Rear of right hand wing valance
1	In luggage compartment adjacent to left hand tail lamp
1	In luggage compartment adjacent to right hand tail lamp

Plug and socket connectors

Plug and socket connectors are shown individually on this wiring diagram, but on the vehicle they are in three separate units under the facia panel

Fig.10.13. WIRING DIAGRAM FOR RAPIER H120 MODELS FITTED WITH TYPE 16AC ALTERNATOR

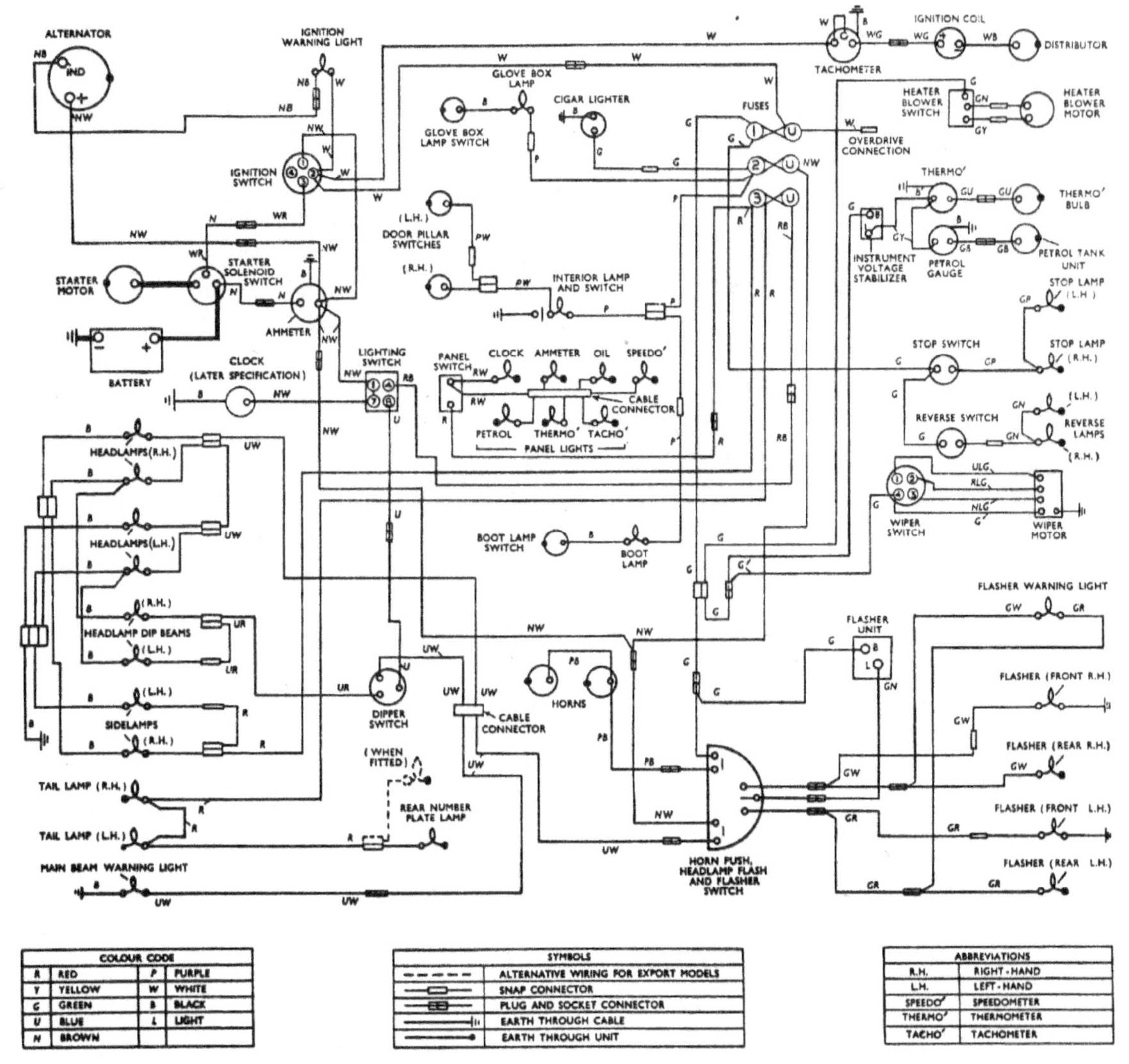

COLOUR CODE			
R	RED	P	PURPLE
Y	YELLOW	W	WHITE
G	GREEN	B	BLACK
U	BLUE	L	LIGHT
N	BROWN		

SYMBOLS	
— — — — —	ALTERNATIVE WIRING FOR EXPORT MODELS
(snap connector symbol)	SNAP CONNECTOR
(plug and socket symbol)	PLUG AND SOCKET CONNECTOR
(earth symbol)	EARTH THROUGH CABLE
(earth symbol)	EARTH THROUGH UNIT

ABBREVIATIONS	
R.H.	RIGHT-HAND
L.H.	LEFT-HAND
SPEEDO'	SPEEDOMETER
THERMO'	THERMOMETER
TACHO'	TACHOMETER

Snap connectors

Quan.	Location
4	Front of left hand wing valance
4	Front of right hand wing valance
1	Behind bumper adjacent to rear number plate
3	Under facia adjacent to blower motor
1	Under facia at left hand side
2	Under facia at right hand side
2	In console on floor tunnel near gear lever
2	Under bonnet near centre of bulkhead
1	Adjacent to lamp in luggage compartment
1	Adjacent to glove box
1	Rear of right hand wing valance
1	In luggage compartment adjacent to left hand tail lamp
1	In luggage compartment adjacent to right hand tail lamp

Plug and socket connectors

Plug and socket connectors are shown individually on this wiring diagram, but on the vehicle they are in three separate units under the facia panel

Fig.10.14. WIRING DIAGRAM FOR RAPIER AND RAPIER H120 MODELS FITTED WITH TYPE 16ACR ALTERNATOR

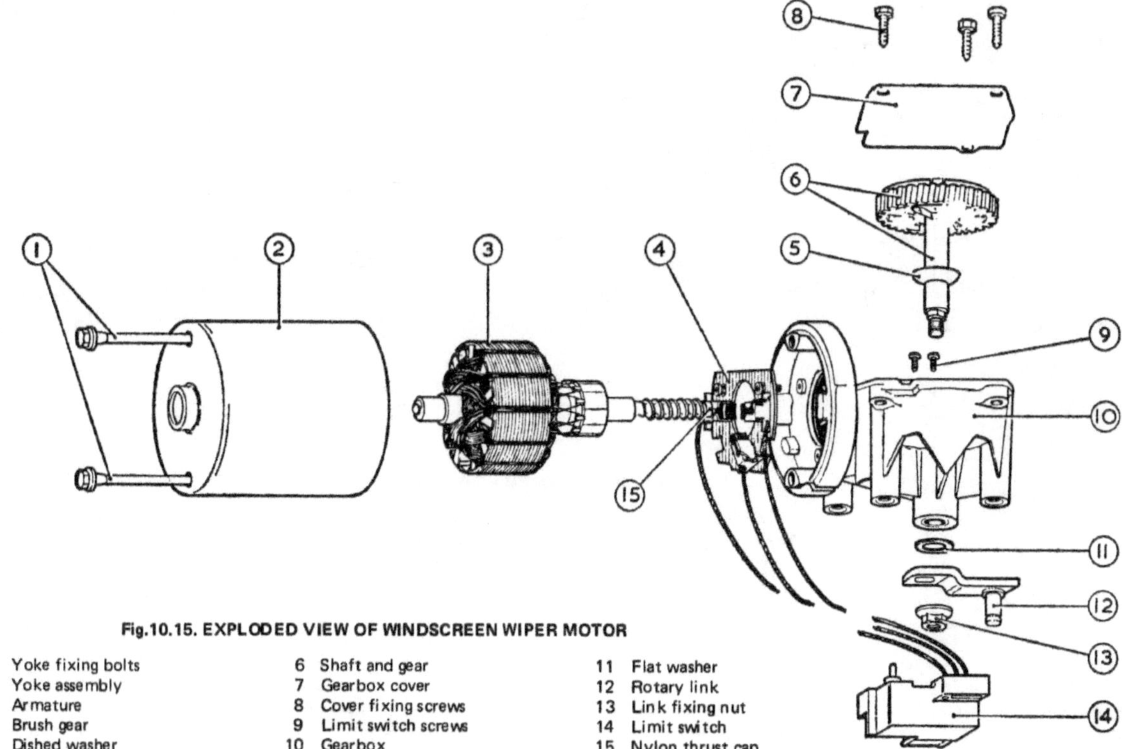

Fig.10.15. EXPLODED VIEW OF WINDSCREEN WIPER MOTOR

1 Yoke fixing bolts
2 Yoke assembly
3 Armature
4 Brush gear
5 Dished washer
6 Shaft and gear
7 Gearbox cover
8 Cover fixing screws
9 Limit switch screws
10 Gearbox
11 Flat washer
12 Rotary link
13 Link fixing nut
14 Limit switch
15 Nylon thrust cap

faulty. If they do not go on, first make quite sure that with the ignition switched on current is reaching the 'B' terminal at the flasher circuit. If it is, then the indicator switch is faulty. If it is not, the the connection from the ignition switch to the flasher unit is faulty (via fuse No.2).

18. Windscreen Wipers & Drive Motor - Fault Diagnosis

1. If the wipers fail to operate first check that current is reaching the motor. This can be done by switching on and using a voltmeter or 12 volt bulb and two wires between the '+' terminal on the motor and earth. On two speed motors ,there are three leads from the motor and there should be a reading from two of them.
2. If no current is reaching the motor check whether there is any at the switch. If there is, then a break has occurred in the wiring between switch and motor.
3. If there is no current at the switch go back to the ignition switch and so isolate the area of the fault.
4. If current is reaching the motor but the wipers do not operate, switch on and give the wiper arms a push - they or the motor could be jammed. Switch off immediately if nothing happens otherwise further damage to the motor may occur. If the wipers now run the reason for them jamming must be found. It will almost certainly be due to wear in either the linkage of the wiper mechanism or the mechanism in the motor gearbox.
5. If the wipers run too slowly it will be due to something restricting the free operation of the linkage or a fault in the motor. In such cases it is well to check the current being used by connecting an ammeter in the circuit. If it exceeds three amps something is restricting free movement. If less, then the commutator and brush gear in the motor are suspect.
6. If wear is obviously causing malfunction or there is a fault in the motor it is best to remove the motor or wiper mechanism for further examination and repairs.

19. Windscreen Wiper Motor & Mechanism - Removal & Replacement

1. Disconnect the battery and then remove the air intake grille in front of the windscreen. It is held in position by three screws. Detach the water pipe from it at the same time.
2. Remove the wiper blades and arm assemblies by pulling them off the splined spindles. Be careful not to bend the arms - the boss should be levered a little if it is tight.
3. Remove the nut, washers and rubber bushes holding the spindles to the bulkhead.
4. From inside the car, remove the screws and studs securing the parcel shelf and also the R.H. demister air tube which is held on to the heater box by two nuts.
5. Remove the glove box lid by undoing the five screws and unhooking the check strap. Then remove the two screws holding the box itself in position and lift that out.
6. The cables leading to the motor are next disconnected and the large self tapping screw which holds the motor and mechanism to the bulkhead bracket is then removed. The whole assembly can then be lifted out.
7. When refitting the assembly make sure that the earthing cable is refitted to the securing screw and that the rubber bushes are fitted exactly as they came off.

20. Windscreen Wiper Motor & Mechanism – Dismantling & Reassembly

1. The exploded drawing indicates the layout of the motor and by removing the through bolts it is easy enough to examine the commutator and brush gear. Normally, however, if a wiper motor fails it is usually for reasons of excessive loading due to wear or jamming of the wiper arm link mechanism and consequently the renewal of the complete motor is the best answer. Brush gear can be

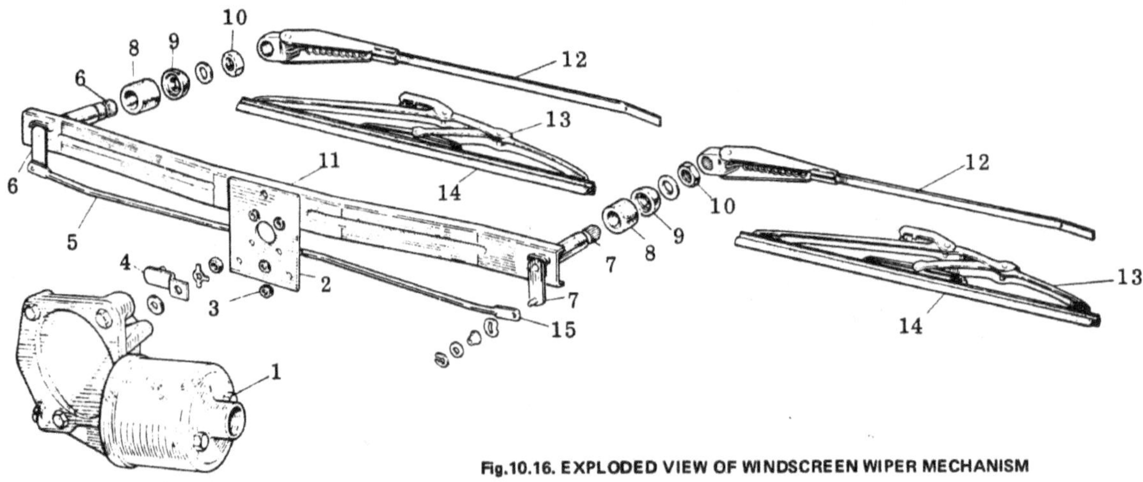

Fig.10.16. EXPLODED VIEW OF WINDSCREEN WIPER MECHANISM

1 Motor unit
2 Mounting bracket
3 Nut
4 Rotary link
5 Primary link LH
6 Spindle LH
7 Spindle RH
8 Bush - rear
9 Bush - front
10 Locknut
11 Link set
12 Wiper arm
13 Blade assembly
14 Squeegee
15 Primary link RH

obtained separately if it is conclusive that this is the only fault. Similarly, the large gear wheel and spindle can be obtained. Any serious wear in the armature spindle bushes, however, is not a matter of simply renewing the bushes as these are part of the end covers.

2. If a new motor is fitted (or the old one successfully repaired) it is important to make sure that the wiper arm mechanism operates smoothly and freely, otherwise the motor could be ruined yet again. The nylon crankpin bushes should be renewed if worn and the wiper spindles should be a good fit in the sleeves (Fig.10.16). If in doubt renew the whole assembly.

21. Windscreen Washer - Fault Finding

1. The washer is a simple pump which draws water from a reservoir and pumps it along a pipe which goes to the jets. It is operated by the combined wiper/washer switch.

2. If nothing comes out of the jets when the pump is operated, disconnect the pipe from the jets. This will soon tell you if the jets are blocked or not. If no water comes down the pipe trace all the pipes and connections to be sure that there are no breaks or hardened kinks or flattened sections. Blow through the pipes to make sure they are clear.

3. As a last resort, remove the pump from the back of the instrument panel and check its operation with a piece of pipe in a bowl of water. If it does not pump you will have to buy a new one.

22. Horns - Fault Finding & Remedy

1. Should either or both horns fail to work the first thing to do is make sure that current is reaching the horn terminals. This can be done by connecting a 12 volt test lamp to the feed wire and pressing the horn button with the ignition switch on. If the bulb lights then the fault must lie in the horn or the horn mounting. The tightness and cleanliness of the horn mounting is important as the circuit is made to earth through the fixing bolt. The connections should, of course, be a clean tight fit on the horn terminals.

2. If no current is reaching the horn check the fuse (No.1) and wiring connections as indicated in the wiring diagram.

3. Having established that the fault is in the horn the adjusting screw can be used. Do not touch the centre screw which is pre-set and is not to be adjusted. The adjusting screw is near the terminals and can be turned in either direction. Anticlockwise turning reduces and eventually cuts out any sound, and the correct setting is at a point where sound becomes correct just after cut in when turning clockwise. When doing adjustments the fuse is likely to blow, so fit a piece of heavy wire across the fuse bridge temporarily.

4. If a satisfactory note cannot be obtained then the horn must be renewed.

23. Headlamps - Adjustment, Removal & Replacement

1. Twin circular Lucas F575 sealed beam headlamps are fitted to all models, although some export models have a similar unit with replaceable bulbs.

2. To remove a lamp unit for renewal or bulb replacement first of all remove the grille by undoing the crosshead screw as shown in Fig.12. xx in Chapter 12.

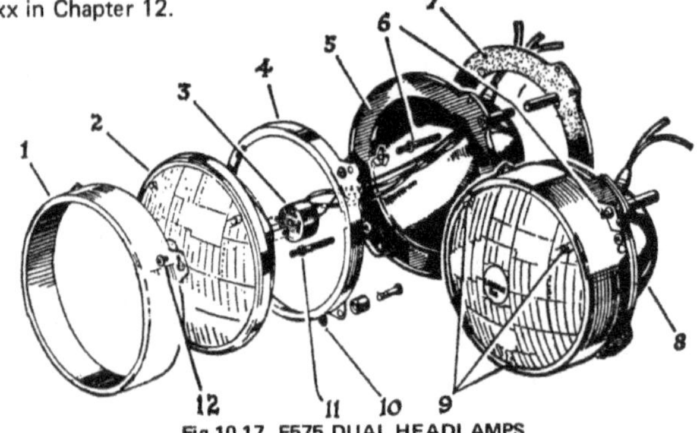

Fig.10.17. F575 DUAL HEADLAMPS

1 Front rim
2 Light unit (2A)
3 Cable adaptor
4 Seating rim
5 Lamp body
6 Beam adjustment screw (vertical)
7 Sealing gasket
8 Lamp body
9 Aiming pads
10 Retaining ring
11 Beam adjustment screw (horizontal)
12 Rim retaining screw

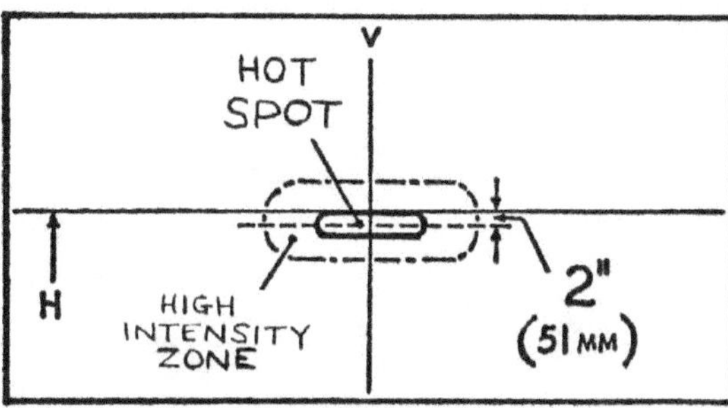

Setting for inner lamps

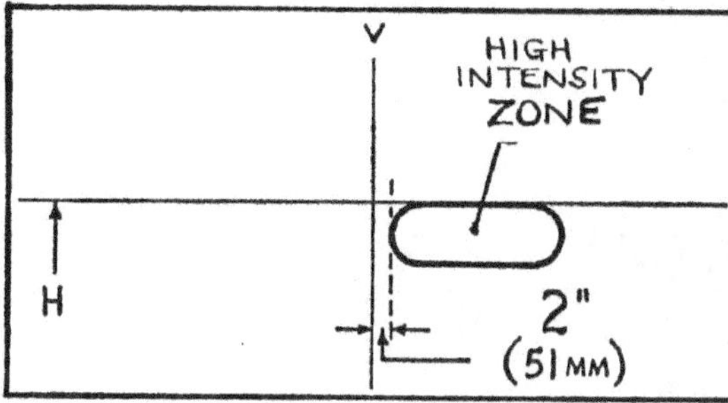

Setting for outer lamps
(right hand rule of the road)

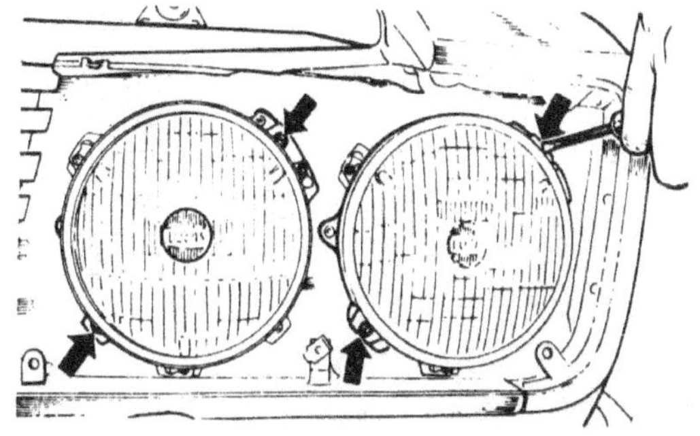

Adjusting screws

Fig.10.18. Headlamp alignment
H Height of headlamp centre above ground
V Vertical line through headlamp centre

3. Remove the screws holding the unit rim, being careful not to confuse these screws with the two adjusting screws which should not be disturbed. Then draw the unit forward away from the car.

4. With the lamp unit clear the connector plug at the rear may be detached, or in the case of replacement bulbs the holder may be unclipped and drawn from the reflector. The bulb may then be taken out (Fig.10.17).

5. Beam setting should normally be done with the proper optical equipment but a good guide can be obtained by using the alignment diagram as given (Fig.10.18). This shows how the lights should aim in the main beam condition with two people in the front of the car. The car should face squarely a vertical surface at a distance of 25 feet (7.6 metres). Each lamp should be masked whilst the other is adjusted by means of the vertical and horizontal adjustment screws provided.

24. Front Side Lamp & Flasher Assembly

1. The units are not interchangeable from one side of the car to the other.
2. To renew bulbs first remove the two screws which hold the two colour lens in position. Do not disturb the rubber lens seal unless it has deteriorated and needs renewal (Fig.10.19).
3. The bulbs may then be removed by pressing and twisting anti-clockwise.
4. Both bulbs are single filament and the bayonet caps will fit either way round.
5. When replacing the lens do not overtighten the screws or the rubber seal will be over-compressed and made less effective.
6. It is important for correct completion of the circuit that the bulb holder sleeves and the unit fixing screws are all quite free of any signs of corrosion or rust. Also they must be tight. Intermittent operation or lamp dimness is usually caused by these faults.

25. Rear Side, Stop & Flasher Lamp Assemblies

1. Undo and remove the three screws, one at the top, two lower down, holding the lens to the body and lift the lens away.
2. Bulbs are removed by pressing and turning anticlockwise. If they are very tight it may be necessary to remove the bulb holders from the rear of the clamp (Fig.10.20).
3. The stop/tail lamp bulb is a double filament type with an offset bayonet pin so it will only fit the holder one way round.
4. When replacing the lens do not overtighten the screws.
5. In cases of malfunction make sure that the lamp fixing nuts and the earth wire connection to one of the fixing studs are all corrosion-free and tight before checking the wiring circuit.

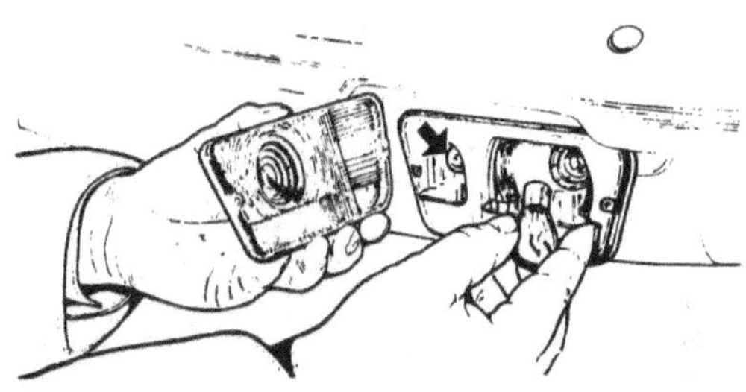

Side and flasher

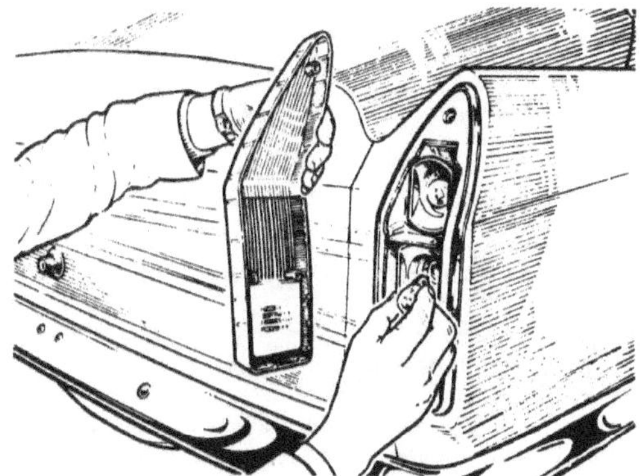

Rear side, stop and flasher

Fig.10.19 Renewing bulbs

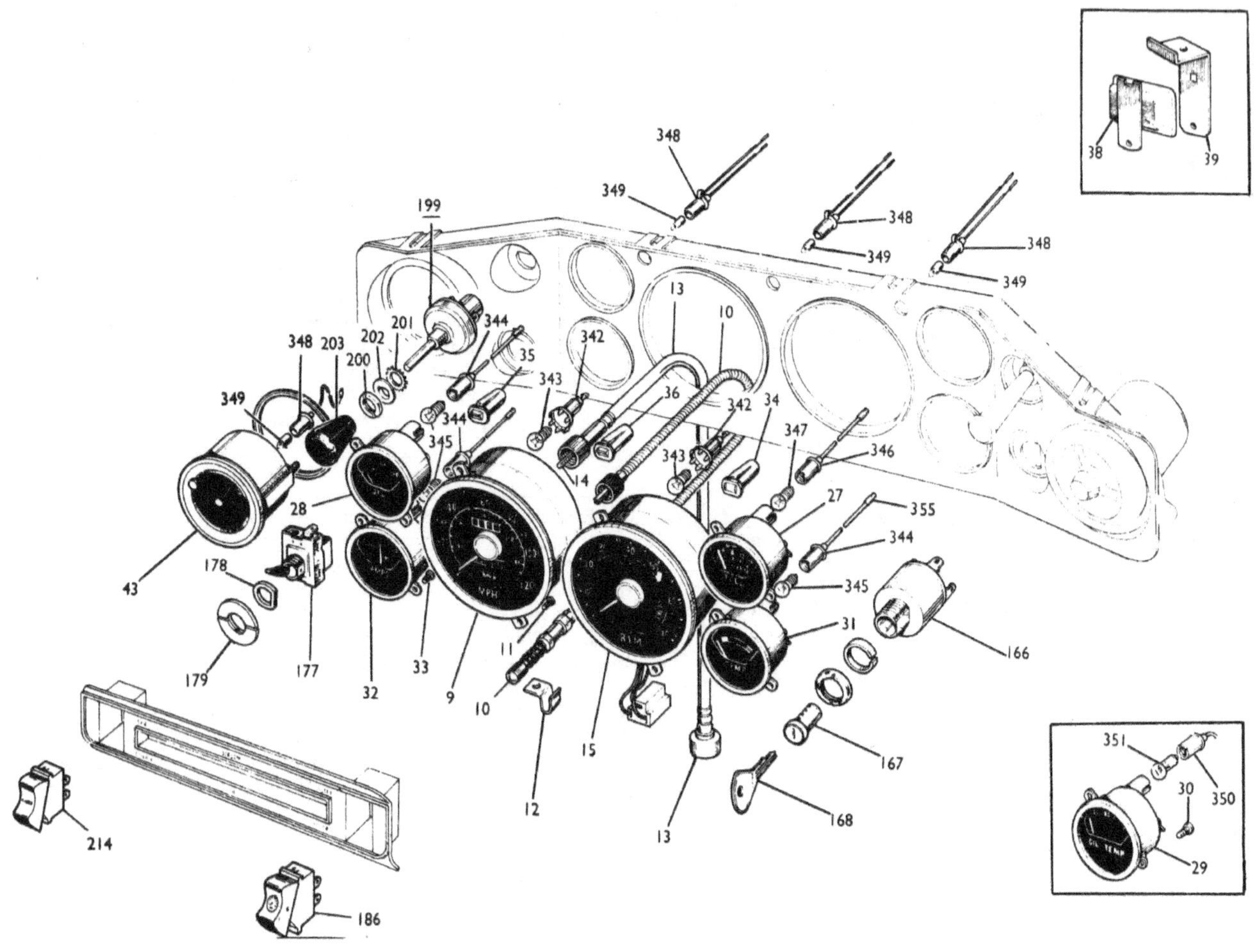

Fig.10.21. EXPLODED VIEW OF THE INSTRUMENT PANEL

9 Speedometer
10 Remote trip cable
11 Screw
12 Clip
13 Speedometer cable
14 Inner cable
15 Tachometer
27 Fuel gauge
28 Oil pressure gauge
29 Oil temperature gauge (H12)
30 Screw
31 Water temperature gauge
32 Ammeter
33 Screw
34,35 & 36 Warning light bodies
38 Voltage regulator
39 Bracket
43 Clock
166 Ignition switch
167 Lock
168 Key
177 Lighting switch
178 Spacer
179 Circular nut
180 Panel light switch
199 Wiper switch
200 Circular nut
201 Shakeproof washer
202 Spacer
214 Blower switch
342 Bulb holder
343 Bulb
344 Bulb holder
345 Bulb
346 Bulb holder
347 Bulb
348 Bulb holder
349 Bulb
350 Bulb holder
351 Bulb

26. Dip, Flasher, Main Beam & Horn Switch

1. The switch is mounted on the steering column and if any or all of its parts go wrong, it has to be renewed as a complete unit.
2. To test the switch, the cowl round the steering column should be removed and the wires disconnected at the nearby snap connectors. By bridging the appropriate wires according to the colour coding in the wiring diagram, each part of the switch's function can be verified.
3. The switch is held to the steering column by two screws securing a clip and can be removed by simply unscrewing them.
4. When refitting a switch it should be positioned so that the flasher self cancelling cam is set centrally when the wheels are in a straight ahead position.

27. Instrument Panel & Instruments – Checking, Removal & Replacement

1. The Rapier instrument panel is made of a black moulded non-reflective construction, being slightly curved. To get at any of the instruments the whole panel must be withdrawn in the following way (Fig.10.21).

2. Disconnect the battery by removing the earth lead and disconnect the choke cables at the carburettors.
3. Disconnect the speedometer drive cable and the speedometer trip control cable from the rear of the speedometer by undoing the knurled nuts.

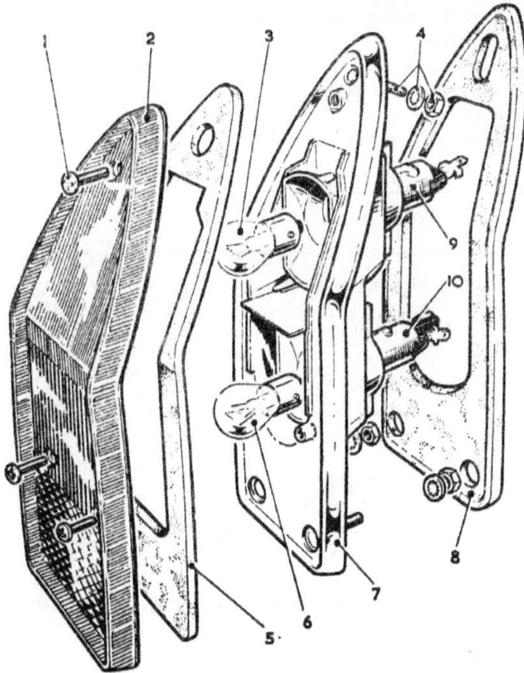

Fig.10.20. DISMANTLING REAR SIDE, STOP AND FLASHER LAMP ASSEMBLY

1 Lens fixing screw
2 Plastic lens
3 Single filament bulb
4 Lamp fixings
5 Lens sealing gasket
6 Double filament bulb
7 Die-cast lamp body
8 Lamp body gasket
9 Flashing indicator light
10 Stop-tail light

4. Remove the oil gauge pipe from the rear of the gauge and disconnect the screen washer pipes from the pump on the rear of the wiper/washer switch.

5. From a central position behind the panel unplug the multi-pin harness cable plugs.

6. Detach the fresh air vent pipe from the diffuser on the extreme right of the panel, then remove the steering column cowl by undoing the six small screws from the lower half.

7. Remove the overdrive switch and the indicator and horn switch from the steering column by undoing their two retaining screws.

8. Release the four spring clips from behind the lower edge of the panel and undo the four crosshead screws securing the top edge of the panel to the facia.

9. Withdraw the panel a short way, then unscrew the windscreen washer pump from the back of the switch, and disconnect the wires from the panel light switch and the clock.

10.The panel can now be drawn further into the car, or if required out of the car, taking care to guide the choke cable gently through the bulkhead.

11.With the exception of the clock which is attached to the panel by a stirrup clip and knurled nuts, all other instruments are attached to spigots on the panel by two crosshead screws.

12.Replacement of the instruments and panel is a reversal of the above procedure.

Note: Section 28 - Fault Finding - will be found on the next page

28. Fault Finding - Electrical System

The following chart does not include fault finding in connection with starting failure or engine running, covered in Chapters 1 (Engine) and 4 (Ignition). **It also assumes that a good battery is fitted and that the earth link strap is properly connected from engine to body frame.**

Before anything else **always** check that the battery terminal connections are clean and tight.

Note that fault finding in alternators is difficult; it is best to entrust the work to a qualified electrician.

Symptom	Reason/s	Remedy
When the ignition is switched on the oil and generator warning lights do not light	Blown bulbs Broken circuit wire or loose connection Defective oil pressure sender	If engine starts anyway the bulb(s) will be defective. Check oil sender by touching wire to earth. Check fuse box and alternator connections
When engine speeds up generator light stays lit	Loose or broken fan belt Defective alternator Defective control box on alternator	Check fan belt tension Test alternator in car
When engine is running the oil pressure warning light stays lit (check causes in sequence given)	No oil Severe leak in lubrication system Oil pressure switch defective Oil pump defective	Stop engine Check lubricant level and system for leaks Check lead is fitted to sender switch tightly. Change sender switch Check oil pump by slackening oil filter and and running engine to see if oil is pumped out
Battery goes flat after a few days, yet generator warning light goes out normally	Loose fan belt resulting in alternator not turning fast enough Alternator output inadequate Control box malfunctioning	Check fan belt Test alternator output in car and overhaul as necessary
No road lights at all when switched on	Broken feed wire (the headlamps are not fused)	Trace wiring circuit to headlamp switch
No side lights	Blown fuse or broken connection	Check fuse. Trace which bulb causes failure if fuse keeps blowing and then check circuit
Some bulbs fail to operate	Blown bulb Bad or dirty bulb holder connection Broken feed wire to circuit in question	Remove bulb and test and clean up bulb holder Check earth connections of units which complete the circuit to earth through the body of the unit Check circuit
Stop lights do not work	Blown bulb(s) Defective switch Broken wire	Check bulb and connection Short out terminals of switch and see if lights come on when ignition is switched on. If they do switch is U/S Trace wiring circuit
Fuel gauge registers incorrectly	Faulty voltage regulator, sender unit or gauge	Check as described in this Chapter
Water temperature gauge registers incorrectly	Faulty voltage regulator, sender unit or gauge	Check as described in this Chapter
Horn faulty	Switch defective, bad earth connection or broken circuit Faulty horn	Bypass switch to check if horn is all right. Then check feed to horn See details in this Chapter
Windscreen wipers not working properly	Mechanism jammed Mechanism worn out Defective switch Defective motor	Give wipers a push to see if they will start. Then check out as described in detail in this Chapter.

Chapter 11 Suspension, dampers and steering

Contents

Specifications

Front Suspension

Type	Independent MacPherson type strut with anti-roll bar	
Damper	Armstrong telescopic, integral with strut	
	Standard	**Heavy Duty**
Spring - Inside diameter	4.5 in (11.4 cm)	4.5 in (11.4 cm)
Free length	14.15 in (35.9 cm)	12.9 in (32.8 cm)
Laden length	7.2 in (18.3 cm)	7.7 in (19.6 cm)
Laden load	625 lb (283.5 Kg)	625 lb (283.5 Kg)
Front hub bearing end float	0.002 – 0.004 in (0.05 – 0.10 mm)	
Toe-in at wheel rim	1/8 in 30 minutes	
Camber angle	Zero	
Castor angle	¼^o negative	
Steering axis inclination	11¾^o	
Toe-out on turns	Nil - parallel at 20°	
Wheel angles at full lock	Inner 35° – Outer 33°	

Rear Suspension

Type	Asymmetric semi-elliptic leaf springs
Dampers	Telescopic, direct acting Girling monotube or Woodhead-Monroe
Number of leaves	4
Unladen camber	1.5 in (38.1 mm)

Steering

Type	Burman F-type recirculating ball worm and nut
Ratio	16.4 : 1
Turns, lock to lock	3½
Turning circle	33 ft 6 ins (10.2 m)
Rocker shaft end float	Zero – 0.004 in (0.10 mm)
Inner shaft bearing pre-load	0.002 – 0.004 in (0.5 – 0.10 mm)
Worm helix lead	5/8 in (15.875 mm)

Wheels and Tyres

Wheel type	
Rapier and Alpine	Ventilated pressed steel disc
H120	Deep pressed steel (Rostyle type)
Rim size	5J x 13

Tyre size	
Rapier and Alpine	155 x 13 radial
H120	165 x 13 radial
Air pressures	
Normal - Rapier Alpine	26 lb sq in front and rear
Laden	30 lb sq in front and rear
- H120 (all times)	28 lb sq in front 26 lb sq in rear

Torque Wrench Settings

Front Suspension	
Crossmember to body	52 lb ft (7.2 Kg.m)
Lower link to crossmember	28 lb ft (3.9 Kg.m)
Brake reaction stay - front nuts - early models	26 lb ft (3.6 Kg.m)
- later models	40 lb ft (5.5 Kg.m)
- rear bolts - all models	68 lb ft (9.4 Kg.m)
Anti-roll bar - mounting bolts	28 lb ft (3.9 Kg.m)
- link nuts	16 lb ft (2.2 Kg.m)
Lower swivel bearing - ball pin nut	44 lb ft (6.1 Kg.m)
- to strut	17 lb ft (2.4 Kg.m)
- to lower link arm	34 lb ft (4.7 Kg.m)
Top strut bearing - centre nut	35 lb ft (4.8 Kg.m) maximum
- housing to body	16 lb ft (2.2 Kg.m)
Strut gland nut	27 lb ft (3.7 Kg.m)
Rear Suspension	
Spring U-bolt nuts	35 lb ft (4.8 Kg.m)
Steering	
Steering arm to stub carrier	38 lb ft (5.3 Kg.m)
Steering box to underframe	30 lb ft (4.1 Kg.m)
Relay lever to underframe	30 lb ft (4.1 Kg.m)
Steering linkage ball pin nuts	40 lb ft (5.5 Kg.m)
Drop arm to rocker shaft	75 lb ft (10.4 Kg.m)
Relay lever to relay shaft	30 lb ft (4.1 Kg.m)
Rocker shaft cover to steering box	20 lb ft (2.7 Kg.m)
Outer column to steering box	20 lb ft (2.7 Kg.m)

1. General Description

The independent front suspension consists of the well tried MacPherson Strut system.

It comprises a single telescopic damper unit, the foot designed to carry the wheel hub and brake assembly. A coil spring surrounds the damper. The top of the unit fits into a rubber mounted thrust bush in a reinforced section of the wing.

The lower end of the unit is linked to the front crossmember at each side by a radius arm, and fore and aft stabilisation is from a rod mounted forward to the side frame members. An anti-roll bar is also fitted across the car between the suspension units.

Rear suspension is by conventional semi-elliptic leaf springs, the springs being mounted on rubber bushed shackle pins. Telescopic hydraulic dampers are used.

The steering gear is a recirculating ball worm and nut unit which connects to the wheels via a drop arm, a centre track rod, a relay lever and two outer track rods connected to the steering arms on each wheel.

2. Routine Maintenance

1. As practically the whole of the suspension and steering connects via either bonded rubber bushes or pre-packed and sealed ball joints, most routine maintenance would be better described as routine inspection. The only two items requiring addition or replacement of lubricant from time to time are the steering box and the front wheel bearings.
2. Every 5,000 miles the filler plug of the steering box and the surrounding area should be cleaned and removed, and the oil level checked. The level should be up to the bottom of the filler hole. Top up with 90 EP oil if necessary (Castrol Hypoy).

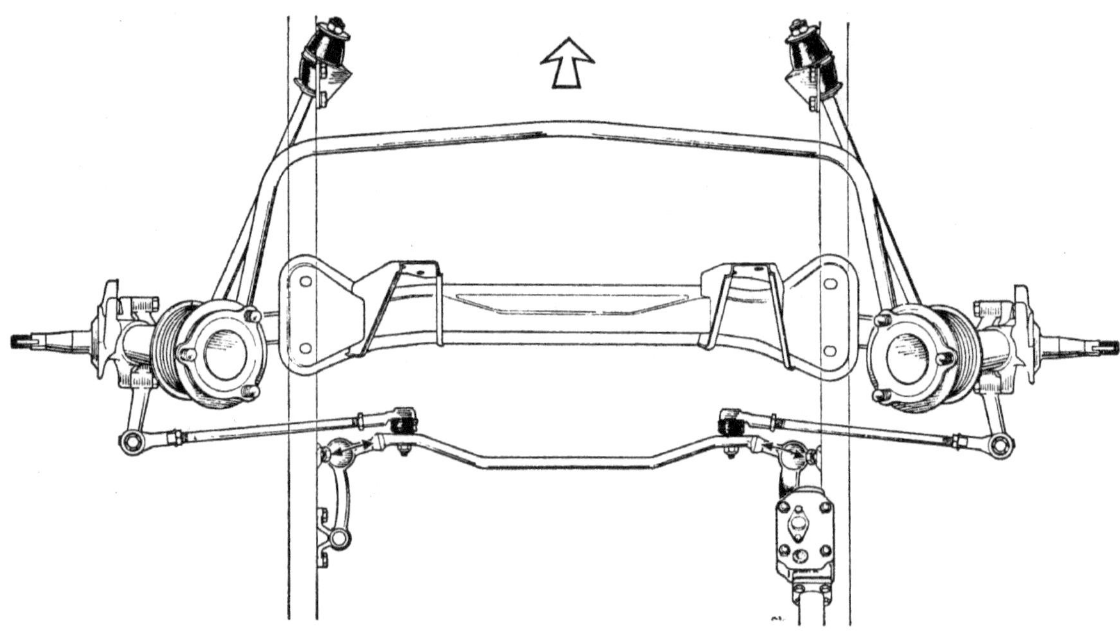

Fig.11.1. Plan view of front suspension and steering layout

3. Every 15,000 miles the front hubs should be removed and the bearings flushed out and repacked with grease (Castrol LM Grease).

4. Inspection of the steering linkage ball joints, suspension bushes and damper mountings should be undertaken at every 5,000 mile service, and components renewed as necessary. (Fig.11.1 shows the general layout of the steering and front suspension.) For the owner who does his own maintenance, this inspection is the one most often neglected. The fact that no grease can be pumped in or no adjustment made anyway tends to deter the owner from going to the trouble of jacking the suspension off the ground and examining the whole system properly. Any fault means expense; the components cannot be repaired - only renewed. This manual wishes to stress the importance of this less interesting aspect of owner car care. The fact that there is nothing to show for one's efforts, except the possibility of further expense and work, will not deter keen owners who are justified in believing they maintain their vehicles really thoroughly. It will be a matter of pride to them that no one else should be able to point first to defects in the steering and suspension, quite apart from questions of safety and roadworthiness.

3. Springs & Dampers - Inspection

1. The safety of a car depends more on the steering and suspension than anything else, and this is the reason why the tests made compulsory for vehicles over three years old pay particular attention to the condition of all the steering and suspension components.

2. The rear suspension should be examined for broken spring leaves. This will usually be obvious as the car will be down on the side affected. Such broken leaves must be renewed.

3. The spring hangar and shackle pin bushes may be checked by jacking up the body and at the same time watching to see if there is any movement between the shackle pins and the frame when the weight is gradually shifted. As mud normally collects round these mounting points a badly worn bush is usually immediately apparent because the movement prevents the mud from caking.

4. Check also for any signs of movement in the 'U' bolts clamping the springs to the axle tube. If any one is loose, check first that the axle is correctly located in the spring seat before tightening the 'U' bolt.

5. The top and bottom anchorage points of the hydraulic damper should be firm. If there are signs of oil on the outside of the lower cylinder section it indicates that the seals have gone and the damper must be renewed. The damper may also have failed internally and this is more difficult to detect. It is usually indicated by excessive bounce at the rear end, and axle patter or 'tramp' on uneven surfaces. When this occurs, remove the shock absorber in order to check its damping power in both directions.

6. The best test of any suspension system is on the road. Static tests of dampers are not entirely conclusive and further indications of failure, either front or rear, are: noticeable pitching (bonnet goes up and down!) when the car is braked and stopped sharply; excessive rolling on fast bends; a definite feeling of insecurity on corners, particularly if the road surface is uneven. If in doubt it is a good idea to drive over a roughish road and have someone follow to watch how the wheels behave. Excessive up and down 'patter' of any wheel is quite obvious and denotes a defective damper.

7. The front suspension should be checked by first jacking the car up so that the wheel is clear of the ground. Then place another jack under the track control arm near the outer end. When the arm is raised by the jack any movement in the suspension strut ball stud will be apparent. So also will any wear in the inner track control arm bush. There should be no vertical or horizontal play whatsoever in either the ball joints or bushes at each end of the track control arms.

4. Stabiliser Bar - Removal & Replacement

1. The stabiliser bar could become ineffective if bent or if its mounting bushes became loose.

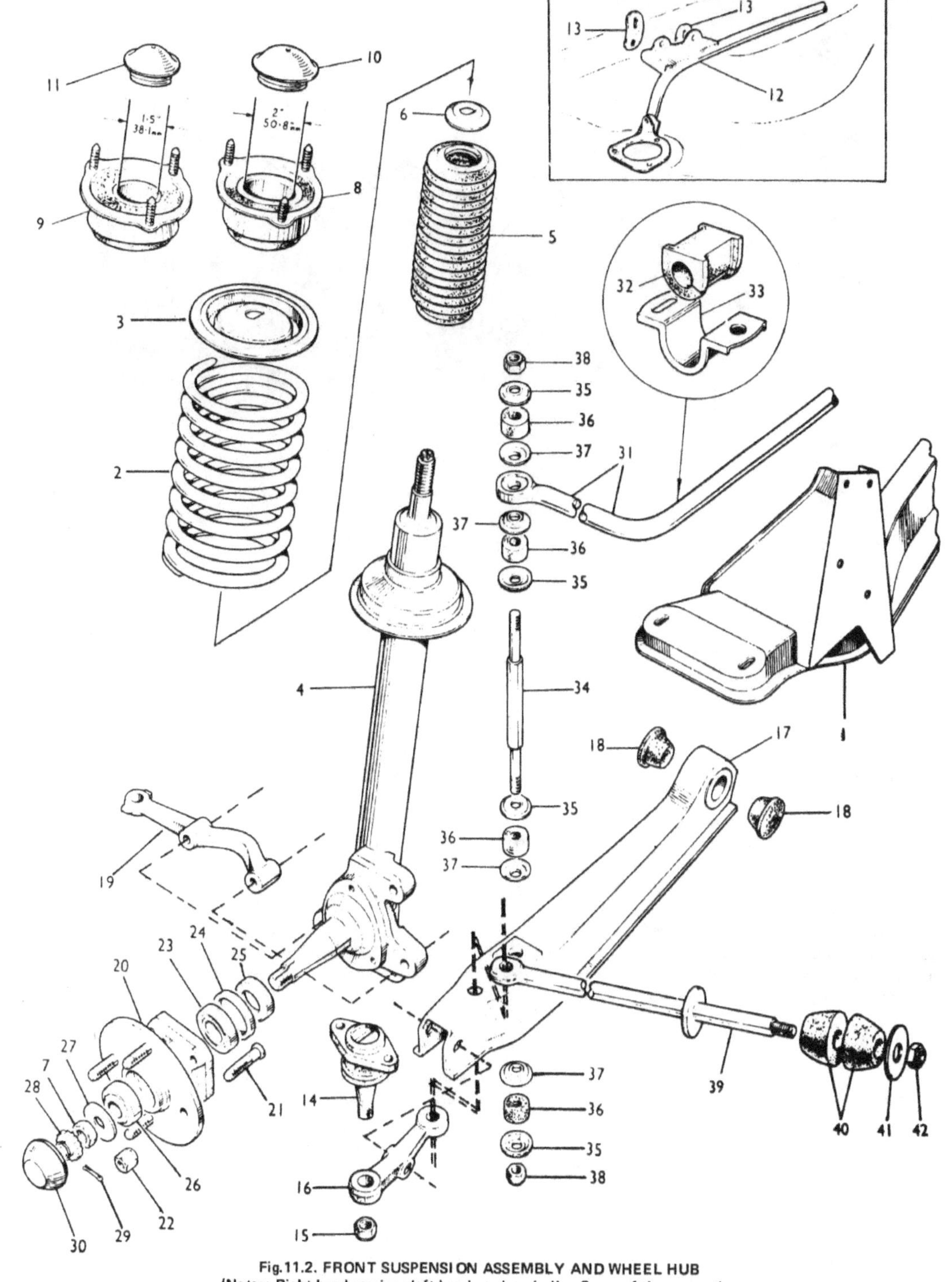

Fig.11.2. FRONT SUSPENSION ASSEMBLY AND WHEEL HUB
(Notes: Right hand version: left hand version similar. Some of the connecting bolts are not shown: lines and arrows indicate linking points)

1 Front crossmember
2 Coil spring
3 Upper spring seat
4 Suspension strut
5 Rubber gaiter
6 Thrust bearing washer
7 Hub bearing nut
8 Thrust bearing unit (machined type)
9 Thrust bearing unit (pressed type)
10 Dust cover
11 Dust cover
12 Strut mounting brace
13 Reinforcing plate
14 Track control arm ball joint
15 Self-locking nut
16 Ball joint carrier
17 Track control arm
18 Bushes
19 Steering arm
20 Hub
21 Wheel stud
22 Wheel nut
23 Inner bearing
24 Grease seal
25 Spacer
26 Outer bearing
27 Washer
28 Lock cap
29 Split pin
30 Dust cap
31 Stabiliser bar
32 Rubber bush
33 Clamp
34 Link pin
35 Washer
36 Bush
37 Washer
38 Nut - self locking
39 Radius rod
40 Rubber bushes
41 Washer
42 Nut - self locking

Fig.11.3. Dismantling front strut, using spring compressor RG251 and special tool P5025

2. Leave the weight of the car on the front wheels and remove from the track control arms the nuts and washers securing the ends of the bar to the top ends of the link pins (Fig.11.2).
3. Then remove the two bolts securing the 'U' clamps and bushes to the side frame members. (These clamps are the ones which need detaching when it is necessary to lower the stabiliser bar for engine removal.)
4. The stabiliser bar can then be removed.
5. Renew any rubber bushes showing signs of deterioration. When refitting, particularly if new bushes have been used on the side frame clamps, it will help if the brackets are compressed by a 'G' clamp to ease refitting of the securing bolts. Tighten the nuts to the specified torque.

5. Track Control Arm Ball Joint - Removal & Replacement

1. Inspection will indicate whether there is any free play in the outer ball joint and if there is, the joint will need replacement.
2. The joint is flanged and bolted to the base of the suspension strut and secured to the lower arm by a taper pin and nut into the eye of the carrier on the end of the arm (Fig.11.2).
3. Jack up the car, support it with a stand under the side member, and remove the road wheel.
4. It improves accessibility if the disc caliper hub and dust plate are also taken off, but this is not essential - especially if you have a pit or elevator. Next undo the two bolts holding the ball joint to the foot of the strut. It should then be possible to move the lower arm away from the bottom of the strut. If any difficulty is encountered, another jack can be placed under the hub or hub spindle to raise the strut a little.
5. The ball joint nut should now be removed from the bottom of the ball joint pin. The tapered pin is often a stubborn item to get out of the carrier. If you do not have a proper claw clamp or slotted tapered steel wedges available to apply the necessary pressure, success can often be achieved by placing one hammer head on one side of the carrier and hitting the opposite side with another. This, in effect, squeezes the taper out of its seating.
6. When fitting a new ball joint make sure that the mating flange faces are clean and free from scores or burrs so that they fit perfectly flush. Fit it to the strut first and tighten the bolts to the specified torque. Then clean the taper pin and the bore in the carrier and fit them together. Tighten the nut to the specified torque.

6. Track Control Arm & Bushes - Removal & Replacement

1. If the inner pivot bushes on the track control arm are worn out the arm will have to be removed in order to renew them.
2. With the weight of the car still on the front suspension, first remove the bottom nut of the link pin which connects the stabiliser bar to the arm (Fig.11.2).
3. Jack up the front of the car and support it on stands placed under the side members. Remove the road wheel from the side being dealt with.
4. Remove the large vertical bolt which holds the eye of the radius rod to the suspension arm; this also goes through the inner end of the carrier arm. Then remove the horizontal bolt that holds the carrier to the end of the suspension arm.
5. If the pivot bolt at the inner end of the arm is now removed the arm may be taken out.
6. New bushes should be fitted to the inner end and in addition all the self locking nuts used should be renewed. Otherwise reassembly is a simple reversal of the removal procedure. Tighten all nuts and bolts to the specified torque. It is advisable to get the steering alignment checked after assembly.

7. Front Suspension Strut Assembly - Removal & Replacement

1. If the damping part of the suspension unit is not working properly, or the spring is broken and needs renewing, it will be necessary to remove the whole unit from the car first.
2. Jack up the front of the car and support it on stands underneath the side members. Detach the brake caliper from the hub as described in Chapter 9.
3. Undo the two bolts which hold the steering arm to the foot of the strut but leave the arm connected to the track rod (Fig.11.2).
4. Remove the vertical bolt holding the radius arm to the track control arm, and then the horizontal bolt holding the carrier to the track control arm. The lower end of the unit is then free.
5. Support the lower end of the strut on a block or jack before the next step of detaching it at the upper end.
6. The upper end is held to the wing valance by three studs from which the nuts should now be removed. The centre nut should not be touched. The whole unit may now be lifted away from the car.
7. When replacing the assembly renew all self locking nuts and tighten them to the correct torque setting. It is important that rubber mountings should not be over-tightened. It is advisable to have the steering alignment checked after fitting.

8. Front Suspension Strut Assembly - Overhaul

1. Unless you are able to borrow the correct special tools needed to dismantle the strut assembly, you could cause damage to both the damper and strut. So unless you are quite sure, we recommend that you get specialist help.
2. To dismantle the unit it is convenient to refit it to a road wheel, place the road wheel on a bench, and steady the strut by putting a wooden wedge between it and the tyre wall.
3. To remove the thrust bearing unit the pressure of the spring has to be relieved with a compressor tool (RG521). If a tool is used other than that specially designed it must be remembered that although the amount of compressing required is minimal, it must be capable of relieving the spring to its free length, and so must have sufficient travel.
4. Fit the tool securely and squarely on the spring, bolt heads upwards, and compress it evenly until the pressure is taken off the thrust bearing unit (Fig.11.3).
5. Remove the dust cap and use tool P5025 to undo the thrust bearing nut. The tool is in two parts. One part is a screwdriver engaging in the slot in the top of the damper piston rod to prevent it turning, and the other is a socket wrench to undo the nut. A suitable tool can be improvised with a long tubular spanner and T-handled screwdriver, but you will certainly need two pairs of hands to deal with it.
6. The washer and bearing unit may then be taken off. The spring compressor should then be released evenly until the spring tension is completely relieved. Remove the spring together with its upper seat.
7. If it is desired to remove the damper unit from the strut, remove the rubber gaiter and push the piston rod right into the strut. Then knock back the staking which locks the sealing nut into the strut tube.
8. The gland nut is one with four dog slots in it to accept a special tool (RG525). Do not attempt to undo this nut with a hammer and pin punch because one slip may ruin the very fine threads and be the virtual end of the whole unit.
9. With the gland nut removed take out the rubber 'O' ring and from inside the top edge of the strut the damper rod should be pulled out, dislodging the guide bush and seal assembly from the top of the strut at the same time. (Fig.11.4).
10. Drain out the oil which is not re-usable.
11. Reassembly is simply a repeat of the dismantling process in reverse, but before commencing operations the following paragraphs should be read and pondered over. Remember that the safety of the car depends much on this unit.

a) The whole unit must be scrupulously clean, inside and out, before reassembly begins. Use petrol to clean out and let it dry off afterwards.
b) 350 cc of fresh oil (Armstrong Fluid 788) is required for each damper unit, and should be initially divided between the damper unit and the strut. It will be necessary to lift the damper guide bush out of the stop tube to get this oil in. The damper should then be primed with one or two long steady strokes of the piston until resistance is equal in both directions.
c) Fit a new seal and 'O' ring and also a new gland nut.
d) Make sure that everything is properly lined up when fitting the gland nut, and keep the damper piston rod pulled out at all stages of reassembly.
e) The threads of the gland nut are very easily crossed unless extreme care is taken. Also make sure that the threads on the end of the piston rod are not damaged during reassembly. Stake the gland nut as before.
f) Always fit a new gaiter to protect the damper piston.
g) Do not refit a spring that does not correspond closely to the free length dimensions given in the specifications. When compressing the spring to refit the upper bearing bush, care is needed to engage the piston rod in the thrust bearing plate and to prevent the piston being pushed back too far into the strut.
h) Observe all the torque wrench loadings on the various nuts with accuracy. If the thrust bearing nut is overtight the steering will be stiff and the thrust bearing overloaded, causing early failure.
i) The special tools required for dismantling will all be required for the same uses in reassembly.

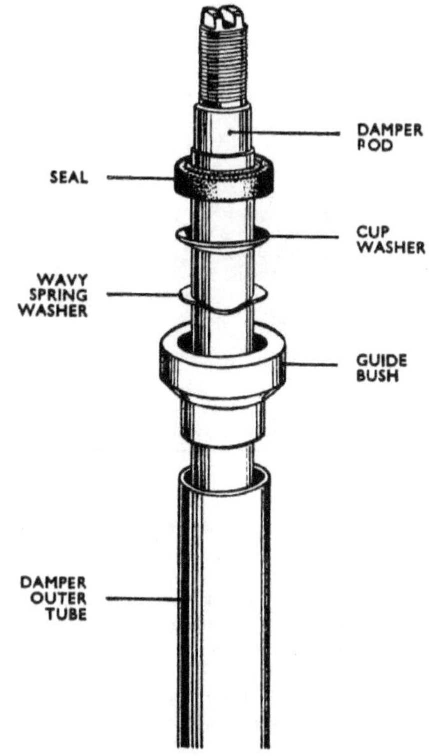

Fig.11.4
Part of front damper rod assembly

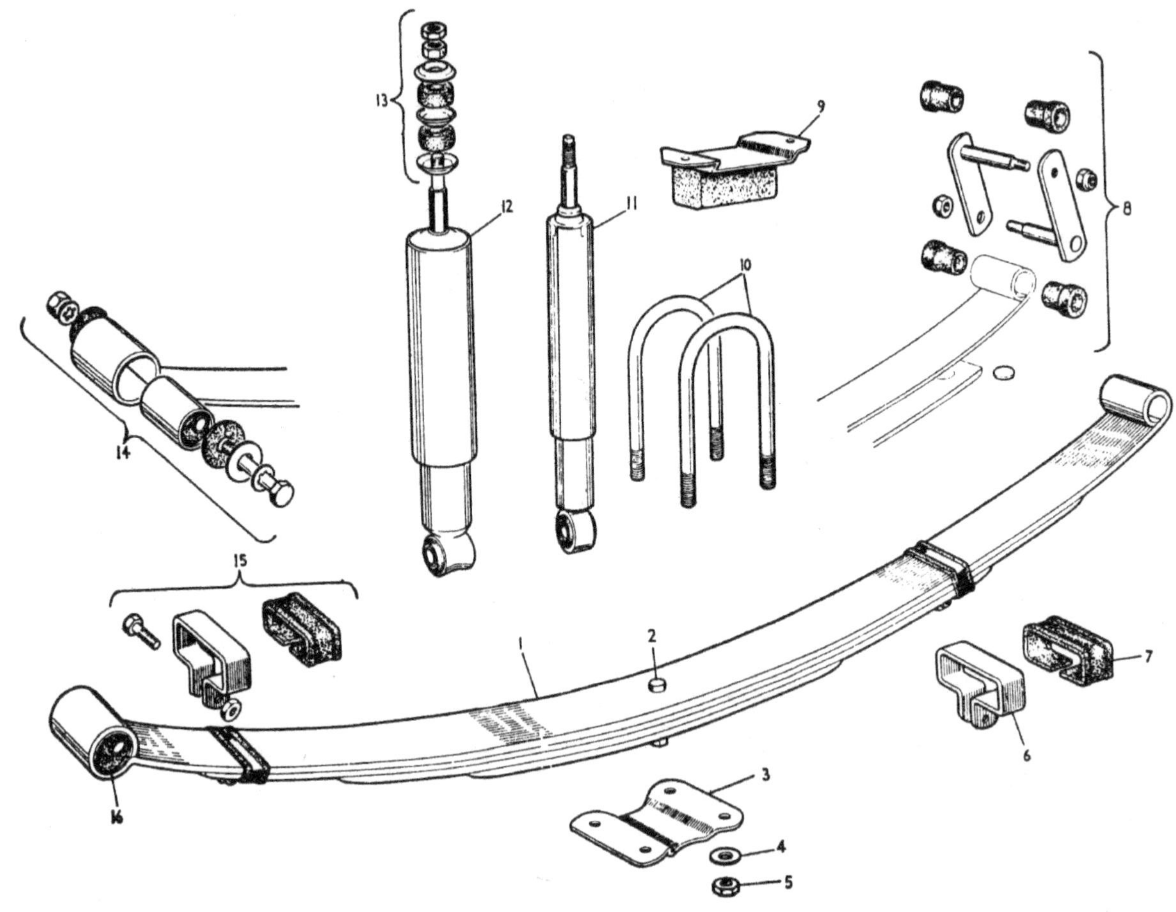

Fig.11.5. REAR SUSPENSION AND DAMPER

1 Main leaf
2 Dowel bolt
3 Spring retainer
4 'U' bolt washer
5 'U' bolt nut
6 Spring clip
7 Spring clip rubber
8 Rear shackle assembly
9 Bump/torque reaction rubber
10 'U' bolts
11 Damper - Girling monotube
12 Damper - Woodhead-Monroe
13 Damper - top mounting assembly
14 Front eye assembly
15 Clip and rubber assembly
16 Eccentric bush - front eye

9. Rear Springs & Dampers - Removal & Replacement

1. To renew the rear dampers jack up the car under the axle and remove the wheel for ease of access. Then remove the lower anchor bolt, nut and lockwasher and pull the bottom of the damper from its location (Fig.11.5).
2. From inside the boot remove the locknut from the top mounting spindle and then grip the flats on the spindle with a suitable spanner so that the second nut can be undone and removed.
3. The damper may then be taken out from underneath. When refitting, first make sure that all the rubber mountings and steel bushes are in good condition. Renew them if necessary. New bushes may come with the damper.
4. The rear springs must be detached either to renew a broken leaf or to renew the mounting bushes at the front or rear. Jack up the car and support it on stands at the rear and then support the axle on a jack at a point away from the spring mountings. Remove the road wheel.
5. Detach the lower end of the damper from the mounting.
6. Thoroughly clean off all the dirt from the 'U' bolts and shackle pins, and soak the nuts and threads with a suitable easing fluid such as 'Plus-Gas'.
7. Remove the 'U' bolt nuts and jack up the axle a little way to separate it from the springs.
8. Remove the nut and washer from the front hangar bolt. This may prove very stubborn, and if it needs driving out replace the nut to try to protect the threads. In any case one should be prepared to renew the bolt.
9. When removing the shackle plates at the rear end of the spring, both nuts must first be removed as the two halves each comprise one shackle pin and plate and need separating. Here again the pins may be very difficult to shift and it is not unknown to have to cut them off.
10. A broken spring can be replaced as a complete unit or the individual leaf can be renewed. If the leaf only is being replaced new spring clips, rivets and inserts will be required to reassemble the leaves. A replacement unit can usually be found at a breaker's yard and this is the simplest and cheapest way to go about it.

11.When reassembling the rubber bushes for the shackles use some soapy water to lubricate them. The front spring hangar bush is a press fit unit into the spring. It will have to be driven out and a new one pressed in if it needs renewal. Note that there were different types of bush fitted to the front hangar over a period of time (Fig.11.6). The very early versions were fitted with an eccentric bolt hole which was positioned at 12 o'clock. These bushes are no longer used and the new replacements, still having an eccentric bolt hole, require that the hole be positioned at 10.30 i.e. 45° up from the horizontal at the front. Other bushes have central bolt holes and others again have a triangular section. The latter require that one lobe of the triangle is positioned at 10.30 in the spring eye like the eccentric version. The point about this variety of bushes in that they must be the same on both rear springs. Otherwise some funny things can happen to the rear axle position under certain load and acceleration conditions. So if a new type of bush is fitted in one spring the same should also be fitted in the other. Another feature which occurs in earlier models is the fitting of a steel wedge between the top leaf and the axle pad. Where these are fitted make sure that the thick end faces forwards.

12.When refitting the spring to the hangars it is usually easier to fit the front end first. Then replace the shackle pins and bushes. Replace the nuts but do not tighten them yet. Then lower the axle and position it so that it locates correctly on to the spring (and wedge if fitted), and put the 'U' bolts and clamp plate in position. Tighten up the 'U' bolt nuts only moderately.

13.The damper should next be fitted to the lower mounting.

14.The car should then be lowered to the ground, bounced a few times to settle the bushes, and then all the nuts tightened to the specified torque.

15.The specifications give the spring cambers, the camber being the amount of 'bow' in the spring - which is measured as the distance between the centre of the top leaf and a straight line drawn through the centre line of the front hangar bolt and lower rear shackle pin. The easiest way to check this is to measure the vertical height of the centre line of the two bolts and the underside of the axle tube from the ground. Put the car on a smooth level surface in order to do this properly. With the known length of the spring between the hangar bolts the dimensions can be scaled on paper and the camber distance calculated.

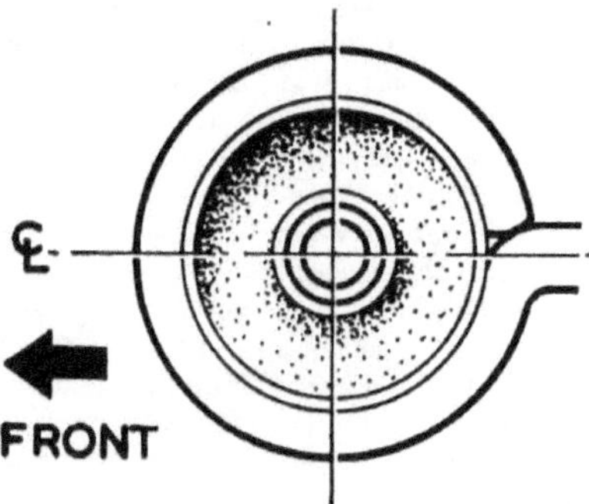

Steel jacketed centre pin

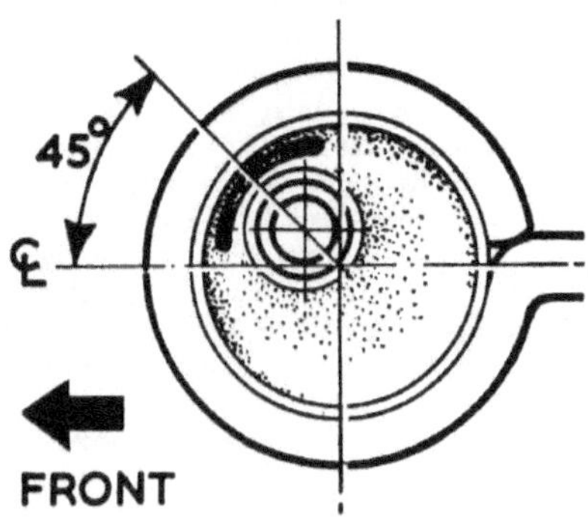

Steel jacketed eccentric pin

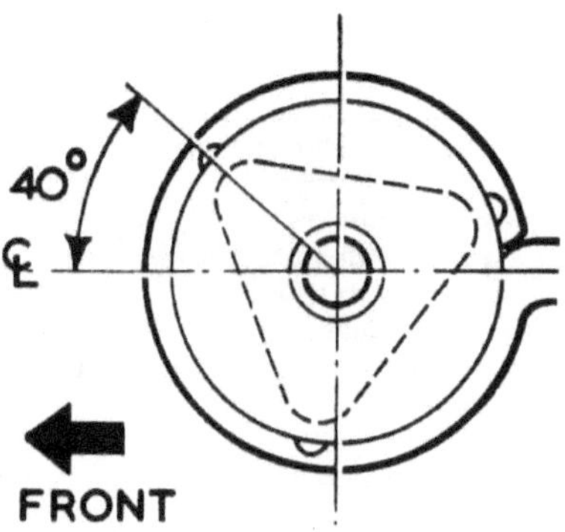

Flanged triangular section

Fig.11.6.
Types of rear spring front eye bushes

10. Steering Gear & Linkage - Inspection

1. Wear in the steering gear and linkage is indicated when there is considerable movement in the steering wheel without corresponding movement at the road wheels. Wear is also indicated when the car tends to 'wander' off the line one is trying to steer. There are three main steering 'groups' to examine in such circumstances. These are the wheel bearings, the linkage joints and bushes, and the steering box itself.

2. First jack up the front of the car and support it on stands under the side frame members so that both front wheels are clear of the ground.

3. Grip the top and bottom of the wheel and try to rock it. It will not take any great effort to be able to feel any play in the wheel bearing. If this play is very noticeable it would be as well to adjust it straightaway as it could confuse further examinations. It is possible that during this check play may also be discovered in the lower suspension track control arm ball joint at the foot of the suspension strut (Fig.11.3). If this happens the ball joint will need renewal as described in Section 5.

4. Next grip each side of the wheel and try rocking it laterally. Steady pressure will, of course, turn the steering, but an alternated back and forth pressure will reveal any loose joint. If some play is felt it would be easier to get assistance from someone so that while one person rocks the wheel from side to side, the other can look at the joints and bushes on the track rods and connections. Excluding the steering box itself there are seven places where the play may occur. The two outer ball joints on the two outer track rods are the most likely, followed by the two inner joints on the same rods where they join the centre track rod. Any play in these means renewal of the ball joint. Next are the two swivel bushes, one at each end of the centre track rod. If play is detected in these then the whole track rod will need to be renewed as the bushes are not obtainable separately. The last point to check is the pivot of the relay or idler arm which supports the centre track rod on the side opposite the steering box. This unit is bolted to the side frame member and any play calls for renewal of the unit.

5. Finally, the steering box itself is checked. First make sure that the bolts holding the steering box to the side frame member are tight. Then get another person to help examine the mechanism. One should look at, or get hold of, the drop arm at the bottom of the steering box while the other turns the steering wheel a little way from side to side. The amount of lost motion between the steering wheel and the drop arm indicates the degree of wear somewhere in the steering box mechanism. This check should be carried out with the wheels first of all in the straight ahead position and then at nearly full lock on each side. If the play only occurs noticeably in the straight ahead position then the wear is most probably in the worm and/or nut. If it occurs at all positions of the steering then the wear is probably in the rocker shaft bush. An oil leak at this point is another indication of such wear. In either case the steering box will need removal for closer examination and repair.

6. Many owners consider removing shims at one of the two places they are fitted, thinking thereby to compensate for wear. This can be done but the beneficial results, if any, will be very short lived. The wear which has taken place and which will be taken up by removal of the shims will not be properly compensated. The top cover shims, which control rocker shaft endfloat, will not rectify wear in the bush. Their removal will merely keep the shaft running out of alignment - albeit with less play initially. But stiffness will probably result and wear will continue at an accelerated rate until the situation will soon be worse than it was originally. The other shims, between the column flange and the box, pre-load the two ball races (which are not adjustable) on the shaft inside the box. If there is noticeable endfloat on the shaft due to worn bearings, the removal of shims will take up the float but the already worn bearings will wear much faster as a result. To sum up, it must be understood that the shims are used to set up unworn components as they should be set up. The shims are not designed as a means of subsequent adjustment in order to compensate for wear. If they are used in this manner, play will be removed initially (with the likelihood of stiffness and steering irregularity), but wear will accelerate and result in an equal or increased amount of play.

11. Steering Linkage - Removal & Replacement

1. The ball joints on the two outer track rods, and the swivel bushes on the centre track rod, are all fitted into their respective locations by means of a taper pin into a tapered hole and secured by a self-locking nut. In the case of the four ball joints (two on each of the outer track rods) they are also screwed on to the rod and held by a locknut. The two other ball joints have left hand threads.

2. To remove the taper pin first remove the self locking nut. On rare and happy occasions the taper pins have been known to simply pull out. More often they are well and truly wedged in position and a clamp or slotted steel wedges may be driven between the ball unit and the arm to which it is attached. Another method is to place the head of a hammer (or other solid metal article) on one side of the hole in the arm into which the pin is fitted. Then hit it smartly with a hammer on the opposite side. This has the effect of squeezing the taper out and usually works, provided one can get a good swing at it.

3. When the taper pin is free, grip the shank of the joint and back off the locknut. Move this locknut just sufficiently to unlock the shank as its position is a guide to fitting the new joint. Then screw the ball joint off the rod.

4. It is most important when fitting new ball joints to first ensure that they are screwed on to the rod the same amount and then, before tightening the locknut, that they are correctly angled. So, after connecting everything up and before tightening the locknuts, set the steering in the straight ahead position and see that the socket of the ball joint is square with the axis of the ball taper pin. If this is not done the whole joint could be under extreme strain when the steering is on only partial lock.

5. If the centre track rod bushes require that the track rod be renewed then it will be necessary first to detach the inner ball joints of the outer track rods from it. The two swivel joints can then be removed from the drop arm and idler arm respectively and the unit removed.

6. As has been mentioned already any play in the idler arm bush means that the centre track rod should be detached from it and the whole unit unbolted from the side frame and renewed.

7. When any part of the steering linkage is renewed it is advisable to have the alignment of the steering checked at a garage equipped with the proper equipment. Although a new joint properly replaced may be satisfactory without further attention there are exceptions, particularly if the recent history of the car is not known. Some misguided individual could have altered the outer track rod settings thinking to cure a steering fault that was caused by wear.

12. Steering Gear - Removal & Replacement

1. The steering gear, or steering box as it is often called, is integral with the steering column and shaft and its removal and replacement is not a quick job. Do not therefore start dismantling it without having first decided what is needed to put it right. Remember that if the bush is worn out the new one could well need reaming out and this involves specialist tools. If the unit is badly worn it is almost certain that the quickest and cheapest repair is going to be the fitting of another one. It is unusual for only one part to be worn and the cost of the component parts together would be little less than that for the assembly.

2. On right hand drive cars it is necessary to lower the front crossmember to provide sufficient clearance to get the whole unit out from under the car. It is also necessary to have at least two feet ground clearance in order to get the column out.

3. First disconnect the battery, and then remove the upper and lower halves of the cowl around the upper end of the steering column by taking out the screws from underneath. Then detach the direction indicator switch and overdrive switch if fitted.

4. Next remove the steering wheel. This can be done by first prizing out the motif in the centre. Then mark the position of the wheel in relation to the shaft - which will simplify replacement if the same shaft is being put back. Undo the nut and the wheel can be pulled off.

5. Move the front seat right back and pull the carpet back from the scuttle. Remove the screws and clips holding the parcel shelf in position and then undo the two clamps holding the column in position.

6. To lower the front crossmember means deatching the engine from its forward mounting, so the weight will have to be supported by other means. In view of the fact that the car has to be raised much higher than usual at the front it is not really practicable nor safe to think in terms of supporting the engine from underneath. It is better to support it from above by means of lifting tackle suspended from a beam or some suitably padded strut across the top of the engine compartment, from which a hook or sling may be attached to the slinging eye at the front of the engine.

7. With the car raised on stands and the weight of the engine supported, the engine mounting bolts should be removed. Then the two bolts on each side which hold the crossmember to the side frame should be taken out and the crossmember allowed to come down as far as it can.

8. Detach the end of the centre track rod from the drop arm.

9. The three bolts holding the steering box to the side frame should now be slackened and, before removal, the position of any shims between the box and the wheel arch noted. The shims must be carefully guarded as they should go back as before, even if a new box is fitted.

10. The steering box and column can now be manoeuvred out from under the car.

11.On left hand drive models the removal of the crossmember is unnecessary. If the air cleaner and clutch slave cylinder are taken off, the whole column can be swung horizontal. The upper end should be protected against oil coming out. The box end can then be lifted upwards inside the engine compartment and the whole assembly drawn out from above.
12.Replacement is a reversal of the removal procedure with the following points borne in mind. Assemble all the mounting bolts and column clamping brackets loosely before tightening anything. The shims between the box and wing panel should be in position, also the rubber grommet round the column where it passes through the scuttle. The alignment of the column with the upper and lower clamps is important, as when everything is tight there should be no twist or stresses built up. This is why it may be necessary to increase or reduce the shims at the steering box mounting. Do not forget to fill the box with oil on completion, and it is advisable to check the front wheel alignment also.

13. Front Wheel Bearings - Adjustment

1. Jack up the front wheels, together or in turn, and remove the hub caps. Then check the bearings as described in Section 10, to verify that they do in fact need adjusting. Then prise off the bearing dust cap. This can usually be dislodged by a few sideways taps with a hammer (Fig.11.7).
2. When the bearing nut is exposed withdraw the split pin and the castellated lock cap that goes over the nut.
3. If it is possible to use a torque wrench, tighten the bearing nut, spinning the wheel all the while, to a torque of 15–20 lb ft. Then back off one flat and refit the lock cap and fit a new split pin. If no torque wrench is available, tighten the nut with a tubular spanner as much as you can without using a tommy bar, and then continue as described.
4. If, during the adjustment and afterwards, the bearing feels rough or the wheel tends to bind in any position, it is possible that one or both of the hub bearing races is worn out in which case they should be renewed.
5. Replace the dust cover, which should not be filled with grease.

14. Front Hubs & Bearings - Removal & Replacement

1. When the 15,000 mile service calls for repacking the hubs with grease the hubs must be taken off the spindles. To renew the bearings is a procedure following on from this.
2. Jack up the car, support it on stands and remove the front wheels.
3. Detach the brake calipers from the discs as detailed in Chapter 9.
4. Remove the bearing dust covers and then take out the split pin and remove the castellated lock cap followed by the nut and washer (Fig.11.7).
5. The hub and disc assembly may now be drawn off and the roller bearing may be taken out from each side of the hub.
6. If flushing and repacking is all that is being done, the inside of the hub should now be thoroughly cleaned out with paraffin to remove all old grease. The roller bearings should be cleaned similarly. Dry them off thoroughly and then work new grease into the roller bearings. The hub should be packed with grease only as much as is indicated in the cross-section drawing. Clean off the spindle and make sure the grease seal is in good condition. Remove the seal and distance piece if the bearings are being renewed.
7. If the bearings are being renewed the inner races of each one will have to be driven out of the hub. This can be done with a suitable drift through the bore of the hub. Be careful to drive the races out straight and square and do not damage the bore of the hub where they fit. Then fit the inner races of the new bearings into the hub, making sure that the larger internal diameter of each race faces outwards.

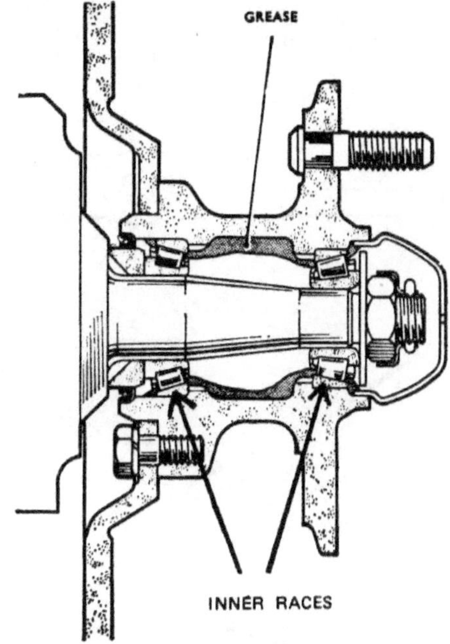

Fig.11.7.
Front wheel hub assembly

8. Next pack the rollers and hub with grease as previously described and place the rollers of the inner bearing in position.
9. The bearing seal should next be pressed into the hub with the lip towards the bearing. Then the special distance piece should be pushed into the centre of the seal with the bevelled side facing outwards.
10.The hub can then be replaced on the axle spindle and the rollers of the outer bearing fitted, followed by the washer and nut.
11.Adjust the bearings as described in the previous Section and replace the dust cap.
12.Refit the brake caliper and road wheel.

15. Steering Alignment

1. To obtain true and accurate steering, correct alignment of the front wheels is essential. Misalignment can be positively dangerous, and incidentally wears the tyres out at a high rate.
2. Before assuming that your steering is misaligned and therefore only in need of adjustment, the following factors must first of all be checked:–

a) Tyre pressures
b) Wheels - trueness and balance
c) Wheel bearings - adjustment or wear
d) Steering linkage - ball joints and swivels
e) Steering box - wear

3. If all the foregoing are in order then the wheel alignment may be checked, knowing that any fault is beyond the scope of visual inspection without special equipment.
4. Steering alignment comprises more than just setting the toe-in of the wheels. Camber angle, castor angle, steering axis inclination and wheel angle on turns are also part of the alignment checking process. Of this total of five alignment features only one can be adjusted - namely, toe-in. Toe-in is adjusted by the outer track rods. All other angles are controlled by the angles and dimensions of the component parts of the steering and the bushes and ball joints which link them together.

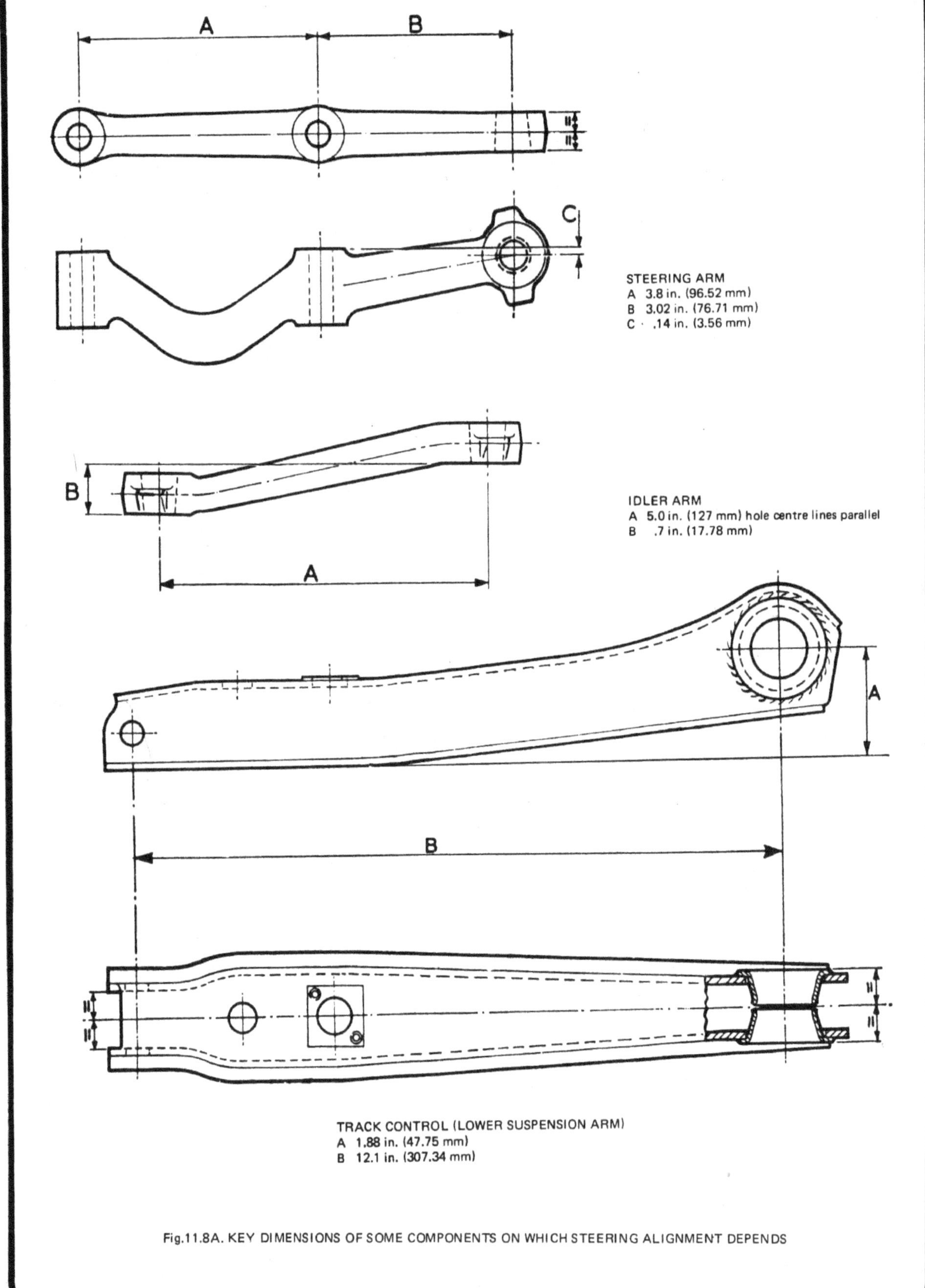

Fig.11.8A. KEY DIMENSIONS OF SOME COMPONENTS ON WHICH STEERING ALIGNMENT DEPENDS

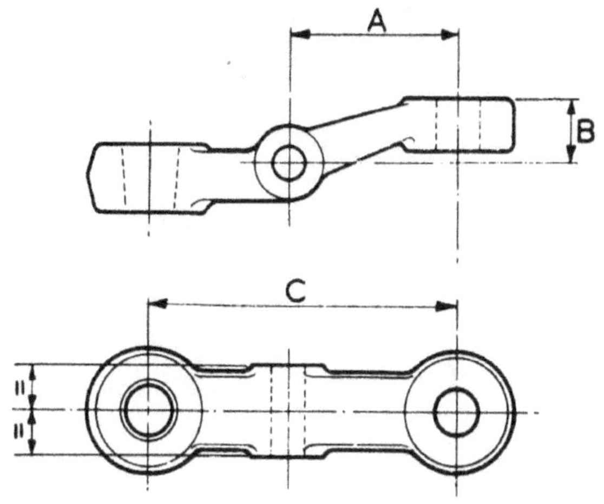

TRACK CONTROL ARM BALL JOINT CARRIER
A 1.96 in. (49.78 mm)
B .72 in. (18.29 mm)
C 3.58 in. (90.93 mm)

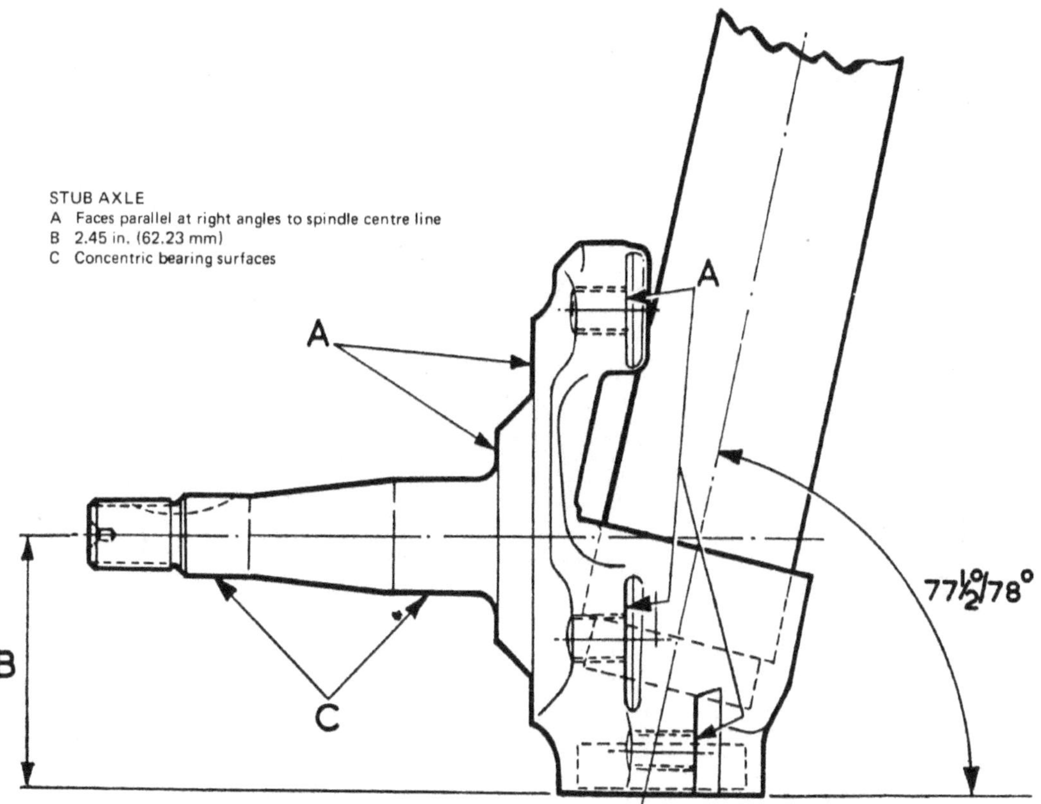

Fig.11.8B. KEY DIMENSIONS OF SOME COMPONENTS ON WHICH STEERING ALIGNMENT DEPENDS

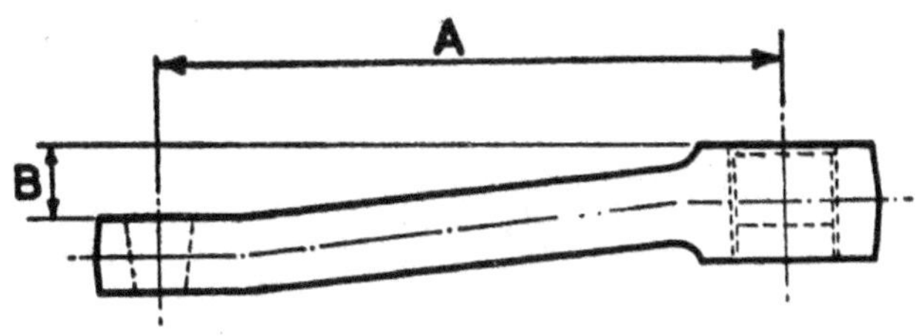

DROP ARM
A 5.0 in. (127 mm) hole centre - lines parallel
B .5 in. (12.7 mm)

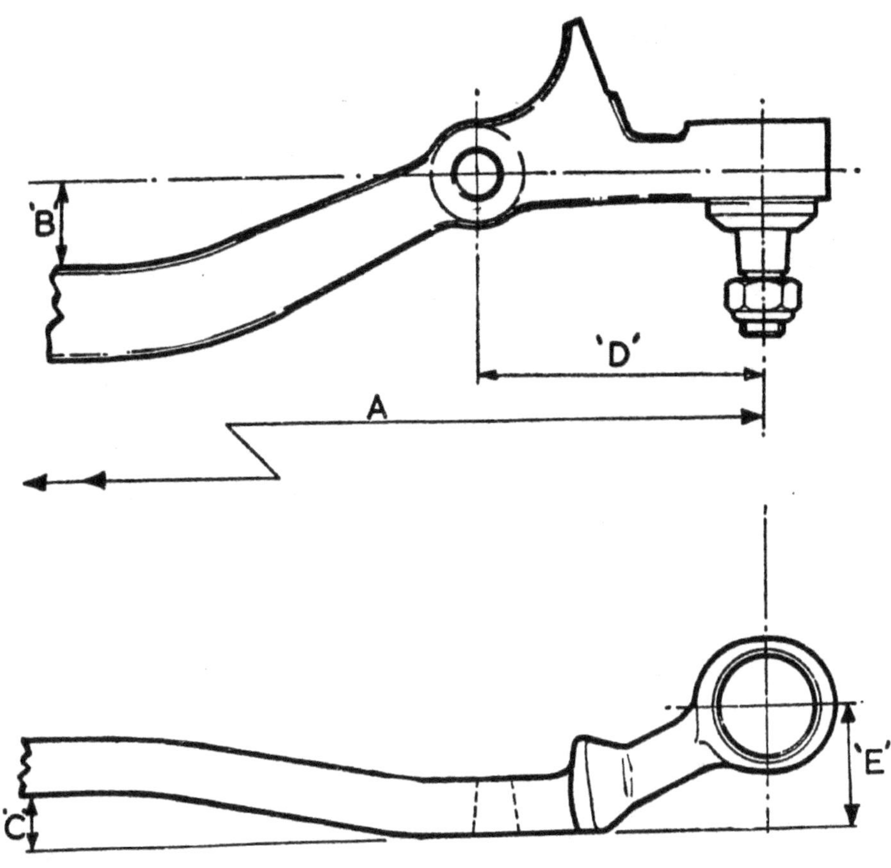

CENTRE TRACK ROD
A 23.75 in. (603.25 mm) between ball pin centres
B .94 in. (23.88 mm)
C .54 in. (13.72 mm)
D 3.21 in. (81.53 mm)
E 1.28 in. (32.51 mm)

FIG.11.8c KEY DIMENSIONS OF SOME COMPONENTS ON WHICH STEERING ALIGNMENT DEPENDS

5. It is not possible to check the steering alignment without proper gauge equipment. It is imperative that any checking is done on the correct equipment and you would be well advised to go to a Chrysler/ Rootes agent for this service. This is because in addition to the alignment measuring gear, the suspension at front and rear has to be pre-set to a fixed datum before checking begins. (This is done by loading the body and fitting special dimension blocks at certain points - details are not given here.) The steering geometry alters under different loads and attitudes and the specifications are at datum position. If the agents should advise that after setting the toe-in correctly some other aspect of the steering geometry is incorrect, then it means that one or more components have been distorted out of shape (provided of course that all the joints and bushes are in order). In such circumstances the components which affect the alignment will have to be removed and their dimensions individually checked. Details of the components and their dimensions are given in Fig.11.8a and 11.8b.

16. Fault Finding - Suspension, Dampers, Steering

Before beginning to diagnose faults from the list below first make quite sure that any irregularities are not caused by:–

1. Incorrect tyre pressures
2. Incorrect mix of radial and cross-ply tyres
3. Misalignment of bodyframe or rear axle
4. Binding brakes.

Symptom	Reason/s	Remedy
Steering wheel can be rotated more than an inch or so before road wheels move	Wear in the linkage or steering box	Inspect linkage and renew parts as necessary
	Steering box mounting bolts loose	Check mounting bolts
Car difficult to keep in a consistent straight line - steering 'wanders'	As above	As above
	Front wheel hub bearings loose or worn	Adjust or renew
	Worn track control arm ball joint	Inspect and renew if necessary
	Steering alignment incorrect (tyre wear will indicate this)	Check alignment
Steering stiff and heavy	Excessive wear or seizure in the steering linkage joints and control arm ball joint	Check all steering linkage and the steering box and renew as necessary
	Steering alignment incorrect	Check alignment
Wheel wobble and vibration	Wheels out of balance	Get professional balancing done
	Wheels buckled	Renew wheel
	General wear	Inspect and overhaul steering
	Broken spring(s)	Renew
Excessive pitching and rolling - particularly on corners and when braking	Defective dampers or springs	Inspect and renew as required

Chapter 12 Bodywork and underframe

Contents

1. General Description

The combined body shell and underframe is an all welded unitary structure of sheet steel pressings. Openings in the shell provide for the engine compartment, luggage bcot, doors and windows. The rear suspension is bolted directly to the side frame members of the unit at each end of the leaf springs. A detachable crossmember is bolted to the side members at the bottom of the engine compartment and this braces the structure, supports the forward end of the engine/gearbox unit and provides the lower attachment points for the front suspension struts. A shorter transverse member is bolted across the transmission tunnel section just to the rear of the engine compartment and this is the third support point for the engine/gearbox unit, the gearbox rear extension being flexibly mounted on it.

The wing aprons are reinforced where the upper bearing thrust units of the suspension strut assemblies are bolted to the bodywork.

2. Maintenance - Body Exterior

1. The general condition of a car's bodywork is the one thing that significantly affects its value. Maintenance is easy but needs to be regular and particular. Neglect - particularly after minor damage - can quickly lead to further deterioration and costly repair bills. It is important also to keep watch on those parts of the bodywork not immediately visible, for example the underside, inside all the wheel arches and the lower part of the engine compartment.
2. The basic maintenance routine for the bodywork is washing - preferably with a lot of water from a hose. This will remove all the loose solids which may have stuck to the car. It is important to flush these off in such a way as to prevent grit from scratching the finish. The wheel arches and underbody need washing in the same way, to remove any accumulated mud which will retain moisture and tend to encourage rust. Paradoxically enough, the best time to clean the underbody and wheel arches is in wet weather when the mud is thoroughly wet and soft. In very wet weather the underbody is usually cleaned of large accumulations automatically and this is a good time for inspection.
3. Periodically, it is a good idea to have the whole of the underside of the car steam cleaned, engine compartment included, so that a thorough inspection can be carried out to see what minor repairs and renovations are necessary. Steam cleaning is available at many garages and is necessary for removal of accumulation of oily grime which sometimes collects thickly in areas near the engine, gearbox and back axle. If steam facilities are not available there are one or two excellent grease solvents available which can be brush applied. The dirt can then be simply hosed off. Any signs of rust on the underside panels and bracing members must be attended to immediately. Thorough wire brushing followed by treatment with an anti-rust compound, primer and underbody sealer will prevent continued deterioration. If not dealt with the car could eventually become structurally unsound and therefore unsafe.
4. After washing the paintwork wipe it off with a chamois leather to give a clear unspotted finish. A coat of clear wax polish will give added protection against chemical pollutants in the air and will survive several subsequent washings. If the paintwork sheen has dulled or oxidised use a cleaner/polisher combination to restore the brilliance of the shine. This requires a little more effort but is usually because regular washing has been neglected! Always check that door and ventilator drain holes and pipes are completely clear so that water can drain out. Brightwork should be treated the same way as paintwork. Windscreens and windows can be kept clear of the smeary film which often appears if a little ammonia is added to the water. If glasswork is scratched a good rub with a proprietary metal polish will often clean it. Never use any form of wax or other paint/chromium polish on glass.

3. Maintenance - Body Interior

Mats and carpets should be brushed or vacuum cleaned regularly to keep them free of grit. If they are badly stained, remove them from the car for scrubbing or sponging and make quite sure that they are dry before replacement. Seat and interior trim panels can be kept clean with a wipe over with a damp cloth. If they do become stained (which can be more apparent on light coloured upholstery), use a little liquid detergent and a soft nailbrush to scour the grime out of

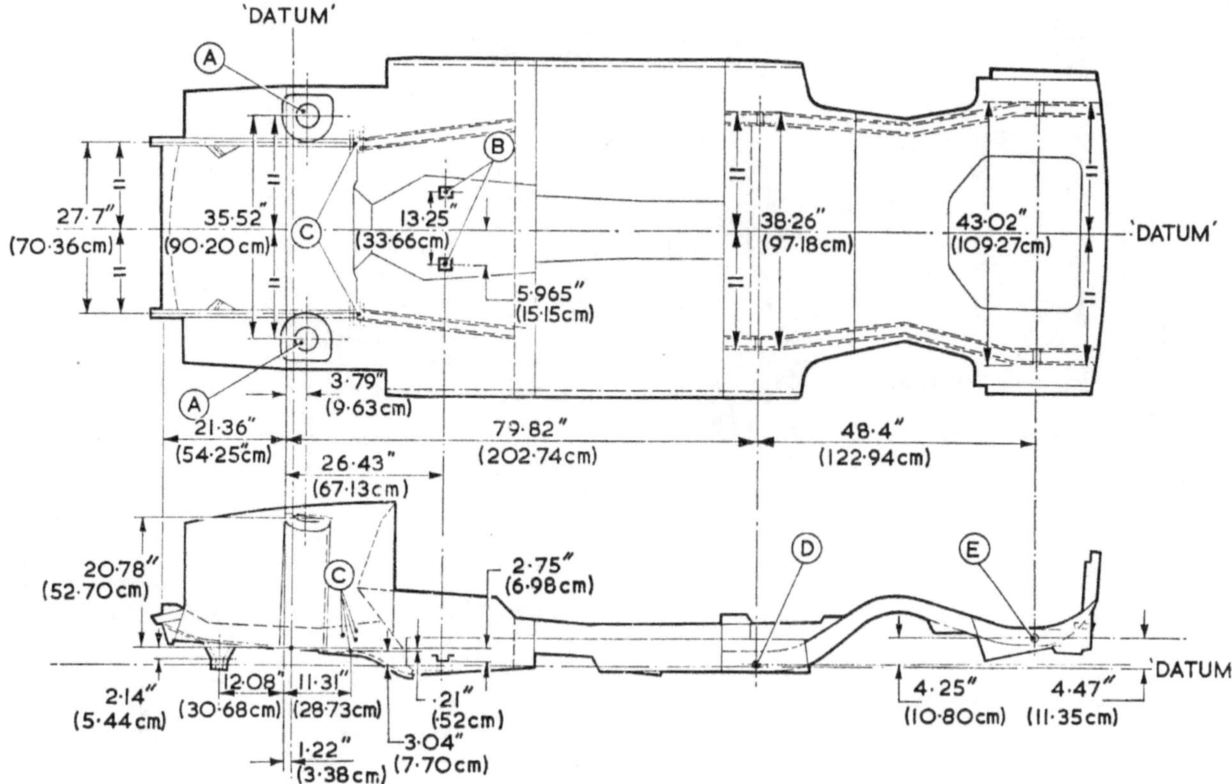

Fig.12.1. Underframe dimensions and fixing points

A Front suspension upper mounting
B Engine rear mounting
C Steering gear mounting
D Rear spring front eye bolt
E Rear spring shackle pin

the grain of the material. Do not forget to keep the headlining clean in the same way as the upholstery. When using liquid cleaners inside the car do not over-wet the surfaces being cleaned. Excessive damp could get into the upholstery seams and padded interior, causing stains, offensive odours or even rot. If the inside of the car gets wet accidentally it is worthwhile taking some trouble to dry it out properly, particularly where carpets are involved. Do NOT leave oil or electric heaters inside the car for this purpose. If, when removing carpets or mats for cleaning, there are signs of damp underneath, all the interior of the car floor should be uncovered and the point of water entry found. It may only be a missing grommet, but it could be a rusted through floor panel and this demands immediate attention as described in the previous section. More often than not both sides of the panel will require treatment.

4. Minor Repairs to Bodywork

1. A car which does not suffer some minor damage to the bodywork from time to time is the exception rather than the rule. Even presuming the gate post is never scraped or the door opened against a wall or high kerb there is always the likelihood of gravel and grit being thrown up and chipping the surface, particularly at the lower edges of the doors and sills.
2. If the damage is merely a paint scrape which has not reached the metal base, delay is not critical, but where bare metal is exposed action must be taken immediately before rust sets in.
3. Most owners will normally keep the following 'first aid' materials available which can give a professional finish for minor jobs:–

a) An anti-rust primer.
b) Cellulose filler (or stopper) for minor scratch filling.
c) Resin filler paste for filling larger areas and depths.
d) Assorted grades of 'wet and dry' abrasive paper.
e) Cellulose primer.
f) Matched finish paint for brush or aerosol application.

4. Where the damage is superficial (i.e. not down to the bare metal and not dented), fill the scratch or chip with sufficient filler to smooth the area, rub down with paper and apply the matching paint.
5. Where the bodywork is scratched down to the metal, but not dented, clean the metal surface thoroughly and apply a suitable metal primer first - such as red lead or zinc chromate. Fill up the scratch as necessary with filler and rub down with wet and dry paper. Apply the matching colour paint.
6. If more than one coat of colour is required rub down each coat with cutting paste before applying the next.
7. If the bodywork is dented, first beat out the dent to conform as nearly as possible to the original contour. Avoid using steel faced hammers - use hard wood mallets or similar, and always support the panel being beaten with a hardwood or metal 'dolly'. In areas where severe creasing and buckling has occurred it will be virtually impossible to reform the metal to the original shape. In such instances a decision should be made whether or not to cut out the damaged piece or to attempt to re-contour over it with filler paste. In large areas where

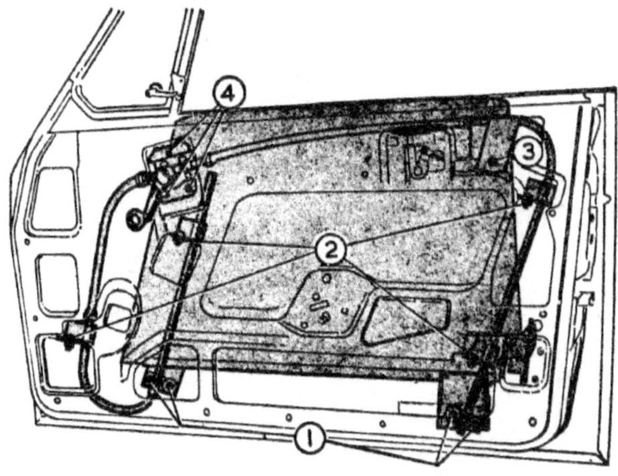

Fig.12.2. Front window winding mechanism

1 Glass to regulator fixing screws
2 Regulator tube mounting bolts
3 Self tapping screw for steady strap
4 Regulator control mounting screws

the metal panel is seriously damaged or rusted the repair is to be considered major, and it is often better to replace a panel or sill section with the appropriate piece supplied as a spare. When using filler paste in largish quantities make sure that the directions are carefully followed. It is false economy to rush the job as the correct hardening time must be allowed between stages and before finishing. With thick applications the filler usually has to be applied in layers - allowing time for each layer to harden. Sometimes the original paint colour will have faded and it will be difficult to obtain an exact colour match. In such instances it is a good scheme to select a complete panel - such as a door or boot lid - and spray the whole panel. Differences will be less apparent where there are obvious divisions between the original and resprayed areas.

5. Major Repairs to Bodywork

Major repairs are required after accident damage or where rust has attacked and eaten away large areas of panelling. Where rust has attacked and weakened structural stress points - such as the front suspension top mountings and rear spring attachment points - and after accident damage, metal work repairs are essential. Accident damage means that the whole structure must be checked for alignment. Damage to one part may affect the whole, due to the principle of construction. If the bodywork is left misaligned the car will be dangerous due to bad handling properties - and uneven stresses will be placed on steering and transmission causing abnormal wear or total failure. Rust damaged stress points may be repairable - it depends on the extent and how much has to be cut away before reaching sound metal to which new pieces may be satisfactorily and safely welded. All such metalwork is beyond the scope of most owners and should be left to professionals. Where large patches of wings or door sills or other non stressed panels need patching, it is possible to use resin filler supported on a wire mesh frame. Here again the deciding factor is whether there is sufficient sound metal in the nearby area on which to hang the repair. In any event all the surrounding area must be thoroughly cleaned or rust and treated, otherwise any repair will eventually be once more surrounded with rusted metal and liable to fall away. Much also depends on the age and overall condition of the car as to what sort of repair is economically suitable.

6. Hinges, Catches & Locks - Maintenance

The hinges and door latches should be wiped clean of grease and grime and a few drops of light oil applied occasionally. An oil with a graphite additive is particularly good. Do not over-oil as the excess merely runs out and collects more dirt. Wipe over after oiling. Other places which often stiffen up unnoticed and need a drop of oil are the bonnet and boot lid hinges and the bonnet release and safety catches.

7. Doors - Tracing & Silencing Rattles

Having established that a rattle does come from the door(s), check first that it is not loose on its hinges and that the latch is holding it firmly closed. The hinges can be checked by rocking the door up and down when open to detect any play. If the hinges are worn at the pin the whole hinge will need renewal. When the door is closed the panel should be flush with the pillar. If not then the hinges or latch striker plate need adjustment. The door hinges are held to the door and frame by three studs on each hinge plate. Access to the nuts is from behind the door and body and the trim should be removed first as described in the next section. The fitting of new hinges requires assistance if damage to the paintwork is to be avoided. To adjust the setting of the door catch first slacken the screws holding the striker plate to the door pillar just enough so that it can be moved but will hold its position. Then close the door, with the latch button pressed, and then release the latch. This is so that the striker plate position is not drastically disturbed on closing the door. Then set the door position by moving it without touching the catch, so that the panel is flush with the bodywork. This will set the striker plate in the proper place. Then carefully release the catch so as not to disturb the striker plate, open the door and tighten the screws. Rattles within the door will be due to loose fixtures or missing anti-rattle pads, and for this the next section explains how to deal with window glass, regulators and so on.

8. Doors – Removal & Replacement of Glass, Quarter Lights, Regulators, Locks & Catches

1. Whatever work is to be done inside the door, the trim panel will have to come off, and this involves first removing the window winder handle. To do this, press back the circular escutcheon behind the handle and push out the pin which will become visible. The handles may then be pulled off, followed by the escutcheon ring. Also remove the two recessed screws from under the arm rest. Slide a flat blade (scraper or putty knife) behind the bottom edge of the trim panel and run it along until it comes up against a clip. Then lever the clip out. Continue like this making sure that the leverage is applied close to the clip, otherwise you might pull them out of the trim panel. Lift the panel to clear the handle spindles and the clips at the top of the door and watch that the locking slide does not fall from the door.

2. To remove the window glass, quarter light and window winder mechanism proceed as follows.

3. Referring to Fig.12.2, remove the glass to winder mechanism fixing screws (1), and from the rear of the door slide out the glass guide. Then withdraw the glass upwards and backwards taking the rear end out first, and making sure that the projection on the glass bottom channel does not foul the weatherstrip.

4. To remove the quarter light, remove the two bolts which hold the quarter light frame from the front edge of the door; on later models these bolts are replaced by a nut and washer inside the door frame.

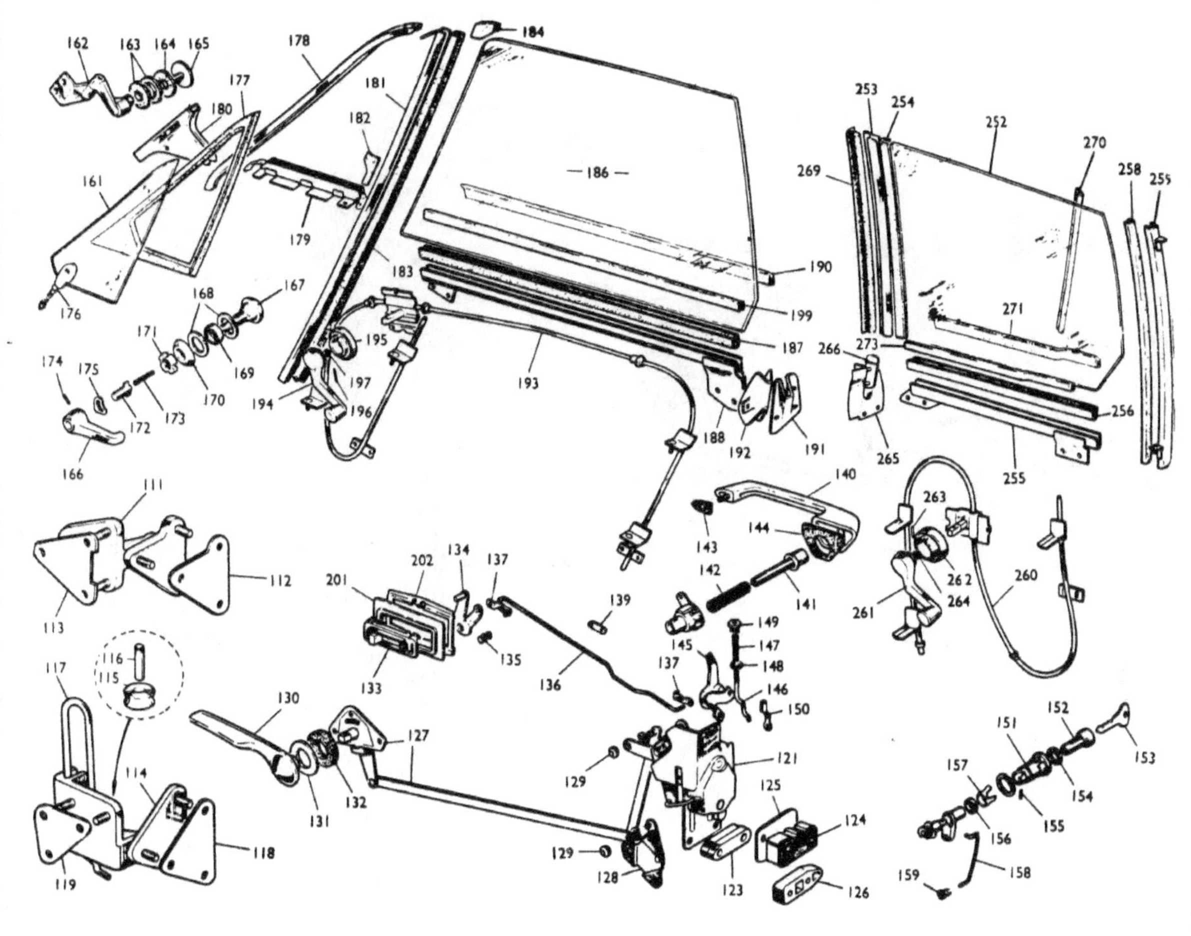

Fig.12.3. DOOR AND WINDOW FITTINGS

111 Hinge
112 Plate
113 Plate
114 Hinge
115 Roller
116 Pin
117 Torsion spring
118 Plate
119 Plate
121 Door lock assembly
123 Dovetail
124 Striker plate
125 Anti-burst plate
126 Striker
127 Remote control
128 Bellcrank link
129 Retaining washer
130 Inside door handle
131 Escutcheon
132 Seal
133 Inside lock
134 Lever
135 Pivot
136 Link
137 Clip
139 Anti-rattle clip
140 Outside door handle
141 Shaft
142 Spring
143 Washer
144 Washer
145 Contactor
146 Link
147 Spring
148 Washer
149 Nut
150 Clip
151 Lock
152 Lock barrel
153 Key
154 Washer
155 Pin
156 Clip
157 Spring
158 Link
159 Bush
161 Quarter light glass
162 Pivot
163 Grommet
164 Fibre washer
165 Screw
166 Locking handle
167 Boss and peg
168 Sealing washer
169 Washer
170 Washer
171 Locking ring
172 Push button
173 Spring
174 Pin
175 Waved washer
176 Pivot shaft
177 Weatherstrip
178 Outer frame rail
179 Lower rail
180 Capping
181 Channel
182 Catch plate
183 Channel
184 Stop block
186 Window glass
187 Rubber channel
188 Plate
190 Sealing strip
191 Stop
192 Glass guide
193 Window regulator
194 Window handle
195 Escutcheon
196 Pin
197 Rubber pad
199 Inner sealing strip
201 Escutcheon
202 Retainer
252 Rear window glass
253 Frame
254 Rubber channel
255 Glass channel
256 Rubber strip
258 Glass run channel
259 Channel support
260 Regulator
261 Window handle
262 Escutcheon
263 Pin
264 Rubber pad
265 Capping
266 Glass guide
269 Weatherstrip
270 Outer weatherstrip
271 Lower weatherstrip
273 Glass seal

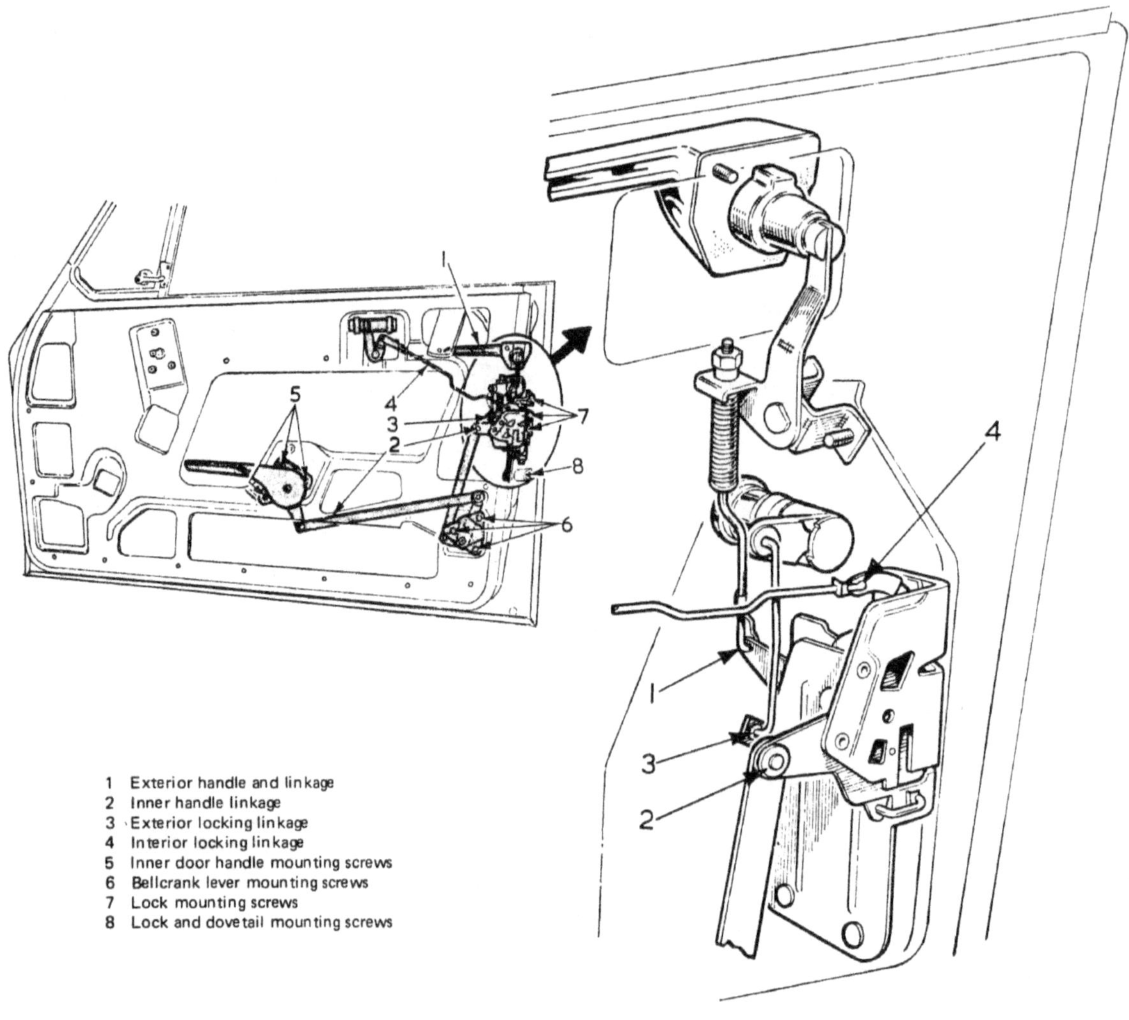

Fig.12.4. General view of door lock mechanism with detail showing disconnection points

5. Remove the nut and washer from the bottom of the glass front channel and the screw from the rear corner of the frame. Lift the assembly up about six inches, turn it through 180° and lift again, leaning the assembly away from the car so that the bottom bracket can come through the gap at the front end of the weatherstrip.

6. To remove the winder mechanism, referring again to Fig.12.2, undo the four mechanism tube mounting bolts (2), then remove the screw (3) securing the steady strap. Finally undo the three screws (4) securing the winder mechanism and withdraw the complete assembly through the large aperture in the bottom of the door.

7. To remove the door lock mechanism, refer to Fig.12.4, disconnect the exterior door handle linkage at the lock end (1), then by prising off the plastic locking washer (2) disconnect the inner linkage from the lock assembly.

8. Disconnect both door locking linkages at the lock end (3,4) and undo the three screws (5) holding the inner handle mechanism to the door frame. Undo the three screws (6) holding the bellcrank to the door frame, and lower the linkage through the aperture in the base of the door.

9. To remove the actual lock, undo the three screws (7) on the rear end of the door and the two screws (8) from the dovetail tongue. Then lower the lock assembly out through the aperture in the base of the door.

10. Replacement of all door components is a straightforward reversal of the removal sequence. When refitting the window glass do not finally tighten down the securing screws until the positioning of the window has been checked to ensure it shuts properly and does not catch anywhere on its run.

9. Bonnet (Hood) - Removal & Replacement

1. When in position and closed, the bonnet should fit centrally in the aperture and line up flush with the surrounding bodywork. The fore and aft and vertical positions at the hinge end can be adjusted by repositioning the vertical slotted bonnet bracket on the horizontally slotted hinge plate. The forward end is adjusted by the position of the catch post in the centre of the bonnet. By undoing the locknut where it is mounted on the bonnet, it can be screwed in or out as necessary, altering the height at which it hooks under the release catch.

2. To remove the bonnet it should be propped open and cloth placed under the rear corners to protect the paintwork. Two people are needed to remove the bonnet easily as support is required while the hinge bolts are undone (Photos). However, it is possible for one person to do it by supporting the rear corners on wooden blocks whole undoing the hinge bolts. Great care is needed as the whole bonnet tries to pitch to one side off the front prop stay, so be warned! Before slackening the hinge bolts, mark the relative positions of the two brackets so that the need for adjustment is minimised on replacement.

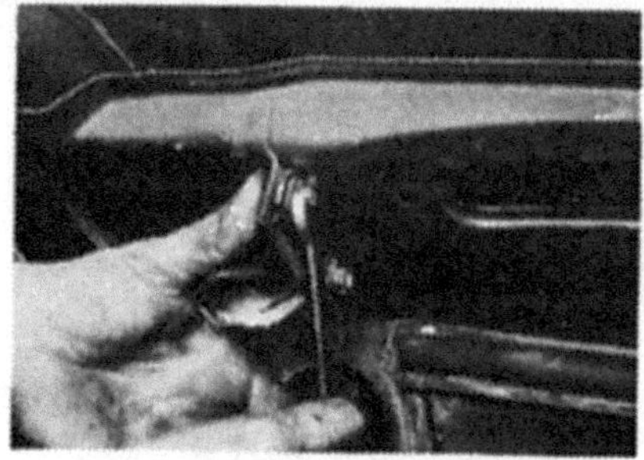

Section 9
Removing the bonnet (hood)

10. Boot (Trunk) Lid - Removal & Replacement

The fitting of the lid into the aperture follows the same principles as for the bonnet, and the hinge end is adjusted in the same way. The height of the closing end is adjusted by raising or lowering the catch post which is clamped to the inner edge of the compartment rear panel.

11. Windscreen & Rear Windows - Removal & Replacement

1. Two people are needed when working on the windscreen, one inside and one outside the car. The screen or window is held solely by the rubber sealing strip, but the lip of the seal is treated with sealing compound where it contacts the glass surfaces and the body aperture flange on the outside.
2. First remove the windscreen wiper arms, rear view interior mirror and sun visors. Then, using a blunt edge, such as the handle end of an ordinary nail file, ease the outer lip of the sealing rubber away from the glass in order to break the adhesion of the sealing compound.
3. Using a similar blunt instrument, next ease the inner lip of the rubber (inside the car) over the body flange at one of the top corners. Once this is started, firm hand pressure applied from inside will force the windscreen out. Make sure someone is ready outside to support the glass when it becomes free.
4. When the screen (or window) is out, remove the weatherstrip and clean away all traces of sealer. In cases of a broken windscreen make sure all broken pieces are removed (if the same strip is being re-used).
5. When fitting a new screen, first make sure that the edges of the new screen are ground bevelled, and that no chips or cracks in the edge are apparent. They are potential starters for future cracks across the screen. This must be watched, particularly if you are getting a secondhand screen from a broken car. Next support the screen on a stand, suitably padded against scratching, front side upwards, so that the edges are not obstructed. Then fit the weather-strip to the screen. Next, the outer face of the strip against the glass should be treated with sealer injected from a flat nozzle that may be inserted under the lip. Such nozzles are usually provided with a good proprietary sealer. Then fit the metal or plastic mouldings into the recess of the strip. This is best done by putting one edge of the moulding or beading under one edge in the beading and then using the same blunt article to ease the other edge in. Do NOT leave the moulding until after the screen is fitted - it will be very much more difficult to fit. With metal mouldings fit the two joining clips afterwards. With plastic beading the join should be in the bottom centre of the glass and the ends cut square to make a neat butt joint.
6. Next find a piece of strong cord which is long enough to fit into the weatherstrip body flange groove with two long ends left over. Do NOT use thin string as this could cut through the rubber. Put this into the groove - a piece of small bore tube through which the string can be fed often helps to get it in position easily. The loose ends should cross at the centre of the top edge. After the string is in position a further application of sealer should be made to the side of the channel which will bear against the outside face of the body flange.
7. The screen should next be placed centrally in the aperture with the ends of the cord hanging inside the car. The inner edge of the strip can then be pulled over the flange with the cord. If difficulty is experienced in keeping the weatherstrip in position on the glass after fitting the string, use self adhesive tape over it onto the glass. This will tear away when the cord is finally pulled out.

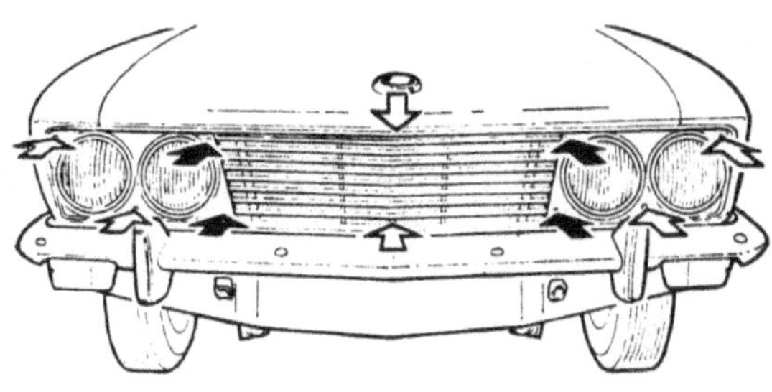

Fig.12.5.
Fixing points of grille assembly

12. Radiator Grilles - Removal & Replacement

All radiator grilles are held in place by self-tapping screws and Fig.12.5 shows where these are located. When removed the grille may be lifted off. Replacement is a reversal of this procedure but get all screws started before tightening any.

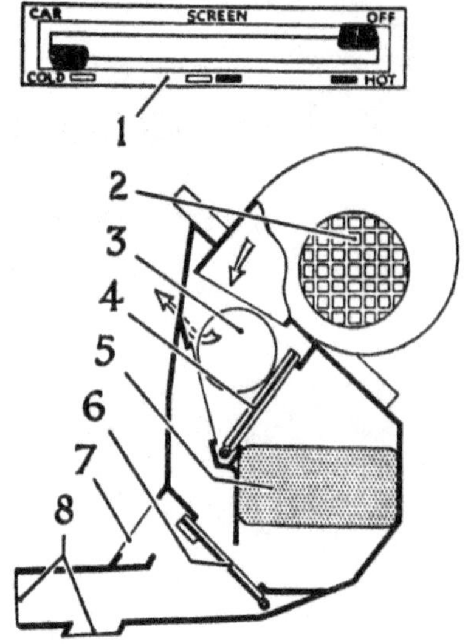

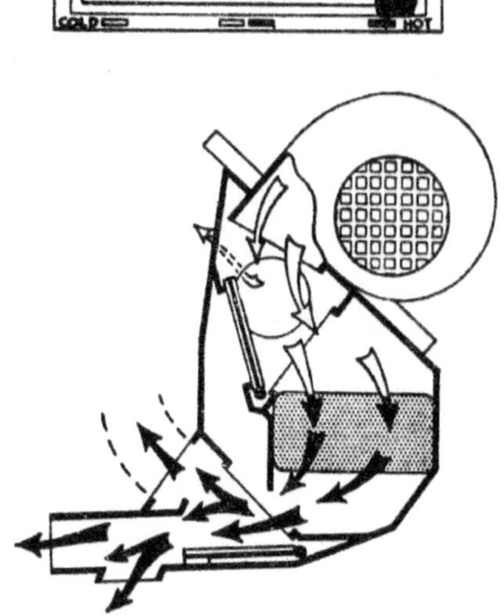

Fig.12.6. Air flow in heater at various control settings

1 Control panel
2 Blower
3 Outlet to face ducts
4 Air mixing valve flaps
5 Heater matrix
6 Distributor valve flap
7 Screen air outlet
8 Car air outlets

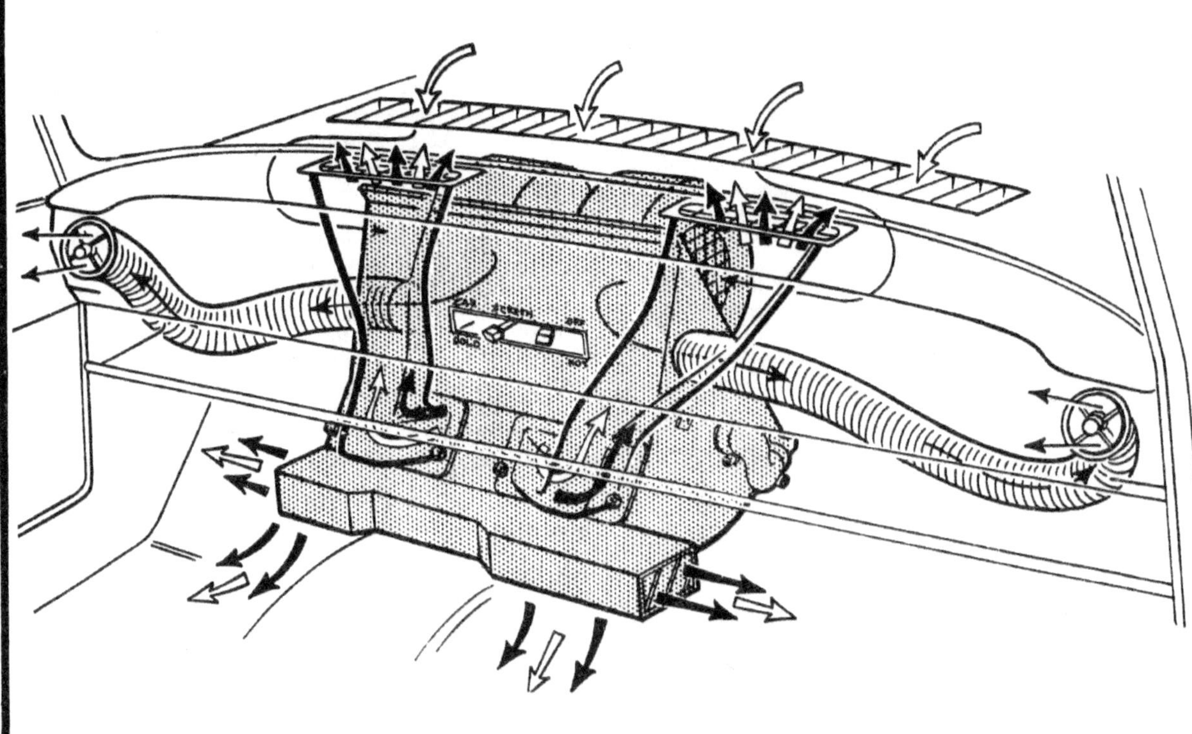

Fig.12.7. Air flow in heating and ventilating system

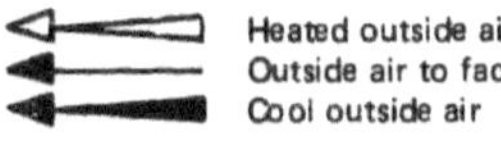

Heated outside air
Outside air to face vents
Cool outside air

13. Heating & Ventilating System - Description & Adjustment

1. The system comprises a water heated matrix, linked into the engine radiator circuit but not controlled by the thermostat so that hot water reaches the heater as soon as it is available. Air enters the system through the grille over the scuttle and, depending on the control settings, is either partially or wholly heated and directed to screen, interior or both (Fig.12.7). The controls operate the mixing valve, distribution valve and water valve. The top lever of the two marked 'off, screen, car' controls the distribution flap (Fig.12.6). In the 'off' position all air is directed to the screen vents for demisting and in the 'car' position most air is directed into the car with some bled off towards the screen. The other lever, marked 'cold–hot' operates both the air 'mixing' flap and the water valve. They both operate simultaneously when the lever is moved away from cold. The water valve lets hot water into the heater matrix and the mixing flap lets a proportion of the inlet air past the heater. In the 'hot' position all air flows past the heater. The water valve is fully open before the mixer flap completely cuts off the cold air inlet. The air flow is boosted when necessary by the twin rotor blow fan. A pair of independent fresh air inlet ducts, with outlets one at each end of the dashboard, is also installed. This is not affected by the controls and cannot be heated. The direction and flow of the air is controlled by the air valves at the ends of the ducts.

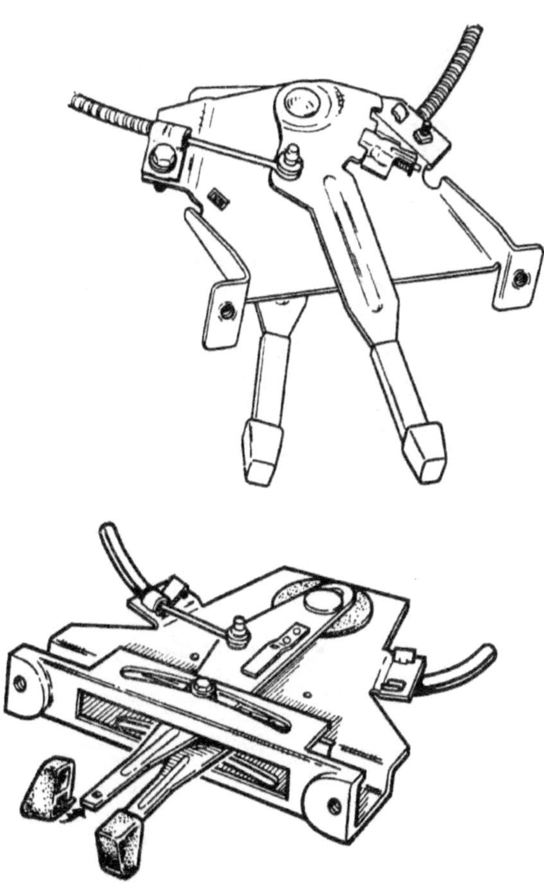

Fig.12.9.
The two types of heater control

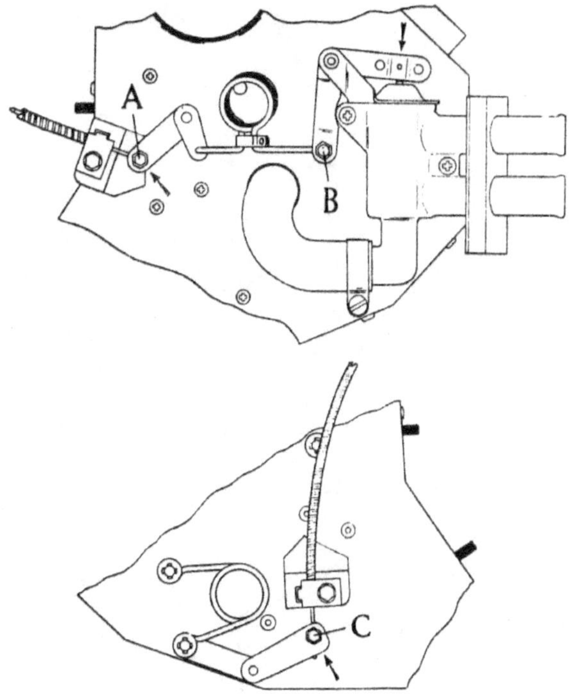

Fig.12.8.
Heater cable adjustment points
A Mixing valve
B Water valve
C Distributor valve

2. If the heater seems to be malfunctioning, make sure that a thermostat is installed in the cooling system and working properly (see Chapter 2).

3. In order to make sure the air valves are working they can be checked and adjusted at the heater ends of the cables. Release the cable at the lever trunnion (A in Fig.12.8), and set the mixing flap control to 'cold'. The lever should then be set as far as it will go in a clockwise direction (as arrowed) and the cable clamped up. The water valve which is operated by the same cable should be set at the same time by undoing the trunnion clamp (B) and pressing the top arm down (as arrowed). Then tighten the clamp once more.

4. The distributor valve cable is set in the same manner but the lever is moved as far as possible clockwise (C). Check the full range of operation after adjustment to ensure the flap valves are seating correctly at each extremity.

14. Heater Controls & Cables - Removal & Replacement

1. To renew either cable, the control assembly has to be withdrawn from the facia panel. First disconnect the battery to minimise the possibility of short circuits behind the facia panel, and disconnect both cables at the heater end adjustment trunnions (Section 13).

2. Remove the radio, console and parcel shelf, and then the escutcheon, held by two screws, round the control levers. On later models take off the detachable knobs (Fig.12.9).

3. Two screws, accessible through the aperture, hold the assembly in position, and when these are removed it can be drawn forward, bringing the cables with it. Each cable is clamped and can be detached, and the inner cable lifted off the lever peg.

4. When fitting a cable make sure the end of the outer does not project beyond the edge of the clamp (or spring clip). Adjust the levers, after replacement, as described in Section 13.

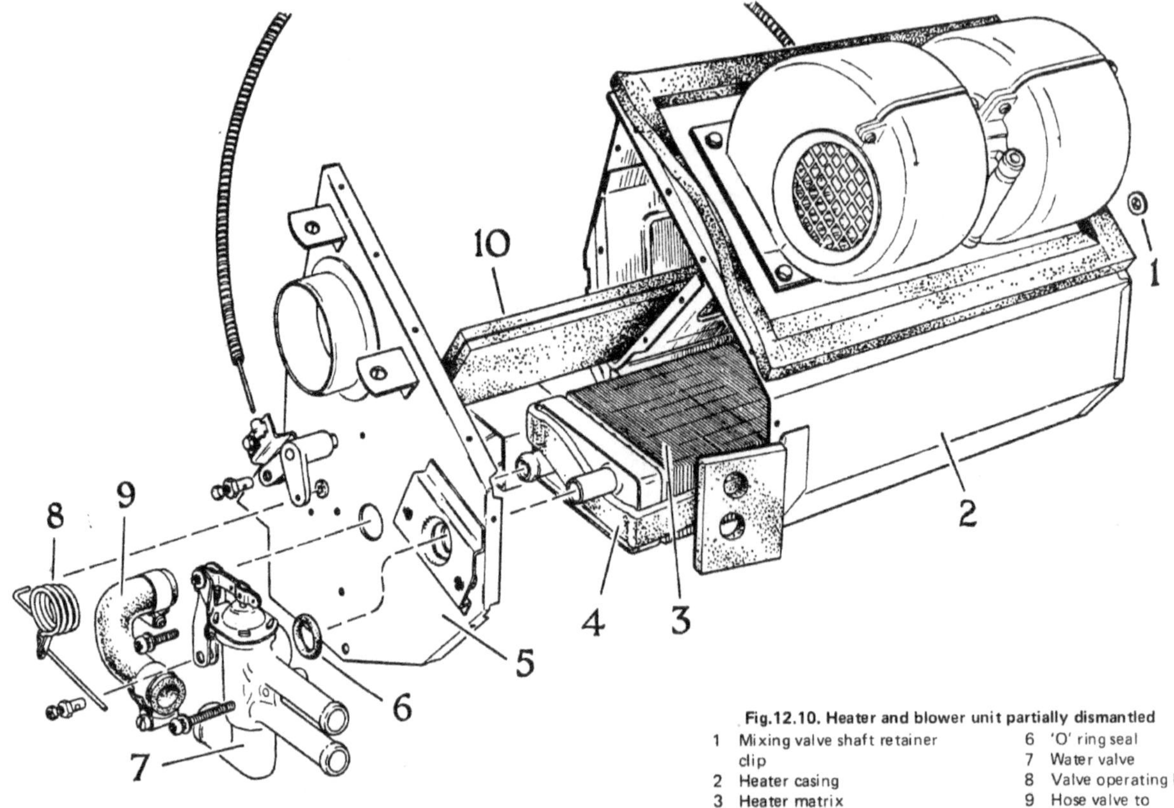

Fig.12.10. Heater and blower unit partially dismantled

1 Mixing valve shaft retainer clip
2 Heater casing
3 Heater matrix
4 Seal
5 End cover
6 'O' ring seal
7 Water valve
8 Valve operating link
9 Hose valve to matrix
10 Mixing valve flap

15. Heater Unit, Blowers & Water Valve - Removal & Replacement

1. Disconnect the battery and partially drain the cooling system, keeping the coolant if antifreeze has been added. Disconnect the inlet and outlet hoses from the water valve.
2. Remove the controls as described in Section 14.
3. Remove the face vent air hoses from the heater end and the demist tubes which run up to the windscreen.
4. Disconnect the two blower cables at the snap connections and release the cable harness where it is clipped to the body of the heater unit.
5. Four screws, two each side, which hold the unit to the mounting, should now be undone. If it is carefully moved to one side it can now be lifted out (Fig.12.10).
6. To remove the water valve, disconnect the short hose between the valve and matrix and release the operating link at the trunnion. The two crosshead securing screws should then be removed and the valve withdrawn. Note the 'O' ring seal which fits between the valve and matrix. This must be renewed when refitting the valve.
7. To remove the heater matrix (having removed the unit from the car and taken off the water valve), take off the air mixing valve shaft retainer clip from the end opposite the lever and then remove all the screws holding the end cover in position. The end cover, together with the mixing valve, can be withdrawn and the matrix lifted out.
8. The blower units are serviced as complete assemblies and no spares are supplied by Chrysler for repair. In fact they are assembled and balanced on original assembly and the clearances between rotors and casings are very fine. Dismantling is not, therefore, recommended. To remove the blowers the heater unit should be taken from the car. Attach a draw wire to each of the cables and then remove the six screws holding the blowers to the casing. The draw wires should be left in position on the casing for refitting the leads when replacing the blowers. Note the earth wire attached to one of the centre screws.
9. When reassembling the unit it is important for quietness and proper operation that all sealed joints are made good and that the foam padding is everywhere in good condition and correctly positioned.

Index

Zeitfracht Medien GmbH
Ferdinand-Jühlke-Straße 7
99095 Erfurt, Deutschland
produktsicherheit@kolibri360.de